Dragons of The Digital Age:

How Unilateral Cryptocurrency Regulation is a Threat to Consume the Entire Global Economy

By

Dr. Christopher W. Smithmyer, LLM

Remi Alli, JD, M.S.

Abdullah Jadoon

Ryan Ashe

Edited By

Prajwith Ullal

Elite exclusivity

Dysart Detroit Dallas

ISBN: 978-1-952651-00-7

"The world governs itself. It doesn't need our intervention."

Renowned author *Tao Te Ching, Lao Tzu*

Table of Contents

DEDICATED TO

The future generations, may we leave them a better world than we live in.

Introduction

Have you ever noticed that in legends, when someone slew a dragon, the world was a better place? Old stories were much better than the modern ones where every bad guy has to be politically correct, mixing good features and bad features to make them "relatable." Old stories did not do this, dragons, vampires, werewolves, and other denizens of the world were bad, and we knew what we had to do. Sometimes blurring the lines between good and evil make for an interesting story, but sometimes you want a story where the hero lays the smackdown on the baddie.

Dragons have always been an interesting element of stories. In the European legends, they were always straight up bad guys, stealing the princes, burning the countryside, eating all the livestock. Even in the Asian stories, the dragons tended to have a hidden agenda. While they may help the heroes in the story, it usually came at a cost. Dragons represent what is problematic in this world- false benevolence, outright evil, trickery, or a giving part of something and watching people fail as they struggle to understand it. This is what makes them such an interesting feature in literature, you know they are bad- you just do not know how bad they are.

In the story of cryptocurrency, there are heroes and villains. Sometimes the difference between the two is hard to define. However, in our story we also have dragons. Regardless of what they are doing, dragons always have an ulterior motive. In our story, the dragons are the government regulators who are trying to take away the freedom of the system and replace it with a controlled system (controlled by the central banking cartels) that operates on the same broken premise the old system we sought to replace was working on.

All stories with dragons need to have heroes. In our story, each person who is in the crypto community has the opportunity to be a hero. Regardless of the backstory, how much money they have, or how they are involved with the system, each person in the cryptoverse has a role to play in dealing with the biggest problem that the crypto community faces, the potential for government overregulation. When we work together, we can help the system to a point where the system itself slays the dragon of over-regulation. We are writing our own legend, and it falls on us to define how the story will end.

The Need for Existing Regulations

Anyone who is involved in finance can agree that any financial system needs some regulation in order for the system to work. While the wild west system can function for some time, they will eventually fail. Charlatans and snake oil salesmen will move into boom towns faster than the people can create rules to regulate the economy. These bad actors remove wealth from the system, which ultimately undercuts the system. There is a need for law; however, we have already defined the laws in this area, we do not need to government to build a new set of laws for an old set of investing. If the community adopts the laws of civilization, taking the good and leaving the bad, we can make the crypto community the community we deserve, not the civilization we inherited because people 4, 000 years ago set up arbitrary rules.

When any system develops, it begins to make its OWN rules. Humanity did it. The explorers of the world did it. The wild west did it. The internet did it. The people of the world (Terrans) have made a pattern of setting up new systems anywhere they go. Usually, the system starts with a vision. That vision is then adapted to the needs of the new community. The community turns to where they came from. Successful communities adopt the alleged good rules from their previous story and abandon the alleged bad rules. Failed communities take the old rules wholesale and just expect things to be different. Einstein is credited to have said, "insanity is doing the same thing over and over again and expecting different results."[1] The insanity in the crypto world is expecting failed governments to make good regulations for a developing field that they do not understand.

The additional danger of new space (which the cryptoverse and metaverse

---

[1] Wilczek, Frank (2015). "Einstein's Parable of Quantum Insanity." Scientific America at https://www.scientificamerican.com/article/einstein-s-parable-of-quantum-insanity/.

are) is that the denizens of the space will think that they do not need any rules. This libertarian streak of new frontiers can cause problems for the occupants. First of all, in a land without laws, the lawless person is king. Most people who are exploring the metaverse are decent people; these people think that "sunshine and rainbows" will allow them to have the "perfect society." Interspersed among these honest people who are moving through the metaverse are drug dealers, human traffickers, scammers, and gun runners. These people love the idea of a society without rules because they had no intention of following them regardless. These are the bad actors that make rules a necessity.

The good news in this space is that we have rules on how currency, assets, securities, and financial instruments work. These laws are already established and on the books in most of the countries where the servers and the clouds for the financial systems are located. We know what the tax and trading rules are for currencies. We know where to find the rules for assets. Securities are managed by a discrete code of conduct. And financial instruments have a specific code around them. There is no need to create new laws to govern this (in fact, there is a question of whether any government has jurisdiction to do so), the laws already exist. Governments just need to enforce the laws that exist and give clarification on how they function in the metaverse.

The crypto community is derived from self-governance, but until there is a "United States of Crypto" or "Crypto Union," we do have to function within the existing framework of laws. This does not mean that we cannot legally pick and choose what works and what does not. Most of the countries in the world that are active in crypto are relatively free, and this means that the people in the community have a voice over how the community is run. Regulators are servants of the people; dragons who are unapproachable. If every crypto user wrote a letter to their representative in a free country, the billions of us around the world could convince them to enforce the laws that are already on the books, and that we do not need new laws.

Parts of the Book

This book follows a very simple three-part structure. Many people who are trading crypto do not understand crypto; therefore, we start with an explanation of the current terms in the crypto community and the upcoming terms from the 3rd Wave of crypto. Part II looks at the specific needs that the crypto community has acknowledged the government has limited authority over. In this part, we take the time to look over those needs and define the limited involvement that the community should allow national governments - over a global system. Part III looks at the actions that the community needs to take to ensure that the system remains functional, and this includes stabilization of the market, introducing derivatives for investors, and expanding the metaverse beyond a social meeting place for the community. All three of these elements are in play. Part III talks about how you can be involved with them.

Part I starts out how any good book on a new field starts, general definitions. If you are a little leery on the lingo, then there is an index and glossary to help you catch up. Crypto, like any field, has trade terms. These terms are the "in" words that show you understand what you are talking about. Part I takes the time to acclimatize you to the system before it really moves into the advanced elements. After establishing the definitions, Part I: Section II goes over the history of the system. While this is "a brief history of crypto time," knowing where the industry came from can be invaluable to understanding where it is going. This section also deals with the ideas of 1st Wave, 2nd Wave, and 3rd Wave cryptos. Part I concludes with an explanation of evolution within the system. As crypto is a digital system, it is constantly evolving. What is cutting edge today may be the "Zune" of tomorrow; the system needs to constantly evolve for the system to be effective.

Part II looks at the element that most of us do not want to deal with: regulation. Regulation never makes anything easier; it just makes it safer. Right now, the community needs a little safety. Part II: Section I establishes some of the protections that the community is willing to accept as it develops. As this is a global community, we need to ensure that no one government "owns" crypto. The rules that we bring into the system can be the current laws, but the community should have a say in how these rights are applied, and not necessarily some bureaucrat behind a desk in Washington, London, Moscow, or Beijing. Part II: Section II next takes a look at dealing with criminals within the system. Since governments have a monopoly over the legalized use of force, there is little that the community can do to bad actors but ban and sue them. This is where the rights of the community members come into play; if any member of the community has standing to ask for their rights to be protected under the current law, then the community has standing. When someone commits a criminal act against the community, that person can be tried for that criminal act in any jurisdiction of the system. Part II wraps up with section III, which looks at the security considerations of the system. The system cannot rely solely on the government for regulation, self-regulation needs to be paramount in how we design our community. This section looks at community rights, institutional duty, and the need for multiple (redundant) access paths for members of the community.

Part III deals with the stabilization mechanisms of the system. One of the key factors in any system is that people understand how valuation is derived. Transitional, transactional, market and inherent valuation are key elements of the cryptosystem. Further, the system needs to place elements that prevent bad actors from manipulating the system. Part III: Section II builds on this idea by adding value to the system. Derivatives stabilize the market and add new instruments to the system to increase the viability of the cryptoverse while limiting the volatility. Finally, Part III concludes with a short walk through the metaverse. Because this is the coming thing, we look at how the metaverse can evolve to be a parallel system to the current socio-economic system in the world. It replaces nothing but enhances everything.

The goal of this book is simply to educate the reader. We want to give the reader the tools that they need to understand what is going on in the cryptoverse. By explaining the system, people can see how it works. By explaining the need for rules, people can build better rules. By looking to the future, we can set our jaws to move into that future and take responsibility for our actions. Understanding is the greatest tool that someone can have when another person (or government) is trying to take away their rights. As long as crypto users are following the rules, governments have no right, let alone a reason, to interfere in a system that is working. We have witnessed 100 years of inflation as the central banking cartel pilfered the wealth of the world, shifting it from 30% of the population to 1% of the population. In two years, the crypto community has shifted trillions of dollars back into the hands of the people who are not considered elite. Now the community that rose from the digital frontiers is claiming its place in history, not as those stuck in a system from the Middle Ages which have failed people for centuries, but a system forged out of the digital age, a system of equality, a system of innovation, and a system where we realize that we are all human and that as residents of this rock we call home (Terrans) we have rights given by God, not by central banks and governments.

Mining, Speculation, and Banking

When we look at the development of any new system, we need to think about how that system is developing. In most cases, we go through a system of discovery, exploitation, then civilization. When this is being taught in one of our classes, we conform this to the “gold rush” mentality, mining, speculation, banking. Systems need each level of this evolution to ensure that the participants have a stable environment in which to work. Thus, we are seeing the same system play out in the cryptoverse.

Mining (discovery) is the phase in the system where people just claim what is out there. Bitcoin claimed the idea of monetizing the blockchain. It is not that no one had the idea before, it was just that bitcoin was first to market. With each revolution of the system, there are early adopters and those who sit back. The early adopters tend to make the big money upfront and become the powerhouses as the system evolves. However, once an idea is discovered, the early adopters need to ensure that they have control of their system, this is when they move the system forward. (1st Wave crypto)

Speculation (exploitation) is the phase where people get other people to do the work for them. Ownership of an asset that can be worked has its benefits, especially if you can get someone else to work it for you. This is where those that earned money in mining (or had money to start with) purchase the assets and then 'allow' others to work the assets for them. This consolidates the power within the system but allows many more people to be involved with the earnings, albeit at different levels. (2nd Wave crypto).

Banking is the penultimate level of the system. This is where we are today in crypto. The miner has become a standard feature in the ecosystem; therefore, people are finding ways to consolidate the speculators into manageable groups. Once enough speculators make money, they decide that there needs to be another level to fight for. This is the banker level. The banker level is the level that funds the speculators to allow them to hire the miners to exploit the resource. Bankers make less off of more people to ensure that they take the lion's share.

While some people (especially late adopters) do not want to see this system take hold (you will find that the people who are late to the game always discount the work of those who were there before them), most people in the system understand that unless we have miners and creators, we will not have a system. They also understand that if no one finances them, then they will not have the funding. Speculators understand that if they have to use their own money, they are taking all the risks- therefore the banks are necessary. The system feeds upon itself; it is not until governments get involved that the system does not bring wealth to the whole group.

Global Access to A Global Market

One of the key elements that the community needs to focus on is that we need global access to the system. This book looks at how the 3rd Wave crypto concept of Global Exchange Tokens (GETs) are allowing more people access to crypto than ever. In tyrannical countries that will not allow crypto, their citizens might use VPNs to get around firewalls, allowing more people financial access just the same. The GET system allows those people to move their wealth to "safe" countries to prevent their own governments from stealing off of them. The community must come together to support these people who are less fortunate than others.

GET is a type of token that is used to give users access to the spiderweb bridge. Building a coded bridge between them is unwieldy because the coding systems of the different blockchains are so difficult. Additionally, these coded bridges are less secure as they become focal points for hackers and spammers. The GET system allows a token to exist on a given chain, but then provides a managed transaction within the DeFi banking system or on an exchange. There is a small fee (which is often lower than a standard gas fee) that is used to maintain the system and build the value of all coins on the system. This is also a transactional token, which means that anyone holding it is in the process of converting it to something else (rather than it being an ending investment).

GETs are a lifesaver (literally) for crypto users in tyrannical countries. Through active use of VPNs, a user can work within the space of the crypto community, then when they would like to withdraw equity, they can use the GET system to convert the equity to their preferred fiat currency. The fiat currency can be transferred to a central bank, and other than the fact that a GET was used, no one can trace (without the help of the system) what funds the person was working with. Since the community is not likely to hand over records to a country that is abusing the rights of its citizens, this allows the community to keep those looking for financial freedom safe, while still turning over the records of traffickers, drug cartels, and other criminals.

Problems of the Market are the Dragons of the Digital Age

Under the current system of laws, the community can take care of itself. As long as governments do their jobs of arresting criminals and providing court systems to enforce contracts, the system does not need any additional laws. No government has the jurisdiction to create a unified oversight body, that duty falls on the collaborative efforts of the exchanges and the DeFi banks within the system. As long as the rules that they create follow the laws of the countries in which they operate, countries have no reason or right to interfere with the lawful commerce of system participants.

Regulation is the dragon hanging at the periphery of the system, preventing it from growing. This boogeyman created by government corruption and incompetence is preventing the system from bringing billions of people around the world out of poverty. While physical goods are a real thing, fiat wealth is just an agreement that wealthy people have supported for centuries. Crypto is a threat to that system; this is why governments want to stifle it. The only saving grace is that the corrupt politicians whom the elites have bought are so greedy (and making money in the new system) that they are hesitant to do their bought and paid for master's bidding. The community needs to acknowledge this corruption and keep the government in its lane.

Jurisdiction is also an issue. While governments have the right to regulate things happening in their borders, they do not have the right to prevent people from trading in legal goods. Taxes aside, governments have no right to regulate crypto outside of the existing laws. As long as people are participating in agreed-upon trades, and those traders are paying the taxes (which are questionable) then people are following the law. Why does a government want to make a law to make law-abiding people criminals? Because they cannot accept a system that they do not have majority control over.

The goal of this book is to help you slay the dragon of over-regulation in your country. This is not an anarchist book; this is a book about freedom. Governments have their place, to protect their citizens and ensure that property rights are followed. Crypto does not violate property rights, it creates new property and wealth that allows a new generation of business people, entrepreneurs, artists, and citizens to work together. Maybe the biggest reason that the governments are afraid is that our ancestors created the dragon of government regulation to alleviate their fear, now Generation X and the Millennials have turned on the light and said, "We are not afraid anymore!" What is the purpose of dragons if no one is afraid of them anymore?

Part I: Cryptocurrency as a Field

Introduction to Part I

Anytime there is innovation, someone tries to claim the innovation. Often the claims are voiced by many "someones," as different fields see value in the new field and want to claim the value as their own. The best fields are the ones that find their identity fast enough that they can survive this onslaught of "progenitors." In crypto, we have claims coming from many fields. The IT field claims that as crypto is a computer process, it should be theirs. Finance claims crypto because of the relationship between exchanges and banks. Governments argue that crypto should be managed by them because it is a type of currency (even though it was created to avoid poorly managed government currencies. Due to its potential worth, dozens claim crypto, but it is a field unto itself.

Part I is designed to help novices and veteran users alike understand what crypto is and why it is a field unto itself. Section I of this part looks at the definitions within the space and how they differentiate between what was, what is, and what is coming. As the lexicon of cryptocurrency grows, so does the argument that cryptocurrency is not part of another field- but a field all of its own. If we want to keep the government regulators out of our market (as it is a contracts-based market), we must first define the field as it is, not what the regulators want it to be.

Understanding the terminology of a field is not enough for the field to "cut its teeth." Section II of this part takes the time to look at the history of what has brought us to where we are. Cryptocurrency is an evolution of money, which means that it is something more than the sum of its parts. Looking at the different levels through which cryptocurrency has passed opens the doors for people to discover where it is going in the future. If you do not know where you are, you cannot plan your journey to somewhere else.

Beyond the past lies the present, and the present is where we are battling regulators for who defines the crypto space. Section III of this part looks at the methodologies that are fundamental to the success of the crypto market. Whether it be the management of information, the types of trades for which crypto is useful, or the internal structures which support the contracts we are creating; the industry should be defining the future- not bureaucrats in a government office.

For novices, Part I is essential for you to "catch up" with the field so you can be effective in the new marketplace. For those who have been with crypto since the beginning, this Chapter can help align the terminology to ensure that we are all on the same page as we move through the evolutionary process. A unified lexicon and a unified resistance to over-regulation will help us keep our system decentralized as we move into the future.

Part I: Section I

General Definitions

Introduction to Part I: Section I

What is the value of a word? Sometimes as people who use a language every day, we do not think about the words that we use. We understand that words have meaning, but we do not look at what that meaning does, and to who it relates. Within the expanding market of cryptocurrency, the words we choose to describe our systems have meaning, both internally and externally. For internal use, the lexicon allows us to understand one another. Externally, the lexicon needs to be functional enough that a potential user can enter into the system without too much fear. Our words define who we are, and the definitions are the key element of Part I: Section 1.

Chapter 1 looks at the big question in the world today, "What is cryptocurrency?" When you are part of a new field, defining the field may be one of the hardest parts of establishing new systems. "That is an IT concept..." or "That is a banking concept..." are phrases that will haunt the cryptocurrency market for decades. As early adopters, we need to be ready to adopt those terms as our own and use them to describe similar things. As the field evolves these terms will have new meaning, but as we build the foundation, understanding of the terminology is vital.

The difference between tokens and coins is another big issue within the field. Chapter 2 discusses what the fundamental elements are of a coin and what the fundamental elements are of a token. While 3rd Wave crypto tends to blur the lines between these macro concepts, there is a simple fact that a coin will always have its own blockchain, and a token will just be a smart contract overlay on an existing blockchain. The other elements are fungible, but this is the key difference that makes the distinction.

Tokenomics is another term that we find is getting shuffled around the marketplace. Tokenomics is still coming into its own, but it has the basic element of how a token or coin is both built and introduced into a system. Chapter 3 looks at the basics of tokenomics, how it adds value to the system, and how the public should analyze how the coin goes into people's hands. Understanding tokenomics becomes vital when participating in the system, where knowing how to tokenomics works can make you a lot of money.

Chapters 4 and 5 look at the concepts and evolution of Stablecoins. For this book, we are looking at the three main variations of Stablecoin, Stablecoin 1.0, Stablecoin 1.1, and Stable coin 2.0. Stablecoin 1.0 is the leading edge of the new type of crypto. Based on fiat currency, Stablecoin 1.0 showed the market that things could be stabilized by linking digital value to inherent value. Stablecoin 1.1 attached the value of coins to a single asset (non-fiat) or a family of assets. This showed the marketplace that fiat currency was not the best attachment and that the system could evolve. Stablecoin 2.0, the current iteration, is based on complex diversified portfolios and ecosystems of cryptos working together. This has shown the industry that all cryptos are entangled and that the success of one is based on the efficiency of all.

Chapter 6 looks at the smart contracts that underpin Ethereum and the 2nd Wave cryptos. The more that the system grows, the more need there will be for smart contracts and smart contract overlays to evolve. Moving into the metaverse increases the utility of the coin, it therefore, falls on the industry for the system to rise to the challenge to meet the needs of the future.

Overall, once you have a basic understanding of the terminology, the more complex concept becomes that much easier to understand. Remember, cryptocurrency relies on two things trade and validation. We all understand the concept of trade in an ecosystem, this is the world that we live in. Validation is the same as it has always been; "trust but verify." This allows the system to be more secure than the fiat system and based on the real value which will (hopefully) stand the test of time.

Chapter 1: Defining Cryptocurrency

In the world of finance, one of the most common questions circling the globe is, "how does cryptocurrency work?"[2] To address the protections that we need against unmitigated regulation in the cryptoverse, a novice reader needs to know the definition of cryptocurrency. Even more so, the community needs to work to build a more unified understanding of the system. In many cases, different platforms are using different terminology, and each of these inconsistencies is a wedge that governments around the world can use to separate the community, giving rise to a pre-constructed "need" for regulation.

Building a better system means that we all need to work from the same lexicon while having the freedom to create new elements as the need arises. This duality of necessity creates the unique dynamic of decentralized management- we need to be working toward the same goal but we can all take different paths. There are several constructs that are constants: crypto, blockchain, and decentralized finance, but the pieces that make up these systems are very open to change. It is in the constants that we need to have the same working definition, however, even if it changes from time to time.

The more consistent the terminology, the more respect the field garners. Trade language becomes common language and common language becomes the soul of the field. As the system evolves, so will the terms. However, in its infancy, those who are using the system need to be using a common set of terms to ensure that we are all working in the same direction. The exploration of space, the metaverse, and the world we live in all rely on our ability to work together, defining the terms that we will be using is the beginning of this process.

What is cryptocurrency?

Cryptocurrency is somewhat hard to grasp for those of opposite

---

[2] Royal, James & Voight, Kevin (2022). "What is Cryptocurrency? Here's what you should know." Nerdwallet at https://www.nerdwallet.com/article/investing/cryptocurrency-7-things-to-know.

generations. Chatting with a person under ten, a simple definition is coinless, paperless money used only online in exchange for what one desires. Talking to a person in their twenties, cryptocurrency is recent technology just garnering respect globally to utilize like cash online that may be the key to a more equitable economy. Chatting with a Boomer, crypto might be virtual money that they may want to avoid as there have been enough hackers who have stolen millions, if not billions from this medium.

Not everything is true. Not everything is false.

> A cryptocurrency is a digital form of money that can be traded online, using encryption to authenticate and secure money exchanges and rely on a connected network of computers. There are thousands of various cryptocurrencies in the world.[3]

"They are not backed by or convertible into a commodity like any fiat currency." Moreover, cryptocurrency researcher Jan Lansky states that "a cryptocurrency is a system that has the following requirements:

1. The system does not require a central authority; its state is maintained through distributed consensus.
2. The system keeps an overview of cryptocurrency units and their ownership.
3. The system defines whether new cryptocurrency units can be created. If new cryptocurrency units can be created, the system defines the circumstances of their origin and how to determine the ownership of these new units.
4. Ownership of cryptocurrency units can be proved exclusively cryptographically.
5. The system allows transactions to be performed in which ownership of the cryptographic units is changed. A transaction statement can only be issued by an entity proving the current ownership of these units.

---

[3] Frankenfield, Jake (2021). "Cryptocurrency" Investopedia at https://www.investopedia.com/terms/c/cryptocurrency.asp.

6. If two different instructions for changing the ownership of the same cryptographic units are simultaneously entered, the system performs at most one of them."[4]

"Cryptocurrency often uses decentralized control rather than a central bank digital currency to work through distributed ledger technology, like blockchain, as a public financial transaction database. (When it is created prior to issuance or sent by a single issuer, it is generally considered centralized.)"[5] A computerized database called a ledger uses cryptography that is quite resistant to cryptoanalysis or secret codes to ensure transaction records are secure in order to prevent additionally created coins and to confirm the transfer of coin ownership.[6]

What is blockchain and how does it work?

"A blockchain is a database that stores information electronically in digital format that offers security and allows for a high degree of trust of a record of data and without a middleman (decentralized)." It stores information in blocks connected to another storage block, forming a chain of data, creating a permanent, chronological line of data filled with "receipts" to look back on.

Initially, a research project from the early 1990s, blockchain allows digital information to be preserved exactly as is and scattered where necessary. These transaction receipts, called Distributed Ledger Technology, cannot be edited or destroyed.[7] This creates a permanent record of the process occurring, which secures not only the network but the system as well. This is one of the key reasons why the myth of "crypto for terrorism" is difficult to believe, why would they use a system that creates a traceable record.

---

[4] Lansky, Jan (2018). "Possible State Approaches to Cryptocurrencies." Journal of Systems Integration 9/1 pp 19-31.

[5] Staff (2021). "What is Cryptocurrency? A Beginners Guide to Digital Currency." Coin Telegraph at https://cointelegraph.com/blockchain-for-beginners/what-is-a-cryptocurrency-a-beginners-guide-to-digital-money

[6] *Id.*

[7] Hayes, Adam (2021). "Blockchain Explained" Investopedia at https://www.investopedia.com/terms/b/blockchain.asp.

Bitcoin made blockchain popular in 2009, "but with cryptocurrencies, decentralized finance (DeFi) applications, non-fungible tokens (NFTs), and smart contracts, it is now widely used."

What is decentralized finance (DeFi)

With decentralized financing, everything happens autonomously; a client anywhere can connect with those globally willing to insure your assets or vice versa. "With smart contracts ensure a more equitable, secure, and trustworthy process while cutting out the traditional middleman like an insurance company."[8]

Unlike centralized finance, decentralized finance or well known as its short form (DeFi), are "financial services that are governed and controlled by a group of participants via decentralized networks while open to anyone to use and allowing its customers to have complete control over their funds." They no longer have to go through a brokerage or a bank, for example, thus an *Investopedia* notes, "a government-issued ID, Social Security number, or proof of address are not necessary to use DeFi."[9]

Further, *Go Cardless* states that

> There are two core components that allow a finance system to work; it needs an infrastructure to operate on, and a currency to operate with. In a centralized system, banks and financial institutions act as that infrastructure, while fiat money, like the US dollar, acts as currency. Decentralized finance must replace these components in order to offer a full range of financial services.

They also remind us that "through decentralized finance, secure a loan in a matter of minutes, without having to go through a complicated or restrictive application process."[10]

---

[8] Staff (2021). "What is Decentralized Finance (DeFi)." Go Cardless.com at https://gocardless.com/en-us/guides/posts/what-is-decentralized-finance/.

[9] Sharma, Raesh (2021). "Decentralized Finance (Defi) Definition." Investopedia at https://www.investopedia.com/decentralized-finance-defi-5113835.

[10] Go Cardless, *Supra*.

Ultimately, decentralized finance is a movement within cryptocurrency online spaces with the goal to add open-source software (**source code that anyone can vet, edit, and update)** and "decentralized networks to turn traditional, centralized financial services and products into trustless and transparent systems that do not require any authority figure to watch over them."[11] Decentralized Finance replaces traditional banks and brokers, allowing for the potential of more efficient monetary transactions, and less tedious headwork - along with not demanding a minimum transaction. As a result, many believe that this will lead to a more equitable economy globally.[12]

Why are these systems important in the modern-day?

Blockchain Council reminds us that

> Users can access their assets straight from their browsers using these wallet extensions. They are installed similarly to other extensions, and usually require users to either import a current wallet or create a new one using a private key. They are also password-protected to ensure high-end security. In addition, some of these wallets come with built-in web browsers.
>
> Furthermore, these wallets often include mobile apps with features to access DeFi projects. These apps are wallets with built-in browsers that can be used to interact with DeFi applications. Users can synchronize their wallets by first creating them on one device and then exporting the private key from another device.
>
> Such mobile applications frequently incorporate Wallet Connect opensource code to make things convenient for users. Scanning a QR code with mobile phones allows the users to connect their wallets to DeFi computer apps.[13]

---

[11] https://itsblockchain.com/top-20-defi-crypto-projects/#:~:text=Well%2C%20DeFi%20is%20the%20short%20form%20for%20decentralized,require%20any%20authority%20figure%20to%20watch%20over%20them.

[12] Sharma. *Supra*.

[13] Banerjee, Avinandan (2020). "Decentralization Finance (DeFi: Digging into the Blockchain Frontier." Blockchain Council at https://www.blockchain-

The evolution of the global system is based on the system becoming more dynamic. The system which has been in effect, because of the global banking cartels, had a purpose for the last 100 years. This purpose has been perverted to the enrichment of a limited cabal of individuals who now run these banks. Decentralization allows us to move away from the power being in the hands of the few to the power being spread across the system. Thus, we can create a system that has more balance than the current system.

Digitization of the banks also allows for more people to have access to the system. One of the greatest shortfalls of the current system is that most people in the world do not have access to financial services. As more of the world acknowledges that access to the internet, in some form, is a human right, more people will have access to do their financial activities on the decentralized system, helping to bring millions out of poverty.

The key reason, however, that the digital system is so important is due to the nature of the system itself. The central banking system has stagnated. Innovations are few and far between, consisting mostly of "rehashed" old ideas with new branding. The decentralized system has the ability to create thousands of banking systems in collaborative competition, which can bring new ideas to the marketplace- helping the system move forward.[14]

Why does this move us toward augmented reality and the metaverse?

Decentralized finance depends on public blockchains like cryptocurrencies, to act as online financial services technologies that offer services such as crypto trading, loans, interest accounts, and more. As a result, governments can benefit from further looking into and partnering with the metaverse for employment, education, health care, urban planning, and many more opportunities. Payment processing, identification verification,

---

council.org/defi/decentralization-finance-defi-digging-into-the-blockchain-frontier/

[14] Rapoza, Kenneth (2021). "What's the big deal about DeFi and how do you invest in it?" *Forbes* at https://www.forbes.com/sites/kenrapoza/2021/03/21/whats-the-big-deal-about-defi-and-how-do-you-invest-in-it/?sh=15d794dde89c

and more could be facilitated if the government plans accordingly.

Crypto is not only the currency of the metaverse, it is the metaverse. Each bit of property, each avatar, each personal item that you buy in the digital space is made up of crypto. Whether something is an NFT or a regular token, it has value in the system and its existence gives the system value. The more we work to refine the system of use of crypto, the more that we will be able to merge the real world and the AR world to expand the human condition.

As we look at how the metaverse is forming, we must also remember that we are a key component in the system. Unlike in the fiat currency system where the users are interchangeable and expendable, in the cryptoverse, we are each a unique point of data. How we interact with other data can define how we function within the system. Crypto is the building block of the metaverse, but it is the users that are the "meta" in the metaverse. [15]

Conclusion

To understand the field of cryptocurrency, you need to first understand what the currency itself is. As we explore the development of the field, we have an obligation to understand where our terminology came from, where it is, and where it is going. Words have meaning, and in that meaning, we find their utility.

The link between crypto, the blockchain, and decentralized finance is central to how the evolving system of cryptocurrency works. One cannot exist (efficiently) without the other. As the system evolves, the linkages will become stronger; however, as it is evolving, we need to understand that an action in one area can cause an unanticipated action in another section. Regulation in one area can cause a market collapse in another.

The more we move away from the central banking cartels and their controlled, centralized system of finance, the more the logic behind crypto

[15] Sudan, Randeep (2021) "How Should Governments Prepare for the Metaverse." Digital Diplomacy at https://medium.com/digital-diplomacy/how-should-governments-prepare-for-the-metaverse-90fd03387a2a.

makes sense. Currency should not be a "thing" for currencies' sake, it should simply be a tool to facilitate transactions across multiple systems. Fiat currency is perceived to have value because we want it to have value; however, its value should be centered in the transaction- not in the actual currency itself.

As we lose the bonds of surly earth, we must realize that space, the metaverse, and even continued human existence on this planet relies on a better system of commerce. A system where people do not hoard the currency as an asset, rather they use the currency as a tool. This flow of the currency will allow many economic theories to function; theories that are befuddled by the concept of hoarding currency and an absolute value of the currency. Change is needed for currency to work properly and help people move toward a better age.

Chapter 2: The Difference Between Coins and Tokens

One of the first concepts that one needs to understand when entering into the forum of digital decentralized currency is the terminology difference between "coins" and "tokens." For 90% of the people who are involved with cryptocurrency, or who want to be, the terms "coins" and "tokens" will be interchangeable. However, if you want to be competent and heavily involved with the system, you need to understand the key differences between the two systems, because in the differences lies the applicability of the system.

This Chapter serves as a primer to introduce you to the concepts of "coins" and "tokens." Because this is a constantly changing field, the definitions vary from day to day, but some core concepts will always stand when looking at the crypto markets. While the definition of a "coin" or a "token" may change over the evolution of the system, one of the first elements that any serious crypto investor needs to understand is that coins and tokens are not, nor will they ever be the same thing.

What is a Coin?

A crypto coin is digital money.[16] This is a universal element that can be exchanged anywhere that it is accepted.[17] At the most basic level, the concept of cryptocurrency is so simple that it hurts. When explaining this in business meetings and lectures, some people have trouble finding the "zen" that cryptocurrency is just another type of money. Once you accept this basic idea, you can move on to the more complex concepts of the coin.

The first of these concepts is that the basic value of the coin is derived from the blockchain, a system of processors which are independently operated, yet connected to create the modern backbone of the digital world.[18] Unlike

---

[16] Crypto 101 (2021). "What is cryptocurrency? A Beginners guide" Cointelegraph at https://cointelegraph.com/blockchain-for-beginners/what-is-a-cryptocurrency-a-beginners-guide-to-digital-money.

[17] *Id.*

[18] Bonpay (2018). "What is the Difference Between Coins and Tokens?" Bonpay at https://medium.com/@bonpay/what-is-the-difference-between-coins-and-tokens-6cedff311c31.

the current fiat currency, which is based on what the government (or the federal reserve) says money is worth, or the classic currency model (where the issuing body held some sort of surety in place for the notes that they issued) cryptocurrency has a constantly growing valuation model, which in most cases will be called transitional value.[19]

The next of the core concepts is the validation. A coin is only valid if the parties to the transaction believe that it is valid. In a common physical world transaction, there are two validators (three if you count the government, but you really should not).[20] The buyer agrees that the currency that they have is worth enough to purchase the good that they would like. The seller also agrees that the currency is valued at a rate where they would like to sell the good. Both are agreeing that the government issued coin or note has the value that is stated. This "two-factor" authentication has been the core of business for centuries.

With digital coins, there is nothing for the actors to look at. This means that there needs to be a secondary form of validation. In this case, most cryptos use three (or more) validating factors on the chain.[21] Each coin is unique (which is a difficult concept as each physical real-world coin is also unique from an existential perspective).[22] The block in the chain validates the coin is the coin that the buyer says that it is, and validates that it is going to the

---

[19] Though this is explained in Chapter 31, transitional value is the flow through value of a specific space. In the physical "real" world, a good analogy is a toll road. While the driver on the road has a use value for the road, the driver never owns or has exclusive ownership of the portion of road that he or she is on, except for the exact moment that the driver is in that position (use value). The space behind them is no longer of value to them, the space ahead of them only has value if is vacant. When transactions occur across the block in the chain, the user only has value applied (for which they are charged) when their transaction is being validated. The transitional value is the value of the use, by that user at the given time. This is the value of the coin (or in some cases the token).

[20] Liquid (2021). "Crypto Coin v. Token: Understanding the Difference." Liquid at https://blog.liquid.com/coin-vs-token.

[21] PWC (2021). "Bitcoin, Cryptocurrency, Blockchain... what does it all mean?" PWC at https://www.pwc.com/us/en/industries/financial-services/fintech/bitcoin-blockchain-cryptocurrency.html.

[22] *Id.*

seller's wallet.[23] The block then uses independent verification from multiple sources. This leads to a system that is more accurate and less prone to counterfeiting.

Finally, the coins are tradable. While this should come as no surprise, many people have a hard time with this concept. The coin itself moves around the digital space, which means that it can be in different places.[24] The Old Guard (OG) programmers and investors tend to struggle with this the most. While physical coins need to move from place to place, the OG seems to feel that the crypto moving along high level of encryptions is less secure when the opposite is true. Coins, as long as you type the wallet address incorrectly, will always be validated in the wallet before the transaction is closed.

What is a Token?

To answer the question of "what is a token?" we have to know that there are two different answers. The first type of token is a transactional token; what a lot of people confuse with coins.[25] The second type of token is a Non-Fungible Token, or NFT, which we cover later in Chapter 48. The reason that we separate tokens and NFTs is due to their nature. Tokens are an investable asset, which can be used as a currency; NFTs, on the other hand, are assets that are kept for their ownership (like art).[26]

Basic tokens do not have their own blockchain.[27] Each token out there operates on another blockchain, like BAT or KIROS, operating on the Ethereum blockchain.[28] In the first and second Wave of cryptocurrencies,

---

[23] *Id.*
[24] *Liquid, Supra.*
[25] Cryptopedia Staff (2021). "Digital Assets: Cryptocurrencies v. Tokens." Cryptopedia at https://www.gemini.com/cryptopedia/cryptocurrencies-vs-tokens-difference; please note that they are using a different lexicon, coins a the equivalent of cryptocurrency in their lexicon, where cryptocurrency covers tokens in modern parlance.
[26] *Id.*
[27] Karamat, Sheba (2021). "What is a token?" Coin Rivet at https://coinrivet.com/guides/guide/what-is-a-token/.
[28] *Id.*

coins could be traded anywhere, but tokens could only be used for specific purpose.[29] With the advent of spider-bridging across the different chains through the use of exchanges, tokens have, in their own right, become nearly as transferable as coins.

Coins also tend to be more complex than tokens. The native smart contracts on a specific chain tend to denote the complexity of a coin; however, the tokens that arise out of that chain or contract can be as simple as cash or as complex as the chain itself.[30] When investing in a token, make sure you understand the complexity and use of the token. Further, if you invest in something make sure that you know what it is designed for, what it is used for and how it should be used.

The big takeaway is that tokens can be more versatile than coins. Whereas coins can only "be one thing," tokens have the ability to expand the definition of what they can do. We have seen this in the development of the NFT market and in the creation of the metaverse (which is just a collection of NFTs interacting.[31] As we explore the crypto space more deeply, we are finding that people around the world will come up with new ways to use coins and tokens as the ecosystem evolves.

Where can a Coin be Used?

One of the biggest questions that are heard from OG investors is, "Where can a coin be used?"[32] This is one of the myths that surround

---

[29] Liquid, *Supra*.

[30] M, Laura (2021). "Toke vs Coin: What's the Difference?" BitDegree at https://www.bitdegree.org/crypto/tutorials/token-vs-coin.

[31] Coinbase (2021). "Why are NFTs important?" at https://www.coinbase.com/learn/crypto-basics/plp-what-is-nft?utm_source=google_search_nb&utm_medium=cpc&utm_campaign=14578273644&utm_content=125317687885&utm_term=nft%20explained&utm_creative=544646171720&cb_device=c&cb_placement=&cb_country=us&cb_city=open&cb_language=en_us&gclid=CjwKCAiAiKuOBhBQEiwAId_sK5w5ly-KZ-gvmuC0BTdlweVd5bdXkSXk3WGIRtIZImVUqLVHK7NOnhoC3ooQAvD_BwE.

[32] Tuwiner, Jordan (2021). "Who accepts bitcoin? 11 Major companies." Buy Bitcoin Worldwide at https://www.buybitcoinworldwide.com/who-accepts-bitcoin/. This list is actually much longer.

cryptocurrency, that you can only use coin if you are in the know. Like many myths, this myth is based a little in fact. The cryptoverse is still developing. There are a limited number of places currently in the world that accept crypto-currency. However, this is not because you need to be in the know to use it, it is because the adoption is a slow process, especially with regulatory agencies looming in the sidelines with no real guidance on how the government is going to interfere.

Coin, just like currency, can be used anywhere you can find another person who would like to conduct business with you in your preferred coin. This can be on exchanges, simple transactions, or even as an investment opportunity. The key factor here is that there needs to be a bargain for exchange, just like in any contract. Thus, as silly as this sounds, you can use a coin anywhere you can use it.

As the ecosystem develops around coins, users are finding that it is easier to use coins. Some exchanges, such as Crypto.com or Binance, have even started offering credit cards that create the exchange for you.[33] While these systems are in the early phases of utility, they are showing the variability of people having wealth stored in various assets that can be intermingled for immediate use and investment. The days of savings being completely separate from your "spendable" are over as the market is making everyone more liquid. But with this change comes more responsibility, you have to manage your finances more readily.

One of the biggest advancements of 2021 was countries that are adopting digital currencies as a secondary currency.[34] While some OG commentators, such as Jeffrey Frankel, argue that it is pure folly for countries to accept crypto, this is the Wave of the future.[35] One of the greatest scams of history is governments issuing currency, it is simply a

---

[33] *See* Binance.com and Crypto.com.

[34] Frankel, Jeffery (2021). "El Salvador's Adoption of bitcoin as legal tender is pure folly." The Guardian at https://www.theguardian.com/business/2021/sep/24/el-salvador-adoption-of-bitcoin-as-legal-tender-is-pure-folly

[35] *Id.*

means of control of the masses. By accepting cryptocurrencies, some countries are giving their people a freedom that they would never experience under the fiat system.

Commentors such as Frankel do have one area right, the countries may have chosen the wrong system.[36] By choosing one coin (or in some cases a limited family of coins), the country is trading one limited system with another limited system. Spider bridge methods have allowed acceptance of any participating crypto across the board, which means limiting to one crypto not only stifles the market, but also prevents citizens from widely expanding their reach globally as potential investors.

To be clear, the OG opinion that crypto coins can only be accepted "if you are in the know," is false, it is a myth that is spread by people who are not "in the know."[37] Anyone can access crypto, and anyone can put it on an exchange and convert it into the currency of their choice. The question is whether you have the time to do that and whether companies are going to continue to make the process easier for individuals. As using your crypto becomes just as easy as using your credit card, accept that you are not debt financing yourself, it will become readily apparent that this is a better method than the 2000 years of relying on colored pieces of paper and shiny pieces of metal.

Where can you spend tokens?

Transactions involving tokens are slightly more complicated than simple transactions with coins. Coins are just like money, which means that they can be traded for goods and services without any real controls being put upon them. While some networks have "gas fees," which are costs that a person pays for the "privilege of accessing the network, many coins are abandoning this model.[38] It is being replaced with smart contracts that "burn" an amount of the coin to ensure that the supply continues to grow

---

[36] *Id.*

[37] Royal, James & Voight, Kevin (2021). "What is cryptocurrency? Here's what you should know." Nerdwallet at https://www.nerdwallet.com/article/investing/cryptocurrency-7-things-to-know.

[38] KIROS White Paper.

in value.

The first type of tokens we look at similarly to regular coins. These tokens are simply soft or hard forks on the chain that allows for added utility. Using KIROS as an example, the enhanced smart contract overlay allows for the coins ecosystem to be maintained through a "smart burn and earn" system that constantly increases each coin and token in the ecosystem's value.[39] Ironically, with this system, it brings up the value of all cooperating cryptos while keeping the entire supply in circulation (with some staking).

The second type of tokens are tokens with hybrid values. Many coins are designed to be functional only on a given network; however, as they evolve in popularity the designers allow them to be used elsewhere.[40] This increases the viability of the coin, but also can make the foundational network unreliable. In many cases, this is an example of designers having an idea and then abandoning the idea as they see the opportunity for the coin to make them money.

The third type of token is a token that is usable only on a given system. These tokens are created to ease transactions for a given purpose (like a gaming community or metaverse system) and stay within these parameters. While these tokens can be traded on some exchanges, they are mostly used for internal transactions. These tend to be the most stable coins in the second Wave system; however, under the third Wave system the stability gap has been closed, and some say even exceeded by tokens that mimic coins. Really, why use a token that is limited to a single system when you can use a token that is usable across all systems?

The final category that we look at are "Stablecoins."[41] While this topic will

---

[39] KIROS White Paper.

[40] David Rodeck, & Benjamin Curry(2021). "An Introduction to Dogecoin, The Meme currency." *Forbes* at https://www.forbes.com/advisor/investing/what-is-dogecoin/.

[41] Stellar (2021). "Stablecoin." At https://resources.stellar.org/what-are-stablecoins?utm_term=%2Bwhat%20%2Bis%20%2Bstablecoin&utm_campaign=Search:+Payments&utm_source=adwords&utm_medium=ppc&hsa_acc=8782384464&hsa_cam=12953021934&hsa_grp=124695784227&hsa_ad=518895296863

get several Chapters (Chapters 4, 5 & 6), the idea of stable coins warrants mention here. A Stablecoin is a token that is linked to an asset. The first edition of stable tokens (called Stablecoin 1.0) were always linked to a currency. The effect of this was much like a company store, once you have the token it can be used anywhere the token is accepted, but in all likelihood, the currency that the token is attached to has the same utility.

Ripple (XRP) experimented with a gold-backed coin, which is a step backward in some commentator's mind.[42] Linking their coin to the value of gold has the potential of the coin to grow in value; however, gold falls victim to the same growth and depreciation cycle that currencies can face so there are problems with that model as well. The gold-backed tokens tend to be more likely to be regulated as they are "shares" in a commodity stockpile, rather than a representation of an economic system.

Stablecoin 2.0 are tokens that are working within a larger ecosystem of investments.[43] The largest family, the family working off of *The Wallet Group* system, attaches the value of component tokens to a large investment portfolio held by a publicly traded company to ensure that the system is always growing. While this system is vulnerable to ups and downs, it simulates the constant growth of a mutual fund that is actively managed- however, with a vastly diversified portfolio.[44]

&hsa_src=g&hsa_tgt=kwd-1211384036608&hsa_kw=%2Bwhat%20%2Bis%20%2Bstablecoin&hsa_mt=p&hsa_net=adwords&hsa_ver=3&gclid=CjwKCAiAiKuOBhBQEiwAld_sK2aleqS3IBDSQqiSnpt5MzfLouevthKxvEkRsrAJXiGVdBameSEg3BoCdloQAvD_BwE.

[42] Mason, Bob (2021) "Ripple XRP price prediction 2022" Yahoo finance at https://finance.yahoo.com/news/ripple-xrp-price-prediction-2022-020451677.html?guccounter=1&guce_referrer=aHR0cHM6Ly93d3cuZ29vZ2xlLmNvbS8&guce_referrer_sig=AQAAAJZm54FhSUZswiF4yHEOawidw4qBUZ6ZpV3iZ3WpA0R7B4tYyYEMvdWIfa0q22FpCKpnoGezg3tW4dtV0egxmBNL4AtX9T_Js5QLWER0HCQF93oW8vuEgz33GwKZJhK2n56H3v00yhjYD5i-hFtcGKkwcL8NOl6rcLM3A_0-0I7G.

[43] KIROS Whitepaper (at *Black Wallet* LTD Website).

[44] *Id.*

What Makes a Token or Coin Valuable?

The valuation of the token can be a challenging thing. Economically, there are four different types of value that can be attributed to a crypto coin/token.[45] These types of value are transitional value, transactional value, market value and inherent value. While each of these topics gets its own Chapter, transactional value is the value of the exchange, the market value is the value the market attributes to the coin/token, transitional value is the value gained by the use of the smart contract overlays and the confirmation of the coin/token's authenticity, and inherent value is the value of the support system. Many tokens or coins only have one or two of these, some of the more advanced system such as KIROS have all four.

Coins values change over time. Market values change on a second-by-second basis.[46] The transitional value changes depending on the time of day and the traffic. "The transactional value changes based on the perceived value of the coin and the usability," the more places that accept the coin the higher transactional value a coin has.[47] The inherent value is measurable in how many coins exist and what the value of the "backing is" less the reserve amount of the coin/token, divided by the number of unstaked coins in circulation.

As the ecosystem for cryptocurrency develops, the value of the coins will increase as the transactional value of the coin outpaces the market value. Investors will always keep the value of the coin in a controlled growth, where transactional value of the coin will rise to meet the need. In an unmanaged market, the coin will always experience inflation. In a managed

---

[45] IPBES (2021). "Economic valuation." IPBES at https://ipbes.net/economic-valuation.

[46] Redman, James (2021). "Stablecoin valuations continue to swell, MIM and MUSD Market Caps increase triple digit in 30 days." Bitcoin.com at https://news.bitcoin.com/stablecoin-valuations-continue-to-swell-mim-and-musd-market-caps-increase-by-triple-digits-in-30-days/.

[47] Redman, James (2021). "Valuation of stablecoin DAI Market Swells- DAI Market cap increase more than 800% in 12 months." Bitcoin.com at https://news.bitcoin.com/valuation-of-stablecoin-dai-market-swells-dai-market-cap-increased-more-than-800-in-12-months/.

market, the coin will always see a value growth. Where coins and tokens choose to affiliate with define which way the value goes.

Difference between coins and tokens for use

When we are looking at how a coin or token is being used, the difference in the coin or token can be negligible or they can be quite important. The questions then become what ecosystem the exchange is taking place in and what use is being conducted (see next section for investing). The more complex the system, the more likely you will want to use a token, the more general the more likely you will want to use a coin.[48]

Token, especially dedicated tokens, thrive in a system where there is a lot of complexity. Tokenomics allow for the token to be constantly updated to the value within the system.[49] These types of tokens tend to rely heavily on their transitional value for their valuation, however, we can see transactional value taking up the lions share of the total valuation. When being used in a closed system, the market tends to have limited, if any influence, on the value of the token. Because they are designed for a closed system, they also tend to have little or no real-world or digital "support" for the stability of the token. In these cases, while the operators would gladly accept coins, tokens tend to be the preferred payment method.

Conversely, when the system is a general transaction, coins or GET (Global exchange tokens or general exchange tokens) are the preferred means of transactions.[50] GET tokens or coins allow for the utmost liquidity of a transaction while ensuring that the transaction is secure. As a general rule, the more types of valuation (transactional, transitional, market, and inherent value) that are present, the more useful the coin is for general

---

[48] Slideshare presentation (2021). https://www.slideshare.net/TrentMcConaghy/tokens-and-complex-systems.

[49] Staff (2021). "Tokenomics: Demand and Supply of Cryptocurrencies." Times of India at https://timesofindia.indiatimes.com/business/cryptocurrency/blockchain/tokenomics-demand-and-supply-of-cryptocurrencies/articleshow/87273549.cms?from=mdr.

[50] KIROS White Paper (*Black Wallet* LTD Website).

transactions. In countries where a specific coin is a legal tender, you generally have to use that coin as a proxy for the national currency.

Difference between coins and tokens for investment

When it comes to investment, the market is still out on how the coins and tokens will perform. From what we have seen, coins tend to be a good long-term investment and tokens tend to be more effective for the short-term investment model. The third Wave of cryptos seems to be bucking this trend with a high reward/low-risk model for coins in the "smart burn and earn" ecosystem. Because the system manages the growth rate to constantly increase the values of the holdings within the ecosystem, the system tends to increase fast enough for short term investment but really shines in the long term.

One totally unknown area is how the derivatives markets within the crypto space will function.[51] Since derivatives are already a volatile market, they seem to be a bad combination with an already volatile alt-coin market. However, because of the nature of derivatives, there is the possibility that the derivatives themselves will actually help regulate the alt-coin market. Though it is not an alt-coin, the market maneuvered to correct before the Bitcoin options went into effect in November 2021.

The question remains: are coins and tokens a good tool for investing? To answer this, we need to look at the markets in general. Whether you are investing in stocks, bonds, commodities, or crypto, you are gambling. In this case, you are taking money that you presently have and buying a bet that the money will be worth more in the future. Crypto plays just like stocks, bonds, and commodities. The only difference is that the casino is not as regulated. There are fortunes to be made in crypto on the open market, but for every fortune made, remember, that one is also lost.

Difference between Coins and Tokens in the DeFi system

One of the most alluring aspects of the crypto ecosystem is the

---

[51] Latham and Watkins (2015). "Client Alert." Latham and Watkins at https://www.lw.com/thoughtLeadership/lw-regulatory-notes-bitcoin-cryptocurrency-derivatives.

decentralized nature of the finance. In most cases, the more decentralized a financial system is, the less likely it is to be universally affected by market changes. That being said, if you look at any set of crypto coins/tokens together in the market, you will see that they tend to follow the same trends.[52] One or two may follow different patterns to the bulk, but the ebb and flow of the markets always tend to mirror one another.

Currently there are enough coins on the market that we have a basic decentralized market. This market is very much like the wild, wild west. As a result, the markets have the ability to act independently but a majority of tokens and coins in play are held by people (or AI) that are trading following the same patterns.[53] Elon Musk tweets something the markets jump or fall. The fed announces interest rates, the markets jump or fall.[54] As we see more coins and more advanced systems of decentralization, we will see more unique patterns and more ability to move coins around to avoid losses.

Tokens also tend to follow the same pattern, though there are more tokens so they can operate more independently. Tokens tend to have followings, and these followings can support a token even in a downturn. Unlike coins, which tend to function like currency, the tokens act as a commodity where the community bands together to help them stay in a good place. This is not to say that tokens will not see double-digit losses, but when it does happen you will have millions of people saying "buy the dip."

Conclusion

So, what is the key difference between a coin and a token? A coin carries its own blockchain, while a token is built on top of another blockchain. Understand this difference and you will be worlds ahead of the millions of people who are just betting systems on the market. Once you can

---

[52] *Infra*.

[53] Altfins (2021). "Crypto chart patterns." Alt Fins at https://altfins.com/knowledge-base/chart-patterns/.

[54] Leach, Ollie (2021). "3 Crypto chart patterns to help make sense of the market." Coin Desk at https://www.coindesk.com/markets/2021/07/06/3-crypto-chart-patterns-to-help-make-sense-of-the-market/.

understand the key difference, the other differences between coins and tokens seem to make more sense. Market patterns and patterns from tokens in the same family start to stand out, you can organize your charts more effectively and see which items are more useful to you to hold.

Likewise, if you are holding coins for purchases, you can see where the modeling is going and see whether today is a good day to buy or if your coin may be worth a little more tomorrow. As long as the world is still using the fiat currency as the "price" of goods, then coins will always be present in a ratio to that currency. When the ecosystem adjusts and companies start listing the prices of goods in the crypto (it is happening) the crypto will be more effective and people will have an easier time using the coin. Coins and tokens are the keys in the world of crypto economics, the more you see the relationships between coins and tokens and tokens to tokens, the better able you will be able to manage your wealth.

Chapter 3: Tokenomics

Why does something have value? When you are looking at cryptos, you need to ask why this item, pulled from the ether of the digital world has value. To understand this value, you need to understand tokenomics. Tokenomics is the practice of assessing the "value of a cryptocurrency based on the valuation," the distribution, the application, the reserves, and the community of the coin. Whenever a coin is launched, its tokenomics should be discussed in the White Paper. This allows the community to decide whether the coin will be valuable or not.

This Chapter breaks down the system of tokenomics so that a layperson can use methods similar to those that a professional will use. Simpler methods do not mean that they are not as successful, just that they are less complex. In the first section, we look at the basics of what it takes to be a crypto. Sometimes we see digital creations enter the market that does not have the elements to be crypto, they may still be valuable assets, but without the key elements- they are not crypto.

There are three general families of analytics that exist in tokenomics (at the basic level). These are the basics, the value to the system, and putting the coin in people's hands. Each of these categories has subcategories that allow the analysis to be more robust, but in this Chapter, we only look at the basics needed to decide if a coin is worth pursuing or not.

The more the science of tokenomics evolves, the less the "art" of tokenomics will be relevant. The basic categories that we cover are only scratching the surface. Each new generation of the coin, each new iteration of staking will change the market. These changes can be major or minor, but the system of tokenomics needs to adjust with each change. As the system grows, we need to grow with it.

What Does it Take to Be a Crypto?

When we look at the tokenomics of a coin, the first thing that we need to look at is whether the coin exists or not. Some of the best ideas for a coin have died on the vine because the creators could not get funding for the coin. Still, others published their White Paper too early and their coin was cannibalized by actors in the space who could build the coin more quickly. Regardless of why many of the best ideas in crypto were not optimized by those who came up with the idea. Therefore, when you look at the tokenomics of the coin, the first question, as silly as it may seem is, "does it exist?"

Next, we need to look at whether the coin has value or not. There are dozens of different systems of code on each of the major blockchains that allow you to spool up a "junk coin" with nothing more than a little transitional value and some of the base coin backing it.[55] This means that the coin has some value, but not much. This is where many coins start because the creators of the coin are not looking at why the coin should be valuable, just hoping that it is valuable. Good coins should enter the market with a good plan in each of the four valuation categories, transitional (what does the smart contract do), Transactional (who will use it), market (what exchanges will it be on), and inherent (what is the reserve system for this crypto). In the third Wave of crypto, it is difficult to find the actual value of a coin that does not have these three valuation methods.

Acceptance is another important element of any coin. Is the crypto a niche coin/token? Does it work in multiple situations? Is it an exchange token to facilitate the spiderweb bridge? Each of these questions will help you find the audience that may be looking at a coin. When it comes to the worth of a coin, if no one wants the coin, then it is worth less than a coin that people want. That does not mean that it is worthless, just that it is not as valuable as other cryptos.

What it all comes down to: the market must accept a coin - and the people must want a coin for it to have value. Clever names, good marketing, well-placed distribution can take a coin with limited transitional value and turn it into a crypto powerhouse, but someone needs to understand the tokenomics of the system for that to happen. Just creating a coin and slapping it on the market may have worked in the 2nd Wave of cryptocurrency, but in the third Wave, the new investors and the OG

---

[55] Unfortunately, the term "junk coin" refers to tokens and coins without value.

exchanges will eat a coin with little value alive.

Basics

Before you run, you need to walk. Before you walk, you need to know the basics. Sometimes in the crypto world, we see people create tokens with amazing utility, but they fail because they have not looked at the basic elements that make a coin viable: the name, the function, and who is putting the coin on the market. These are the first level steps that any crypto needs to look at, without them a coin will have a difficult time entering the market.

Some of the best ideas in crypto have started with a simple placeholder name. "Coin12735" is a great placeholder when you are walking through the design of a coin. You can increase the number each time that you make a change to your design so that you can see what iteration of the system you are resting on. This works great in a lab space, so great that people get attached to names like this. The market does not like generic names. Even very basic names can have trouble on the market. Make sure that your coin has a name that people will remember.

On the other end of the spectrum is coin who have names that are too tricky. Coins that have offensive names, coins that are named based on someone famous, or coins whose names are just too complicated tend to have short lives. They work as pump and dump coins, if you are willing to jump into this casino- more power to you. However, if you are a serious user who wants to work in the market to make the crypto dream a reality, pump and dump coins are some of the most dangerous elements to faith in the system. Look for something with a cool simple name, those are the coins people will remember.

Once you find a name for a coin, the coin then needs to have a function. Even the generic code that anyone can download off the internet to make a coin has a basic function (usually mathematical). The more useful the function, the more your block will be used. The more your block is used, the more the transitional value of the coin will be. Moving beyond the transitional worth of a coin, you also need to have use of the coin once it is created. A block can have great utility, but if the coin has no purpose outside of being created, then it will suffer in its market value. This is where the transactional value of the coin must be developed. People need to use the coin for the coin to have transactional value, so always ask who the users are.

The final basic element that you need to look for is who is putting the coin out. Early in the game, anyone could put a coin on the market and roll the dice to see if it was effective. Some of the best coins and tokens on the market were created by a person known only by their tag. As the market matures, there are several reasons for a coin to be marketed by a company. First and foremost is the liability. If you create a coin that fails and costs people a lot of money, then you may find yourself the focus of a lawsuit. Even if you only use your tag for the creation of the coin, someone will still hunt you down. Having a company gives you basic protections against lawsuits, you may lose the company if there is a lawsuit- but it will likely protect your private holdings.

Another reason that investors are looking for cryptos that are created by companies is that the system is becoming more complex. Companies tend to give the impression that there is a team working on the coin, not just a crypto cowboy hoping to strike it big. Regardless of how many people are in the company, the company name can inspire confidence in the new crypto. Think of this when you are looking at names for the crypto and the company, while a name may be fun talking to your teammates "Mikes Saggy Pants" does not inspire confidence in investors.

Value to The System

Once the basics of crypto are out of the way, creators need to look at what value the coin adds to the system. There are thousands of cryptos on the market today, what makes their coin different from the others. The pump and dump crowd do not care about this, they just want a coin that they can make money off of; however, teams that are building coins that will advance the dream of digital currency need to think long and hard about what their coin will add to the market. As an investor, you too need to look at what the coin brings to the table.

The first thing that you need to look at when approaching this level is the valuation of the coin. Every company on the market comes to play with the value that they think their coin should be worth. Sometimes this number is correct. Most of the time this number is too high. Every once in a while, we see a team that comes to the table with their coin undervalued. Knowing how they valued their coin is paramount in seeing if you agree with the valuation. Does the White Paper tell you how they valued their coin (or are they letting the system value it). If they did value it, what is the transitional value? What is the transactional value? What is the inherent value? How will the market receive it? These are all questions that must be asked if you are going to assess where a coin is going on the market.

Next, is there a way to increase value? This is where tokenomics gets a little complicated, the ability to increase value is not imperative. What is more important is that the crypto is going to be able to retain its value. Stablecoin 1.0 faced the problem of coins not holding value because the coin was based on fiat currency. Stablecoin 1.1 faced a problem when the family of assets to which the coin was attached hit a bear market. Even Stablecoin 2.0 models can have problems if their portfolio is too narrow and it does not hedge against inflation. When looking at the model to increase value, is it trying to increase or is it trying to maintain? When you have the answer to this question you will be able to answer whether they have a good plan to reach their goal.

The "valuation" element that you should look at in any crypto system is what type of reserves or holdings do they have. There are two types of reserve that you should be aware of: static and active. In a static system, the creator keeps some of the cryptos in a reserve account (separate from their private holdings) to maintain the market should there be a need for more liquidity. In an active reserve, the crypto is sold onto the market for value and the asset for which the crypto is traded are then managed like a mutual fund to increase the value of the coin. The best 3rd Wave cryptos use both models to ensure that the system is stable. As a side note, if the crypto lives long enough unless there is a standing burn the static reserve will run out. This is why it is good to have both types, even in a standing burn system.

The last valuation element that you should look at is the number of coins that are on the market. If the creator just picked a number out of the air, that is a problem. If the White Paper discusses why a specific number of coins was created, then at least there is a plan. Take the time to look at the plan and determine whether you think that it is a good plan. The number of coins is only relevant if you know why that number was selected.

The valuation of the crypto is what most people are interested in. The people who are using the crypto want to know what the crypto will be worth in trade. The people who are investing in crypto want to know if the value of the crypto will increase (or at least hold its own). Too often people skip over the basics in their analysis to jump to this stage, which can be dangerous to your funds because those coins without the basics cannot stand on valuation alone.

Putting it in People's Hands

If no one has the crypto, then it has no market or transactional value. This third level of tokenomics is vital for a crypto to be successful. Many good crypto ideas have fallen by the wayside because people cannot get the coins out of the miners' hands and into the users/investor's hands. It would be similar to a person hearing that mining gold is a great way to make money, then going to mine slate. The miner may have the market cornered on the commodity, but if no one wants the asset, then it is worthless. Generally, the more people that hold the crypto, the more it is worth. People always give more value to something that they have as their own, so good crypto developers want as many people to own the coins as possible.

Distribution is key to the whole process of ensuring that people own the coin. Many cryptos jump on the market and think they can get away with giveaways and an ICO. This may have worked early in the 2nd Wave, but there are so many coins out there trying this that people do not have time to "invest" in each and every one of these coins. This means that some good coin ideas fail because not enough people have them. Good plans get the coin in the hands of users, businesses, governments (if possible), and specific industries. This allows the coin to circulate. Once they do this, they have transactional value in play when they release their ICO to establish the market value. Good 3rd Wave coins know what they are worth before they sell coins to the public.

Another fatal flaw of many plans is not working with exchanges and DeFi banks. Yes, any crypto can put itself on a decentralized exchange and simulate an ICO, but a real ICO takes planning and coordination. Just putting a coin on an exchange is an amateur move, the crypto should be co-launched on several exchanges, hopefully with an ICO release on the exchange. This allows people to know that it is a legit ICO, not just a pump and dump. Having a DeFi bank holding the crypto reserve can also increase confidence in the crypto.

Access is another area where many coins have problems. If people cannot access a coin, then they cannot use or trade the coin. Sometimes creators can play things too close to the vest. In these cases, people cannot get access to the coin and the coin dies in the creator's wallet. Security is one thing, but making sure that your target audience can get in to use the coin is vital. Make sure that a person can also get out when they invest, some coins have anti-whale tech that will limit trade potential. This is a sign that the coin may be a scam if it has a blanket ban on large sales. Most legitimate anti-whale tech will have a limit on the amount you can trade in a time period, or force you to make several small trades rather than one large trade.

Rights are the final issue that we are discussing here. Make sure that any coin that you get involved with has full rights to the possessor of the coin. Some coins have the ability to close a wallet if the creator wants. These are not cryptos, they are power grabs. This is the same way the governments freeze your wealth if they do not like you, except in the digital world you do not have recourse. Accounts should be owned by the possessor of the wallet and the key. This is why maintaining your wallet and key in a safe way is paramount to keeping your account safe.

Better Coins through Better Tokenomics

The great thing about crypto is that it will always be growing. Unlike economics, which has stagnated into camps that are over 100 years old, tokenomics is still young and growing. These categories in this Chapter will continue to grow. Some will fade away; others will diversify as people find new ways to work with their cryptos. Evolution keeps the system fresh and the discipline growing. Politicization and stagnation are the enemies of a good system.

One of the big moves that the community can make with tokenomics is forcing the junk coins off the market. While they can be fun to play as a casino, they are hurting the investor's faith in the market. Pump and dumps hurt everyone, even the people who make money off of them because they weaken the system. As tokenomics become more established, the system can start to weed out coins and tokens that are just there to take up space. This will leave more room for the good coins to flourish and grow.

The system is already moving to Stablecoin 2.0. It is not one single coin or token that is moving the system in this direction, dozens of coins in synergy showed the need and the desire for this type of system. The more the coins have inherent value, separate from the exchange value, the more that the system has its own capabilities. Stablecoin 2.0 systems grow if they are properly managed. This means that the value can keep up and sometimes surpass the inflation of the fiat currency.

Tokenomics also allows institutions to gauge whether crypto should be on the market or not. Good tokenomics allows the system to build for a better tomorrow, bad tokenomics are easy to spot. If you look at the coins over the last few years (except the meme coins) the best tokenomics coins had the best runs. Even the meme coins have started to build around stabilization techniques that give them better tokenomics.

Finally, the market will dictate which tokenomics are best. People will use the coins that they trust the most. Even if the central banks try to force a broken Stablecoin 1.0 system down our throats, we can still rise above it by using good coins to establish trade. Each time that tokenomics evolves, it becomes a soft fork for cryptos to follow. The ones that do will survive, the ones that do not will fade into history.

Chapter 4: Stablecoin 1.0

One of the most important improvements that happened during the development of 2nd Wave crypto is the development of Stablecoin 1.0.[56] Before Stablecoin, there was no inherent value in crypto. The system was based on the transitional value and the market value. This allowed the market to be a very wildly fluctuating market. As a result, many investors were leery of entering into the crypto market; remembering the junk bond market of the 90s and its collapse (or the subprime mortgage crisis).

In this Chapter, we look at the development of Stablecoin as a concept in the crypto world. The first key phase in this development is the idea that crypto needs to have some sort of value backing it. Without the value, the coin is simply mimicking the fiat currency system that we sought to replace. Next, we look at the idea behind Stablecoin 1.0.[57] Like the first wheel was not the same wheel that you would put on a Ferrari today, the first Stablecoin was a necessary evolutionary step, but not a final product.

Evolution is a vital concept in the world of cryptocurrency. After Stablecoin 1.0 started to go flat, the idea of a coin linked to something else moved into the market. This was still a mono-asset or a low-volume style of holding, but the system did move the system towards a better idea. This is the foundation of Stablecoin 1.1. While still not a fully developed system, it managed to shake off some of the naysayers who were attacking the stable coin system.

This Chapter concludes with the idea that overly linked currencies are part of the problem. As such, we are looking at how the development of new

---

[56] Stellar (2020). "Stablecoins" Stellar at https://resources.stellar.org/what-are-stablecoins?utm_term=%2Bstablecoin&utm_campaign=Search:+Payments&utm_source=adwords&utm_medium=ppc&hsa_acc=8782384464&hsa_cam=12953021934&hsa_grp=124695784227&hsa_ad=518895296863&hsa_src=g&hsa_tgt=kwd-1211381016448&hsa_kw=%2Bstablecoin&hsa_mt=p&hsa_net=adwords&hsa_ver=3&gclid=Cj0KCQiAlMCOBhCZARIsANLid6YjKVj6V3az1l4VuAnTiJJZnYBPGNTIw7dbtKLjUatjghW5pX5urXkaAgQ0EALw_wcB.

[57] Hayes, Supra.

models, like Stablecoin 2.0, is vital for the survival and evolution of cryptocurrency. The more we allow this type of evolution to take place, the more we are able to ensure that crypto will move along the right path.

The Concept of Stablecoin

When the crypto market was in full flux during the summer of 2020, there was an anchor that allowed serious investors to look at the market and make their plans. This anchor was the Stablecoin 1.0 system. At the time, this system was simply called Stablecoin, so people would see that the coin had a relationship to a real-world asset, thus making them more stable on the market.[58] When the system was ebbing and booming very quickly, this anchor allowed for there to be a "stable" crypto that investors could look at and understand the value of the cryptosystem.

In any Stablecoin relationship, there is something with value and there is a coin that represents that value. This value to coin relationship is vital in fining the inherent value of the coin, which is a valuation method alongside the transitional value and the market value.[59] Oftentimes the market value will hold pace with the inherent value of the coin. There becomes a problem when the transitional value of the coin starts to suppose the inherent value of the coin, when this happens the coin trades at above what the 1:1 ratio would suggest, meaning the coin has more value than the reserve. This can destabilize the system.

The building transitional value of the coin will always be a problem in a Stablecoin 1.0 model. Unless the value of the underlying asset is rising at the rate of inflation and matching the growth in the transitional value of the coin, the coin will see a point where it is overleveraged against its holdings.[60] The only remedy of this is to take value from the transitional value to increase the size of the stake- but that in itself starts to devalue the process of the Stablecoin concept.

---

[58] Ethereum.org (2021). "Stablecoins" Ethereum at https://ethereum.org/en/stablecoins/.

[59] Hayes, Supra.

[60] Ethereum, Supra.

The dual (and sometimes triple) valuation of the coin creates a difficult situation for many traders. While the triple valuation of the coin does give a better triangulation of the actual value of the coin than the single or dual model, it can still be problematic as there is not a safety valve to relieve the pressure created by heavy trading in the market or heavy use in transactions. This can result in an over (or under) leveraged coin.

The Idea Behind Stablecoin 1.0

Stablecoin 1.0 is a proxy for fiat currency. This is why so many countries are clamoring that there needs to be some sort of Stablecoin model for any currency to be used as legal tender. Governments of the world understand the concept of fiat currency; they print it, we get more value (apparent) and the market has to deal with the value (real) of the currency. One of the reasons that they like Stablecoin 1.0 is because it is based on fiat currency.

The most common currency used for Stablecoin 1.0 is the U.S. Dollar. With the dollar being the standard currency for global exchange this makes the most sense. Also, the fact that most rogue regimes attack the U.S. dollar, means that it is a good target for linking currency (fake money for staking). This allows corrupt people and regimes to use the Stablecoin 1.0 model to launder money. Print fake money in a third-world country, use the money to buy crypto in a Stablecoin 1.0 system, then dump the Stablecoin for fiat currency and let the holders deal with the fake bills. This is one of the key reasons that Stablecoin 2.0 models do not allow 1 for 1 trade (a third party holds the value system, see next Chapter).

When a currency is linked to a single asset, especially a single currency, the market movements in the currency markets can devalue the currency. A fiat currency is always going to face inflation, because they are always printing more than they destroy. This means that there will always be a drag on the currency. In the early days of crypto, this drag was acceptable because the market was growing so quickly. Once many of the Stablecoin reached their plateau, the inflation started to reduce the value of the coins on a daily basis.

Novice traders also tend to look at the U.S. Dollar as a static value. It is not.

Just like any currency, the U.S. dollar fluctuates in value in relation to other currencies.[61] With a Stablecoin that is linked to the U.S. Dollar, when there is a major movement in the dollar (in a downward direction) the holder of the coin can see a rapid drop.[62] Even if they exchange directly for the dollar their coin is worth, they are losing value quickly. Stablecoin 1.0 is just fiat currency with a few extra steps.

It was, however, a necessary step in the evolution of cryptocurrency. Without Stablecoin 1.0, the system would have never fully developed. The need for an inherent valuation of a coin is now apparent to most serious traders on the market. While linking to dying fiat currency is an evolutionary dead end, the concept is a sound one. The market knows that there needs to be some inherent value behind the coins. Now with the 3rd Wave crypto, we are exploring those methods of valuation.

The Idea Behind Stablecoin 1.1

Stablecoin 1.1 took a new direction from Stablecoin 1.0. In the Stablecoin 1.0 system, the asset chosen for which the currency was linked was a fiat currency. This was all and good until the coin plateaued in value. Then when the ratio stagnated, the coin began to lose value as inflation undermined the value of the coin. Stablecoin 1.1 pioneers realized that perhaps fiat currency was not the best asset to which to link the coin.[63] This led them to move on to other assets, which had variable markets.

The most common asset for a Stablecoin 1.1 to be linked to is a precious metal. Ripple was among the leaders with a precious metal linked Stablecoin 1.1. Linking their coin to gold (with other coins linked to other metals) showed the crypto world that a coin could be linked to something other than a currency. The model was quite effective, but also quite limited. When the commodity was up, the coin was up. When the commodity went down, the coin went down. For many people, this led them to wonder why they would not just invest in gold, and skip the steps

---

[61] Hayes, Supra.
[62] Stellar, Supra.
[63] Hayes, Supra.

of dealing with the crypto.

Single asset linking, while better than fiat linking, is still not a very good model. Even when you link to an entire family of assets, that market can move up and down and that can cause the value of the coin to fluctuate. When the market is in a rally, this can be a great thing for the crypto; however, when you are losing money, the crypto does not look like a good idea. While this did enlighten people that they could move beyond fiat, it still falls flat as an ecosystem management device.

Stablecoin 1.1 is necessary to the system, however, because it showed what direction the system needs to go. Moving away from fiat currency is a good idea, moving to a single asset (or a single family of assets) was not a good idea. This opened the door for Stablecoin 2.0 to link currencies to many different assets combining a money market, a commodity market, and a mutual fund all under one general holding scheme.

Overly Linked Currencies

The Achilles heel of the Stablecoin 1.0 and Stablecoin 1.1 families is that they decided to hitch their horse to one wagon. While the concept was there, they did not realize that this was just making the coin or token a proxy for the underlying asset. This is another reason that the governments of the world are so interested in Stablecoin systems, they want them to be attached to a single underlying asset so that they become securities. Once we make the move to a Stablecoin 2.0 system, they are attached to several different markets- which make them what they should be, a currency.

Single asset cryptos are an anchor. When the market was rapidly moving, they were something that secured the market against rapid changes. This was much needed at the time and was a lifesaver. However, when the market started to rise, the Stablecoin found that they only had so much chain. Soon the rising tide of the market submerged Stablecoin 1.0, and then Stablecoin 1.1.[64] The market indicated that the system needs something to keep it steady but allow it to rise with the market. This was

[64] Hayes, Supra.

Stablecoin 2.0.

Stablecoin 2.0 was a system designed to hook the market to a rocket, not to an anchor. While this still gives the system some control in troubled times, it also keeps the crypto moving up when the market settles down. This is the best of both worlds and the best model we have right now. This does not mean that this will be the only model in the future, it just means that it is what we have now. For right now we need to be willing to ride the rocket into the future while we watch those who are not willing to change sink beneath the tides of the market.

Crypto owes its success to the lessons and legacy of Stablecoin 1.0. Stablecoin 1.1 was built on the shoulders of these giants to move the system another step forward. It is not time to embrace the next level of evolution and look at how Stablecoin 2.0 can maintain the stability in the system that is needed to increase the transactional value of all coins in the market, while still bringing enough diversity of assets to the market to ensure that the market continues to grow. Crypto is a quickly growing market, the sooner we embrace the new systems that benefit the whole of crypto the better.

Conclusion

When looking back at Stablecoin 1.0, the fault in this coin is that it was out for itself, not the community. The crypto community is quickly learning that fighting amongst ourselves only benefit the regulators and the central banking cartel. This system is creating wealth at a rate the world has not seen since the dot-com boom of the 1990s or even maybe the industrial revolution. While competition is good to ensure that the evolution of the system continues to grow, we also need to work together to ensure a better system for the future.

No crypto is for every. This is because crypto is currency, and no currency is forever. The better we understand how currency works (Chapter 7), the better we can understand that currencies can compete and work together at the same time. Each currency is working to make the most for its users and traders, however, it is also constantly working to increase the value of the system. Stablecoin 1.0 did not do this. Nor did Stablecoin 1.1. Now as we move to the 3rd Wave of crypto, we can only hope that more coins will join large ecosystems which benefit all of the crypto community.

Chapter 5: Stablecoin 2.0

Now that you have a strong conception of what Stablecoin is we need to look at the problem with Stablecoin 1.0. Stablecoin was an excellent concept for its time, however, the growth of the market quickly outpaced the Stablecoin concept. Not only that but the Stablecoin 1.0 concept was built around the OG market. Protect the fiat and allow the coin to be a proxy for central banks in the crypto space. This was a system of quasi-centralization which was destructive to the philosophy of the crypto market.

Stablecoins being pegged to fiat currency made Stablecoin 1.0 a 2nd level fiat currency, a trojan horse if you will. This is a vehicle for monetary controls, used by the central banking cartel to increase their worthwhile "mining" the people of the world for money.[65] Most of the Stablecoin 1.0 systems did not realize this when they started, they only wanted a coin that was stable in the market and attached to something. This is why Stablecoin 2.0 is so important, it gives the market the stability it needs while avoiding the fiat attachment that it does not.

This Chapter starts off by looking at conditional staking. Optional staking, the vouge model in 2nd Wave cryptocurrencies, was a process where people would "invest" coins in a static wallet to grow the value. Conditional staking is a staking system based on burns where the system itself "stakes" holdings to increase the value of the system. The Chapter then goes on to discuss the standardization of burns when working within a conditional

---

[65] Behrens, Alex (2021). "USDC: How the most stable cryptocurrency is impacting crypto users." Circle at https://www.circle.com/blog/usdc-how-the-most-stable-cryptocurrency-is-impacting-crypto-users?utm_term=&utm_campaign=G_USDC_Leadgen&utm_source=adwords&utm_medium=ppc&hsa_acc=2894751369&hsa_cam=12300337439&hsa_grp=127699796383&hsa_ad=556684387886&hsa_src=g&hsa_tgt=dsa-1456110646459&hsa_kw=&hsa_mt=&hsa_net=adwords&hsa_ver=3&gclid=Cj0KCQiAlMCOBhCZARIsANLid6ajjbVFgeVgsISv8-obgiq1iDJOet9CYKtMFtZt2tu-mUdhlbjVxnoaArqyEALw_wcB. Please note that calling a coin stable because it stays at the same basic value as the fiat currency that it is pegged to is setting the bar very, very low.

staking system. The burn rate must be visible and stable so that members of the community see what is going on.

One of the key features of the Stablecoin 2.0 system is that the project is decentralized. The coin is an entity unto itself, the community builds itself, and the burn company and the portfolio companies are separate entities. This allows for several different communities to have a say on how the system works and allows for the interests to be diversified that the focus stays on the growth of the portfolio, not on any specific set of actions. This will result in the next topic of this Chapter, diversification.

Separation of the pieces from the platform is vital to ensure that the platform functions properly. The value of the system is not based on what the people can take out of the system (like Stablecoin 1.0) but on what the people put into the system. Standardization of the burn rates allows for the system to continually grow with just a minor tax or toll placed on transactions. When we are looking at paying up to 50% on our income, up to 10% on our sales tax, and 33% on our capital gains, a 1-2% (total) system maintenance fee (that eliminates most of the capital gains and sales tax) seems quite reasonable.

Conditional Staking

Conditional staking is the process of staking regardless of the investors movement.[66] In a traditional staking system, the investor chose to stake their crypto for interest in return. This worked well for the people who did not stake, the system grew and they still had their coin to use. In the Stablecoin 2.0 model, the system has a "tax" (burn rate) which is much lower than most gas fees, which allow the system to invest in itself. Conditional staking is superior to the classic burn strategy because the crypto is in an active wallet, not a dead wallet that is doomed to fail. Overall, conditional staking is more balanced and allowed everyone to pay their fair share while using an advanced system.

---

[66] Coinbase, (2021). "What is Staking?" Coinbase at https://www.coinbase.com/learn/crypto-basics/what-is-staking.

The traditional staking system was voluntary. People would invest (for a reasonable return) their stake into a wallet and make it unusable for some time. This helped coins with no reserve create a pseudo reserve to increase their stability and value. The problem with this was that the people who staked the coin saw, in general, a lower return rate than those who kept their coin. This allowed those that did not stake to increase their returns while someone else's crypto did the work! To make matters worse, many cryptos used their limited reserves to pay out the interest on the stake.

Stablecoin 2.0 solves this problem with a standard burn.[67] The standard burn is a tax that everyone pays when they use the coin. Rather than be a voluntary system where individuals invest in a dubious system, everyone using the coin works together to build the value of the coin. Not only does this allow the system to compound the value in the holdings, it also allows the system to recycle without taking coins out of the system.

The tertiary advantage of the conditional staking system is that it places the holdings in an active wallet. Think of when you save money, is it more effective to hide it under the mattress where someone can steal it, or is it more effective to put it in a money market or mutual fund where it can grow. With dead wallets, the system was basically putting a coin under the mattress. Not only did the value constantly decline as the inflation rate rose (whether the coin was mine or reserves were released), but there have been times when people stole from the dead wallets to get rich quickly. Conversely, when savings are put into a mutual fund or a money market, they increase in value (most of the time) and can hedge against inflation by moving money around. Stablecoin 2.0 uses the later method to ensure that the coins within the Stablecoin 2.0 community are continually growing.

Standard Burns

This book discusses standard burns several times in different Chapters. Each time, the book looks to come at the topic from a different viewpoint. In this Chapter, the viewpoint is why standard burns are so much more

[67] KIROS White Paper, Redefining the term burn.

effective in the Stablecoin 2.0 model than general burns. General burns are burns orchestrated by the creators of crypto to increase value (or the community). Standard burns are also created by the crypto creators, but they are a constant force in the market. Whereas a general burn can go to a dead wallet, standard burns must go to an active wallet (or the coin will cease to exist). This allows for the system to be more efficient and continually grow.

A general burn is a useful strategy in a 2nd Wave crypto that was created with too many coins/tokens.[68] When there is more supply than demand, the value of the asset stagnates. In order to decrease the supply to comply with the demand, some coins burned coins into a dead wallet.[69] This method was more effective than destroying coins, because destroyed coins make the coins more like an NFT than a Fungible token. Thus, moving them to a dead wallet put them in a "Schrodinger's box" situation, the coin was both living and dead at the same time.

The disadvantage of the dead wallet system, other than the fact that the dead wallet can resurrect and tank the value of the coin, is that the coins in the wallet are not active. These "coins under the mattress" just sit there and do nothing but maintain a pseudo-reserve. The coins are no good to anyone and simply are increasing the value of the investor's portfolios at the expense of the users, this is a zero-sum gain where the users of the coin are getting the "zero."

A standard burn fixes the two keep problems of the general burn. First, it eliminates the arbitrary nature of the burn system. In a general burn, the creator decides when and how much of the coin to burn, along with how the coin will be acquired. In a standard burn, the creators announce, in the White Papers that there will be a standard or variable burn rate. In a standard burn rate, the rate is always the same. In a variable burn rate,

---

[68] Lyle Daly (2021). "What is Cryptocurrency coin burning?" The Motley Fool at https://www.fool.com/investing/stock-market/market-sectors/financials/cryptocurrency-stocks/coin-burn/.
[69] *Id.*

when the market is trading up, the burn rate goes down. When the market is flat, the burn rate is medium. When the market is in a decline, the burn rate goes up. Generally, the swing is around 1-2%, so that the movement is minimum. The increase in rate discourages whales to sell off during a short decline. The decrease in rate opens the market up to allow the system to grow when it is rallying. All variable rates should be controlled by an AI.

The key factor that differentiates a standard burn from a general burn is that a general burn can go to a dead wallet, a standard burn cannot. If a standard burn of 1% would go to a dead wallet, soon it would eat away at the supply of the coin until there was no coin left. Conversely, if it goes to an active wallet, the crypto is re-introduced at market value to "buy" a larger share in the holding system. This increases the value of the cryptosystem continually, but still maintains the stability of the coin value on the market.

Decentralization

Another key factor of Stablecoin 2.0 is that the system needs to be decentralized.[70] Be wary of cryptos where the creator of the coin, without corporate structure, controls the portfolio or holdings. Portfolios or holdings should be managed by an independent (preferably a trust or publicly traded) company. This allows for the interests of the ecosystem to be taken into account, rather than simply increasing the wealth of the creator. Through a decentralized (preferably diversified account) the system can be more stable and have a steady rate of growth increases the value of the crypto.

When the creator of a coin holds all control over the portfolio, this signals trouble for the system. While the creator can be involved in the portfolio control (after all they are the brain behind the system) this should be no more than 20% of portfolio control. Likewise, the sponsoring company behind the crypto should have less than 50% control over the portfolio. This means that at least 41% of the portfolio company should be publicly

---

[70] Kharif, Infra.

traded (eventually, not at the start). The only exception to this is if the portfolio is managed by a trust, which should be managed by a separate company from the trust holding company.

The diversity of the company is also something that should be taken into consideration. Closely held companies are less stable than publicly traded companies. This is a fairly good general rule to follow. Looking at Stablecoin 2.0 holding companies should be a litmus test in how much control the investors have, how much control the creator has, and how much control the community has in where the coin is invested. The more the power is spread across the system, the more effective the system will be.

When creators are building their coin, they should look very hard at whether they want to create their own ecosystem, or join an already existing ecosystem. Established ecosystems can immediately add value to the new crypto, though a portion of the coin needs to be invested in the ecosystem. New coins cannot expect that their coin can gain the benefits of an established ecosystem (which has endured countless burn cycles) without a true stake. The stake should be no more than 10% of the coin to join the group, though some of the bigger ecosystems have a rate of between 5-7% depending on how the portfolio is trading. This adds another level of decentralization and joint ownership to the cryptos system, making it more reliable and less affected by quick market changes.

Diversification

Not only should the management structure of the crypto's stake be diversified, but the stake itself should also be diversified.[71] As noted above, sitting on a coin under a mattress does nothing but promote theft and increase vulnerability to inflation, the system must be active. An active system can be mono level or multi-level with the multi-level systems being more stable. When a crypto creator decides whether to build their own system or join an ecosystem that is already established it is important to

---

[71] Dilallo, Mathew (2021). "Understanding Portfolio Diversification." The Motley Fool at https://www.fool.com/investing/how-to-invest/portfolio-diversification/.

know which kind of ecosystem you would like to be part of.

The ecosystem should be completely separate from the coin itself.[72] The ecosystem is the generator that develops the power that the inherent value of the crypto represents. Stablecoin 1.0 systems where coin owners can "draw" against the holdings were a broken system, ecosystems are symbiotic with the crypto, not interchangeable. Interchangeable systems seem, on their face to be more stable, but in effect act like a bank. When there is a panic in the community, the bank can have a run, which decreases the value of the coin in real terms. When the system is separate, the holders must sell the coin to "cash out," this means that the value stays stable even when there is a panic, allowing the system to recoup its losses fairly quickly.

There are two coins in the system, uni-level or mono-level systems (we will call them uni-level system) and multi-level systems. In a uni-level system, the portfolio only holds one type of asset. Now a uni-level system is not a uni-asset system, which should be avoided. In a uni-asset system, the system only works with one asset, such as gold. This is merely one step away from a fiat system. In a uni-level system, the system will invest in different assets across the type. An example would be a system that only invests in precious metals. While they are similar to gold systems, these systems have the option of looking at other metals as the system becomes more complex. Less stable than multi-level portfolios, these are a vast improvement over uni-asset systems.

Multi-asset systems have the top level of diversification. These systems invest across all asset families to be as productive as possible. These systems invest in currencies (money markets), cryptos (exchange markets), stocks (and mutual funds), derivatives, land, commodities, and even in companies, bonds, and ventures. The level of complexity of multi-level portfolios makes them much more difficult to understand and manage, but their increased diversity makes them much more stable on the market.

---

[72] KIROS White Paper.

While 3rd Wave crypto accepts both uni-level and multi-level portfolios, the uni-level portfolios are only useful in a small number of niche markets. While nothing is stopping a coin from being involved in more than one ecosystem (because of the spiderweb bridges), it can be cost-prohibitive as being involved with a static system (1% burn) and a variable system (1-2.5% burn) can lead to high-level burn rates during periods of decline. However, this can also be strategic as it does limit sell-off viability for the sellouts.

Separation

It cannot be overstated how important it is that the systems remain separate from the creators and the coin.[73] When the systems are linked too closely it gives the opportunity for "rug pulls" and the coin and the ecosystem to be liquidated.[74] However, if there is not enough communication between the investment groups and the sponsors, the coin can lose progress and focus. This is one of the reasons that *The Wallet Group* has been so popular. Allowing portions of the system to be publicly traded, some to be closely held, and others to be market-driven has allowed unparalleled shared governance while still maintaining a joined corporate vision.

It is a fact that the sponsor and creator should have some control over the portfolio (as long as they want it). However, in the case of most systems, the creator may not have the corporate knowledge to manage what amounts to a hedge fund. This means that total control by the creator not only poses a conflict of interest, but also a viable threat to the stability of the system. By using a subsidiary or trust, the creator and the sponsoring company can have a well-managed fund while still keeping the modicum of control they need and deserve.

Allowing the management of the system to go completely public can also cause problems. While some will argue that if a coin holder wants to have

---

[73] Kharif, Olga (2017). "The Bitcoin Whales: 1, 000 people who own 40% of the market." Bloomberg Business at https://www.bloomberg.com/news/articles/2017-12-08/the-bitcoin-whales-1-000-people-who-own-40-percent-of-the-market

[74] *Id.*

a say in the company that they should buy shares too, for many holders that are not possible. While crypto worth $2 may be within the budget of a user, buying a share that costs $1,200 may not be. This limits governance to the wealthy, this is why only a portion of the governance should be through shareholders (also why the sponsor should hold up to 49%, the sponsor then gives voice to the holders). There is also something to be said about the wealthy having a voice in how the fund is managed, they are rich for a reason.

Combining the two worlds is very important in Stablecoin 2.0. The holders and investors need to have a voice in how the fund is run. The overarching goal of the fund is to increase the value of the system. The more we can increase the value of the system, the better off the people using the system are. While the creator, the investors, and the users may have differing opinions, they should all be able to agree that they want the coin, the ecosystem, the family, and the portfolio to grow to make the coin healthier in transactional, transitional, market, market, and actual value.

Chapter 6: Smart Contracts

A contract in one of its simplest definitions is simply a promise, going a bit further, it is an offer, acceptance, and consideration (a bargain for exchange.).[75] Using lines of code and ready-made phrases, often called "boilerplate terms" in the legal world, they are filled in automatically. Therefore tech is used where humans once had to deeply contemplate certain executions and transactions of a regular contract.

Smart contracts are an evolution of the concept of a contract operating on the blockchain.[76] For the blockchain to function, it needs to do something. Smart contracts are the code that tells the block what to do. While the original Bitcoin chains simply did validation, Ethereum introduced new elements into the system. This allowed the system to evolve and become more complex.

This Chapter starts with the idea of access to the system. Without access to the system, no one has the ability to use the system. Access also creates one of the important legs of contractual development, it is part of the bargained for exchange. When a person accesses the system, they are consenting to the smart contract. What contract a person is agreeing to depends on the system that they are entering. Each system has its own rules, those rules define the nature of the smart contract.

"For a smart contract to be functional in a system, it needs to have two key elements." The first element is the exchange disclosure requirement. Without disclosing the information, the contractee cannot have informed consent. Likewise, if the information is not in a common language, if left completely to the base code of the system, then people, once again, cannot make informed consent. These ideas are central to the functionality of any smart contract.

Building better smart contracts allow for the creation of more complex smart contract overlays. This is vital for the development of the 3rd Wave

---

[75] Wex Law (Contracts) at https://www.law.cornell.edu/wex/contract.
[76] Staff (2020). "What are Smart Contracts on the Blockchain?" IBM at https://www.ibm.com/topics/smart-contracts.

of cryptocurrencies. "The more complex the system, the more stable the system is." As long as the foundational smart contracts are functioning properly, the smart contract overlays can open whole new worlds in crypto-economics.

Access to how the System Works

To experts, smart contracts are "simply programs stored on a blockchain that run when predetermined conditions are met."[77] This process is not only technical but also legal. The system includes an I/O (Input Output) part of a system where when the unsorted data is present, the system inputs or starts the contract.[78] When the sorted data outputs or exits the block, the system has completed its task.[79]

Regardless of the conditions that need to be met, the system reacts to stimulus, which allows the system to be defined in its actions.[80] If a system is coded properly, the chain runs smoothly, or else the system can collapse.

The legal element of the smart contract is the formation (offer, acceptance, consideration) and actual use of the contract. In a smart contract, the system allows for the user or contractee to enter into and be bound to a boilerplate agreement (general, fixed contract language) with a contractor. Thus, the contractee enters into the agreement by consenting to have their function serviced by the block.[81] Once this relationship is confirmed by the smart contract, the contract is executed. This process is generally quick.[82]

The relationship within the dynamic of the smart contract shows how integrated the digital world is. The system relies on traditional legal elements while using modern technical systems to create, populate, and execute the agreement. This marriage of the "old" and "new" allows for

---

[77] IBM, *Supra*.
[78] Mearian, Lucas (2019). "What's a Smart Contract and How does it Work?" Computerworld at https://www.computerworld.com/article/3412140/whats-a-smart-contract-and-how-does-it-work.html.
[79] *Id.*
[80] *Id.*
[81] IBM Supra.
[82] *Id.*

the world to compute more elements, and have those elements validated by the chain.[83] These chains allow the digital world to complete millions of tasks a day.[84]

Multiple Systems Mean Multiple Different Rules

Because the cryptoverse is made up of many different blockchains, there are many sets of rules on the market for which these contracts operate. Please note that the use of the blockchain is different from simply trading currency on the blockchain. Each chain has its own smart contract (or smart contract overlay for a token). This means that each chain has its own rules. Just like an arbitration, the rules of the chain create the universe for the completion of the contract.

Understanding that the use of a block is different than the system trading of coins on an exchange. When trading on an exchange, the exchange validates the possession and validity of the coin. This is done (sometimes through another blockchain) to ensure that the trade is valid. In a wallet-to-wallet exchange, the validity is checked by the block of the original currency. This means that the transaction is validated by the smart contract to ensure that the coin is real.

Each chain within the cryptoverse has its own smart contract under which it operates. Some blockchains within the system operate on very similar smart contracts, especially chains that are forked off of older chains. This creates a system of evolving smart contracts, which may at some point be able to be replicated by AI to create better and faster blockchains. Regardless, the more efficient the smart contract, the faster the block will be able to process the data.

When looking at how the system works, you need to look at what the smart contract does, this can mean that you need to research the blockchain you are using. This is another difference between using a blockchain and just trading its requisite crypto. When you are trading all you care about is

---

[83] Mearian, Supra.

[84] *Id.*

value. When using the chain, you need to take into account the utility of the coin. Knowing what the contract does allows you to see if it will be useful to you, paying the fees for a transaction you do not need is never a good business move.

The rules set the digital world for any actions arising from a contract. Just like in an arbitration, where the rules are set by the four corners of the contract, the system operations are defined by the smart contract. This is another reason that you should know the contracts you are dealing with. Ignorance is never an excuse for the law; in cyberspace (where information is almost always available) it will not save you if your funds go to the wrong place. Taking the time to do the research allows you to be prepared for what happens after the contract is completed.

Eliminating the Middleman

Smart contracts remove the middleman, including payment processors since no one can alter the records, smart contracts, providing higher fiduciary regulations. This decreases the cost of executing a smart contract because it limits transaction fees and more. Companies can use it for various aspects including regular client business.

Most include "if/then" (complex or simple) statements which check whether predetermined conditions are met. If the conditions are met, a specific action is executed by the smart contract. The outcome of the action is then automatically updated in the blockchain.

According to, *CryptoWrecked*, smart contracts offer a wide range of benefits, including:

1. Increased speed and efficiency
2. Accurate transactions with no human error
3. Enhanced security and fraud protection
4. Superior transparency and trust
5. Reduced costs for handling transactions

After a condition is met, the contract immediately executes the required action. As the actions are executed automatically, no humans are involved.

While a major aspect of blockchain technology and most cryptocurrencies, the use of smart contracts precedes blockchain technology.[85]

Executing a smart contract with blockchain technology offers less likelihood of major errors and provides increased transparency when used for a cryptocurrency. Thus, smart contracts could revolutionize the way people handle agreements[86]. Marrying efficiency and agreements creates smart contracts.

Language Requirements

Creators of smart contracts must ensure that the contract has terms that users can understand. An important aspect of a smart contract is that users are able to understand what they are signing and being bound to during the duration of the agreement.

Courts currently are already hesitant to allow the cryptosystem to function on its own, if the contract language is not sufficient for people to understand what they are getting into, the courts will reject them.

The requirement of exchange disclosures is vital for the understanding of the contract. For the contractee to enter into the agreement knowingly, they must have the ability to find out what the smart contract is doing. Just because they have the ability to learn what the smart contract is doing, does not mean that they have the obligation to do this for the contract to be valid. This is a choice that the user needs to make, if they do not look to see what the contract is doing- then they cannot complain when it does not do what they want.

In the same vein, the creator of the smart contract must make sure that the disclosures are understandable to the people who are using them. Making something intentionally so complex that a person using the system would not understand it will not make for a valid contract. This means that it behooves the creator to work within common language requirements to

---

[85] Staff (2021). "What is blockchain?" Cryptowrecked at https://www.cryptowrecked.com/what-is-blockchain/.
[86] *Id.*

make the basic function of the smart contract understandable. Since smart contracts are generally simple programs, the output of the program should be understandable to the layperson (or a tradesperson for a field-specific token).

While there is not a uniform language requirement across the cryptoverse, there is an international agreement on what contracts should be like. Boilerplate contracts are already suspect. Crypto contracts are suspect. Therefore, crypto contracts based on boilerplate are going to receive additional scrutiny from the courts. This means that as cryptos build new and better smart contracts, they need to make sure that they have proper disclosures and a common language so that users can understand what they are doing.

Conclusion

Smart contracts are a tool. Just like any other tool, they need to be properly used to be effective. In the space of crypto contracts, people need to know what they are doing for access to the system to be real. If they do not know what they are getting into, do they really have the mental ability to knowingly enter into a contract? Likewise, if they do not know when they are leaving a system or staying on the same system, do they really know what system or rules they are under?

The cryptoverse can do itself a lot of favors by making sure there is an industry-standard to have disclosures on how the exchanges work. Clarity eases confusion, which helps prevent lawsuits about poorly written contracts. Add to this a requirement that new cryptos have a plain language disclosure about what the smart contract does, and new crypto will be in a very strong position in regards to the legality of its smart contract.

Part I: Section II

A Brief History of Money and Cryptocurrencies

Introduction

"When educating yourself about anything, it is important to understand the history of the model." Unfortunately, many institutions of learning (primary, secondary, and higher) have accepted the 1970s mantra, if it happened before the 1960s it does not matter.[87] This type of generational thinking is highly disruptive to the evolution of society, not to mention that it creates generations of drones who move through life without learning the history that is needed to keep them from falling into their parent's traps.

In this section, the history of money and cryptocurrency is brought to life. This is not an exhaustive history, the book only has so much space; but this is enough of a history for you to see where different models come from and why we do things the way that we do things. We will also see some of the "forks" in history that were ineffective, along with those that were effective. Building this knowledge, you will be ready to see which coins entering the market are making changes that are new, and those that are just repeating history's old mistakes.

Chapter 7 is dedicated to the history of money and credit. This "60-minute" history of money will explain why we do some of the things that we do, and why we still do some of the silly things too. Unfortunately, not everyone learns from their mistakes and that can be quite costly, not only to investors but also to people who have to live in the markets around the world. We start with the accumulation of wealth and move through the system until we arrive and the broken fiat currency system that we are forced to accept. Well forced to accept until the advent of cryptocurrencies.

Chapter 8 builds around the first Wave of cryptocurrencies. This means that we look at Bitcoin, its creation, and the concept around the crypto

---

[87] Kaines, Malcolm (2018). "Baby boomers, critics of millennials, once advised 'ignore anyone over 30" Medium at https://www.coinbase.com/learn/crypto-basics/what-is-staking. See here is the problem, boomers and millennials thinking medium is a good place to put non-factchecked articles. Cited Ironically.

ecosystem. While most people call Ethereum an "Altcoin" its wide acceptance has earned it a place in the first Wave of crypto-currencies. The main reason for this inclusion is because it sets forth some of the key smart contract concepts that are being used in other blockchains and coins. The roots of the system demonstrate the utility of the system, sometimes when we get caught up with the different manifestations of the systems, we can lose sight of what things were set up to do.

Chapter 9 discusses the Altcoin revolution. While it started gaining steam in 2018, the real catalyst for the alt-coin explosion was the COVID pandemic of 2020. This placed people at home for long periods of time where they could learn about this new model of wealth management. OG investors were among the crowd of "If you did not learn a new skill during the lockdown, do not beat yourself up over it; we were going through a pandemic, a global crisis." Meanwhile, millions of new millionaires were created from the crypto boom. These were the people who took the time to learn the new system and how to navigate the changes in wealth management. Those who learned moved themselves into a better position, those who relied on the government to save them are behind even further than when they started.

Chapter 10 is an introduction to the third Wave of cryptos. Seen by many as the golden age of cryptos, the third Wave is defined by stable currencies (not Stablecoin 1.0) that are built around security management. Another defining feature is that the spiderweb bridge technology that supports the third Wave cryptos allowed for a second (and even first Wave cryptos) to hard fork into the new era, raising the value of coins across the board while the ecosystem gained wealth. The third Wave of crypto has the potential (as it just started in January 2022) to bring people around the world together in a way that nothing has done in nearly 100 years.

Seeing where we have been as a global economic system has the potential to help us see where we are going in the near future. Crypto has the potential to bring people together, to give freedom to those who are oppressed by tyrannical governments, and to highlight the failings of past economic systems- but it will take people to build a better world. This means that the more people that understand how we have moved from where were in history to where we are now, the more people who will be able to see where we are moving in the future for the betterment of humankind.

Chapter 7: History of Money and Credit

What do humans and mythical dragons have in common, well we both like shiny things? The amassment of "wealth over the course of human history has been nothing short of obscene." People living in castles while people froze outside,[88] to the vomitorium at Roman festivals while people starved,[89] to the ill-thought out "Squid Game" party hosted by failed Hollywood socialites,[90] humanity has shown that the worst people can appear to have the most wealth. But then again, appearances can be deceiving.

While they may not have been people who were going to be nominated for sainthood, Rockefeller, Carnegie, and other robber barons built some of the great wonders of the modern world.[91] Billionaires have donated fortunes to see the betterment of mankind and the richest organization in the world provides more aid to the poor and oppressed than all of the governments of the world combined. This means it is not the possession of wealth that makes a person bad, but the lusting after wealth above their neighbors.

Wealth is a good thing for society. While it is in the "vouge" for college professors and other talking heads to mock Kennedy's "A rising tide lifts all ships..." trickle-down economics has worked better than the more

---

[88] Histories (2021). "Medieval Castles" Histories at https://www.english-heritage.org.uk/learn/histories/medieval-castles/.

[89] Please note that I am using Vomitorium in the pop culture sense. An actual vomitorium was a path to get into the theater when you arrived late. While it was not a room used for throwing up, the concept of vomiting between courses at meals did exist, though not as prevalently as pop culture would have you believe. For more information look at, Marchetti, Silvia (2020), "Laying down and vomiting between courses: This is how Romans would Feast." CNN at https://www.cnn.com/style/article/ancient-roman-feasting-history/index.html.

[90] Ibrahim, Samantha (2021). "Squid Game' fans mad at Chrissy Teigen's theme party:'So beyond Tone Deaf." New York Post at https://nypost.com/2021/11/16/fans-angry-over-chrissy-teigens-squid-game-theme-party/.

[91] Sollinger, Marc (2015). "What the Robber Barons gave us- after they took from us." The World at https://theworld.org/stories/2015-09-23/what-robber-barons-gave-us-after-they-took-us.

socialized systems in the vouge right now. The one area where the United States has lost the most ground is in education, which is why we should question those who are questioning the system. The truth is that you do not see caravans of the poor and oppressed fleeing the United States to socialist countries. You only see the entitled elite who are being held accountable for their crimes "running away." The reality is that people try to get to the United States, the UK, and Australia because of the opportunity that these countries offer.

Shiny Heavy Things

One thing that we have to face as humans is that we like collecting things. Whether it be baseball cards, cars, or jewelry, people have always wanted to get things that they like (or see as valuable). As we look at the oldest human histories of wealth, we see that as society developed people started amassing more than they needed. This led to people who had more stuff than others. As this system developed, we saw the beginnings of the modern economic system.

One of the best authors on the subject was Adam Smith. Smith wrote "Wealth of Nations" during the American revolution (he was in the UK). One of the best images from the book is the image of how wealth develops. Smith noted that one person's labor can produce a little more than their family needs (which now is two people's labor barely meets what a family needs). This means that when several people are working in a group, the group size will eventually reach the size where someone in the group will not need to work and there will be enough for society to continue. This is when a society begins to create wealth.

Now if we assume that this person accumulates some of the largesse that they live on, then they are not giving it to other people- for they are exploiting people by not working why would they give away what they have illicitly gotten. In this case, they start to build a stockpile.[92] People around

[92] Cerullo, Megan (2020). "US Mint to American: Stop Hording your coins- go spend them." CBS News at https://www.cbsnews.com/news/coin-shortage-spend-us-mint/.

see that they are building a stockpile, so those that can also save. Now here comes the problem, what do you do with a stockpile?

At this point in history, most of the goods were food and tools. While tools were being used, the food would only store for so long. This meant that if you saved all your food, your wealth would rot. People, being the ingenious animals that we are, found that if they traded their excess for things other people would want, then if they needed something else, they could trade for those. This was the basic barter system. Eventually, people needed something that they could easily keep without the risk of others taking it. This is why gold and silver were good items. They were heavy, easy to work, had no real use in society at the time other than for a currency. If a person stole your gold, then they would be moving slowly (because of the weight, assuming you had enough to be worth stealing) and others could see them carry it. Heavy and shiny was the currency of the day.

As wealth developed, some people became wealthy (not by comparison to today's wealth). These people would have massive piles of shiny, heavy things and would be able to use their wealth to acquire more things. It is the same thing we do today, but we use paper. Now if two very rich people needed to trade things, how would they know what the value of the shiny heavy things was. The agreed-upon means was weight. People would give so much weight of one thing for whatever they were trading for. The system worked pretty well, except that everyone needed to carry a device with them to measure or rely on a money changer. As a result, powerful people started making coins of the heavy, shiny stuff so that trade could be accommodated.

Coins

Coins were a major invocation for humanity. Rather than carrying around big chunks of shiny heavy stuff, we could carry small pieces around that were "minted" to be about the same size. The uniformization of the system allowed for commerce to be more than just the local villages. Merchants could carry coins between regions and, if the minter was famous or powerful enough, the coins would be accepted based on their weight. Now, this was not an entirely honest process, forgery and milling of the edges were common, but by and large, it worked.

This also created a system where not only the wealthy person living in an area could be wealthy. Traders could trade and build up their own wealth, not dependent on a given location. A good trader could raise as much wealth as a king, and if the rulers of a region would give them too much trouble, they would quit doing business there (or take their business underground). Ironically, this is where taxes started to come from too, the government interfering with wealth and commerce.

Eventually, people started to reach a new level of wealth. Merchants and those collecting taxes (kings and tax collectors) would acquire vast quantities of coins. When you could carry your net worth on your person, there was some security; however, when you had to leave it at home, you risked someone stealing it (which also brought new industries of professional thieves and highwaymen). This meant that merchants who were traveling needed another way to store/transport their money, and the regional barons who were making fortunes off of them needed a way for the money to keep flowing. This is where we see the birth of a banking system.

The Banking System

For this discussion, we are looking at the banking system as something very different from what it is today. When we think of a bank, we think of a lender of money. These money lenders were another business model entirely, more like a loan shark that owned you if you failed to pay. The banks that developed in this timeframe were simply that, a bank. The services that they provided were storing your money and confirming that you had money in a bank. The idea of interest was alien at this point, you paid to have your money storied (to pay the guards).[93]

In this model, only the rich had the money to keep money in banks, but they did evolve the system of commerce once again. Before, if you had to

[93] COBALT (2021). "The Five Oldest Banks in the world." Cobalt at https://www.cobaltrecruitment.co.uk/blog/2019/01/the-five-oldest-banks-in-the-world.

move your wealth to another person for a large purchase, you needed to hire guards, make sure the path was clean, and sometimes the problems would lead to war. With the advent of banks, banks could let one another know that a transaction occurred (with a piece of paper that was only worth something to the bank[cheque]) and the banks could then "balance the books" by exchanging money owned, not actual money. The basic plan was for business to go both ways.

If one bank owed a lot of money to another bank, then a small military would be mobilized to move the money from one bank to another, usually hired from the highwaymen who would have tried to steal it anyways. This allowed for the system to evolve. Business was good, and the traders realized that there had to be a better way to store their wealth and move it from place to place without the massive fees of the banks and money lenders.

Bank Notes

If you were a bank, why let the wealth out of your vaults at all? Eventually, traders and banks realized that if a bank issued a note of the value, that note of value could be exchanged among traders and people who held value at the bank. Similar to a modern check, you would put your gold and silver into a bank and the bank would issue you a note. This note could be traded and if someone wanted the gold, they could come to the bank and get it.

Now for the banking industry, which was starting to form at this point. This was a major win. No longer did they have to hire armies to move gold from one point to another, they could let the traders carry little pieces of paper. This increased the ease of trade and started to break down barriers. As traders could carry a lot of value in notes, they could take the risk and the transaction would be cheaper.

This also meant that highwaymen could steal more, since the whole point of the heavy shiny things was to make it hard to steal, but by this point nations of the world did not want highwaymen out there, so the main roads were patrolled. Robberies still happened, but highway robbery was a dangerous job, and merchants, for their part, did defend themselves.

Government Currencies (Wealth Backed)

Here we see the currency system wrap back around on itself.[94] Banks were great at issuing currency, however, too many banks issued currencies in an area could be confusing. Also, counterfeiting was a problem as people could accept money from a far-off bank. As a solution, the world took a giant step backward and allowed governments to mint the money again. Under this model, governments in the region would print currency, and (eventually) bank notes were not accepted. People traded pieces of paper and coins printed by governments to have a trade.

The problem with this system is the same problem we face today. If you have a government that does not understand how money works, then they will just continue to print money so they can spend it. Inflation was a major problem in the 1700s, 1800s, and early 1900. Treasuries for countries would print money, backed by gold, to finance wars. However, with each note printed the value of the other notes dwindled. As a result, we saw countries where you needed a wheelbarrow of money to buy a loaf of bread.

Fiat Currencies

In the early 1900s, there was an idea. Who had the idea no one really knows, but the idea was simple? What if we move away from the gold standard and allow central banks to dictate the value of the currency?[95] The central banks would work together around the world, and the individual nations would have oversight over how the banks operated. While the system was designed to be the best of government faith and credit merged with banking efficiency, that was not the case.[96]

For the first thirty years, the system seemed to work. Then an American

---

[94] Beattie, Andrew (2021). "The History of Money." Investopedia at https://www.investopedia.com/articles/07/roots_of_money.asp.

[95] Beattie, Andrew (2021B) "How the federal reserve was formed." Investopedia at https://www.investopedia.com/articles/economics/08/federal-reserve.asp.

[96] *Id.*

president started printing more money to buy his way out of a financial crisis created by a failing stock market (which the government was just starting to interfere in). As a result, the central bank was told to print money. The central bank, a for-profit institution, was glad to oblige. For every 10 bills they printed for the government they took one for themselves. Millionaires were made overnight.[97]

Over the next 80 years, we have seen each crisis the world faces be used as a reason to print more money. Some countries, like the UK and the United States, managed their money better than others. Others like Zimbabwe saw runaway inflation that had comical monetary notes (100 trillion dollars was worth $0.40 American). Some experts even suggest that bad monetary policy caused the U.S.S.R. to lose the cold war. All because of the collusion between central banks and the state. Even now the US and UK are printing money and their currency is losing value- the only silver lining is that other countries are doing it faster.

Checks

As the fiat currency lost value, people needed to make transactions without having large amounts of money on them. The banks dipped back into history and created checks. Checks, for those that do not know, are semi-single-use documents for individual transfers. A bank would have a person's money (like a debit card) and the person would write a check. The check would be guaranteed by the bank (though if you had insufficient funds it could bounce).

This was a system where people would no longer have to carry a lot of money with them when they walked around. It was a boon for people, a windfall for the banks, and a slight thorn in the side of the robbery industry that was, for a while, doing quite well. Governments loved the idea because it created a record, which could help them collect taxes (the income tax came around about the same time as the fiat currency).

---

[97] *Id.*

Credit Cards

Around the 1950s, banks had a brilliant idea: "Why do we have to make sure the people have the money to buy something before they buy it?"[98] If the person did have the money to buy something, a credit card could be used and the person would not have to carry a checkbook (which could be stolen) around with them. The person would pay the card off at the end of the month and the bank would get their money (plus a small fee). If the person did not have the money to buy something, then the bank could issue them credit.[99] The person would still have to pay the fee at the end of the month, but they would have extra time to pay off the debt (plus interest).

With credit cards, the banks had people coming and going for their money. The more money that they spent, the more fees the banks collected. The less money they could pay off at the end of the money, the more interest that the bank collected. It was a win-win for the banks and created the system of "debt financing" that has the world in so much trouble today. Once again, however, the system created new millionaires.

Debit Cards

It took society about 20 years for people to realize that credit cards were not a great idea (well the rich people realized it anyway). Because of this in the 1970s, debit cards came into existence.[100] Debit cards were like credit cards, you could go places without carrying money. However, with a debit card, you could spend money that you had, not money that the bank lent you. This means that while the poor and middle class were spending money they did not have, the rich could spend the money that they did have and look like they were part of the same system.

Debit cards were a good deal for those who could afford them and the banks. There were still fees with the cards, (mostly collected from

---

[98] Steele, Jason (2021). "The History of Credit Cards." Credicards.com at https://www.creditcards.com/credit-card-news/history-of-credit-cards/,

[99] *Id.*

[100] Collins, Jennifer (2011). "A Short History of the Debit Card." Marketplace.org at https://www.marketplace.org/2011/08/18/short-history-debit-card/.

merchants). Merchants did not have to carry large amounts of money on hand, and people could just carry that piece of plastic with them. As the system developed, more people shifted from credit cards to debit cards (which did cause some banks problems), but it also helped people move away from debt financing.

Digitization of Currency

With the advent of computers that we carried in our pockets (smartphones), the world saw a new way to exchange money in the world, digital currency.[101] Apps and applets on phones allowed people to buy virtual currency to help them get ahead in their games. Then came Bitcoin, which allowed people to buy digital currency for the real world.

The difference between bitcoin and the game currency was that bitcoin derived its value from the transaction itself. The more people used it the more it was worth. For a coin that was worth less than a dollar 10 years ago, to the $60, 000 juggernaut that it is today, people see the value in the coin and how it revolutionizes the system. As blockchains become more efficient, the system will find new ways to make money (for people, banks and governments.)

Conclusion

Getting from piles of shiny, heavy stuff to the modern human economic system has been an exciting ride for a lot of people. As you read history, you will see empires rise and fall on their monetary policy. This is why the history of money is so important for people looking to get involved with cryptocurrency. If you do not know why money has value, then you cannot know why the new stuff has value.

As we move into the digital era, we have to avoid making the mistakes of the past. Just because a past system (such as gold-backed currency) failed more slowly than the current system, it does not mean that we need to

---

[101] Kay, Gary (2021). "The Many Alleged Identities of Bitcoin's Mysterious creator, Satoshi Nakamoto." Business Insider at https://www.businessinsider.com/bitcoin-history-cryptocurrency-satoshi-nakamoto-2017-12.

take a step in that direction. Successful monetary systems have always moved towards the future. Some will succeed and some will fail, but if we turn our sights on the past then we will be doomed to repeat the mistakes of our forebearers.

Chapter 8: Wave 1 Cryptocurrencies

When in the process of creating a new world, we see that something from nothing is never a good start. Even in the Bible, God brought to light from darkness to create a new reality. When we look at the digital world, in the beginning, there were botnets. Botnets were individual systems working within systems to complete small tasks which would be added together, in aggregate to create a bigger network. Blockchain technology took these illegal botnets and turned them into something that is defining the internet of things and the world we live in. Each block on the chain is set, and this setup is creating a global computing system that is bigger (and in most cases better) than any single computer that we have in the world today.

Our take on 1st Wave cryptos will be a little different than some other analysts. Most analysts place only Bitcoin in the first Wave. We are adding Bitcoin's little brother, Ethereum to the mix. Both Bitcoin and Ethereum added enough new things to the system that they deserve to be seen as the first Wave. While Bitcoin will always be the "first to market" we should not ignore the contributions of Ethereum and how it moved crypto more into the mainstream.

This Chapter starts by looking at what a Wave one cryptocurrency is. This is defining and defending the standards that we are setting that Bitcoin and Ethereum both deserve to be within this system. Being both a curse and a blessing, being in the first Wave of crypto means that you will be one of the big dogs for the foreseeable future, but also that every new coin is being built because it does something better than the original system. Bitcoin and Ethereum have been good parents, rather than fighting against their offspring for a place in the market, they welcomed their children to the system and have helped them grow in use and number.

Next, we take a walk down memory lane and look at how the system is built. While the White Papers for bitcoin and Ethereum look at the technical issues of each coin, these Chapters look at how they developed, how the concept grew, how it was brought into the market, and where the coins stand today. As the spiderweb bridge brings coins across the spectrum together, the backbone of the crypto community is bitcoin and Ethereum (but even that is becoming more decentralized).

Finally, this Chapter looks at one of the greatest accomplishments of the first Wave cryptos, aiding and supporting the growth of the second Wave. One of the greatest reasons that markets fail is because of the progenitors of a market fight against evolution. Being based in the digital world, crypto is always welcoming newcomers to the field. This is why the "killer" coins are so silly, why fight the groups that are welcoming you into the market. Crypto creates wealth, it does not horde it. This is why so many cryptos have found a home in the market.

What is a Wave 1 Cryptocurrency?

The first Wave of crypto is the genesis of the system, but where did it start. One of the basic concepts of crypto is that access to the blockchain has value, a toll if you will, for using the services it provides. Just like any tool, this money should be used to maintain the system. Bitcoin and Ethereum created a system where users could give access to the chain to allow their processing power to fuel the chain. This community-sourced project worked because when the value was added to the system, the value was given to the miners (in the form of coin). This allowed millions of people to join the network building the blockchain.

Once the blockchain was starting to develop, the method of valuation became paramount. This transitional value (the amount of information moving across the system) became the underpinning of the 1st Wave of cryptos. Because the use had value, the coin had value. This was the birth of cryptocurrency.

In the original system, the value was converted into a coin. This meant that there was no capital (or asset) reserve for the system. This was one of the biggest attacks on the system (which led to Stablecoin 1.0 and 1.1. However, Transintestinal value proved to be enough that when the coin was placed on exchanges to trade, that the market took notice. People traded (mostly decentralized) the coins and the market value grew.

The transactional value was limited in the first two Waves also. The transactional value of a coin is based on how many people, companies, and countries are using the coin and the value that they place on the coin. In the beginning, both Bitcoin and Ethereum were only done in the wallet-to-wallet exchanges and had a very low value, but as the market grew- so did their value. Once the 2nd Wave hit, the transactional value evolved as they accepted the evolution into the 2nd Wave.

Before the 2nd Wave, the valuation of the 1st Wave currencies was almost entirely based on the transitional value. This limited the investment potential of the coin (in theory) because there were only two supporting valuations. Bitcoin and Ethereum both took years to break out of the low-value category. Now they sit as two of the most valuable coins on the market.

Elements of 1st Wave Crypto:

1.) Built on Blockchain (all cryptos)
2.) Dependent on Transitional Value and Market Value
3.) Limited Transactional Value
4.) Starting point for other Chains (either in theory or practice).

Bitcoin

Being first to market is always a boon for any product. With Bitcoin, this has proven to be true. Bitcoin was the granddaddy of them all, and as such holds the (rightful) place as the current king of cryptos. However, the design of Bitcoin is limited in utility and will eventually be replaced by another system. Bitcoin will, always, have value because of its transitional value. Most likely, it will also always have value because of its relationship to the system. When the market value for use starts to fade, there will be digital collector's value. The first FT NFT.

The concept of bitcoin was quite simple, an electronic peer-to-peer currency system.[102] The founders of bitcoin knew that the fiat currency

[102] Haar, Ryan (2021). What is Bitcoin? NextAdvisor at https://time.com/nextadvisor/investing/cryptocurrency/what-is-bitcoin/.

system was having a negative effect on business growth.[103] Bitcoin kept its concept simple, this allowed the system to start without too much competition.[104] At first, it was traded as a novelty, but as more and more people mined the coin and used it valuation became important. Bitcoins spawned other coins and tokens that have helped stabilize its system.

Arising in 2009, Bitcoin took several years to start to grow.[105] No one really noticed it until about 2011, when it started to rise in value.[106] In 2011, the coin was worth $1.[107] By 2013 it crossed the $100 mark.[108] Now in 2022, the value is well north of $40, 000, think of what you would have if you would have dropped $100 on bitcoin when it was under $0.01. Bitcoin blazed the pathway for other coins to gain value. Unless Bitcoin had taken its knocks over the years, we would still be stuck with the fiat system.

One of the reasons that Bitcoin is still a market force is because it continues to evolve with the community. While the underlying code stays the same, we are seeing that bitcoin enthusiasts are introducing it to new markets. While moves, such as being legal tender in El Salvador, are problematic because of the underlying value of the coin, opening the crypto markets up to being legal tender is a major step forward in the field.[109] Bitcoin was the leader and is still pushing forward so that other cryptos can enter new markets.

---

103 *Id.*

104 Bitcoin White Paper.

105 Haar, *Supra*.

106 ET (2021). "Boom and Bust: Bitcoin Prices have swung wildly since 2010." Economic Times at https://economictimes.indiatimes.com/markets/stocks/news/boom-and-bust-how-bitcoin-prices-have-swung-wildly-since-2010/whats-behind-the-big-bitcoin-crash/slideshow/82790287.cms.

107 *Id.*

108 Edwards, John (2021). "Bitcoin's Price History." Investopedia at https://www.investopedia.com/articles/forex/121815/bitcoins-price-history.asp.

109 Reuters (2021). "Bitcoin Use in El Salvador grows amid setbacks since its adoption as legal tender." NBC at https://www.nbcnews.com/news/latino/bitcoin-use-el-salvador-grows-setbacks-adopting-legal-tender-rcna2743.

Ethereum

Ethereum was the second real crypto coin to the market. It entered into the market to challenge Bitcoin, but not in the way that hostile "killer" coins enter into the market. The founders of Ethereum understood that there was a lot of room in the market. Ethereum brought forth improvements on Bitcoin, especially the ability for new tokens and forks to be done easily. This opened the door to the second Wave and is the reason that Ethereum has a deserved place in the first Wave of cryptos.

Whereas Bitcoin just used the blockchain for the transactions of the system, Ethereum was the founder of the smart contract idea that allowed more to be done with the blockchain.[110] Why allow the system to just create coins, when the system could be used to do services (paid) which add value to the coin.[111] This really enhanced the transitional value, well beyond the market valuation model used by Bitcoin.[112] Ethereum also increased the amount of data going through its blocks (which would be increased by others). This allowed the system to process more data.

Being founded in July 2015, Ethereum had the ability to look at the way that bitcoin grew.[113] This led to slightly more rapid growth of the Ethereum network compared to the Bitcoin network. The was, of course, facilitated by the fact that Cryptocurrency was already beginning to be used around the world. Once people are already using something, it becomes much easier to be adopted. Ethereum also paved the way for other tokens and coins built on its network to be heavily used.

Ethereum now stands as the second biggest crypto on the market, a title it seems that it will hold for at least a few more years. Like Bitcoin, even when

---

[110] Reiff, Nathan (2021). "Bitcoin vs. Ethereum: What's the Difference" Investopedia at https://www.investopedia.com/articles/investing/031416/bitcoin-vs-ethereum-driven-different-purposes.asp.

[111] CMC (2021). "What is Ethereum?" CMC at https://www.cmcmarkets.com/en-sg/learn-cryptocurrencies/what-is-ethereum.

[112] Frankenfield, Jake (2021). "Ethereum" Investopedia At https://www.investopedia.com/terms/e/ethereum.asp.

[113] Reiff, Supra.

the use-value of the coin starts to drop- there will always be a collector's market for Ethereum. If Bitcoin is the granddaddy of the cryptocurrency, Ethereum is definitely the grand momma.

Evolution to Wave 2

Bitcoin and Ethereum have survived because they did not fight against the evolution of the system. There has been some community "defending territory" but largely the crypto community is becoming coin/token agnostic. If we ensure that all coins rise in value, then regardless of what coin we are holding, the general system will continue to see rises. This is a good thing for everyone. As first-year investing students are taught, if the percentages are going up in your portfolio, it does not matter what you are holding. The numbers only matter when the percentages are going up (or down).

Each time a new idea or new system comes out, there is a fork in the blockchain. Those coins that fight against these forks are the ones that are seeing problems increasing value. If you see a soft fork that works for you, then join in on it and ride the Wave. If you see a hard fork coming, get ready to adopt it. While changing the overlay of the smart contract (the actual data on the block cannot be changed but how it is interpreted can), you can continue to evolve with the system- ensuring that whatever coin you use, invest in, or create will stay caught up with the pack.

For those that are just entering the system. Learn how the first Wave worked. Just like knowing what is in the lobby of your building, you should know what is in the foundation of your system. Just like you would not open a children's movie theater over an adult bookstore, make sure you know what is going on the ground floor. You can learn from the mistakes of those who came before you, I assure you those lessons are much cheaper than mistakes that you learn on your own.

2nd Wave crypto is a hard fork in the system. Currencies that are not moving up in valuation techniques are dangerous investments. 2nd Wave cryptos have 3-3.5 valuation techniques, 3rd Wave cryptos have all four. The more valuation that you have in a system the better. As 2nd Wave developed,

Bitcoin and Ethereum both updated the way they did business (not the chain but the actual service) to ensure that they could meet the needs of the evolving system. They appear to be doing it again as the third Wave develops. Those who hide from forks in the system will be forked by the system.

Evolution will always be crypto's biggest strength. With millions of people and thousands of cryptos on the market, we have the ability to evolve the system each time there is a change. Hiding behind a system is dangerous, being part of the system is how you make money. As the 2nd Wave gives way to the third Wave, it is best everyone takes a look at the 1st Wave. By knowing where we have been, we can better plan on where we are going.

Chapter 9: Wave 2 Cryptocurrencies (AJ)

Background

The earlier Chapter explores some of the definitions and mechanics behind Wave 1 cryptocurrencies, which we deem to be Bitcoin and Ethereum. These founding fathers truly set the breeding ground and the technical infrastructure in place for the rise of Wave 2 cryptocurrencies, more commonly known as altcoins.

Before we explore the magnificent rise of altcoins, it may perhaps be best to explore the nature of these Waves. The true beauty in cryptocurrency and decentralized financial instruments lies in its cyclical nature. Much of the cryptocurrency world adheres to the laws of mathematics and physics, and this is perhaps what makes it so compelling and beautiful. That despite the chaos and confusion in the crypto sphere, there lies simple mathematical efficiency.

Figure 1 outlines Sinusoidal Waveforms. Waves are circles and cyclical in nature. This is important to understand because the crypto market moves in cycles and this sets the true pretense for Wave 2.

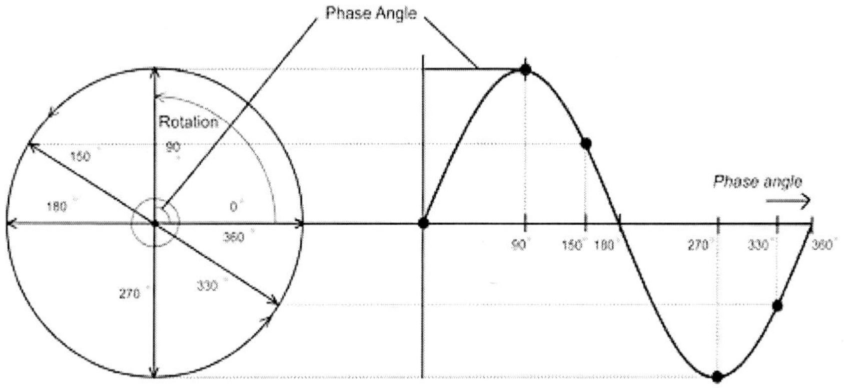

Figure 1 - Sine Wave Forms

What is a Wave 2 Cryptocurrency?

Wave 1 set the scene for the rise and intermediate link between blockchain technology and financial instruments. While Bitcoin and Ethereum laid the foundations for what was to come, they built an infrastructure and ideology as opposed to utility in the early stages.

With a small community and little to no developers, the early builders were exploring mainly theoretical concepts and applications setting the infrastructure of what would later change the world forever.

As Bitcoin and its early counterparts began to be picked up attention, by gaining early usage on the darknet due to its unique anonymity. It eventually attracted the interest of early cyberpunks and techno-associated groups as they sought to apply the infrastructure of Bitcoin/Ethereum to 'fix' or 'solve' other issues and gaps.

This is where altcoins were well and truly born, and it is what we call Wave 2 cryptocurrencies. These altcoins were a bridge between blockchain and utility, and many were and are still vaporware with just a mere connection. We will dive into that later as we discuss the ICO mania fueled by Wave 2 Cryptocurrencies.

The time-period of Wave 2 cryptos is vague and up for discussion, but it is commonly described as the period between 2015-2019. Although one could argue that the period began as early as the creation of Ethereum and continues till this very day. This would be true, but this Chapter will outline the period in which the most significant and notable activity took place.

Why Altcoins?

Bitcoin and Ethereum are truly magnificent inventions of our modern era, and perhaps some of the most influential. However, as described earlier, in the early stages there was a great lack of utility and services built on these tools. This would of course later change in 2020+, but the period of 2015-2019 saw the creation of thousands of new cryptocurrency altcoins that aimed to bridge the gap between blockchain and "insert industry here."

The rise of altcoins cannot be explained without the mention of centralized exchanges, which were perhaps the fuel to the fire and caused the explosion of Wave 2 crypto. The early stages of crypto markets were P2P, much like the technology it was built on. Most of the transactions occurred on the deep/dark web and there was no real significant money markets or exchanges geared towards this new asset class.

After the initial interest and rise of Bitcoin and Ethereum, new businesses and exchanges sought to bridge the gap between retail money and this new brewing asset class and create digital exchanges, centralized in nature. These exchanges not only created liquid markets to initiate transfers of value seamlessly, but they were also the early onramps to allow for the facilitation of fiat to crypto transfers.

There are many early exchanges that can be named as being some of the founding fathers of this crypto revolution, but some of the biggest ones to mention are Coinbase (founded 2012), Kraken (2011), Huobi (2013), Binance (2017), OKEx (2017), Mt Gox (now defunct by launched 2010), Bitfinex (2012) and many more. As of 2022, at the time of writing this, CoinMarketCap lists 451 total exchanges and a 24-hour volume of over 86B. To date, cryptocurrency exchanges have facilitated value transfers worth trillions and therefore it comes as no surprise that many of these exchanges are now some of the largest companies on the planet.

So now we had the infrastructure set by Bitcoin/Ethereum, growing mainstream interest, retail exchanges that could allow anyone to participate in the market, and a unique asset class that was completely different from anything we had ever seen. Although it was unclear in the early stages, these factors would eventually lead to the explosive rise of altcoins.

Altcoins/Wave 2 cryptocurrencies can be categorized in the following brackets:

- Utility/service-based cryptocurrencies (Filecoin etc.)
- 'Killer' cryptocurrencies (Litecoin etc.)
- Meme cryptocurrencies (Dogecoin etc.)
- Forks (Bitcoin Cash etc.)

Altcoins capitalized much on the Wave 1 cryptocurrencies and improved on the flaws of Bitcoin and Ethereum. The key improvements looked at maximizing the speed, reducing the cost of transactions, and changing the mining structure.

Altcoins allowed the retail market to enter crypto through CEXs and increased the competition in the market which eventually led to the breakthroughs we have seen today. On a whole, altcoins lowered the transaction costs within crypto, gave more mining opportunities to the retail community, and unlocked a whole host of use cases. This represented a shift from cryptocurrency being a payment mechanism, to cryptocurrency being a store of value, asset class, and utility assets.

CoinMarketCap lists a total of 16,425 cryptocurrencies, so the rise of Wave 2 cannot be undermined. It truly changed the game for the cryptocurrency market and made it primed for adoption.

'Killer' Coins

The earlier section talks about some of the issues these new altcoins began to tackle. These new altcoins that built their ethos and mission on the underwhelming performance/mechanics of other cryptocurrencies are called 'Killer' coins. As suggested by their names, these tokens sought to 'kill' and 'destroy' their predecessors which they deemed to be not providing the best value.

ICO Mania (2016-2018)

AS the market became more developed, people began to notice that there was money to be made in cryptos. Rather than follow the mining pattern, second-Wave investors started seeing the potential to trade the coins on the market. Bitcoin and Ethereum were expanding rapidly, mostly on trading through decentralized platforms. Investors realized that arbitrage was now a viable option and they took to the market in droves, driving up the value of crypto and helping cryptos become more mainstream.

During this market gold rush, people realized that the tokens and the coins were both growing in value rapidly. The difference between tokens and coins had not been made apparent to the new investors, and regardless of the utility of the crypto, anything digital was hot. This resulted in an explosive valuation of the crypto market, causing some of the companies in the market to believe that there may be a better way to make money off of crypto than selling mined coins, the ICO craze had begun.

An ICO (Initial Coin Offering) is the process of releasing According to Investopedia, "Interested investors can buy into an initial coin offering to receive a new cryptocurrency token issued by the company. This token may have some utility related to the product or service that the company is offering, or it may just represent a stake in the company or project." the versatility of the ICO process, coupled with the ability to "stake" or "no stake" made the cryptocurrency market more appealing to many investors.

When crypto developers saw the money that could be made through ICOs, the movement was born to increase the number of coins. The boom of the 2020-2021 creation of coins would not have been possible without the ICO craze two years prior. Junk coins hit the market (coins with no backing), utility tokens joined the market from almost every industry, and creators started experimenting with cross-chain methodologies. Booming creation led to a massive expansion of our understanding of the field- and massive over-investment in coins with no reserve.

Bear Market 2018 – 2020 (Rise of Wave 3)

Anytime there is a boom, there is always the risk of a bust. When the market started into the 1st quarter of 2018, it was apparent that there were some hard times coming for the crypto market. Nearly half of the gains of the ICO craze were nearly wiped out in just a few months. This bear market continued well into 2019 when the bottom began to form. People who were watching the market were interested whether the system was creating a new pattern with bullish intentions or simply forming a cup and handle leading to a drop in the market.

There were many things that contributed to the bear market of 2018-2019. Even into 2020, the market had not recovered. Cryptos with no backing was one of the key factors that undermined public confidence (along with the scams in the system). This was the beginning of people taking note of stable coins. US Dollar Coin USDC was founded in September of 2016 but did not reach a viable market cap until mid-2019. Seeing that cryptos could be backed by something allowed for renewed confidence in the system.

The influx of the stimulus checks into the American market was another driving factor of the recovery of crypto in 2020. Many Americans received the equivalent of a month's rent in a free free tax-free check from the government. This check was intended to ease the pain of the pandemic and stimulate the economy. One of the biggest economies that it stimulated was the crypto market. Billionaires were made overnight as cryptos saw 10, 000% rises. Each additional stimulus check issued by the U.S. government caused another, albeit smaller, boom. Coupled with the benefits other countries were giving created a perfect storm for crypto.

But this cycle was not without its lessons. Stablecoin 1.0 and Stablecoin 2.0 cryptos tended to have steady increases, even during the mini- "boom and bust" cycles of the rise. This led people to understand that the third Wave of crypto demanded something better than Stablecoin 1.0 or 1.1. Creators also began to see that there needed to be more utility in their cryptos, the inability for cryptos to connect over the spiderweb bridge left them isolated to whales and governments. The more closely the cryptos worked together, the more likely they would be to succeed as the system moved forward.

Chapter 10: 3rd Wave Cryptos

Bringing ourselves to the moment, it is not time to discuss the current Wave of cryptocurrencies. 3rd Wave cryptos began, in earnest, in January 2022. The shift from 2nd to 3rd Wave was not instant. All through 2021, and even in 2020, we saw some of the base elements of the 3rd Wave start in their prototypical form. Items such as staking, cross-platform utility, and dynamic trading we starting to develop in the 2nd Wave. It was just that they did not all come together until the beginning of 2022.

Growth in a communal system that is as complex as the cryptocurrency market does not all happen at one time. Each generation of coins, in fact, each coin, is based on the coins that came before it. Ironically, in cryptocurrency, this is more evident than in other systems. If you know where to look, then you can look at the forks and developments and how the system evolved, layer over layer, token over the token.

While the 2nd Wave was loaded with "killer" tokens and coins (Doge killer, Ethereum killer, etc.) the 3rd Wave is defined by the idea that all coins can work together for mutual benefit.[114] Coins are not set against each other in the current market. Coins are set against fiat currency. Make no mistake, the OG and the governments of the world are working to protect the dying system of fiat currency, not to ensure a fair marketplace for crypto exchanges. Too many wealthy executives, bankers, despots, and western politicians get millions of dollars each year from the status quo. To change the system, the system must simply be better and efficient enough to overcome the roadblocks that the OG put in the way of progress.

This Chapter takes the question of government regulation directly into the mouth of the government. If the December 2021 Congressional Hearing in Washington D.C. and the legal arguments in India during the same time

[114] Nahar, Pawan (2021). "After a 17,500% rally in 2021, does the 'Ethereum Killer' have more steam left?" The Economic Times at https://economictimes.indiatimes.com/markets/cryptocurrency/after-a-17500-rally-in-2021-does-the-ethereum-killer-have-more-steam-left/articleshow/87584692.cms.

showed us anything, the question was not, "How do we make a better system?" but "How do we stop this threat to the present corrupt system?" Dealing with the problems in the system is vital to ensure that our system can work well enough to deal with the present corruption in the fiat system and open doors to the crypto ecosystem.

Next, to identify why the 3rd Wave is different, we need to look at some of the problems that arose out of the 2nd Wave. Actions such as the creation of junk cryptos, trade wars between currencies, whale manipulation, and lack of a coherent community policy on proof of stake and proof of utility hurt the entire community. To deal with this, this Chapter looks at each of these problems, in-kind, and looks at how 3rd Wave cryptos deal with these problems.

Ensuring the utility and tradability of all coins from their inception is a very important element of 3rd Wave cryptos.[115] Without some system of utility (transitional and transactional value) and tradability (market and inherent value), there is no way to get a proper valuation on crypto. Next, we look at the concept of spiderweb bridging through the exchanges. For years, the holy grail of crypto was a smart contract overlay that would allow a coin or token to be used to trade between different platforms with strong verification. Taking a step back and looking at the system rather than the code allowed for KIROS to bring the idea of spiderweb bridging and global exchange tokens to the market, allowing for better trading and confirmation across different levels. Anti-whale technology has been a big topic over the last few years, while the main "look" at this system is in Chapter 35, this Chapter does provide an introduction to novices in the area.

Staking and Stablecoin 2.0 rounds out the discussion topics of this Chapter. Staking and how the stake is held are vitally important to the stability of a coin in the modern era. Prior to the 3rd Wave, stakes could be worth a

---

[115] McEachran, Rich (2021). "For Long Term Crypto Gains, Look Utility." Raconteur at https://www.raconteur.net/finance/investing/cryptocurrency-utility-investing/.

fraction of a value of the coin's "face value." Under the era of Stablecoin 2.0, it is very possible that the "face value" of a coin could actually be less than the actual value of a coin. As the ecosystem around crypto grows in value, so does the utility to society. Bitcoin was founded to break people away from the broken system of fiat capitalism, now the 3rd Wave coins and tokens are giving people the chance to make that choice.

The Need for Evolution and the Specter of Government Regulation

When you learn about the market in college, there should be some basic psychology that is taught with market classes. So many people follow the *Wall Street* philosophy of Gordon Gecko that, "Greed is good..." and that greed drives the market.[116] While greed is a factor in the market, it is usually an indicator of mistakes, nothing more. Greed is a secondary vice, meaning that it comes from somewhere. When we look at the market there are two human emotions that control movements that cannot be explained: Hope and Fear.

Starting with fear seems like a good place to start because that is where any beginning investor starts. We move into the market with a tenuous understanding of the system, placing our small stake into the market and yanking it out soon after. The reason that most people start trading with mutual funds and money markets is that someone else has to watch the market. Many people put their money in and do not look at it again for weeks or months. Why? Because of fear. People are afraid to watch the markets for the same reason that we think we need to watch our favorite sports team because we think watching makes a difference.

In all reality, fear is what causes people to make mistakes in the market. If you are afraid of losing what you have placed in the market, then you have placed too much of your money in the market and are gambling.[117] Investing your money consists of placing your excess (that you can afford

---

[116] The Movie *Wall Street*, not the place.

[117] Sherwood, Christina (2010). "Not the Gambling Type? Scientists Link fear of money loss to brain structure." Opentext World at https://www.zdnet.com/article/not-the-gambling-type-scientists-link-fear-of-money-loss-to-brain-structure/.

to, do not want to, but can afford to lose) into the market to create some growth. This is a system of hope where you hope things get better but do not need them to. "When you invest more money than you can afford to lose," then you will be afraid that you will lose that money, fear causes people to make bad choices and this can cause you to fail in the market.

This is why a person working within the system should only be playing with the money that they feel they can lose.[118] While 3rd Wave cryptos are establishing value in the world, having a foot in fiat and a foot in crypto is the best move to keep your accounts stable. Do not take the plunge until you can do so without fear, only the hope of being part of a better world. People make the mistake of getting into deep too early because of fear of missing out (FOMO). The crypto market is here to stay, learn about the market and move in slowly. Start with safe (or low value) cryptos and then move up in complexity as your level of skill increases. Fear will hold you back, hope will set you free.

One area where fear in the market is being weaponized against the people is in the coming government regulation model. The government understands that people overleverage themselves and are afraid of losing what they have staked. They use this fear to create a ghost of a "corrupt market" to scare people into supporting government controls on a system that already has community controls. The specter of government regulation is fiat currency 2.0, where the government controls the crypto markets and takes the control away from the people.

One of the most prevailing myths in the world today is that the government has the "right" to control the currency in their territory. Governments have no right, only privileges. The century-long experiment in government currencies and fiat currencies has failed, government has proven that internal corruption and cronyism make the government a bad steward for the currency. The fact that many people in government are the least common denominator in society ensures its failure.

---

[118] *Id.*

Cryptocurrency is a clean slate that we have to give the opportunity to write itself. With it be the currency forever? Not likely. Humanity is always evolving and we may not have the ability to conceive what people will come up with in 100 years, 10 years, or even next year. One thing that we know is that the experiment in government-controlled currency has failed and it is time to move to the next experiment for the betterment of humankind.

Problems with 2nd Wave Cryptos

Second-Wave cryptocurrencies were an improvement over the first Wave. They brought more stability, more utility, and dealt with some of the problems of the first Wave. However, they were not perfect in their conception. Some of the infighting from the first Wave of cryptocurrencies found its way into the system. New models without value or with value that failed entered into the market. The diversity of the market became a virtual tower of Babel, where systems did not talk to each other. New people and new money entered into the market making it more volatile and people started to demand that the value of the coin be defined, not just speculated upon. Each of these problems has been addressed in the 3rd Wave of crypto.

Junk cryptos were one of the biggest problems in the 2nd Wave.[119] People would create a coin with a theme and the value of the coin would blast past the transitional value of the coin based on market pressure alone. These coins would see meteoric "pump and dump" cycles then the coins would plateau around the market value of the coin. Some would even drop back to their base transitional value, leaving millions holding the bag. 3rd Wave cryptos took care of this by looking at the utility and tradability of a coin.

Another problem that was seen in the 2nd Wave was the trade wars between coins on the market. Because many coins needed the hype to grow, they branded themselves against other coins. This type of action

---

[119] Yago, Glenn (2020). "Junk Bonds" Econlib at https://www.econlib.org/library/Enc/JunkBonds.html.

created factions in the market, factions that the government is using to attack the market in general. Divided crypto space is a vulnerable crypto space, the government knows this and has been using divide and conquer tactics since before Rome was an empire. The 3rd Wave of crypto is dealing with this problem by introducing spiderweb bridging through the system rather than through the coding.

As new money came into the market, new methods of market manipulation became prevalent.[120] Whales (whether by influence or by pure cash) could manipulate the smaller coins. Smaller coins had an effect on the market and the large coins would move due to the manipulation. The result was a whale could sell-off on a small coin to buy in big on the dip with a large coin. This created a very volatile market space. 3rd Wave cryptos are now using smart contract overlays to ensure that this practice is difficult to do while maintaining the protection needed so that the whales will stay in the pool.

The staking process in 2nd Wave crypto was in its infancy. Some coins would have one for one stake, others would have stakes that were less than the market value of the coin. Both of these problems cause a lack of faith in the coins that led to many small collapses. Understanding that all four valuation methods are needed for a strong coin is one of the hallmarks of a good 3rd Wave crypto.

Utility v Tradability

One misconception that 3rd Wave cryptos have taken head-on is that utility and tradability are on opposite ends of the spectrum. Users and investors have been placed at odds with one another since the beginning of crypto. This division has caused there to be deep rifts in the 2nd Wave community around how coins should be used. Philosophically, users and investors should help each other to build a better system because we are all in this

---

[120] Davies, Pascale (2021). "Bitcoin and other cryptos have slumped after record highs. Is market Manipulation the reason why?" Euronews at https://www.euronews.com/next/2021/11/17/bitcoin-and-other-cryptos-have-slumped-after-record-highs-is-market-manipulation-the-reaso.

together. We cannot let "pre-planted" divisions keep us apart, we need to look past the media/government smokescreen and work together.

The concept that a use-value coin is less tradable than a coin that is simply security is a false statement. For the government to place heavy regulations on crypto, they need to define crypto as a security, which it is not. While the community should acknowledge that any derivative of crypto is a security, we need to fight tooth and nail against the classification of the coins and tokens themselves as security. Coins in use are more valuable, thus traders should welcome the boost in value. Likewise, coins that are trading high are worth more, once we "de-peg" from the fiat currency, cryptos can be worth more in trade goods if the market is trading high.

The philosophy that users and investors are different is really a false comparison. They use the coin differently but are technically doing the same thing with it. A user trades the coin for a good or service. An investor trades a coin for another coin/token or fiat currency. Both are trading for something else; both want the value of what they have to be more than what they are trading for. The open market and the trading market are two different markets, which make it silly for the sides to be at each other's throats.

So where did these misconceptions come from? They came from governments around the world. Nearly every government hearing and media outlet have said at one time or another," how can we protect people using the coin from unscrupulous investors..." or "how can we ensure that investors are protected from lack of liquidity because a coin is being used to trade." The community is not asking these asinine questions, the government that wants to regulate the coin is asking the question. The government needs the division so that the users and the investors will vote for regulation to protect their interest from members of the same community, it is a trick and we are the ones being tricked.

The crypto rush is similar to the early years of gold mining in the United States. 1st Wave crypto users were the miners, they had a great potential to make quick money but were taking the highest risk. The government moved in and taxed them to where it was hard for them to make a living. The second level was speculators, people who did not do the mining themselves but made money from production. The government taxed them to where they made less money through dealing with securities. Finally, the banks moved in and made a steady rate of return on their investments, then the banks bought the government to protect their interest. Crypto needs to work together, not using a corrupt system of cronyism to work the system, but to protect their system from over-regulation.

Spiderweb Bridging

Throughout the 1st and 2nd Waves, people were looking for that elusive code that allowed people to move from one platform to another without much stress. Systems watered down their code to make them fairly generic hoping that a highlight secularized industry would comply with their generalization move to make the system easier. These failed because people approached the problem through a coding method rather than through a business method. The answer was out there the whole time, no one wanted to do it because they had to give up more control than they wanted to.

The answer was not coded, it was the tokens and the markets themselves. Free trade within a decentralized system does not need to have a special code for free trade, just an understanding in the community that there is something to do with the open trade, and it comes with a slight fee. Global Exchange Tokens (GET) allow for groups to use exchanges to cross-platform lines while maintaining the confirmation needed for the security of the system.

A GET exists specifically to be confirmed that it exists, this is what the chain validates. Regardless of the chain that it is on, its sole purpose is to exist in a secure state. Its secure state of existence makes it the perfect coin for trading across platforms. The trades allow the individual platforms to confirm the existence of their coins, then use the GET to confirm the transfer. Thus, there is a strong confirmation of the GET via its home platform and the coin that it is converted from and the coin that it is converted to are confirmed on their own platforms. The market then facilitates the exchange and everyone is happy.

Spiderweb bridging is an advancement over simple exchange bridging because the confirmation bias was always on the receiving party. With GETs, traders can trade to GETs or keep the GETs in reserve for trade. This allows the markets around other coins to stabilize and to make the market more secure over the long run. As businesses like stability, GETs can also be used to trade crypto for real-world goods, leaving stores to be able to base their prices on a stable market rather than a constantly changing market.

Antiwhale Tech

As there is a full Chapter on the subject, we only briefly touch on the problem of whales here and how to deal with the problem.[121] Whales have the ability to change the market (through influence or investment). To deal with this system, 3rd Wave cryptos built-in specific tech to deal with the system. The lockdowns of the 2nd Wave were a broken system, therefore we needed to move away from that. Limits are a more effective system and a system that allows the community more control while not being prohibitive from an investor's standpoint.

Time-based limits limit the amount of coin/token that can be traded within a given time. They are less desirable than limit-limits, however, they are also easier to manage and have more control. Limit-limits limit the amount of coin/token that a person can trade in a single trade. Whereas the time limit affects only those holding large amounts of the coin, limit-limits can affect regular traders. Both can be headaches for the community, but it is a small price to pay for stability in a market without direct manipulation.

Staking and Stablecoin 2.0

Stablecoin was present in 2nd Wave cryptos. In this iteration, the coin was

---

[121] Wigby, Miles (2021). "Stopelon Explained- An Anti-Whale Crypto designed to surpass Tesla." HITC at https://www.hitc.com/en-gb/2021/05/21/stopelon-explained-an-anti-whale-crypto-designed-to-surpass-tesla/.

linked to a currency to stabilize the coin. It had problems but was effective.[122] 3rd Wave cryptos expanded on this system to increase the diversity of the stake to increase the value of the ecosystem. An additional innovation of the staking system is that communities of coins and tokens could work together to build a bigger general ecosystem. Overall, this decentralized system seems to have given inherent value to crypto while still keeping the spirit of a decentralized crypto viable.

In the original Stablecoin system, the coin was pegged to a currency. This was effective at stabilizing the coin, but the stabilization was linked to a declining currency. Since many people are using crypto as a hedge against inflation, linking it to the very fiat currency that was deflating was problematic as best. 3rd Wave crypto sought to break the link between crypto and fiat currency, so 3rd Wave cryptos are based on portfolio holdings, not a single currency or commodity.

The philosophy behind the 3rd Wave system is that diversity breeds strength in investment. The wider the holdings of a portfolio are, the less likely that the whole market will collapse. Even if the market collapses, the diversified holdings should allow the system to decline more slowly than the surrounding market. This makes the holdings like a boat in a rough sea, it should always be on top. Likewise, when the waters start to rise, the smart nature of the portfolio allows the system to rise with the top of the Waves.

Perhaps the biggest advancement of 3rd Wave cryptos is that they are willing to work with other cryptos in the system. Towards the end of the 2nd Wave, cryptos started associating with each other based on family and platform. Now in the 3rd Wave, the communities are open to anyone who wants to be involved. The group-managed portfolio (generally managed by a third party to maintain the decentralized nature) works together to grow the entire ecosystem. These systems are "joint" holdings, like joint ownership but owned by a third party in trust. This allows the system to

---

[122] Hayes, Adam (2021). "Stablecoin." Investopedia at https://www.investopedia.com/terms/s/stablecoin.asp.

grow (and gives good tax benefits).

A better system benefits all cryptos

The common theme of the 3rd Wave is that we are all in this together. Yes, there are still going to be "killer" currencies that are out to knock off the big dogs, but these currencies are little yappy purse dogs in comparison. When the cryptos work together, everyone gets to eat- thus everyone gets bigger. By breaking down some of the competition, we allow for cooperation- and this will help the system grow.

3rd Wave does not eliminate all the competition. This is not a "Borg" mission. Third-Wave coins do not seek to assimilate. The coins seek to raise the value of all coins to make the system stronger. This means that some coins will do their own thing to make the system better. Innovation is still at the heart of the 3rd Wave, an innovation that will make the system better.

Part I

Section III: Evolution of the Regulatory System

Introduction to Part I: Section III

All systems evolve. Evolution requires stimulus. This means that we must identify the stimulus that is causing the present system to move forward and see whether it is the type of stimuli that will make a better system. Looking at the regulatory system, truth is the best stimuli to increase the viability of the system where lies and fear-mongering can cause the system to collapse upon itself as its foundations are based on fiction.

This portion of the book is an examination of how the system is evolving within the current regulatory framework. The systems dynamics around crypto are interesting. In some cases, we see that the systems are difficult to manage because of the misinformation. In other cases, we are seeing that the system is able to react so quickly that even misinformation may not be enough to stop the juggernaut. However, ensuring that the system receives proper stimuli is imperative to see that the system moves in the proper direction.

Chapter 11 looks at the regulatory framework that is coming for crypto, and what we need to do to make it support the freedom of cryptocurrency. Chapter 11 is broken down into two parts, the myths, and the truths. The myths sections will look at the lies that are being told to bring down the public confidence in crypto and how we need to address them. The truths are items that we need to ensure that the world knows about to make the system work more efficiently.

Chapter 12 looks at how the crypto markets have adapted to the spot trading markets. Spot trading is a system where one person has a currency that another person wants. That person offers to trade that currency for crypto or stock that the other person has. When they reach an agreement, that agreement is the spot rate for the exchange. The spot rate for crypto is the general value that the market will pay for the coin, so it is a very important indicator of price and thus a vital part of the framework.

Chapter 13 looks at one of the newcomers to the crypto market in 2021. Derivatives have been a staple of the stock industry for decades, but they are relatively new to the crypto market. Derivatives are values that are placed secondary to an asset and allow traders to trade not only the present value but the future value of the crypto. This is a great way to make/lose money and makes the market more exciting.

Chapter 14 looks at the internal structure of the industry under current contract law. This Chapter looks at how contracting between two people is a fundamental right and how the government should not interfere with that. This Chapter also looks at some of the rights that citizens have to be more successful in business and how the privileges given to the government via the social contract do not take away a person's human rights.

Overall, the regulatory structure of the current market is more than enough to manage the crypto markets. If the governments of the world just enforced the laws that were on the books, they would not need new laws. When the crypto community comes together to protect its interest, the system can be more efficient and can protect the rights of everyone, equally.

Chapter 11: Regulatory Myths and Truths and Government Fearmongering

Understanding the framework of something is vital to understanding the way in which the system functions. This section is going to look at how these pieces of the framework interact with each other. However, before we embark on this journey, it is imperative to set the record straight with some of the common issues that people hear about cryptocurrency. The myths that are out there today are very damning and prevent many people from investing in the system.

In addition to the myths around the field, we also have three key truths that the system needs to get out there to the masses. Each of the truths eliminates several of the myths and helps bring the efficiency of the system to light. This Chapter does not read like the other Chapters, it identifies a myth and disproves it. In the later part of the Chapter, identifies a truth and explains why it needs to be introduced to the market.

Myth 1: Crypto Has Value

If you are reading this book, by this point I hope you can see through this silly myth. This is a myth promoted by the OG billionaires who are heavily invested in crypto.[123] The goal of this myth is to keep the masses out of crypto until the system has been "milked" for its big growth potential. The part of this that the OG does not understand is that crypto has years of growth if it is managed properly.

By preventing people from entering the market, the OG is preventing the market value and the transactional value of the system from growing. This not only hurts their bottom line but retards the growth of the entire ecosystem. The more people understand the transitional value and the transactional value of crypto, the less this myth will affect people.

Myth 2: Crypto is just for Arms Deals

I am not sure where this myth came from. It is true that crypto was used

---

[123] Gupta, Sumit (2020). "Bitcoin has no intrinsic value.' Then what gives bitcoin value?" AIthority.com at https://aithority.com/guest-authors/bitcoin-has-no-intrinsic-value-then-what-gives-bitcoin-value/.

on the dark web for a while, but one of the problems with crypto for criminals is that the validation records of the crypto are present.[124] It is difficult to do a crypto trade without validation, and if you do a direct-to-wallet transfer with no validation that is like taking a briefcase "full of money" and not checking it.[125] Arms dealers are savvy and are unlikely to use something that can be tracked across exchanges as easily as crypto.

Further, it is much easier for them to use currency and bearer bonds to transfer wealth. These methods do not leave a trail, so it is easier for arms dealers to get away Scot free.[126] The myth is promoted to increase the "scary" nature of crypto so that people who can see its worth can milk the value out of it before the market stabilizes.

Myth 3: Crypto is used for Human Trafficking.

Like arms deals, human traffickers will likely stay away from crypto.[127] Virtual transactions create a record on the system. People who are watching a system can see when amounts move from one wallet to another. With the market constantly watching for when whales make a big move, people are watching the markets all the time to see when there are transactions.[128] Dark web transactions are watched too, so this is a bad place for bad guys to be using.

One danger that is seen is when a wallet key is transferred from one person to another. This is the area where there are problems in tracking the information. However, this is an area where bad guys will likely stay away from. If you are a bad guy and you are dealing with a bad guy, are you really

---

[124] Early on this may have been true. NewsBTC (2015). "Illegal Weapons Dealer Uses Bitcoin for Transactions." NewsBTC at https://www.newsbtc.com/all/illegal-weapons-dealer-used-bitcoin-for-transactions/.

[125] Prasad, Eswar (2021). "The Brutal Truth about Bitcoin." Brookings at https://www.brookings.edu/opinions/the-brutal-truth-about-bitcoin/.

[126] *Id.*

[127] Wolfson, Rachel (2019). "Anti-Human trafficking Agency Trace Crypto to Fight Modern-Day Slavery." CoinTelegraph at https://cointelegraph.com/news/anti-human-trafficking-intelligence-agency-traces-cryptocurrency-to-fight-modern-day-slavery.

[128] *Id.*

going to trust that person to have the key to the wallet while you are driving away?[129] If you do not trust the other bad guy, then you have to transfer the funds quickly (letting watchdogs see it), if you do trust them, then they can simply do the transfer on their own as soon as you no longer have a gun on them. It is a lose-lose situation as the market is developing.

This does not mean that bad guy will not find a way to get around these difficulties, it is just easier for them to use ART, drugs, and diamonds like the CIA.

Myth 4: It is used to steal money from retirees

Accusing crypto of being created to steal money from retirees is kind of a stretch, but I have heard financial advisors say this.[130] The truth is that the retirement market is a very small percentage of the business market. Financial planners see this as a big part because that is what they deal with. Corporate accounts, hedge funds, and government accounts make up a much larger portion of the market. Government accounts and taxation alone steal more for retirees than retirees have invested in crypto.[131]

In the beginning, if you were to invest $1, 000 in Bitcoin, you would be amazingly wealthy right now. Even investing $100 would have netted you $50 million in 2021.[132] This tends to indicate that those who invested in bitcoin did quite well. So why does this myth persist? The elderly tends to have problems with market movement (mainly because they do not have the opportunity to put more money in). This means when there is a dip and bounce, a lot of people sell on the downslope and buy on the way up. That is not how you make money and can cost big bucks. Good investors can put money in and let it set. Day traders lost a lot of money in crypto, but the

---

[129] *Id.*

[130] Locke, Tayler (2021). "Over $10 billion was stolen in Defi Related theft this year." Make It (CNBC) at https://www.cnbc.com/2021/12/14/common-defi-crypto-related-scams-and-how-to-protect-your-wallet.html.

[131] *Id.*

[132] Reinicke, Carmen (2021). "Bitcoin hits another record. Here's how much you'd have if you invested $100 in 2009." CNBC at https://www.cnbc.com/2021/02/12/how-much-youd-have-today-if-you-invested-100-in-bitcoin-in-2009.html.

longs have made out like bandits.

Myth 5: It is too Complex to Work

Maxine Waters' work on the Congressional finance committee has been met with much controversy, but still, there is an argument to be made that crypto is not as complex as she might have been led to believe - along with others.[133] For anyone who has studied the Federal Reserve System and the global economic system, crypto is a walk in the park. Modern monetary policy in governments is too complex, crypto is a simplification of a system that is hopelessly broken.

Crypto is quite simple. There is a transaction. The blockchain validates the transaction. This validation has value. The Coin is minted with this value. Five sentences that explain transitional value. Transactional value is the same as money, so it is neither more nor less complex. Market value is the same also. Inherent value is pretty simple too, what are the holdings that the coin is based on. If they are good, it has good value- if not, well it cannot be worse than fiat currency that is simply based (literally) on politician's promise.

Myth 6: It takes away the government's Right to print currency

First of all, governments do not have rights.[134] They have duties and privileges. Crypto does not take away either a duty or a privilege. What crypto does do that governments do not like is it forces the government to have a stable economic policy. The competition created by the crypto increases the efficiency of the system. If the government's fiat currency cannot keep up, that is on them.[135]

Crypto does not remove money from circulation. It simply moves it around. This is dangerous for bought and paid for politicians because they cannot

---

[133] Iansiti, Marco & Lakhani, Karim (2017). "The Truth About Blockchain." Harvard Business Review at https://hbr.org/2017/01/the-truth-about-blockchain.
[134] Snowball, Tim (2018). "Government is not the source of Our Rights." Pacific Legal Foundation at https://pacificlegal.org/government-is-not-the-source-of-our-rights/.
[135] *Id.*

control where the money is going. If the government does not have poor people to scare, how will it function?

Myth 7: It undermines freedom

Ironically, the area where you see this claim being made is not in the free countries around the world, but in the 3rd world despotism where freedom is a bad word.[136] Many dictators hate the idea of crypto because it gives people access to money to live off of. One of the cardinal rules of socialism or fascism is to keep the working poor so poor that they are afraid to lose the little that they have. When they get comfortable, that is when they rise against tyranny.[137]

Despots hate crypto because it actually gives people freedom. A decentralized system prevents any government from harassing people in the way they do their business. This is scary to a system that relies on the fear of people looking over your shoulder to keep everyone in check. Bad governments will always oppose anything that promotes freedom, so if you see a dictator hating something that everyone else likes, then you should get on board.

Myth 8: the creators of the coin can shut off the coin for no reason

This is a first Wave problem. At one point, the blockchain could be shut down by the creators to shut the coin off with no recourse for the people on the chain.[138] Now for a blockchain to shut down it would create billions of dollars in liability issues. Blockchains are integrated. Just like the US government can no longer "shut down" the internet without destroying the infrastructure. Blockchain companies could not shut down the chain without destroying billions (sometimes trillions) in infrastructure.

---

[136] Armstrong, Brian (2021). "How Crypto Enables Economic Freedom." The Coinbase Blog at https://blog.coinbase.com/how-crypto-enables-economic-freedom-7dee35d8f0e0.

[137] *Id.*

[138] Also dealing with the hacking misconception, Bitpanda (2021). Can Cryptocurrency like Bitcoin get hacked or shut down?" Bitpanda https://www.bitpanda.com/academy/en/lessons/can-a-cryptocurrency-like-bitcoin-get-hacked-or-shut-down/.

There is also a sub myth here that the government could shut down the internet.[139] The modern web is built of levels on top of levels. Any of those levels can operate independently. Even if a nation were to EMP communication hubs around the world, certain networks would still work. It would be easier to shut off the power grid than to shut down the internet of things and the crypto world (as some people suggest happened in Texas in the winter of 2021).

Truth 1: Crypto Destroys Cronyism

Politicians are afraid of crypto because it destroys cronyism.[140] With regular currency, it is easy to see who is donating to unseat them. With crypto, these numbers can be tracked but it is a lot more work. There is no open federal disclosure that allows a politician to take revenge on those who supported their opponents with crypto, and this scares the corrupt.

The more decentralized the system is, the harder it is for crony capitalism or crony socialism to take place. People need to be able to control the flow of cash to create corrupt markets, decentralized markets allow corrupt markets to die. It is a win-win for the world. People need to know that the market punishes those who are bad actors when the government is not protecting them through cronyism.

Truth 2: It gives people a voice in world economic policy

It is said that if your name is not Rothschild, Soros, Branson, or Rockefeller (Maybe the Vanderbilts) then the truth is that under the fiat currency system, you do not have much say in the world economic policy. When it comes to crypto, it does not matter what your name is- you can buy the crypto with the policy that you like.[141] Ever since the introduction of fractal purchases, anyone can own part of any crypto. When you are part of the community, you have a say in where things go. If you do not like it, then you can move to another crypto that you do. The market will decide.

---

[139] *Id.*

[140] Gladstien, Alex (2018). "Why Bitcoin Matters for Freedom." Time at https://time.com/5486673/bitcoin-venezuela-authoritarian/.

[141] Time.

The era of the fiat monopoly is over. Governments kept people out of economic policy by devaluing their money. None of them ever expected that the people would create their own money. Give it value. Then have enough pride in their product to allow it to become a global phenomenon. As long as we do not "give it back" (technically they never had it) to the government, this will be a long-term improvement.

Truth 3: It is more Stable than Fiat Currency.

Fiat currency is only stable because the government has a monopoly on the lawful use of force to collect the debt. If you do not pay your debts to the government, you can go to jail. In the civilian world, there is nothing like this, you can be ordered to pay a debt but if you do not have it, then the order is just a piece of paper.[142] Governments do not like having their power taken from them, but as fiat currency is slowly being overpowered by crypto in some sectors, they (legally) can only watch the old system pass them perhaps. Crypto is based on the market and three other kinds of value, fiat currency is just based on the government's promise to pay you with more fiat currency. It is a broken system and will eventually fail.

Conclusion

The more people know about crypto, the less scary it is. People need to take time to educate others about the system. If you can, give them a copy of this book. While it may seem, a little self-serving. This book is written to help people understand what crypto is and why it is the future. The more people that understand this, the fewer people will be screaming for the government to regulate something that is already working.

The power of crypto lies in the global community. The more we work within the system, the more we can function as a community. We are all human, why is everyone's voice not worth the same? In crypto, that can be a reality; you can voice your opinion with your wealth. From the greatest to the smallest, the market listens to all. It may hear some more loudly, but there are many more small voices than there are loud voices. These can

---

[142] Emirex Group (2020). "Why cryptocurrency is more stable than fiat." Emirex at https://blog.emirex.com/why-cryptocurrency-is-more-stable-than-fiat.

drown even the biggest voice, for they need our air to breathe.

Chapter 12: Spot Trading Currencies

As we enter the world of trading, it is best to start at the very beginning and work our way to more complex strategies. The first step in any trading lesson is how to spot trade. A spot trade is the trading of stock at the present market value. Spot trades occur immediately. Understanding this basic element of how to trade a stock helps you understand when you move to more complex elements.

In this Chapter, we take a moment to look at some of the elements that can help a person become a good spot trader. Making sure that you understand exactly what a spot trade is can help you if you decide to move on to more complex strategies like shorts, margin trades, and derivatives. Once you know what a spot trade is, it is also useful for you to understand the difference that you will see between spot trades, shorts, margins, and derivatives- because different types of trades require different strategies.

After working on the "what" of spot trades, this Chapter starts looking at some of the elements that will help you "see" the market working better. One of the first things that most novice traders look at in the stock world is the patterns. Patterns are movements in the market that traders look for when they want to know if there will be a market reversal. One of the biggest mistakes that novice traders make is relying on the patterns alone, understanding the interplay between patterns and volume is essential to making good stock trades.

Something else that a lot of traders miss is the markets within the market. There are times when areas of the market are going to run, even while the general market is in a downturn. This is where many people can make fortunes on relatively safe spot trades, you use the rallying market within the market to hedge your bets and maintain value in your portfolio. Finally, this Chapter concludes by looking at the needs for both centralized and decentralized exchanges. As government regulators are clamoring for only centralized exchanges, this is why you should know that decentralized exchanges are needed.

Overall, the spot rate is the basic building block for any trading ideology or methodology. Without spot trading, then there are no advanced trading methods. This is why understanding the foundation is important before you move on to more difficult trading methodologies like shorts, margins, or derivatives. This is a "walk before you run," situation because if you move too fast when learning about stocks you can find yourself falling flat on your face.

The Difference between Spot and Derivative Trades

One of the biggest traps that novice traders get caught up in is trading securities that they do not understand. Even most children can understand the concept of a spot trade, "I give you X dollars, you give me stock/crypto/commodity."[143] This is the foundational system of our global economy, and kids pick this up when they realize that they need money if they want new toys. What catches a lot of traders is when they start to look at shorts, margins, and derivatives- which can quickly drain their brokerage accounts of all equity.

Shorts are perhaps the way that we see most people bankrupt their brokerage account. When a person gets involved in a short, they borrow a stock/crypto from someone who has the currency (and unlocks borrowing in their account) then sell that stock/crypto. The first step sounds like a good deal to most people, you get to sell stock that you do not hold when the value is high. Sounds amazing. However, this is where things get a little heady. Each short has a time limit. The new "friend" you made who let you borrow his toys wants to be paid back (with a slight fee). This means that before the end of the short contract you need to buy back an equal amount of the stock/crypto that you borrowed. The lender expects every share/coin/token back. If the value of the stock/crypto goes down (like you predicted) you buy it back at the lower rate to return it to the lender, then you pocket the difference (which is how money is made). If the rate goes up because you are wrong (and let's face it novice traders are wrong a lot), then you still have to buy back the stock to return it to the lender, regardless of whether you have the money in your account or not. This is

---

[143] Chen, James (2021). "Spot Trade." Investopedia. At https://www.investopedia.com/terms/s/spottrade.asp.

where people can lose money that they were not planning to invest by using an investment tool that they do not understand. To make matters worse, even if you lose money, you still have the pay the "interest" on the amount borrowed.

Margins are also a dangerous tool for people who do not know how they work. In a margin trade, the trader borrows funds from the brokerage account to make a trade that they normally cannot afford. These trades are usually done on "sure things" which generally turn out to be busted. The good news is that in most modern countries you can only trade on the margin up to the value of your brokerage account, which means if you fail to cover the brokerage will liquidate your account and take that as payment, leaving you to only owe the difference. In the past, people used to be able to buy the margin up to 10x the value of the trade (which put many people in the poorhouse). Just like with shorts, not only do you need to pay back the full value to the brokerage (regardless of how your trade does), you also have to pay their interest fee on the margin loan that you took out (always watch what the fees are).

Derivatives (Chapter 13) are securities based on the underlying value of other assets. These can come in many forms, which we cover in the next Chapter. The most common are options (put and call), forwards, futures, swaps, and warrants. Each of these has their own ins and outs, but basically, you are buying the right to do something with a stock in the future at the present price. This allows you to speculate on where a stock is going, without having to take the risk of actually buying the security. Remember, in most of these derivatives you are only buying the right to do something, you still have to have the funds to cover if you want to actually execute the derivative.

Once you understand the difference between a spot trade and any other type of trade, the other types of trades become very tempting. However, if you are a novice trader who is just learning how things work, you want to start with the easier methods of trading before you move to the more complex methods. The patterns tend to work across all markets because the patterns are based on the human traders, not the stock/cryptos themselves. This means that if you take your time to learn your patterns on spot trades, you can be slightly safer when you move on to other trading methodologies.

The Patterns

If you combined a fortune teller, an old Greek oracle, and a 1970s clairvoyant, you would have one heck of a traveling carnival show, but not much of a trading strategy.[144] If you look on Facebook or any other social media platform today, you will see dozens of companies and people telling you that they have a full-proof system for predicting how stocks/cryptos are going to move. What they are doing is following the patterns. These modern oracles have about the same track record as the old oracles, their pages are corrected two days after movement to look like they predicted what happened- and anything future-focused is usually written so vaguely that no one can really "prove them wrong."

Patterns are a useful tool when you are looking at what trades to make and when to make them. However, there are certain things that you need to remember when you are looking at these trades. First, the patterns represent the market, not the asset.[145] This means that they are vulnerable to human error, human manipulation, and human stupidity. Just because a pattern appears does not mean that it will definitely react the way it has in the past (at best it is 60/40). Another danger that people face is that they start seeing patterns everywhere. A pattern in the 1-minute chart is not as indicative as a pattern in the 1-hour chart, but people treat them the same. When comparing patterns, you need to compare apples to apples, not apples to oranges.

So, what are the patterns? If you go online, you will find hundreds of patterns that fall into about 7 different categories. People who sell this system tend to find the same patterns people have been using since the

---

[144] Illev, Georgi (2020). "Edu Campaign Four: Technical Analysis." Applications in Life at https://lessonsfinancial.com/2020/03/31/edu-campaign-four-technical-analysis/?gclid=Cj0KCQiAlMCOBhCZARIsANLid6anwNM5iHZESsy5n-tnBx0l81YQymcpLUXd4yHtjBomQlBQN2G6QNsaAqZAEALw_wcB.

[145] *Id.*

1950s and call them something new so they can package them differently. The big patterns that we look at are:

1.) Double tops or bottoms (and triple)
2.) Three candles/crows
3.) Japanese Candlesticks
4.) Head and Shoulders
5.) Cup and Handle
6.) Pivots
7.) Flags

Each of these patterns has something that it tends to indicate and they can be useful when looked at in the proper context.

A double (or triple) top (or bottom) is one of the first patterns that people learn to look for.[146] This pattern tends to be replaced with trends as someone becomes a more savvy trader (trends can be slightly more reliable types of patterns. A double top is when the trading hits a wall, retreats, then hits the wall again. In a triple, this pattern repeats a third time making it more likely that it is true. Double tops are a bearish signal, which means that the stock is likely to stop.[147] On a double or triple bottom, the stock tests the support line rather than the resistance line and the double or triple bottom is a sign that the stock is likely to have a rally after the second or third peak.[148]

Crows and candlesticks are another popular pattern to look for when you are trading.[149] Showing a reversal is likely coming, crows are when bears beat back the bulls three times in a row (black/red crows) or when the bulls

---

[146] Hayes, Adam (2021). "Introduction to Technical Analysis Price Patterns." Investopedia at https://www.investopedia.com/articles/technical/112601.asp.
[147] Cliffe, Callum (2020). "10 Chart Patterns Every Trader Needs to Know." IG at https://www.ig.com/us/trading-strategies/10-chart-patterns-every-trader-needs-to-know-190514.
[148] Please note some people will also look for quadruple bottoms and tops, which tend to be even more reliable (however, these usually fall into a trend pattern, which is an evolution of this system.).
[149] CMC (2020). "11 Most Essential stock patterns." CMC at https://www.cmcmarkets.com/en/trading-guides/stock-chart-patterns.

beat the bears (green crows). In this pattern, the trader will see three peaks of about the same size forming in the five-to-ten-minute charts. These indicate that a rally in the market is coming to an end and that those who are selling (cashing out) are outpacing those who are buying with the hopes of a continuing rally.[150] When you see the three peaks rising, that generally means a downturn. When you see three dips starting to bounce, that generally means an upturn in the market.

Japanese candlesticks are not a pattern, per se, but are a way of marking your charts. Developed by Japanese rise merchants centuries ago, these types of charts can be used like crows as indicators of market direction.[151] Candlesticks show the open, close, high, and low points for a given period. This allows traders to see what the spot trades are, but also to see the high and low offers (wicks). Looking at how the high and low offers are moving can often be a good tool to see market confidence.

Head and shoulders are another strong reversal sign that many people look for in trading. Unfortunately, many people tend to look at them in the wrong light. Generally, a true head and shoulders pattern is the same as three black (rising) crows. It indicates the end of a rally and the beginning of a downtrend. In this pattern, the left shoulder sets the boundary, the head is the high point, and the right shoulder is the last high before a decline. With an inverted head and shoulders, you see the opposite.[152] The left shoulder is a slight dip, the head is the largest dip, and then the right shoulder is the last dip before a rally. This is an easy pattern to see (normal) but can be tricky to see inverted.

Cup and handle are an often-misrepresented signals on the market. A cup and handle are formed when there is a "U" shaped bowl followed by a slightly downward "handle" which looks like another "U" shaped bowl.[153]

---

[150] Hayes, Supra.
[151] Foot, Patrick (N/A). "What is a Japanese Candlestick." IG at https://www.ig.com/en/trading-strategies/japanese-candlestick-trading-guide-200615.
[152] Hayes Supra.
[153] CMC supra.

In the stock market, this is often seen as a bullish signal as the market tends to rally out of the handle. The key difference between the cup and handle in the stock and crypto market is that in the crypto market, the cup and handle tend to form over the space of a few hours- in the stock market a cup and handle are not reliable unless they have been forming over a period of weeks to months.[154]

For those that are good at math, there is also a pattern called pivots. A pivot is "a technical analysis indicator, or calculations, used to determine the overall trend of the market over different time frames. The pivot point itself is simply the average of the intraday high and low, and the closing price from the previous trading day."[155] This point is used as an indicator as the following trading session starts. If the value is below the pivot point, it is thought to be bearish. If the value is above the pivot point, then the market should be bullish.

Flags are somewhere between a pattern and a trend. Because flags are so short, we have included them here in the patterns section (which tend to be shorter, or spot looks). In a flag, you see a consolidation of the value of the stock.[156] A downward trending flag tends to be the indicator of a large rally coming. An ascending flag tends to mean that the asset is going to take a downturn.[157] Flags are great points in which to make your trades, just do not "force" a flag to be somewhere that it is not.

Patterns are useful tools, but make sure that you are using them as the tools they are. Patterns are not magic; the market can still move whichever way that it would like. Patterns simply increase your odds of following a movement in the market that can help keep your numbers in the black for your trader. As a general rule, the longer the pattern plays out, the more

---

[154] Chen, James (2021). "Cup and Handle Definition." Investopedia at https://www.investopedia.com/terms/c/cupandhandle.asp.
[155] Mitchell, Cory (2021). "Pivot Point." Investopedia at https://www.investopedia.com/terms/p/pivotpoint.asp.
[156] Callum, Supra.
[157] Scott, Gordon (2021). "Flag." Investopedia at https://www.investopedia.com/terms/f/flag.asp.

likely it is to be a true pattern.

Trends

Whenever you are ready to put on your big boy shorts (or big girl shorts as the case may be), you may want to start looking for market trends rather than just patterns. Patterns get a lot of the hype because so many people create the systems and they are popular among day traders.[158] However, when you are looking at trends, you are looking at the "longs." Trends tend to form on the longer charts (1 hour to 1 week) and can be fairly reliable (70:30) that something is going to happen in line with past situations.

Before you can understand trends, you should have a basic understanding of resistance and support lines. A support line is formed when many people make the same offer for a stock, which creates a basement for the stock value. Likewise, the resistance line is what happens when many investors make a demand at a specific price, which creates a roof for trading.[159] Both of these lines are very important because they form a range in which the asset will likely stay.

Once you have established your resistance and support lines, then you can look for trends. The most common types of trends to watch for are:

1.) Rectangles,
2.) Wedges,
3.) Triangles,
4.) Channels.

Each of these tends to show a market direction. As noted, it can be difficult to pick these up on the short charts, which is why any stock analysis should involve looking at the short, medium, and long-term charts.

Rectangles are the easiest of the trends to see. A rectangle tends to show that the stock is going to continue the pattern that it was in before it entered the rectangle.[160] By and large, a rectangle is a consolidation of the

---

[158] *Id.*
[159] Callum Supra.
[160] *Id.*

stock's value before continued movement. Rectangles are formed by peaks and valleys that are approximately the same size continuing in a pattern of four or more. If an asset was in the decline as it enters a rectangle, then it will likely continue down. If it was rallying a rectangle can show that it is going to rise.[161]

Wedges and Triangles are very similar. The great thing about triangles and wedges. In both wedges and triangles, you see increasing peaks (upward) or decreasing peaks (downward). The support and resistance lines tend to point towards an intersection. However, triangles are dangerous for people who are looking for a wedge. Wedges tend to be indicative of a reversal in a system. A rising wedge tends to show that the market is about to take a downturn. Descending wedges can indicate a bull market is coming. However, wedges change direction before the cross of the indicator lines. This means that if the lines cross, you have a triangle.[162] A triangle just shows a change in the market but does not indicate which way it is going. While it will, more often than not (52:48) show a reverse if it is going up or down, when it is level, it indicates that the market will change but not which direction it will change- so it acts mostly as being a false wedge.

Channels are a day trader's dream, but are also valuable to along. A channel is an ascending or descending rectangle that indicates the movement of the market. The direction of the channel tends to indicate a continuation of the pattern in the short term, but a reversal once the channel breaks. A static channel can maintain the same direction for a period of time, but will eventually break leading to consolidation.

The best traders are able to combine trends and patterns to look for short and long-term movement. Remember, you do not have to be a day trader or a long, you can combine the two. The better you get at spotting differences in the market, the better you will be able to capitalize on those changes. Trades should not be gambling; they should be measured risks

---

[161] Hayes, Supra.
[162] Callum, supra.

you know when to take.

Volume Watching

Anyone who is looking to be a strong trader needs to make sure that they learn about how volume affects a market. A low-volume market can have the best patterns in the world. Most strong traders will take a high-volume channel over a low volume cup and handle it every day. Why? Because the channel on the high-volume charts shows that it is the market making the choice, not just a few traders. This is vital for anyone who wants to have a good market sense.

Low-volume markets depend on what is being traded. In some areas, 100K shares being traded a day is considered a high-volume day. In others, if you are under 100 M trades you are having a slow day. Know your market. When you jump from one market to another, you need to learn the market dynamics to ensure you know what you are doing. Too often people treat the market like it is a constant, it is not. Trading involves using your knowledge to get what you need (which is value). The more you know the better trader you are.

The market is like buying a used car. You can get a winner or you can get a melon. When you go with no knowledge, then you are simply rolling the dice. However, when you take an expert with you (or gain the expertise needed), you can have a better chance at finding a winner. Take the time to learn the ins and outs of the market in which you are trading. This will open new doors to you and help you be a better trader.

The Growth of a Market Separate from the Growth of THE Market

Another quick area that can be the difference between a good trader and a great trader is the understanding of the difference between individual markets and the market in general.[163] The market will always has its patterns, but it will always be an amalgamation of the different areas of the market. Individual markets will have their patterns, which may be affected by the general market or maybe not. To ensure that you have the

---

[163] CMC, Supra.

best understanding of how the market works, you need to understand the whole market and your little slice that you trade-in.

The best indicators of the crypto market are the currency markets. When a currency dives, the crypto market tends to see a rally. This is because people are changing over from fiat currency to crypto. This is a general rule, not an "always" thing. When Serbia had its currency collapse, there was a nationwide rally in crypto. While this would seem to indicate a rally, there was already a bearish sentiment because of the end of the year, so the rally only slowed a bear market. Understanding relationships and how one pattern can be superimposed on another will give you a deeper understanding than 90% of the people on the market.

The Need for Centralized and Decentralized Exchanges

Since crypto has both centralized and decentralized markets, pattern trading can be difficult. Patterns on decentralized markets are, at best, hit or miss. Because the trades are based on individual interactions, not the computers and AI of big trading companies, the patterns can create false signals across the board. The problem is that, as computers move into this space, we are seeing computers react to false trends, which can cause reversals where there should not be reversals.

This begs the question of why there need to be decentralized exchanges. The answer to that is simple. We need decentralized exchanges so that the market can grow. 1 in 100 new cryptos gets to start on a centralized exchange, and most of the ones that accept new cryptos are newer exchanges. Fortunately, cryptos can move quickly to a centralized exchange once they prove themselves. This makes decentralized exchanges vital incubators for innovation in the field.

The decentralized exchanges are more volatile, but the volatility shakes the errors out of the system. This allows the market to be "surer" that something on a centralized exchange is viable crypto. This added level of protection is much better than the fiat system, which test things with the simple statement "trust us, we are the government." The dichotomy forces both sides of the centralized and decentralized markets to improve on the other's features, creating a constant system of innovation within a field of constant evolution.

Chapter 13: Derivative Trading of Cryptocurrencies

In Part III we look at the concept of derivatives in detail and how they interact with the crypto markets, but here in Chapter 13, we are going to hammer what derivatives are and how they are affecting the market. This is a survey Chapter to help you understand the concept of derivatives so that when the topic arises in other Chapters, you will recognize them easier.

To start off, derivatives are a way for people to make more money trading securities. One day, someone said, "Hey, what if I could lock in a price on a stock now and pay it when it comes upon a future date?" It just so happened that someone was sitting there and said, "I think that is a good idea; I will let you do that, but you have to pay me for the option." The options market was born. It likely did not happen exactly like that, but it was something close. Derivatives give people more options in how they can trade securities, and now that this option has opened up on some crypto exchanges, the wild, wild, west of crypto is about to get a whole lot wilder (Maybe).

This Chapter looks at four very important issues around derivatives. In section one, the current volatility of the market is examined. This volatility is one of the key reasons that derivatives seem like such a risk in the crypto markets. Section two takes things a step deeper and looks at the decentralized nature of crypto. Decentralization and derivatives have the potential to be a disaster, but they also have the potential to synergize in a way no one sees coming. Section three questions the ability of new traders to use derivatives. While spot trading crypto only lets you lose what you have put in, some derivatives can allow you to lose more than you are willing to bet. The regulatory miasma is addressed in section 4, looking at how the SEC and congress in the United States are holding back on what exactly cryptocurrencies are (they are currencies, and the derivatives are securities, by definition, but congress is still arguing). Finally, section 5 looks at why derivatives are not always a bad idea and how derivatives in the volatile crypto market could actually bring stabilization to the market. Are derivatives good or bad, neither, they are simply another tool allowing people to trade their wealth freely?

Challenges Related to the Volatility of the Market

If you were to take a college stock trading class (as many of you may be doing now), then you would likely hear your professor tell you that derivatives add to market volatility. While terms such as margins, options, forwards, and warrants sound complicated, they are really not that complicated. Each of these is simply another way that a person may trade on the open market looking for patterns within the systems. Options give you the options to buy or sell, forwards move the process forward, warrants give you a chance at new offerings and margins let you bet with other people's money (that you will be called in on if you lose). Once a derivative is created, that derivative can be traded on the market (with the exception of forwards). This creates a volatile market where billions are made and lost each year.

The scary thing from many of the OG traders is that the crypto market is already volatile.[164] In the stock market, if you see double-digit gains or losses on a stock, it can either make or break your year. As this is being written, there is double-digit movement on at least three of the twenty stocks on my current watch list! Crypto is already something that will move about quite rapidly, and this scares a lot of investors away from the idea of crypto derivatives.

The question that any serious investor needs to ask is "why?" No one is ever forced to buy or sell a derivative. They are securities just like anything else. The danger of a crypto derivative is that when it matured is that it will be worthless. However, the same thing can be said about stock derivatives. When you buy an option, you take the risk that you will never execute that option. When a warrant comes out, you calculate whether the stock will be worth the amount of the warrant, or whether you should just buy the stock on the open market.

Derivatives in the crypto market are just the same as derivatives in the

---

[164] Woebbeking, Fabian (2021). "Cryptocurrency volatility markets." NCBI at https://www.ncbi.nlm.nih.gov/pmc/articles/PMC8326316/.

stock market.[165] They are high risk, high reward. If you are involved with stock derivatives, then you need to accept that the crypto version just offers higher risk and higher rewards. When you follow the golden rule that you should not gamble with more than you can afford to lose, then you realize that if you can afford to lose the stake, the derivatives market in the crypto space offers the opportunity to make more money than you could ever make trading regular stocks. (It is also riskier, remember that).

Challenges Related to the Decentralized Nature of Cryptocurrency

One of the chief concerns over derivatives in the crypto market is the nature of the crypto market itself. As crypto is decentralized, the market tends to favor decentralized exchanges, while investors tend to favor centralized exchanges. It is an interesting tug of war that is increasing the value of crypto across the board as trades move between decentralized and centralized exchanges. With the advent of third-Wave cryptos, the spiderweb bridge GET tokens to allow for the trades to operate smoothly. So why is this a problem with derivatives?

Most trade contracts are unilateral contracts, in this case, one party pays, and the other party transfers the stocks/bonds/crypto to the buyer. This is an efficient system because once the trade is done, the contract is complete and both parties can move on. Derivatives follow the pattern of a bilateral contract where one party makes a payment for a promise. In a derivative, the party receiving the money promises to sell/buy stock/bonds/crypto at a given point to the paying party. Herein lies the rub, the person receiving the money needs to have the ability to comply with the agreement.

In the 1980s, scammers would use options to make billions off people who did not know any better. Companies that did not have the ability to cover their options would pop up, sell the options, then disappear into the 3rd world, never to be seen again. Even as recently as 2020, we saw the certain options and stocks in areas were oversold (meaning more stock was sold

[165] Fernando, Jason (2021). "Derivative." Investopedia at https://www.investopedia.com/terms/d/derivative.asp

than existed). It was thought that the "squeeze" would drive the prices through the roof (it did just not as high as people thought it would.) People also thought that it would make regulators fix the market, but other than handing out some fines nothing happened, and the meme stock crusade failed.[166]

This does highlight the danger of a decentralized derivatives market. There is the potential for new derivative exchanges to pop up, allow millions of dollars in derivatives to be sold, then disappear into the ether leaving empty hands in the bag holders. In the ultra-regulated world of derivatives for stocks, these problems still arise, how can we prevent it with cryptos. NFTs are the Wave of the future. Each type of derivative is minted, there is an NFT created of the contract. The NFT contract must contain the location, accounts, and ability to cover the person selling the derivative. When the derivative expires or is claimed, the NFT is destroyed. The NFTs need to be held on a third-party server, not a proprietary server of the issuer, and they can be traded like normal derivatives (with the exception of forwards, of course).

The very digital nature of crypto allows for new options in ensuring that people do not abuse the fledgling system. Better yet, the issuer can be required to keep insurance over the NFT, which will have a fallback if they are unable to cover the derivative. This means could allow the market to regulate itself with a simple code change in each nation's rules.

"Any issuer of derivatives within the cryptospace or metaverse must carry insurance which can cover the sum amount of the issued derivatives, incompliance with the derivative contract which must be memorialized in NFT form and stored/traded on an exchange unrelated to the issuing entity."

---

[166] Stempel, Johnathan (2021). "Robinhood, others win dismissal of meme stock 'short squeeze' lawsuit." Reuters at https://www.reuters.com/markets/us/robinhood-others-win-dismissal-meme-stock-short-squeeze-lawsuit-2021-11-18/.

And

> Should any entity intentionally create a derivative that they do not have the ability to cover, that entity is prohibited from trading crypto within the territories of [NAME OF COUNTRY HERE] ad infinitum. No entity created by the creators of the original entity, which has more than 50% of the original creators or is made up of more than 50% original creators shall be able to be formed for the purpose of doing business within [NAME OF COUNTRY HERE].

These simple two sections of protection, if adopted around the world could allow for the derivative market to thrive, without the hyper-regulation that we see of currency derivative markets globally.

Challenges Related to Lack of Sophistication in Traders

One of the biggest dangers of derivatives is the money that can be lost by unsophisticated traders. Derivatives can be daunting to understand, especially by people who are newly entering the game to trade stocks and cryptos on the spot. This fear has led many to worry that the derivatives of cryptos could be exploitive for new traders. As you must understand, if someone is making millions, those millions must come from somewhere.

Derivatives are complex, but they are not evil. While it may be tempting to say "Caveat Emptor" and let the good times roll, this is not the best way to ensure that the market is not overly regulated. The market itself must do something to make it known to new traders that derivatives are more complex than spot trades. In trying to be a good community, however, we must also acknowledge that it is the trader's responsibility to learn about the system in which they are trading. If we take all of the responsibility away, then we are not fixing the problem.

One of the best ways to deal with this issue is to educate the traders.[167] While there will always be people who are too eager to "make the big bucks" and will rush right into trading without knowing what is going on, most people will take "free" lessons when they can get them. The crypto

[167] Fernando, Supra.

community needs to band together and create a database of good articles and webinars on what derivatives are and how they should be traded. There are several articles out there already explaining the derivatives for stocks, to expand upon these resources and give people information on cryptos would be easy.

If the community comes together to educate people, then we can stave off one of the big attacks that the regulators are going to make. If we are accused of taking advantage of people and do nothing to prevent this abuse, then we are doing what the regulators say. As crypto is a community, it stands to reason that the community should work together to ensure that community members, new and old know what they are doing when they are trading derivatives.[168]

Challenges Related to the Regulatory Makeup of the System

One of the biggest challenges currently in the marketplace is that there are no real rulings on how the system is set up. Regulatory agencies have taken a "wait and see" approach to crypto. The courts have ruled that it is something different, but even the courts have not defined what it is. This means that there is a legal vacuum where people do not know how to treat cryptos in their taxes, in their finances, and within their businesses. For the system to work properly, the crypto community needs to deal with this problem.

By definition, coins and tokens are currency and derivatives are securities. This means that coins and tokens should fall under the laws the guide the exchange, possession, taxation, and transportation of currencies. Likewise, derivatives should be governed by the same rules that govern other derivatives in the securities markets. When the governments of the world will not make these rules standard, the community itself needs to do so in the trade journals, books (like this one), and other places. Business thrives when the definitions are known for a marketplace, it is time that the

[168] To contribute to this effort, several of the authors have published articles discussing derivatives on free to access sites to ensure people have access to the information.

community names its marketplace.

Since regulatory agencies have taken a backseat in the crypto space, it is time for the community to step up. Write your representatives if you are in a free country with the following statement:

"Mr/Mrs Representative,

My name is [NAME HERE], I am a citizen of your district and I have a concern. I invest in cryptocurrency and the regulatory agencies in our country/state have not given us proper guidance. The only recourse is to treat it like wage income and pay the highest tax rate available to ensure that I am not in violation of the law. This is not right! Cryptocurrency is a currency and should be taxed as a currency. Derivatives in crypto should be treated like other derivatives and be taxed under capital gains. I am not asking for a pass on my taxes, only that the regulatory agencies do their job and affirm that crypto is currency and that the derivatives are derivatives. I do not think that this is too much to ask since the crypto community is putting billions of dollars into our country's economy. Please, have your office call and ask that the [Regulatory agency in your country] define crypto as a currency and derivatives as a security under the law so we can know how to pay our taxes."

If millions around the world send similar letters in, we can force representatives to make changes that will benefit the market and allow the system to thrive.

We also have a duty to use the courts to ensure that our rights are protected. When laws that are against constitutions and public policy crop up (usually because the fiat lobby wants to quash crypto) we need to take the courts, not just the internet. The right to contract is a human right, in the United States it is seen as an inalienable right and by the UN it is seen as a human right. We need to fight to protect this right. If a regulatory body files a definition of crypto or derivatives that is contrary to the rights of the community to contract, we need to sue to get the courts to support the definitions. The crypto community is accepting that we will be taxed on our gains, we just want to be taxed at the proper rate than other securities and currencies are taxed at. If we use the courts, then we can protect our rights.

Finally, the crypto community must militarize. Not in some socialist Antifa way, but the way real companies mobilize, through lobbying groups. GreenWallet is the lobbying wing of one of the major crypto communities that can help smooth progress in the United States. They also, where legally permitted, make donations to other lobbying groups in other countries. The crypto community is not asking for special treatment, just that they are treated equally to other commodities and securities around the world.

Overall Benefits of Derivative Trading and Stabilization

Before we move away from this topic, look at the benefits of derivatives to the overall crypto community:

1.) Derivatives will Bring in Hedge Funds- Hedge funds will stabilize the market as huge swings are harder to manage when using larger funds.
2.) Derivatives will help make cryptos retirement income- Once there are derivatives, retirement funds can use the derivatives for structured investment policies.
3.) Derivatives are viable trading too- as noted above, they are a viable tool, it should be at the behest of the educated investor whether they want to use the tool or not.
4.) Derivatives will help stabilize growth as rapid growth and decline are against the market- the open market derivatives will help stabilize trade to ensure steady, rather than rapid, growth in the market.
5.) Derivatives allow the centralized exchanges to stay active while keeping the decentralized exchanges focused on spot trades.

If we can realize that these benefits will help people around the world, and help the market grow. It seems like it is a good idea to bring derivatives to the marketplace.

Trading derivatives will always be a risky business. If the community can band together and understand that for the decentralized system to be maintained, there will be elements that need to be centralized. Derivatives are one of these systems. A centralized derivative market can give the regulators something to focus on. The centralized market will also ensure that issuers of derivatives will have the capital and the security to cover their offers. The community itself can expand the efficiency of the system by making sure that people are educated as to what derivatives are, so they do not just become a get-rich scheme. While these are not the "be-all and end-all" of the crypto market, they are a tool that people should be allowed to use to increase their trading capacity, which can help the community in the long run.

Chapter 14: Industry Internal Structure within Current Law

The law is one of the fundamental structures that makes a society civilized. Too often, when new industry comes into play, they worry about the new laws that will be created to govern the new industry.[169] This is a situation that can always be problematic, however, one of the problems that we face in this paradigm is that people never look at the current state of the law and how the new industry can be managed by the current set of laws in effect.

Crypto is not anything new. The coins and tokens are currency and the derivatives are securities. Why then do we need the world to start looking for new laws to govern the system? The answer is that we do not. The system of cryptocurrencies has been in place for nearly a decade, operating under the existing legal paradigm. The only reason that the governments of the world want to make a new law to control the industry is that people who are not part of the "elite" are starting to create generational wealth.

Societies, whether eastern socialisms or western democracies, only work when there is a working-class that is managed by the elite class. All the high school and junior college mumbo jumbo about a "middle class" and "working poor" are simply methods to divide the people in society (and for the unqualified to get doctorates). There are only two classes of people in this world, the people who have the wealth to manage their own lives and those that do not. The problem we face as a society is that most people do not want to admit that they are in the latter class.

Laws are what divides society from being Barbarians. In Rome, if you were Roman, you were civilized. If you lived outside of Rome, you were a barbarian. In the modern world, if you live outside of the accepted paradigms of law and order, you are a barbarian. This Chapter looks at some universal truths in the law that allow society to be civilized. It may

---

[169] Puterbaugh, John (2021). "Two Things Crypto Investors should know about the infrastructure bill Biden just signed." Next Advisor at https://time.com/nextadvisor/investing/cryptocurrency/infrastructure-bill-crypto-taxes/.

offend some people and some leaders who live in countries where these are not standard, but in the digital age, any country that does not support basic human rights law does not deserve to be a county- and we need to quit pretending that they do.

This Chapter focuses on the property rights that people around the world have inherently. This is not an exhaustive list of rights (That is the space for another book). The first of the rights that we look at is the right to contract. Though we talk about his in bits and pieces throughout the book, the right to contract is one of the fundamental human rights that no one talks about. You have a right to decide what you are going to do; those decisions should be based on your needs. No one owes you anything, but the respect of the right for your self-determination. The right to contract is the legal memorialization of that right to self-determine in your own life.

Next, we take a moment to look at your tight security. This is security in your person and your papers. People have been abused and assaulted over their involvement in crypto, mainly because governments do not understand it. Some say that people who follow the rules are harassed because they may not be considered "the right people to make big money." For some reason, the governments of the world reserve that right to celebrities, athletes, and drug cartels. People have a right to be secure in their persons, home, and papers- which includes the right to make money.

People also have a right to use what they need to use to barter. Governments have successfully worn down what people can use to conduct trade in the world over the last 100 years. Now it is time for the pendulum to swing back in the other direction. The country only has to accept one currency, the people can use whatever currency they like. If the government fails to recognize these currencies, then it is on the government to explain why the people should pay taxes on the unrecognized currencies. If they cannot explain this, then why (other than the monopoly on force) should people pay taxes on currencies.

The big difference that needs to be defined in the coming years (or re-defined) is the difference between currencies and securities. Currencies should not be taxed; securities should be taxed.[170] It is as simple as this. While the people of every nation have the right to define what is a security under their laws, the idea that one currency is a currency and another is security shows a deviation in the law. It also violates the rights of the people.

Next, we look at some of the privileges that governments have. To be very clear, governments are formed under the social contract, they have no inherent, inalienable rights.[171] Everything that a government has the power to do is derived from privileges under the social contract or abuses under a system of tyranny- there is no other power in government. The COVID crisis showed us that governments will abuse their powers when they have the opportunity, the people of the world need to work together to ensure that these abuses never happen again.

Lobbies and citizens around the world need to work together to build a better world. This is not a question of capitalism v. socialism, or nationalism v. internationalism, this is a question of the difference between oppression and freedom. The more the lobbies that support crypto around the world empower people to be free, the more governments will allow people to live within the social contract that has been in place. Eliminate the idea of government rights, they do not exist. The government only has duties and privileges that are clearly defined. Even countries with bad constitutions need to understand that power comes from the people and must be returned upon their request.

The Right to Contract

As odd as it sounds, the fundamental right that makes us human is the right to contract.[172] The foundations of society are built on the social contract (though it has evolved through the ages). Each individual has the right to possess and protect what they own, they also have the right to place

---

[170] Liebkind, Joe (2021). "Taxes and Crypto" Investopedia at https://www.investopedia.com/tech/taxes-and-crypto/ .

[171] Pacific Legal Foundation, Supra.

[172] Wexlaw at https://www.law.cornell.edu/wex/freedom_of_contract.

encumbrances on it, sell it, rent it, or divide it. For this to be true, people must understand one major point- no one person or government owns any other person, but for due process of the law. The more the crypto community fights to ensure that each person is free to contract, the more stable the world economy will be.

Society is built on a contract, the social contract. The social contract has evolved over the years, but the basic understanding is that government only has the power it needs to protect the individuals in society. No society has the privilege of unilaterally acting to take rights away from one person for the greater good. Even though billionaires have a lot of money, we do not have the right to take that money away from them because we want it. Whether that is done through force or bill of attainder, that is still theft. The only way wealth can be "taken" from another person by society or the government is if that person commits a crime. Existence is not a crime. Underlying the social contract is the duty of government, protect the people, protect their property. When a government makes a law that protects the property of some people more than the property of other people, mainly because they were paid more, those laws are invalid. The human right to be secure in their property and person is universal- this is the foundation of the social contract.

Expanding upon the social contract, each person has the right to buy, sell, and transact as they need to in society. Some things in society are illegal, however, one must always question why they are illegal. Are they illegal because they make other people suffer (the majority of the time)? Then the making of those goods illegal is within the social contract. Are they illegal simply because they cause pain to the person who chooses to use them, or because others are afraid of them? Then their illegality is beyond the social contract. Each person has the right to use their goods and property in a way that does not directly/intentionally contribute to the pain or injury of other people. If pain or injury is a side effect, then there is a question of civil claims against the person, but the illegality of the possession is a violation of the social contract. When the government restricts our use of what we own, the government is violating the rights of the people.

This brings up another very volatile matter. A person cannot own another person.[173] This is a universal truth. A person can have control over another person, such as a parent having control over a child, a government having control over a prisoner (with due process), or a state having control over someone with a mental deficiency, but no adult can own another adult. We are all born free people, and that is how we should live our lives. The only time that we can give up this freedom is if we commit a crime. The only limit on the control that we have over ourselves is that we cannot commit actions that will or have a high likelihood of causing harm to other people (physical), and we may not sell ourselves into slavery. No person owns another person, and until this is true in the world no one is free.

These are the basic tenants of contracting. Each country can have its own caveats around the idea of contracting, but the general rule is you can do what you need to as long as it is not intended or extremely likely to harm another person. This means people have control over their bodies.[174] Building our system based on people having control over themselves (and responsibility for what they do) is fundamental to building a better world and preserving the freedom to trade using cryptocurrency.

The Right to Be Secure in Our Papers

Governments around the world have always been interested in what is going on inside one person's house or another.[175] This is akin to a curious neighbor wondering what you are doing when the blinds are drawn. Just like the neighbor has no right to know what you are doing in your house; the government does not have a right to know what is going on in your

---

[173] *Id.*

[174] Under the current court rulings in Alabama a child within its mother is a person, as long as one jurisdiction sees a biological human being as a person, then there is no right for other jurisdictions to deny this right.

[175] Goitein, Elizabeth (2019). "The FBI Violated the privacy rights of tens of thousands of Americans. The Brennan Center at https://www.brennancenter.org/our-work/analysis-opinion/how-fbi-violated-privacy-rights-tens-thousands-americans.

house or your papers. There are limited exceptions to a government knowing what is in your house; however, the exceptions are even more limited when it comes to seeing what is in your papers. Income taxes around the world are one of the most invasive invasions of privacy in the world. These invasions need to stop for the world to move forward.

First of all, the government does not need to know what is going on in your home. Unless there is clear and pressing evidence that there is a crime being committed (a crime that harms another human being or a human being inside of the house), the government has no right to enter your home. This is why most civilized countries have a system of warrants where the government needs to show "reasonable cause" to violate a person's privacy; however, they are showing "reasonable cause" to THE GOVERNMENT, so the system is highly suspect.[176] In an ideal world, a panel of citizens would issue warrants, not judges (citizens who do not work for the government). The foundation that a person is secure in their home is the basis of our hierarchy of needs.

This situation goes double for being secure in your papers. Each person has the right to conduct business in their own way as long as:

1.) It does not violate the just laws of the land;
2.) It does not cause harm to other people;
3.) It deals only with their property or person (environmental laws, riparian laws, etc.).[177]

This is a simple proof system that enables people to be secure in how they do business. However, the governments of the world have created thousands of special cases where people's rights are abandoned because of the common good, because of paranoia, or simply because a despot or crackpot says so. People should only have to turn their private information over to the government if there is a crime being committed, or reasonable suspicion of a crime.

---

[176] Liebkind, Supra.

[177] *See Also* Descartes First Meditation.

This brings us to the topic of income tax. The income tax is not about the money that the government can take off of you, it is about the information that they want to have access to. Originally (on the global market), the income tax only affected the top 0.5% of the income earners in the world. Then the system was expanded to the upper class, then to the middle class, then to the working poor. Eventually, the government expanded it, even more, looking at people's investments. Why did the government need to do this, because the government needed to expand growing war machines and growing invasions into people's privacy? The United States alone went from having two federal law enforcement agencies (the FBI and the Department of Treasury's secret service) to 65 agencies and 27 offices of the inspector general's in just over 100 years. For the first 150 years, the US only needed on law enforcement agency at the federal level (Secret Service). This massive expansion in the United States was not needed, nor is it needed around the rest of the world

Every person has the right to be secure in their papers. Unless there is a specific reason that the government needs to see your papers, they should not have access. Tolls, fees, and tariffs ran the country for 150 years, they could run it again if we get rid of the excess. If the country needs a balancing tax, then have a national sales tax on goods and a luxury tax, it is much more progressive than an income tax and encourages people to save money. Poverty is the natural state of people, we come out of the womb naked and afraid, it is not the government's job to keep us in that position.

Adoption of Legal Tender: The Privilege to Regulate National Currency

Countries have the right to determine their legal tender. When we say countries, we mean that the people have the right to decide what their legal tender is. If they want to use fiat currency, then that is their choice. If they want to use cryptocurrency, more power to them. Even if they want some system where they use goats and F150s, that is the choice of the people. The government does not need to have a specific currency that people use in day-to-day stations.

The only use of national legal tender is for the paying of taxes to the government.[178] A government may determine what type of tender that it wishes to have its taxes, fees, tolls and tariff paid in- but that is a private given to them by the social contract. The misconception that a government needs to print and coin money for use is simply not true. Societies existed around the world for millennia without this system being fully enforced, and humanity saw exponential growth in these times.

Nation-states have shown that they are not the best place for currency to be regulated. For years, they have been the "only choice" because there was no one else to regulate the currency. Now with the advent of the digital age, the community has the ability to regulate the currency. 200 years ago, when there were dozens of currencies in a given country, no one was able to regulate them all and define what they were worth in comparison to one another on an adjusting scale. Now people carry a device around in their pocket that can do this very quickly, it is called a cell phone. The need for the government to be the sole arbiter of currency value has ended, now it is time to let the market build a better economy.

Governments still have the privilege to define what type of currency that they will accept when someone is paying their bills to them; however, each entity in the society also needs to be able to define what it will accept. The national legal tender must be accepted within the bounds of a nation; however, entities can accept other forms of currency at their discretion. Just like my local gas station could accept dollars and yen, a Dollar General store could choose to accept all cryptos or no cryptos (based on corporate policy). As long as the system is accepted equally without discrimination against the people spending the money, then the system should be allowed. Governments have the privilege of regulating trade with the government, not regulating trade from peer to peer.

Currency v. Security: & the national Privilege of Taxation

One of the biggest battles looming for the crypto world is the discussion of the definition between a currency and a security. Many people are using crypto like a security, and this is creating a window for the government to

[178] Liebkind, Supra.

define it as a security.[179] The community needs to come together and make sure that more places are using cryptos as a currency so they are not defined as a security.

The key reason for this distinction is that currencies are not taxable under most countries' laws, securities are. When the government is trying to make crypto a security, it is not because they want it regulated as a security- they want it taxed as a security.[180] Capital gains tax is a silly system. If corporations pay taxes and individuals pay taxes, then no one should be "double taxed" based on the security where they have their money; however, that is the current law. If crypto is a currency, then it should be outside the tax system.

Nations have the privilege of creating their own tax codes. The people of the world need to come together to ensure that these tax codes are just. 70% taxes are never the solution to anything, other than making people dependent on the government. The social democracies of the world are having massive problems with suicide, depression, and worse when people are denied the majority of their income for the job they have done. People have a right to contract, and no one has the right to take the majority of what they contract for just because they have a monopoly on legal force.

The Need for Crypto to Work Together Globally

Not since the human race walked out of Africa have the people of the world had the ability to communicate with each other so directly. The internet has allowed the people of the world unprecedented access to each other. Now is the time that we use this access. Crypto is not a call to overthrow governments or replace them with something else- it is a call for the people to demand that their governments comply with the social contracts and give people back their rights. We may not like all the rights that people get; however, we owe it to ourselves and each other to see that all human beings have rights.

---

[179] *Id.*

[180] *Id.*

As members of the crypto community, we have a duty to be good stewards of this earth. How we do that depends on what area of our lives we are living in. If you live in a country where you can vote in free elections, use that power. If you live in a country where you can lobby your representatives or leaders, take the time to do this. It is time that we quit looking at humanity as a collection of disconnected mobs, and start looking at it for what it is, a group of individuals with the common goal of a good life.

Every time a new law is passed, someone's rights die somewhere. Governments cannot give people rights, rights are inherent. When a government returns a right to someone, it is always with caveats and strings that hold them back, the simplest of these is having to admit that the government had the power to do so. Each and every person has the right to be free, it is time that we help others achieve that right. Until the last slave is freed, we are all slaves; until the last person has the right to determine their own lives, we are all oppressed; until the last person realizes this, we are all asleep.

Conclusion Part I

By understanding, we build our ability to change. By accepting our past, we build our ability to change the future. By seeing our evolution as it happens, we are able to change for the better. Cryptocurrency has come into the world at a time when things are changing quite rapidly. As a Terran global society, we need to look at where we are and where we are going. The best way to plan out where we are is to understand where we have been. Hopefully, the first part of this book has helped you with that.

Understanding the field in which you are working is vital to understanding how it works. Too often we are only given enough information to be dangerous. To acquire enough information to make a difference we cannot rely on any system and must do our own study and research. Understanding the delicate interplay between coins and tokens allows us to see how cryptocurrency can be useful in the coming years. Looking at the tokenomics of a system lets us understand the utility of the coin. Finally, understanding the evolution of the Stablecoin model allows us to see why the system needs to have more security to function properly. The interworking of the system is what makes it move forward, we just need to understand that we are part of that system.

With crypto, we need to start our understanding with the history of money and credit. We build a system that was doomed to fail because we wanted everything to be too easy. Society gave control of everything over to a few elites, and they did what humans do, they stole and controlled. Our goal now is to look at the foundation of the 1st Wave of cryptocurrencies and see what the goals of the system are. We need to look at the 2nd Wave and see how diversification of the system is a strength of the system. Finally, we need to look at the 3rd Wave and see how we must work together to ensure a better future.

The system itself is based on systems we have had for years. The challenge that the present generation has is to take the good and leave the bad. While this seems like a simple task, generations have failed at this since time immemorial. As the system grows people must realize that people having more does not mean that they, themselves, will have less. It simply means that humanity is evolving. There will be a time when people will not have to work 40-hour weeks to survive. That time may be near, but it is not here yet. Those of us who have the ability should be working 80-hour weeks to ensure that our children will have a better life.

PART II:

The Needed Regulatory Framework by the Industry

Introduction to Part II

One aspect of the market that very few people want to deal with is the need for a regulatory framework in the industry. There are millions of investors, traders, and users out there that want the market to stay as it was, a wild, wild west industry. However, this is living in a fantasy world. The world of crypto was never a wild, wild west industry- the contract laws that govern our industry have been in place for decades. The companies that entered into the field stayed within the bounds of the law, and this allowed them to exist without being overseen by the government. Now we need to accept that the industry must fully mature in various respects before it will be able to have a chance in this respect.

Section 1 of this part looks at the market protections that the industry needs in order to be successful. This section does not imply that there need to be new laws overseeing the system, just that nations need to do their duty and maintain the laws that are already on the books. As the crypto community evolves, there will doubtless be bad actors that prey on the people within the community. These bad actors need to be brought into line and turned over to the law. The smoke and mirrors effort of some governments, suggesting that the crypto marketplaces are corrupt, need to be brought to heel and the system needs to take accountability for itself.

Section 2 of this part looks specifically at the already existing criminal and laundering protections on the market. Globally, there are already systems in place to deal with criminals and money launderers. If the crypto community cooperates in these endeavors, our systems will be less likely to be used for nefarious acts. Crypto, because of the validation process, is one of the hardest areas for criminals to move monies without them being tracked, collaboration with governments can keep some of those criminals out of our markets.

Section 3 of this part concludes with a discussion of the security requirements of the industry. As crypto is a digital industry. There is a need for the industry to stay on the cutting edge of security measures. In this section, we look at the different types of security, why human security is so important, dispel the myth of the "wallet and key" shell game, concluding with the idea that we need redundant systems to maintain the access of all crypto users.

How we interact with governments is very important. Representatives who want to over-regulate the system and turn it into Fiat 2.0, are the enemies of the crypto community. However, as the government has a monopoly on the lawful use of force against criminals, we need to ensure that we do collaborate with the government to remove criminals from our midst. However, this collaboration should not lead to new regulations when the current regulations already on the book will keep the people of the community safe for years to come.

Part II:

Section I: Market Protections

Introduction to Part II: Section I

Regulations are one of those things that either a market with doing, or the government will do. Markets that decide not to properly regulate will find themselves looking in devastation as the government heavy-handedly tries to "fix" what may or may not be broken. One way to think about this is your parents tell you to clean your room or they will do it. If you wait the time to allow your parents to clean your room, nothing is in the right place, things that are useless are prominently displayed, and some of the more important stuff in your life is thrown out. The government does not know or care what is needed for the system to work efficiently, they only know what is needed to keep the people paying for the government making money in the black.

Chapter 15 looks at the proposal, by the market, for one primary regulator and one rule book for the system. This is really the only place where the government needs to be involved in the system. There does have to be an oversight body that ensures the rules are being followed; however, the government does not need to make new rules for this system to work. Trading already has a set of rules. Currencies are currencies. Derivatives are securities. As long as we operate under the current rules, there is no need for a "more enhanced rulebook" by the state."

Chapter 16 discusses the need for any regulations to be market structure agnostic. If a specific set of rules are created for crypto, then the structure is no longer agnostic. Crypto should be treated in the same fashion as the current stock market. The existing rules are enough, we do not need new rules. Just require that the SEC or national oversight boards define the rules under which crypto falls. The "grey area" treatment is simply an excuse for regulators to harass crypto traders. Define the market and let the rules do their job.

Chapter 17 looks at how the market itself must create rules. These rules should come from the exchanges and global associations for crypto traders, such as the BPSAA.[181] Homegrown rules, from valid associations will allow the system to evolve in an equitable fashion while preventing government bureaucrats from interjecting the system of corporate cronyism into the field. Developers know more about what needs to be built. Traders know more about how the markets must function. Users know how they need the transactions to occur. Government has no place in this but to enforce the current laws (or simplify them).

Chapter 18 looks at the specific point when a transaction is settled. This is a very important point in the crypto exchange because this is when the validation is complete. Different points in the transactions are considered settlements, so the industry needs to come together to look at the different places and work to ensure that they have a unified definition. Once a transaction is settled, then the transaction cannot be reversed.

Chapter 19 looks at the accessibility of spot and derivative trades. This accessibility question must be overseen by the exchanges. Market access becomes a human right. Those that want to trade should be allowed to trade. Restrictive policies, such as China's policies or the proposed Indian policies, are human rights violations and need to be fought by all elements of the market. Anyone who has the ability and the desire to trade should have the option to trade.

Chapter 20 looks at the right that traders have to review trade policies and trade confirmations. The fees, rates, or burns for a specific trading platform or currency should always be available for traders to review. Until everyone can see policies, easily accessible on the platform, there is not a true bargain for exchange. Traders have the right to know how currencies and exchanges are managed. This provides for educated traders and empowers the community.

Chapter 21 discusses the general risk disclosures that need to be contained on the exchanges. While trading and access is human right that should not

---

[181] Blockchain Privacy, Security & Adoption Alliance (2021) at https://bpsaa.vision/.

be denied by the government, people must have access to information as to how the system works. Different exchanges are different, and even savvy traders still need to see how the system works to make educated decisions. This is where disclosures are so important. Just as crypto need to have a White Paper to be transparent, an exchange needs to have a set of disclosures so that everyone can trade equally. These disclosures should be written simply in common language so that more people can trade with confidence. Exchanges should also list what protections they have for the customers and the token/coin issuer.

Chapter 22 takes on an elephant in the room, minimum capital requirements. Cryptocurrencies develop along four different sets of valuation, therefore, they can be difficult to wrangle when it comes to capital requirements. Starting off, crypto should have to show some transactional value. As they grow they should need to show that they are building some sort of Stablecoin 2.0 system to ensure inherent value; however, the industry must also accept that this is a growing value. Once they enter the market, they need to show that they have market value and are not manipulating the market. Finally, as crypto matures, they need to show that they have transactional value to stay in business. Each of these items should be used to show "value" which can be combined with capital reserves to show the validity of a currency. Exchanges should have enough reserves to "cash-out" traders should they wish to make a withdrawal.

Chapter 23 concludes Part II Section I by restating the need to avoid the Stablecoin 1.0 model. Stablecoin 1.0 was a necessity in the early days of the 2nd Wave, but it is broken as new systems have risen to the top. Basing crypto on fiat currency is the system the community is trying to break away from, not reinforce. Stablecoin 1.0 was needed to grant some stability in the volatile market to get new investors, but with the advent of Stablecoin 2.0, this system needs to be put to rest. Mono-currency reserves are not as safe as multi-currency reserves. The more safety we have in the system the more confidence we can have.

Overall, this section of the book looks to help make the case for why there are already enough laws surrounding the investment space and that the only moves investors need the government to make are to simplify laws. The community itself needs to work together and build strong associations to ensure that rules can be created and followed within the crypto space. If the community does not do this, then we deserve to be regulated. We must avoid letting fear force us to "run to the nanny state" to do what we can do ourselves. Crypto is made up of adults, it is time that we start acting like it.

Chapter 15: Proposal for One Primary Market Regulator with One Rule Book for Spot and Derivative Listings

One of the greatest dangers in any market is the people who do not know how the market works going to the government for clarification. The government will always give its advice, even if it does not know what it is talking about. Novices in any market will always eat up the drivel that comes from the government because they do not know any better. The result is people that know nothing leading people that will believe anything. Getting market advice from the government is like getting financial advice from a Hollywood celebrity, the advice "Just look good," can only get you so far in this world.

The crypto market needs to have a set of rules and regulations under which to operate. The problem with the current movement for the government to get involved is that the government is already involved. There are rules and regulations that involve trading, the government just needs to indicate its support to the market that it is going to operate under these rules, and not go off on some backward plant to make new rules.

This Chapter discusses why rules and regulations are needed. You cannot have a civilized system without rules; however, how the rules are framed is very important. The Chapter then goes on to deal with the question of whether the government or an association should be the regulator, the short answer is both but it is significantly more complicated than a one-word answer. The arguments for government involvement are outlined, then the arguments for association regulation are outlined. The reader can make their own choice, but in the end, we need to turn to the community of crypto creators, users, holders, and investors to ensure that there is a free market for all.

The Need for Regulations

Ladies and gentlemen, the wild, wild west was fun, but it has to end sometime. The market is always going to grow in sophistication and stability. There will still be 1000% daily runs for new cryptos and the exciting drops where you can buy the dips, but these need to be overseen so we do not see a repeat of SQUID.[182] To be honest, the wild, wild west was never really that wild. Crypto was always traded under some regulatory regime, so it is not that big of a shock to move into a more structured system.

To move to level two as an industry, crypto trading needs some controls put upon it. The fiction that it is operating in the cracks between government regulation is simply false. Traders who break the rules have been convicted for years in the crypto market. We just like to keep the wild, wild west atmosphere because it feels like a portion of life that is out of government control. What we have to understand is that if we keep the fiction going, the idiots in the capitals will start to believe that they need to get involved.

Any system needs rules. We already have them.[183] Crypto is a currency, currency trading is already a regulated market. We currently work under this system of regulations; therefore, there need not be any new rules introduced to manage crypto, the government just needs to acknowledge that crypto is a global set of currencies and treat it like other currencies. This means favorable taxation and the right to speculate.

On the other side of the coin, the crypto community needs to realize that derivatives are securities and fall under security laws. Most of the community is already treating derivatives this way (for no other reason than avoiding a huge tax penalty. If the governments of the world would define crypto as currency and derivatives in crypto as securities, the world could breathe easily and the market could continue to develop with the security of knowing what the rules are.

In addition to the "necessary" government rules, the community also

---

182 Yoon, John (2021). "a Cryptocurrency inspired by 'Squid Game' crashes. The industry has questions." New York Times at https://www.nytimes.com/2021/11/02/business/squid-coin-crypto-scam.html.

183 Cornell Law School (2021). 15 U.S. Code Chapter 2B- Securities Exchanges. https://www.law.cornell.edu/uscode/text/15/chapter-2B. Specifically for derivatives.

needs a standard set of rules from within. Associations and exchanges need to get together and make a set of rules that everyone needs to play by. Association rules can adapt to the changing system faster than government regulation while still allowing the structure needed for business to thrive. It is the best of both worlds, where we can adapt but have faith in the market.

The Question of Whether the Government or Associations should be the Regulator

Where the rules come from is always important. Unless someone is given tablets from the sky with divine crypto rules on them, we should follow the old rules that we have. Societies around the world have operated with a given set of "base rules" for centuries. Do not steal. Do not lie. Do not kill. Do not manipulate and covet. These are rules that most societies can agree upon. If we hold these for the base rules for the marketplace, then we really have a limited need for government or association rules.

Should government or an association have control over the crypto marketplace?[184] The answer is both and neither. Regarding both, we need a set of ground rules and specific regulations that guide the industry. These will increase industry confidence and allow the system to be more functional. Regarding neither, the community has done a good job of controlling the market on its own. While there has been a setback, one only needs to compare the crypto community's track record with the government's track record to see that we are vastly more qualified to keep crime down.

The government has a place in the crypto community. The place is to keep its distance. As we will see in the next section, there are jobs that the government needs to do to keep the market functioning. The problem arises when the government tries to be too many things to too many people. The government's job is to protect the people and protect their property. When it moves beyond this role into morals, aggregate rules, and

---

[184] Davis-Sterling (2021). "Quasi-Governmental Nature of HOAs." Davis Sterling at https://www.davis-stirling.com/HOME/Q/Quasi-Governmental-HOAs.

other areas it fails. It was not built to do things beyond protect people and their property, and it should not be put into that role.

Likewise, the associations have a specific role in the development of the crypto community. They have the duty to create moral boundaries for what is acceptable. This should not be one person's interpretation of what the rules should be, but the crypto community. We have already seen this in multiple exchanges, where they have banned crypto companies that are built on gambling or pornography.[185] This does not indicate that the community is not engaged in these activities, but it does show that they do not want these things associated with their business.

When we suggest that the community is able to self-regulate, we mean it. However, the community needs to know what interference the government is going to have and what the ground rules are from the associations. Clarity breeds confidence in any business system and right now we do not have clarity. Governments are being sheepish about how they are involved and associations are afraid to make moves before the governments define the system. We need to stabilize these areas before we move to the next level of crypto success.

Arguments for the Government Involvement

Most of the crypto community understands that the government will only hold back the community if it gets overly involved. While some are starting to move to the "we have money camp," most people know that the crypto community does not have the type of money (yet) to dictate government policy. This means that we want the government to do its job and let the people in the community do theirs. If the government stays in its lane, it can be a powerful partner in the development of the cryptocurrency.

First of all, the idea that the crypto community can control the government is still a little out there. While we can lobby in civilized countries, the amount of money needed to turn an election is more than the community has in any individual country. Add to that the division within the

[185] www.coinbase.com

community on economic and social issues, and you see a deep divide that would split the already limited money in the system. Billionaires will donate to their politicians, but the community is not going to compete (yet) with big communication, big oil, or big media. This means that the community needs to be smart.

The government has a role in crypto. Its role is to enforce the current laws.[186] We often forget that the law is already well defined in the field of trading of assets. Crimes and civil torts exist. If we have the government work in these areas, instead of dealing with things as vendettas, we can show that the government already has the pieces to deal with the problems that we are facing. Using the tools that we have is vital, and we all know that the governments of the world are made up of a bunch of tools.

One area where the government needs to be utilized is when there is a crime. When there is a scam or a rug pull, the crypto community needs to put pressure on the government to do its job and investigate the crime. Because many of these crimes occur internationally, countries are keeping them at arm's length. If the government wants to be more involved with crypto, let the government show that it can do what it is currently required to do! The government is the body that deals with crime, the community needs to let them deal with crime.

The government is also where we look to deal with civil issues in the system. The courts, mediation, and arbitration are vital parts of the cryptosystem because people have civil rights. There are breaches of contracts that happen every day. While the ones that can be dealt with internally should be, the ones that cannot be dealt with internally should

---

[186] Boucher, Jamie et al (2021). "Cryptocurrency Regulations and Enforcement at the US Federal and State Levels," Skadden at https://www.skadden.com/insights/publications/2021/09/quarterly-insights/cryptocurrency-regulation-and-enforcement-at-the-us-federal-and-state-levels. See Also NYU (2021) "Can Governments Regulate Cryptocurrency?" NYU at https://wp.nyu.edu/dispatch/can-the-government-regulate-cryptocurrency/.

be dealt with through the courts. Once again, this gives the government the appearance of being involved, which means that they do not need to "flex" as much where they do not belong.

Overall, the government has a role in crypto. This role is to do as little as possible unless asked. One of the problems that we see in the modern world is that the nanny state does not know what it is doing and thus causes more problems than it solves. The crypto community needs to move beyond this, and keep the government at arm's length. Let the government do its job, as long as we are doing ours.

Arguments for the Associations

If the world community is looking for an association to model the system on, it could take a look at the American Bar Association.[187] The United States has the best lawyers in the world, do not believe me then challenge one in court. Whereas the rest of the world makes law a 4-year degree, American lawyers have four years of undergraduate school, three years of law school (with many doing an additional two years of master's work), five years of slavery as an "associate" and then they are ready to play in the court system. They also work in other areas of dispute resolution helping the courts move forward. The USA also has an overly complex legal system, which means many of these people with 12 years of training need to specialize to be taken seriously. The more complex the system, the more need there is for an association. In the USA that is the American Bar Association.

Full disclosure, I am not a big fan of the bar association. The idea of a two-day test to represent 19 years of education is problematic. It is even more problematic when law schools spend three years telling people not to memorize things, then give a test on logic and memorization. These are problems, however, for the state bar associations. The national bar association creates rules and guidelines for operation and training across the field and works well, for what it does. If the crypto community wants to be taken seriously, it needs to have serious associations to protect the

---

[187] www.aba.org.

system and its users.

First of all, the crypto community needs to have an association with teeth. In a community-driven field like crypto, this can be a little difficult to do. Most crypto users want as little governance as possible. Less government is always good, but there are areas where the system needs to step in. Associations provide a middle ground between community lynch mobs and government shock troopers. A good association can punish people who break the rules without sending them to jail or banning them from the system (though they should have bans as a final resort).

The key element, however, of an association is that they need to set the ground rules. Once people know what the rules are, they can find new and innovative ways to get around them. This is the life cycle of an association: create a rule, the community gets around the rule, correct the rule to make the system work better, repeat. Please note that the third step is not "make a new rule" it is "correct the old rule." This keeps the association from becoming too overbearing in the administration of its duties.

The association also needs to protect the community from the government. The association acts as a shield against the members and a buffer for the enforcement of rules. If we are doing what we should be doing, then the government has no reason to get involved. This keeps the government at arm's length and allows the system to function more smoothly.

Strong associations, more than anything, keep the system in the hands of the community. Governments tend to avoid confrontations with groups of people, they like to single out small communities and prey on them. When a large community, like the crypto community, works together, they become a harder target. Legislatures around the world will still harass industry leaders, but they will be less willing to make a move against the industry when untold numbers of voters are represented by a strong association.

The Community Built a Viable System

Our biggest asset as a crypto community is that we have built a variable system, despite of, not because of, government interference.[188] Crypto developed from a single system to a wonder that is part of the internet of things. The more that we work together, the more that we can achieve. Crypto efforts, to this point, have made some of the biggest donations in the history of the world, directly to people and businesses to bring society out of the current dark age and into the bright future of the digital age. If we work together as a community, humanity can reach for the stars and someday, maybe touch one.[189]

Bitcoin started something beautiful, and we have the opportunity to be part of that. Bitcoin envisioned people working together in a non-government controlled system where people could trade freely. This system is being built before our eyes. Many of the roadblocks in research and development are caused by governments not doing what they are supposed to do, they create a dependency rather than an ascendancy, and that is killing development. Massive crypto donations in early 2022, allowed for businesses to join the crypto movement around the world, helping to make the world a better place.

The key factor in the crypto community is unity. The more that we work together, the more the industry can achieve. The Stablecoin 2.0 model is building up massive reserves that underpin the value of the cryptosystem Industries are coming into crypto compliance, allowing people to use their crypto while funding human rights successes around the world. When people have a voice, they will use it for good and do what they can to help their neighbors.[190]

---

[188] Chainanalysis Team (2021). "Crypto Crime Summarized: Scams and Darknet Markets Dominated 2020 by Revenue, but Ransomware is the Bigger Story." Chainalysis at https://blog.chainalysis.com/reports/2021-crypto-crime-report-intro-ransomware-scams-darknet-markets/.

[189] This is not a literal suggestion to touch a start, you will die if you try.

[190] This is why public voices are so good, people tend to do good things when others are watching.

If the governments of the world allow the current trading systems to stay in place, including spot and derivative trading policies, then crypto knows what crypto can do. When government defines crypto as currency and derivatives as securities, then the industry can work on a solid legal framework. When the associations set the ground rules but allow the community to control the day-to-day operations, the system can grow. And when the community comes together to function as an integrated unit, no one knows what great things people around the world will achieve.

Chapter 16: The Need of the Market to be Structure Agnostic

One of the biggest challenges that are facing the associations and regulators in the crypto space today is the need to regulate the markets when the markets are still developing. One of the most impressive elements of cryptocurrency is that crypto is highly adaptable. As the markets change, the coins, tokens, and markets change with the system to make the system more efficient. When an association or regulator tries to make a rule about a system, the system may have already changed. When there is an established rule, then the system may need to move in a way that is counterintuitive to the existing rule. Crypto is flexible, therefore the system needs to be flexible.

The second reason that crypto needs an agnostic market structure is because crypto, by its very nature, is decentralized.[191] Since most of the market rules in the current system are built around the central market and banking cartels, the monopolistic rules in the system do not always translate well to the crypto market.[192] This is why there is a strong bias in the community against the government managing the crypto market. Associations are better suited to deal with the changes and exceptions needed for the market to continue to grow and thrive.

This Chapter looks at the reasons why government overregulation is a problem. In the last Chapter, we defined the purpose of government in the crypto space, in this "crypto bill of rights," we look at the four key areas that the governments need to prevent to ensure that the market grows. The first element that governments need to avoid is national favoritism, which is the process of giving an advantage to cryptos that are founded in a given country. The second major hurdle that the crypto markets are facing is favoritism toward the banking cartel. Many of the myths and rumors against crypto were started by the banking cartel to stymie the

---

[191] Livni, Ephrat & Lipton, Eric (2021). "Crypto Banking and Decentralized Finance, Explained." New York Times at https://www.nytimes.com/2021/09/05/us/politics/cryptocurrency-explainer.html

[192] *Id.*

crypto market.

Another area that the government needs to stay away from is letting politicization affect the crypto markets. In the United States, the UK, India, and China, we have seen political parties already draw lines in the sand around the crypto market. Neo-classic liberals are saying that the decentralized system is a threat to the central banking systems that have kept the world running. The conservative movement is arguing that, while they neither support nor decry the crypto market, the economic system of the world has functioned despite the central banking cartels, not because of them. This political bickering is holding up progress in the crypto market. The final area that needs to be addressed is a direct agnosticism toward class in the crypto market. The crypto market is generally a classless society, no one cares who you are if you have the coin; however, some governments want to regulate the system (like day trading) so that only those who can keep $25, 000 + in their account can trade crypto. This type of classism is simply a direct effort to keep savvy traders from the 90% from improving their wealth.

Understanding the problems that are faced by government overregulation is a key part of making sure that when the system overlay is created, it is specifically created to ensure these rights (along with the right to contract) are not infringed upon by the government. The global community has a right to trade, and governments need to quit interfering because of the political wars of the last century. The best way to stop oppression is to give the people freedom, crypto gives millions that freedom and that is why it does scary to the politicians who feel they have their thumbs firmly upon the people.

Dangers of Government Regulation Part I: National Favoritism

When the government puts its fingers on the scale, it is always a problem. In some industries, like farming, production, or service industries, the government has a vested interest in ensuring that the domestic market is not overwhelmed by the international market. Therefore, they use a functional system of tariffs and taxes to ensure that their people have the advantage in that specific marketplace. Even the people who are being advantaged by the taxes and tariffs tend to complain about this system that is protecting them. What this shows is that people do not understand how taxes work.

Within the crypto space, there is no national market. Anyone who says that their coin is limited to a specific country is so niched that their coin is not generally part of the global ecosystem. The vast majority of coins and tokens, they are currency; which means that they are traded all around the world. This eliminates the "homecourt advantage rule" and is why the government should be agnostic about where the coin was developed.

Governments, sometimes because of benevolence and sometimes because of ignorance, see the cryptos that are developed within their borders as "domestic cryptos." Once a coin goes live, it becomes part of the global system.[193] The efforts of a government to pin down the coin, generally for tax reasons, will likely cause the coin to underperform, rather than expand. Protectionism of a coin is like a helicopter parent hovering over their kid, it rarely has the effect that they are looking for.

There is one caveat in this area that deserves to be noted, countries can ban coins from some areas. If there is a country with which a country is having a conflict, not dealing in their crypto can be a good plan. While the crypto community hopes that these problems will cease to exist in the near future, right now there are rogue states that we should not be helping their economies. This is the only reason that a country should ban all currencies from a specific state.

Another instance where a government should ban a currency is when it comes from a known scammer. There are several developers who have made coins just for pump and dumps around the world and then vacated the coin as soon as they made their money. These groups should be banned universally by the market and countries around the world as they are hostile to the development of the field.

---

[193] *Id.*

National agnosticism is important to the market because no one knows where the next good idea will come from. If we ban small countries, a small country may have the next great idea. If we ban countries of an ideology, this may stop a coin from brining freedom to that country. The government cannot predict the future, nor can it regulate how people spend their money. The right of everyone, unless they are a criminal or politician, to participate in the cryptosystem is one of the fundamental cornerstones of the cryptonomic system.

Dangers of Government Regulation (Lobbying)

Lobbies are one of the most interesting features of western governments.[194] If I give you money and you are in a position of power, then I ask you to do something for me, you and I both go to jail because it is bribery. If a person gets the title "lobbyist" and they do the same thing, neither person goes to jail. It is kind of the difference between prostitution and porn, as long as there is a title it is Ok. One of the most ironic rights of the crypto community is to lobby so that lobbying goes away.[195]

The difference between lobbying and bribery tends to hinge on registration and who is in power. Honestly, lobbying is one of the most dishonest systems in the world. Crypto hopefully will change that because it has to change it. Right now, the banking lobby is trying to get crypto hyper-regulated so that the new exchanges and proto-banks cannot function. As a result, the crypto community needs to band together in each country to protect the market. The faster we do the less damage will be done by the banking community.

Many politicians are whores, they will do what they are told by the people who are paying for them. If anyone thinks that this is a good system of government, then they are probably the ones writing the checks to the

---

[194] Staff (2021). "Crypto Lobbying Going Balistic" The Economist https://www.economist.com/finance-and-economics/crypto-lobbying-is-going-ballistic/21806674.

[195] *Id.*

lipstick politicians.[196] Crypto lobbies around the world need to make their donations and their suggestions very clear. These should be:

1.) That crypto remains a free market with coins and tokens traded as currency and derivatives trading as securities;
2.) That the human rights of all people are accepted around the world, and that no one is put to death or has their rights to property, privacy, or their person removed without due process of the law;
3.) That every person has an equal voice in governance and the process of paying for political votes be ended as soon as possible.

This is a very simple universal platform that most people involved with crypto can support around the world.

Dangers of Government Regulations (Idiots and their Affiliations).

The politicization of money has been a problem for years now around the world. Anti-capitalist groups have attacked money as the root of all evil (desire for money is the root of all evil).[197] They make these claims as they amass great fortunes bilking the poor who support them. Within the United States, political system monetary policy is always to blame if there is a social problem. For crypto to become a successful alternative to the fiat currency system, we need to work together to take the politics out of currency. The less they can attach crypto to a single side of the political spectrum, the less they will be able to complain that the side to which it is attached is evil.

The politicization of crypto has been a problem for decades. Some link the politicization to Saul Alinsky's book, others link it to the writing of Karl Marx.[198] Still, others link it to the religious theory that is between 2, 000

[196] Leventhal, Dave, Et Al (2021). "Bitcoin and altcoin are campaign fuel for these 25 campaigns." Business Insider at https://www.businessinsider.com/altcoins-bitcoin-crypto-cryptocurrency-politics-congress-elections-2021-10.
[197] Macaulay, Michael (2021). "The Socialist Case for Cryptocurrency." Medium at https://medium.com/geekculture/the-socialist-case-for-cryptocurrency-f162b8c1508. (When socialists start making the case for something, this is a red flag that we need to have internal regulation or they will destroy it)
[198] *Id.*

and 5, 000 years old. Regardless of who says money is evil, they are wrong. How people use money can be evil or good, it just depends on who controls it. History has shown us when the control of the money is more spread out (it has never been flat), the better off the world is. The more the money is condensed at the top, the more it is used for nefarious measures.

In the United States, politicization of money is almost comical. Regardless of which party is in office, the problems of the country are always based on the monetary policy of the other side. The minority party will always say that the current economic woes are due to the current monetary policy. The party in the majority will reply, "No, it was your guy that screwed things up." Both parties are to blame because they are taking bribes in the form of lobby dollars from the same people. If you take a moment to look at the donation charts for each party, it is the same people who are donating to both parties. To make matters worse, for every other country in the world where this information is available, the situation is the same.

For us to make real progress in the world, we need to quite polarize money. Money is a tool, just like a hammer or a screwdriver. Could you imagine if a politician stood up and said, "my opponent is a fraud because he likes hammers; we all know that screwdrivers are best." He would look like a fool, especially in the age of cordless drills and impactors. It is the same problem with currency: politicians scream about how the other side is "doing it wrong," when they are both still singing the virtues of the failed fiat currency system.

Dangers of Government Regulation (Inherent problems in the system of classism).

The greatest threat to the security of the system is when the government puts its fingers on the scale. We note this in the first section of the Chapter that looks at how a government favoring their own citizens is problematic for the growth of the system. However, that was only the penultimate problem that we face. More often than not, the government places its fingers on the scale in a very different way. It is when they create a preferred class that the entire nation suffers.

By this point, everyone has seen the charts and memes about government elitism. The "if we all stand the board on our backs will be flipped," or "it is not workers v. management, it is regular people v. elites." Are some of the best imageries to discuss the situation of the world today. We are told what to like, who to look up to, and how to live- all the while the people doing these things are telling people the exact opposite.

This is nowhere more apparent than in the world of cryptocurrency.[199] Talking heads around the world are shouting how crypto is unreliable, even as their hedge funds, banks, and corporations are buying crypto at a record pace. Then end of the year 2021 was announced as a "massive correction" or "people getting out of a scam," when it was people cashing out their crypto so that they could pay corrupt taxes on their gains for the year. Major cryptos grew over 60% in the year 2021. Some of the smaller cryptos grew over 1000%.

Keeping the working class from growing their wealth as crypto grows has to be a goal of the managers of the fiat system. If people become self-sufficient, not living paycheck to paycheck, the current economic system will change.[200] For many, they believe that this will be a collapse, but in all actuality, it will simply be a collapse for the rich. Those who are growing in the new digital system will see great growth, while the old system will see exploitive markets start to decline. People will be able to make choices that best suit them, not choices that will determine their survival. Crypto has the ability to break people out of the current loan, debt, death cycle- and those who own the loans and the debt are worried.

The New System Overlay

Crypto is a new system with the idea of a better world in mind.[201] If the regulations are left to be system agnostic, then the system can grow for the betterment of all people. The truth of the matter is that the majority of people dabbling in crypto are good people, they make up a cross-section

---

[199] Economist, Supra.
[200] Macaulay, Supra.
[201] Levinthal, Supra.

of humanity- a Terran alliance for the betterment of people. As such, the goals of crypto are lining up with the goals of a better society than any economic system in the history of the world.

Crypto does not care about race. It really does not. A person with dark skin can make as much money in the system as a person with light skin. The exchanges do not care who you are, they just care how much money you put in. A wealthy person with a low-risk margin may only make a little, whereas a poor person who risks all they can risk can become wealthy. The system does not care, it just wants people to work together. The same can be said about gender, religion, hobbies, ethos, ethnicity, ethics, or nationality. Every person that enters the market is just ones and zeros, just like every Terran on planet earth is made up of the same base chemicals guided by adenine, cytosine, guanine, and thymine.[202]

Crypto does not care about the goals of the people. It is not a monetary system with the underlying vices and goals which corrupt the central banking cartel. Once a currency is turned over to a system, especially a Stablecoin 2.0 system, morality quits being an issue. The currency, at that point, is just a tool. Some people will use it for good things, some people will use it for bad things. The key factor is that while the fiat system is weighted against the people who are working for good things, the current cryptosystem is morality agnostic, allowing the community to regulate the good and the bad.

Crypto is not bound by region. For too long the ideas and ambitions of people around the world have been chained to the small corner of the world in which they live.[203] This is no longer the case. Crypto has broken this system and allowed people from around the world to work together. Women in Iran can take college classes in secret because the crypto gives them access.[204] Refugees can build wealth that will not be attached to their

---

[202] These are the elements of DNA *See More at* https://www.cancer.gov/publications/dictionaries/genetics-dictionary/def/base-pair.

[203] Economist, Supra.

[204] Levinthal, Supra.

current home but can travel home with them when they return to their country. Victims of domestic violence can have wallets only accessible by a code known to them so they can escape from their abusers. All because the system allows people to move around. Anywhere there is internet access, people can access their personal wealth.

Finally, crypto is not political. Crypto is a creation of the human race so that all Terrans can have a better life. The left, the Right, Conservatives, and liberal are all concepts that are used to divide people and make the working class, the poor, and even the upper-class fight against themselves. All the while, the top 10th of a 1% collect the interest from the loans of the wars being fought. People can work together. Crypto has shown that people are willing to risk what they have for a better world. By working together, we can build that better world, both in the digital space and the real world, so that future generations do not have to suffer as past generations have.

Decentralization has no masters; decentralization asks for no slaves.

Chapter 17: Policies for Governing Token Issues

For the industry to maintain homeostasis, there is a very strong need for a set of rules on the release of tokens (and to some extent coins). The rub here is that part of the reason that cryptocurrency has been so successful is because of the variety of ways in which companies have gotten the tokens into the hands of users and investors. Therefore, the crypto community is faced with the challenge of building a set of rules for the release of tokens without stifling the new methodologies that are arising with every new coin.

To this effect, the crypto community needs to consolidate behind the idea of "keep the good and ditch the bad." In this philosophy, each of the 8, 000 coins and tokens that are in existence can be an example of what is effective and what is not effective.[205] Unfortunately, the burden for this analysis falls on the exchanges, realistically the community cannot tell creators how they need to distribute their coins; however, the exchanges have the ability to tell the coins whether they are allowed on the exchanges or not.

The real danger here is that the industry moves too far toward restricting the release of coins. As this is a fledgling industry, we have not learned all that there is to learn yet. This means that we need to leave room for development. As such, we need a strong system of categories that exchanges look at for the development of coins, but we cannot create them in such a way that the rules do not prohibit the development of new ideas.

One of the first elements that most members of the crypto community can agree upon is the need for White Papers. White papers, or white pages, are proposal documents that outline the management, tokenomics, and market of a cryptocurrency. Next, there is a need for third parties to be able to assess tokenomics; no coin or token should be trusted to work just

---

[205] Hayes, Adam (2021). "10 Important Cryptocurrenicies other than Bitcoin." Investopedia at https://www.investopedia.com/tech/most-important-cryptocurrencies-other-than-bitcoin/.

because someone says it does.[206] Likewise, the burn system needs to be audited to ensure that: A.) the coins go where they say they go when they are burned, and B.) the management of the burned coins is explained, in detail so there is no doubt how the ecosystem works.

Auditing advertisement is another big step in ensuring that the market stays where it is supposed to stay. In many cases, developers are marketing the coin as a commodity, or worse a security. Cryptos are currencies, and for the market to function we need them to be advertised in such. Once the analysis of the system is complete, then the system needs a method for dealing with bad actors. The exchanges, the DeFi banks, and the community need to work together to deal with people who are abusing the system for personal gain. To address bad actors, the system needs to look at the absence of the right to use legal force. Governments have a monopoly on the use of force to correct bad actors; therefore, the crypto community needs to have a methodology for dealing with bad actors.

Insulating this system from outside involvement will be difficult for the crypto community. With governments already trying to interject poorly thought-out policies, it behooves the crypto community to work together to ensure that centralized governments do not overwhelm the DeFi system. This is one of the areas where the entire crypto community should be able to find common ground and work together. While these four areas are a necessity to ensure positive token and coin releases, these are not the only areas that need scrutiny.

The Need for White Papers

One of the most important foundational documents for any coin or token is the White Paper.[207] A White Paper is a formal document, published on the currency's website and third-party websites, to allow potential users, current users, and auditors (both public and private) to look at the

---

[206] This is what got us in trouble with the central banking cartels.

[207] Foleon, (2022). "2022 Ultimate Guide: How to Write and Format a White Paper" Foleon at https://www.foleon.com/topics/how-to-write-and-format-a-white-paper; *See Also,* Hayes, Adam (2021B). "White Paper" Investopedia at https://www.investopedia.com/terms/w/whitepaper.asp.

proposed functionality of the crypto. White pages are a “future perfect” document, discussing what the creators believe that the currency will look like when it is fully developed.[208] While the document can change during the development, the changes from the plan in the original White Paper should be noted in appendixes or amendments. This allows a potential user or investor to understand what they are working with before they invest their hard-earned money into the system.

The first thing that a crypto White Paper needs to outline is the problem that it seeks to solve. In many cases, cryptos are created to deal with a specific problem in a portion of the industry. This problem should be narrowly defined so that a solution will be a direct solution rather than a direct solution. Further, the notation of the problem allows investors to see where the utility of the currency will develop, or whether it is a “junk coin” with no utility beyond trading on the market.

Second, the White Paper should address the specific solution that the currency is using to solve the problem. Solutions can be code solutions (like bi-lateral bridging),[209] use solution (dealing with how the coin interacts with the real or digital world), systematic solutions (how the coin is used within the system to increase functionality, or hybrid solutions (a mixture of the three). The solution should define where and when the coin should be used to maximize utility, and also address other ways that the coins can be used to increase value.

Next, the White Paper should look at competitors and alternative solutions to the problem.[210] No coin is absolutely perfect; the more a creator understands this, the more effective the implementation of the coin can be. This also forces the creator to look at other coins or tokens on the market and how they function in the same space. This can allow for synergy systems to be created within the marketplace, increasing the vitality of the non-fiat system.

---

[208] See Hayes (2021B), Supra.

[209] More primitive than spiderweb bridging.

[210] See Hayes (2021B), Supra.

Most White Papers will also look at the need for blockchain technology for the coin or token. This is an area of White Papers that the industry may be moving beyond. Before people knew how blockchain would function, this was a necessity to educate investors; however, as the market becomes more savvy the need for this has diminished. When dealing with OG investors, there may still be a need to mention how the blockchain works; for most cryptos, this will simply be a statement about validation or how the smart contract overlay works for this specific coin/token.

Following the technology discussion, 3rd Wave cryptocurrencies need to discuss their staking/holding system. These generally fall into the categories of Stablecoin 1.0, Stablecoin 2.0, and individual investor reserves. Stablecoin 1.0 is a system where there is a unit per unit relationship between the coin/token and a fiat currency or commodity. Stablecoin 2.0 is a system where there is a growth model holding system that gives value to the underlying ecosystem of coins. Both Stablecoin 1.0 and Stablecoin 2.0 maintain their reserves in the third-party system, either holding or investing the reserves to manage value. Individual investor staking is dangerous as an investor can "pull" their investment at any time. While there is usually a penalty for doing so, this can still destabilize the coin.

Next, the coin creator may discuss the tokenomics of a coin. Tokenomics is a subset of crypto economics that looks at the supply and demand of the coin, specifically the factors that impact the supply and demand of the tokens. This can include quality, distribution, and production of the coin or token. Including the tokenomics of the coin in the White Paper allows investors to look at the model being used to see about the stability of the coin.

While the entire tokenomics of the coin does not need to be included in the White Paper, the aspect of the token issuance needs to be within the paper. How the coin is going from the creator of the coin to the users and investors of the coin is very important. Some coins will have a single method for distribution (ICO), other coins will have multiple methods of distribution. The White Paper should be very clear about how many tokens or coins can be issued and how they will be issued. Modern 3rd Wave coins should also note how the coins will be related to the Stablecoin 2.0 ecosystem.

Finally, the White Paper should look at the team and its experience.[211] As the team develops, this is the one portion of the White Paper that can evolve without the amendment of the document (though amendments are suggested to let people know the team is improving). The team's experience should not just look at their experience in crypto, but also their experiences in finance, economics, the area of the market that the coin deals with, and any other relevant information about the team.

A good White Paper can be worth more than a few initial investors who want you to sell coins to them other than how you had planned. White papers show planning and planning is an important part of ensuring that the coin is going to be successful. When you look at the "junk coins" on the market today, you will see a common thread that most of them do not have White Papers, or that their White Paper is incomplete. The stronger the White Paper, the stronger the users have for a claim to ensure that the coin/token is managed as it is designed.

Auditing Tokenomics

While no one today can imagine all the innovative methods that will be used for different areas of tokenomics in the future, one thing is clear- that the exchanges and DeFi banks need to look at the tokenomics to see if they are functional.[212] Stakeholders in crypto need to know that a tokenomics system is realistic, meaning that the ideas presented by the creators can be done. DeFi Banks need to know that the tokenomics will be done so that they can manage holdings in the specific areas.[213] Exchanges need to know the number of tokens/coins in play, because without that the market

---

[211] *Id.*

[212] Smith, Samuel (2018). "Fixing Broken "Single" Utility Tokenomics: Part 2- HODL Powers." Difuon at https://medium.com/difuon/fixing-broken-single-utility-tokenomics-part-2-hodling-powers-83b2ca569a3.

[213] Binamon (2022). "Official Audits" at https://docs.binamon.org/features/audits./

cannot make an educated decision on how to price the crypto (outside the transitional, transactional, and inherent value of the coin/token).

The first element that needs to be looked at is the realism of tokenomics. Some token creators hope that an existing community will rally around their coin because it is designed to "kill" one of the rival coins. We saw this with Ethereum killers, DOGE killers, and SHIB killers. Building a coin around the concept of hate is antithetical to the crypto community. We are building a system to move beyond the fiat system, not because we hate the fiat system, but because we understand that it is not a functional system. Good tokenomics will have a reliable distribution mechanism (exchange/drops/ICO/partners) and a plan of dispersal. Bad tokenomics will just hope someone famous talks about your coin.

The second reason that there needs to be an audit of the tokenomics system is for the stability of the coin. Banks and investors need to know that the creators are going to do what they say. Having a great idea is one thing, having the ability to pull off the idea is another. There are many people who have had very good ideas for the tokenomics system, only to find that they do not have the real-world support to pull it off. Banks and investors need to know that the people have the skill and ability to pull off the tokenomics, this is why the team is so important in the White Paper.

Finally, the amount of token/coin is vital for the market value of the coin (not to mention the inherent value of the coin). While the transactional value of the coin is based on how many places use and accept the coin, the market and the inherent value of the coin are based on the ratio of market cap/holdings to the number of coins/tokens. When an exchange (or worse yet the creator) does not know the number of coins, then there is a severe problem with pricing the coins. We have seen how coins in the quadrillions start a thousandth of a cent, trillions of coins put you in the $2-$3 range, and billions of coins let the value rise between $10-$100. This can only be managed when people know how many coins are in the market.

Tokenomics can be as complex or as simple as the creator wants, but those who are auditing the coin need to know how it will obtain value and how that value will be passed on to the user.[214] Pump and dump coins are dangerous on the markets, and the exchanges are right to delist them. Auditing of the tokenomics is vital for the system to be stable, and this is one of the key aspects of token issuance governance.

Auditing the Burn System

When a coin is created, it has a static number of coins. That static number of coins related to the transitional, transactional, market, and inherent value of the coin dictates the actual value of the coin. Every coin, at some point, reaches a plateau where the value follows a rectangle pattern and can stagnate the value of the coin.[215] Until there is some stimulus, this coin will stay in the rectangle. Usually, a stimulus is another coin in the same space which causes a bear market for the coin the rectangle. This almost always happens when a coin allows its value to stagnate too long.

The other way to stimulate a coin is to initiate a burn. Burns can be standing burns or conditional burns, but the theory behind burns is that reducing the number of coins/tokens it increases the value in the market and inherent values. This increases the actual value calculation which helps the coin break out of a rectangle pattern in a rally. Choosing the right kind of burn for the coin should be done at the White Paper stage, but can be changed with the amendment.

A conditional burn is a type of burn instituted by the community or the controller of the coin. In a general burn, a dead wallet is used to "dump" coins. The concept behind the dead wallet is that it is a bottomless pit from where the coins cannot come back. We saw on November 19th, 2021 that this myth was not true. This created some doubt in the dead wallet system, including calls for a "proof of burn system." While some 2nd Wave coins embraced the proof of burn system, most (if not all) 3rd Wave coins moved on to standing burns and *Black Wallets*.

A standing burn is a burn rate on every transaction within a crypto

---

[214] Smith, Supra.
[215] Binamon, Supra.

ecosystem. Standing burns constantly reduce and increase the number of coins on the market. Each transaction has a small burn rate, usually under 2%, which is used as a "tax" for ecosystem maintenance. This burned coin/token goes into a *Black Wallet*. A *Black Wallet* is a system that distributes the coin back into the market in a way that increases the value of the coin. Since the market takes into consideration the value of the holdings, the simplest way to increase the general value of the coin is to increase the value of the holdings.

Regardless of where the money in the burn system goes, it needs to be clearly defined. Though the wallet address should not be disclosed (it will be in the code but it should not be publicly announced), the controllers of the *Dead/Black Wallet* should be named. This way, if the wallet activates (dead) or uses the crypto in a way not specified (black) the community can come after the controller for violations of the terms of service. Ensuring this is part of the community's responsibility to the stability of the crypto.

Auditing of Advertisement

This is a minor issue for most investors, but a major issue for the industry in general. In most cases, investors will have already entered the market before they look at the advertising of crypto. People tend to "jump in" with crypto after it already is on an exchange and being traded. This makes the advertisement secondary to the performance of the token/coin. However, when it comes to the stability of the industry, advertisement is a very important factor.

Generally, when dealing with governments, what something says it becomes what it is. Even though Musk's "Not a Flamethrower" does throw flames, because it is not a flame thrower, it avoids many of the laws around actual flamethrowers.[216] With cryptos, government tends to treat them as advertised. When a coin issues itself as a currency, then it is usually treated as a currency (overseen by commodities regulators for some reason).

[216] It is not simply a naming issue; an actual flame thrower uses a jellied combustible which sticks to targets. Musk's "Not a Flamethrower" uses a gas propellant system.

When a coin puts itself out there as a security, it is treated as a security. This is where things become dangerous to the industry as a whole.

Security, specifically a derivative, is the image that the crypto community is trying to get away from. Derivatives have value only related to the underlying asset. If crypto is treated as a derivative, then the underlying asset for most cryptos would be the fiat currency to which they are most often compared. This makes all cryptos like Mickey Bucks. However, when cryptos are defined as currency, then they fall under currency regulation which makes them much more useful to the market.

Exchanges need to make sure that they are preventing false advertising in crypto communities. While many people use the currencies as an investment tool, they are not, in their face security. They are an asset that is constantly growing in value. This is similar to a currency in an economy that is quickly growing. In fact, this is exactly a currency in an economy that is growing, the digital economy is growing faster than any other segment of the market (except perhaps poorly tested vaccine treatments). Exchanges need to take the time to define advertising rules so people know crypto is a growth currency, not a derivative of fiat currency.

Dealing with Bad Actors.

In every market, there are going to be people who break the rules. Crypto is no different. Every day there are people who try to create scam coins or create scams to rip people off. The community needs a way to deal with this. Banks can blacklist currencies that are being used for scams or pump and dump. Exchanges can delist bad actors and take away the market value (and to some extent the transactional value) of coins controlled by bad actors. The community can exile members who participate in schemes to rip off other members of the community. This triune system of bad actor management can help stabilize the community.

First of all, DeFi banks can create blacklists of currencies that are violating industry standards. While DeFi banks cannot really remove a currency from circulation, they can let their users know who is playing by the rules and who is not. This allows the market to go “grey” instead of “black” for bad actors. Investors that want to take the risk can always choose to work with anyone; that is the privilege of DeFi. When a DeFi bank blacklists a bad actor, however, it will, in all likelihood, tank the value of the coin/token.

Next, exchanges need to delist "pump and dump" coins as well as scam coins. Throughout the history of crypto, the major exchanges have done a good job with this. Though Citadel may be questionable on stock practices related to meme stocks, they and their subsidiary Robinhood are very picky on what coins they allow on the platform. Strong analysis by exchanges allows for the system to be more secure and safer for everyone.

Finally, the community needs to exile members who take advantage of others. By working together, we can remove bad actors from the system to ensure that it is equitable for everyone. Once bad actors are off the exchanges, it is easy for members of the community to not interact with them. Avoid wallet-to-wallet transfers and they eventually fade from the community. The only question after this is how do we look for rehabilitation to allow someone back into the community?

The Absence of the Right to Use Force

One of the most aggravating elements of dealing with bad actors is that the crypto community does not have the ability to use force to deal with bad actors.[217] Neither legal force nor physical force is usable as this is the monopoly of the governments of the world. This means that the crypto community needs to work with the governments when there is a bad actor that they cannot control. The willingness to work with governments should not be seen as a problem, in fact, many of the bad actors use this as a way to keep the community from seeking help. Cryptocurrency is a business as well as a community, which means that we have legal rights that we can enforce within national courts should there be a need.

First of all, the crypto community needs to work with the governments of

[217] Munro, Andre (2021) “State Monopoly on Violence.” Britannica at https://www.britannica.com/topic/state-monopoly-on-violence.

the world. This relationship should be entered into as equals, not as a system where the governments of the world have control over crypto. Crypto is an extranational system, which means that they exist beyond the jurisdiction of countries, except where they choose to do business in a country. When a user decides to do business in a country, they do not create a binding relationship between a crypto company and the country, the crypto itself needs to have an agreement with that country, an agreement entered into as equals.

Next, we need to remove the stigma of users exercising their rights in their countries. Too often, bad actors convince people that working with the government means that you are betraying the crypto community. Crypto users are citizens of their home country and the crypto community. As such, they should use their rights in their home country when they are exploited by a bad actor. When we deny these rights because of stigma we are letting the bad actors win.[218]

Finally, crypto companies, especially ones that function internationally, need to act as independent actors when dealing with governments. Crypto companies are registered in countries, which means that they have to follow the laws, but they also have the right to demand representation. Once an entity is taxed, it should have the right to be represented. If it is not represented, then the country is in violation of the social contract. Crypto companies should specifically work with nations that will give them equal footing as corporate citizens.

Conclusion

Once we establish the relationship between crypto and the world, then the world can deal with crypto as a supernational entity that fights for the rights of people around the world. While each individual crypto has its own goals, we have a general goal of making the world more accessible by people who are using the coins/tokens. This means that crypto exchanges need to require White Papers to be listed. Companies should have their tokenomics audited to ensure that they have a plan for their crypto. There

---

[218] *Id.*

needs to be continual auditing of burn systems to make sure coins are going where the controller says they should be going.

Looking at those who are semi-bad or bad actors is also vital to the evolution of the community. Advertising guidelines should insist that coins be truthfully advertised and treat coins/tokens as currency. Bad actors need to be removed from the system so that the governments do not have any reason to put extra regulations on crypto operations around the world. Finally, the global community needs to enter into discussions as a community- we cannot let outdated methods of governance deny us the future that we deserve.

Chapter 18: Settlements of Transactions (When the Settlement is Final)

Crypto is contract dependent, which means that the settlement of a transaction is the termination of that agreement. Each cryptocurrency transaction is validated before the transaction can be settled which then marks it complete. As crypto evolves, this is one of the key areas that the cryptoverse needs to explore.[219] Additionally, exploring why settlement points are imperative to the system is equally as important.

What is a settlement of transactions?

In the world of understanding cryptocurrency transactions, the settlement point is vital to the system. *Investopedia* states that:

> The settlement layer is also referred to as Layer 0 because it is the base layer upon which other DeFi transactions are built. It consists of a public blockchain and its native digital currency or cryptocurrency. Transactions occurring on DeFi apps are settled using this currency, which may or may not be traded in public markets. One example of the settlement layer is Ethereum and its native token ether (ETH), which is traded at crypto exchanges. The settlement layer can also have tokenized versions of assets, such as the U.S. dollar, or tokens that are digital representations of real-world assets. For example, a real estate token might represent ownership of a parcel of land.[220]

Settlement is the central notion that the transaction has been completed. It is the agreed-upon terms of the contract. Whether this is a smart contract or a traditional contract, the settlement point is important because, at that point, the parties no longer have an active relationship between them. This establishes that the parties to the contract are former business contractors/contractees and not current ones.

Ultimately, blockchain provides the ability to transact and accept payments

---

[219] Law Insider (2020). Settlement Schedule" Law Insider at https://www.lawinsider.com/dictionary/bilateral-settlement-schedule.

[220] Sharma, Supra.

directly instead of working through a middle man as anyone on the network has the ability to view the activities within the chain. As with any system, middlemen increase corruption and cost, two of the key elements that the smart contract system was designed to eliminate. Proponents state that cryptocurrency offers increased security and transparency through a payment process. This makes finance less of a "smokey backroom" system and more of an "out in the open" digital system.

Why is the settlement point so important?

Credit and debit cards settle transactions using batch processing, where companies send batches of all transactions to respective banks at the end of the day.[221] In March 2021, Visa announced that it will "allow the use of the cryptocurrency USD Coin to settle transactions on its payment network."[222] This appears to be the first traditional card accepting the potential of crypto. According to *CNBC*, Crypto companies Binance and Crypto.com, have advocated for crypto cards almost all through the year 2021. Companies must work together to agree on a standardized system of settlement times in order to have a more unified approach to how settlements are handled.

A settlement is considered simple. Generally, a buyer initiates a transaction with a business, sending them cryptocurrency at the point of sale versus a credit card or similar. The transaction is then sent for confirmation to a waiting area so miners may need to resolve issues, which can have different timeframes for cryptographic proofs.[223] Then, if confirmed by others on the network - along with the miners, the transaction is added as

---

[221] "Can Cryptocurrency Disrupt Payment Settlement?" at https://www.gocurrency.com/can-cryptocurrency-disrupt-payment-settlement Cryptocurrency transactions rely on blockchain for settlements due to the efficiency and transparency allowed through technology.

[222] Reuters (2021). "VISA moves to allow payment settlements using cryptocurrency." Reuters (Via CNBC) at https://www.cnbc.com/2021/03/29/visa-moves-to-allow-payment-settlements-using-cryptocurrency.html.

[223] Frankenfield, Jake (2022). "Bitcoin Mining: A Primer of the Process and Profits." Investopedia at https://www.investopedia.com/terms/b/bitcoin-mining.asp.

a block to the chain. The merchant/recipient then receives the funds in their cryptocurrency wallet from the sender.[224]

Why is there a question about settlement points?

Investopedia confirms it too: "Visa says it plans to support new central digital bank currencies as they become available in the future."[225] Settlement points are important for tracking information and determining what each point means and how they differ. The key questions revolve around where the settlement happens just like a bank payment. These include:

1. When the Payment is Sent;
2. When the Payment is Received;
3. When the Payment is Acknowledged.

Each of these points has its advantages and disadvantages, which makes for robust arguments in DeFi circles.

One that is often quoted by buyers in the crypto marketplace is the argument that the payment is settled when the payment is sent. This is based on a common-law rule called "the mailbox rule" In the mailbox rule, once a payment is sent (confirmed by a postmark) the payment can be considered "paid" by the payer. The advantage of this, especially for commerce is it takes a lot of pressure off of buyers, allowing them to start work again faster. The disadvantage of this system is for the payee, who is always being stuck with "It is in the mail" when payments are late. Most of the time, once a payment is received, they do not check the postmark, therefore, it is difficult to argue in court that the payment was late.

When the payment received seems to be the frontrunner in the crypto world, the sending and the receipt of the payment may be delayed by the block. Once the receipt is concluded, then both parties know that the payment is made. The advantage of this is that both parties can confirm the contract is completed. The disadvantage of this is that the buyer can

---

[224] *Id.*

[225] Luthi, Ben (2021). "VISA adds Cryptocurrency to its settlement platform." Investopedia at https://www.investopedia.com/visa-adds-cryptocurrency-to-its-settlement-platform-5181149.

have a "late payment" through no fault of their own- if the usage for the block is high at a given time, then the transaction may take a while to process.

The last "regular" argument for when a settlement is complete is when the payee acknowledges receipt of the payment. For day-to-day transactions, this process is quite cumbersome, but it holds merit for larger transactions. In the real world, this would be akin to having the receiver sign for the receipt of the payment. While this does take more time, this also has the added level of security of someone having to acknowledge the payment for the transaction to be settled.

Each of these systems has its own merits and drawback, and it should fall on the industry to decide which is the best and which should be brushed aside. This is one key area where the governments of the world can be problematic. If one nation sets the settlement conditions in category one, and another sets the conditions in category 2, then there can be a difference of opinions in where the settlement takes place. Even worse, there is no international court that does (or should) have the authority to rule on this. As a result, the need to define when settlements are complete falls on the DeFi banks, the exchanges, and the crypto community in general.

According to *Sofi*, "while some people only want to invest in cryptocurrency for price appreciation, others might find benefit in the ability to use crypto as a medium of exchange."[226] Cryptos transactions like Bitcoin and Ether could cost anywhere from nickels and dimes to several dollars or more.[227] Other cryptocurrencies like Litecoin, XRP, and others can be sent for pennies or less. Payments for most cryptos settle in seconds or minutes.[228] Wire transfers at banks can cost significantly more and often take three to five business days to settle.[229] Settlement points appear to

[226] SoFi (2021). "Investing in Cryptocurrency." Sofi Learn at https://www.sofi.com/learn/content/investing-in-cryptocurrency.
[227] *Id.*
[228] *Id.*
[229] Sofi, *Supra*.

be handled in many places shown above and can begin popping up in unexpected places, including gun exchanges and more.

Identifying a universally accepted settlement point for international cryptos.

Identifying a universally accepted settlement point for international cryptos may just be similar to the points Journalist Randeep Sudan tells us about the metaverse itself, including:

> The metaverse will require many new technologies, protocols, enterprises, breakthroughs, and discoveries to function. For instance, several companies are developing hardware for virtual, augmented, and mixed reality. This includes headsets. Much of computing power needs to be embedded in a frame of glasses to make the technology convenient to use. Computer and networking chips, holographic Waveguides, sensors, batteries, and speakers have all to be crammed in a tiny space.[230]

As the settlement points within the cryptosystem are defined, so too will they be defined in the matrix of the metaverse. As a result, people will have more security in the system.

The arguments over where the points of the settlement become fairly dogmatic in their use. Every system can operate with any of the settlement points currently being argued. While there are advantages to each, these advantages are so minor that it would behoove the community to get past the argument and build the strong foundation that the system needs. If you would like to get even more meta- does the idea of temporal settlement mean anything when time is a construct that is being manipulated by the system. If we are using the real-world time to settle transitions in the metaverse, then should we be using something other than time to define the point of settlement.

---

[230] Sudan, *Supra.*

Chapter 19: Accessibility of Spot and Derivative Trades

As we look at government and industry regulation, one of the most important things to consider is the functionality of the system. On one hand, we are looking at a system that levels the playing field for billions of people around the globe. On the other hand, we are looking at a system that is unreachable by many because of poverty and poor internet access. Whereas at one-time internet access was a luxury, we are entering a period in human history where internet access is becoming a right.

As we move past the first two decades of the new century, our understanding of human rights and business rights needs to continue to evolve. Just as people from the 1920s looked back on the people of the 1820s as little more than barbarians, the shortcomings of our past century, the generation of our grandparents and great-grandparents, need to be examined. This is not a political statement, but simply a statement of what we need to do better. This is not a time to blame, but a time to move forward to a more unified future.

This Chapter starts off with a look at the rights to trade and the right to internet access. As humanity evolves, so too do our rights. Conservatives and liberals alike are looking at the wrong rights that we should be embracing. While LGBTQTIP+ issues, gun issues, green energy issues, and moral issues are issues for another book, there are strong issues that we need to look at in the world today. Access to resources, access to valid voting systems, and access to information are among the top issues that face the globe today. Next, we need to look at accessibility in the secondary meaning of the world, as in the ability of differently-abled people to exercise their rights within the system.

The crypto community has an unprecedented ability to deal with another major problem in the world, countries restricting human rights. Rogue nations are very problematic on the global system. Whereas the antiquated agreement of autonomous authority based on region protects bad actors for old school government policy, the internet of things opens new doors to prevent abuses of citizens by their leaders while improving the lives of the citizenry.

To move forward with a better world, we need better rules. We need universal rules that the whole world can agree upon and the global community enforces, not a powerless organization like the UN or an overreaching government. The digital Terran community needs to blacklist those that deny rights and promote business in regions that support the rights of all mankind. Finally, we need a unified lobbying system for access and right around the world. The one thing that the union movement of the 1920s had correct was that people around the world need a forum to communicate that governments do not censor. However, they were infiltrated by socialists, communists, and fascists who use censorship as a means of control. The digital age needs to step away from the old tropes of wages (which are an antiquated method of payment), borderless society, and class warfare and move toward the concept of universal access to information, protection of property rights (not government rights), and the globalization of society.

Access to information breeds success in people. Human rights enable us to be successful people. When we combine these two things, we have the ability to make a better world. Cryptocurrency, when done properly, helps in both of these categories. To ensure that it can function to the best of its ability, we must ensure that everyone has the ability to access the market and that the access to spot trades and derivatives are protected in their own systems.

Right to Trade (and the Underlying Right to Internet Access)

One of the great social myths is that there is a fallacy in capitalist systems that a person has a right to trade, but the system itself does not give the person the ability to trade. Anti-capitalists around the world use 5-second soundbites, like the minimum wage, to impress upon people that it is another's duty to make sure that an individual has the ability to trade. This, of course, is a problematic fallacy, because it is preached to college students around the globe and not exposed by underqualified academic staff. Dealing with this issue is important to understand why access to spot rates and derivative trading is so important to a new class of wealth.

First of all, the problem of the statement is that no other person inherently owes you anything. The late 1900s tropes that you are owed respect, a fair chance at life, and equity are false. No one owes anyone anything that is not contracted for. When we see people who attack someone because they feel "disrespected" we see a failing of society to teach children that sometimes you will hear things that you do not like. When we see people rioting because someone did not get a fair chance, we see a group playing right into the oppressor's hands because they are showing why certain rights should be denied to a group. When we see people saying that "equity," not "equality" is the future, we see people who believe that some are slaves to others, because their work will be distributed to others without their consent.

Respect is earned, not given. The belief that everyone should treat us like royalty needs to be deposed for society to move forward. Influencers, reality TV stars, athletes, politicians, and celebrities have been placed on a pedestal that society must tear down. Teach children that people who work in the skilled trades are just as important as those who go to college. Teach children that a hard day's work, regardless of the legal field, is something to be proud of. Teach everyone that "getting rich quick" rarely happens. Society needs to move the focus away from people who do nothing useful for a living toward people who learn and evolve society for a living.

For anything to happen, people need access to information. If 2020 and 2021 taught us anything, the greatest fear that governments have is an informed populous (followed by an armed populous). Not since the 1930s has the world seen as broad a misinformation campaign as was seen around the U.S. Presidential Election and the COVID crisis. Both were real things; both will have lasting effects on the world for years to come.

With the presidential election, "fact-checkers" became a normal part of the human lexicon. This bachelor degree-holding employees of tech companies created a world of "privileged" information. If they agreed with the posts that people were making, they were allowed to be posted.[231] If they disagreed, then the post was restricted and marked as false.[232] This created a reality during the election where "trusted sources" were actually manipulating the people of the United States. Whereas the American people had been focused for 4 years on false Russian Collusion stories, they really should have been looking at the corruption coming from 1 Hacker Way.

This pandemic of misinformation then spread to the COVID crisis. COVID is a real disease and has killed millions of people, please do not dismiss it and consult with your physician. However, we also cannot forget that we were lied to (globally) by leaders during the crisis. When COVID first was suspected, we saw leaders who attempted to close borders being called "racist" and that "it was just a ploy"; meanwhile, politicians around the world stockpiled supplies and stocks to make fortunes off the pandemic. We were told that "masks were not needed" till the market was cornered and then they became mandatory, a mask that was $0.01 in January 2020 was soon $3.25 (or more) in May. When leaders tried to keep people off the streets after the George Floyd Murder in 2020, some saw this as a racist act, suppressing the voice of a community. An argument could be made that these selfsame politicians making these accusations were told, ahead of time, that the riots would spread COVID. Still, some on news networks told people that the protests were not spreading the disease, yet COVID rapidly moved across countries while potentially professional protestors were said to have been moved around the country. Even life-saving medicines were said to have been denied to people, while a vaccine with a dubious success rate was marketed to millions. Anyone who challenged the narrative was called anti-science and was given a "Fact-checkers have

---

[231] Editorial Boad (2021), original story in Reuters, "Facebook admits the truth: 'Fact Checkers' are really just (lefty) opinion." New York Post at https://nypost.com/2021/12/14/facebook-admits-the-truth-fact-checks-are-really-just-lefty-opinion/. *See Also* Boyd, Jordan (2021). "Facebook Quietly Admits its Third Party 'Fact-Checkers' are 'Opinions" The Federalist https://thefederalist.com/2021/12/13/facebook-quietly-admits-its-third-party-fact-checks-are-opinions/.
[232] *Id.*

found this to be the untrue" label. COVID is a real disease, but the propaganda machine built over the last two years is also a major problem.

So how does this relate to crypto? This is not a political book, so why are we looking at political items. We challenge the idea that the government is the only group that can regulate the market. One of the key factors needed for the industry to maintain some market equilibrium is that people have access to information. Information is a human right; we cannot make decisions without information. Unfortunately, during the cold war, governments acquired the "right" to hide things from the public for national security. While some things need to be kept private (like nuclear bomb plans, or bioweapon recipes), things that are embarrassing to political figures need not necessarily be kept away from the public eye. However, this has even been extended to market features that the government may not want people to access immediately. To bring this to a point, it is said that many millionaire or billionaire politicians made that money by leveraging information that they had, while delaying the release to the public. They may have cashed in on "classified" or "privileged" information, and once the money was made, then released the information to the populous to collect any scraps.

Information is a human right. Globally, people in free countries need to demand that their representatives quit restricting access to non-military information. Anthony Weiner's Laptop, Hillary's Hard Drives, Trump's Tax Records (while he was in office), these are all items that should be completely open to the public. Now the illegal stuff should not be out there on the internet, but the people have the right to know that it is there. The same goes for trade agreements and treaties. Governments' making back door deals in closed chambers is a violation of the rights of every citizen in those countries. If the people do not know what the government is doing, then they are not really free.

This is why the right to information in trade is so important. If the crypto community believes that a person has the right to trade, then it is inherent in that right that people have access to information. When the old-style governments of the world are keeping secrets, then they are putting their fingers on the scales at the market. When they are using those secrets to enrich themselves, then they are defrauding their people and should be removed from office. When the government withholds information, they are stealing from the people. When the government supports false information and propaganda, they are defrauding the people. As every human being has the right to trade goods and cryptos, every human being should also have access to good information.

Accessibility as the Duty of the Exchange.

Accessibility is an interesting concept. In general, accessibility is assuring that differently-abled people have the ability to work within a system. In some cases, this is providing written materials for those who have an impairment of their hearing. In other cases, it is providing recordings for those who have a visual impairment. Regardless of the abilities of the person trying to access something, those who are providing the service should make a reasonable effort to ensure that anyone can access their materials.

Crypto trading platforms need to make sure that they are doing this in the spirit of open access. Too often, we think of crypto traders as Gen X businesspeople who are staying on the cutting edge or Gen Y millennials who are living a jet-set life. Unfortunately, when we think of this, very rarely are we thinking of those who are differently-abled, both physically or financially. For crypto to forge a better world, we need to look at some of the problems in the current world.

Dealing with differently-abled people is the easier of the two conundrums. The way that we treat people with a different set of abilities has moved forward monumentally in the last three decades. Computer systems have been created that give sight to the blind and hearing to the deaf, miracles of the modern age. Exchanges and wallets need to ensure that they use this technology to make sure that everyone has access to information.

Dealing with people who are differently-abled financially is another story. When we think of crypto traders, we think of western men and women who have access to the internet everywhere, trading on their cellphones. However, do we ever think of college student in Nigeria, doing their trading on a school computer? Or do we think of a poor person in India, who has built together with a computer from discarded laptops in a landfill? Even when we think of third-world trading, we tend to think of the system the way we see ourselves in the system. When we are building a better world, we need access to platforms around the world.

One of the great things about the KIROS development plan is the enhancement of crypto accessibility. Businesses around the globe who would have never thought of becoming crypto accessible have grants and loans to allow them access to the modern world. Even better were the loan system where crypto access points would allow people to access their wallets securely and participate in the market on equal footing. Giving people access to the system is one of the main ways we can ensure that everyone can participate in the system. The more exchanges that work with the KIROS access points and crypto-compliant companies around the world, the more people will be able to move into the future.

Countries Restricting Human Rights

One of the most dangerous attacks on the internet of things and the blockchain system is countries that will not allow new technology to thrive. China, Iran, North Korea are all major offenders that are preventing progress because they do not want to give up control over their people. One of the chief concerns of the crypto community is opening up these markets. Once people have devices, then they have information. Once they have information, then they can trade and participate in the global economy. Once they can participate in the global economy, then they can assert their freedom. Once people assert their freedom, countries become more free. Until all people around the world are free to grow their wealth, none of us is truly living in a free world. This is why the crypto community must establish a bill of rights and use its combined economic power to bring nations into compliance.

What does a country have to gain by excluding devices and crypto? They really gain nothing; they only maintain control over their people. When a country denies devices (like Iran), then the people cannot see what is going on in the rest of the world. When a country (Like North Korea) restricts internet access to its people, then they only see the information that the Government Controls. When a country (like China) shuts down the use of cryptocurrency (poorly), then they are forcing the people to rely on a broken fiat system.[233] Crypto represents countries giving up control over people, which for oppressive regimes is a very scary thought.

Allowing people access to information is always a scary thought for a country. Even in the "free" western democracies, so much information is held back from the people. Now nuclear weapons designs and bioweapons are things we can all agree should not be on the open market; however, why do governments need patents? The government developed the patent with the people's money, should not the people be allowed to use that patent to profit? Everything that is not a weapon design or something we are doing in the espionage/military world should be accessible to the people. Further, the government should not be able to "classify" information just because it embarrasses someone in power. The fact is if that information is released then that person can no longer be blackmailed with it.

Once people have access to information, then they can start to use that information to better their lives. In the crypto world, this means trading and using crypto. Fiat currency survives because government prop it up. Fiat policies are never the market policies, they are simply Keynesian efforts to "tell" the market what to do. While this works from time to time as companies have been "trained" to follow the trends, most of this movement are despite the market. Government's retard markets, and to free these markets we need decentralized systems. The information allows people to pick the system that works best for them, which is why

---

[233] Staff (2021). "How the fiat system works." Dummies at https://www.dummies.com/article/business-careers-money/personal-finance/investing/general-investing/how-the-fiat-system-works-198367. This citation was chosen because you would have to be a "dummy" to believe that the fiat system works.

governments are so afraid- they are becoming obsolete.

The biggest fear that governments have is that a new generation of billionaires will be created. For nearly two centuries, governments have dealt with the Rothchild's, the Rockefellers, and the Vanderbilts of the world. World War II gave us the Koch and Soros empires, which threw the world into disarray. The Silicon Valley boom also caused the system to change. Each time, the people got new freedom and the government went from being the savior to the oppressor a little more. Crypto is this type of paradigm shift, government's want to suppress this because they like the system the way it is, broken and oppressive.

Universal Rules

As this book developed, we have built a Crypto Bill of Rights. These are some of the principles that everyone in the crypto community should be able to agree on. While some of them will rub some people the wrong way, there is a common theme that runs through them. This theme is that all people have the right to exist, the right to survive, and the right to better their place in the world. Breaking away from the OG economic ideals of wage slavery, nanny-state policies, and communal property rights, the crypto universe sets forward rules that will help make the world a better place.

1.) Information- every person should have access to information. Governments should have libraries where people can come to research. These libraries should provide access to the internet, through relatively modern computers and research should only be restricted by preventing access to illegal or pornographic material.
2.) Valuation for Jobs- Wage slavery is one of the greatest problems in society. A specific job has value, the person doing the job should be paid the value of the job. The payment should not be based on gender, race, ethnicity, or other demographic factors. The question should be whether the person can do the job. All people in the same job (doing the same thing) should be paid equally.
3.) Self Determination- Each person should have the choice of the job that they are going to do (if they are qualified). Persons should also

have access to health care and time off during the year. The crypto community should be working toward the 30-hour workweek by 2030 (though people should be allowed to work more if they would like to).

4.) Due Process- no person should have access to any right denied them without due process of the law. For rights that require payment (like travel), a person still must work to earn money to pay for the elements around the right. Rights removed because a person committed a crime should be restored no earlier than 20 years after the conviction. Societies may give back rights as "privileges" within the interim, but they may be revoked at any time.
5.) Travel- Every person has the right to travel to any place that they can afford. No country should restrict access based on gender, race, religion, or any demographic factor.
6.) Access the Internet- By 2030 every person on the planet should have access to the internet, whether through a personal device (paid for) or free public access points.
7.) Education (not indoctrination)- Every student should have access to the following education (at government, home, private, or charter schools), writing, reading, research methods, basic shop skills, basic finance skills, basic home skills, history, civics, science, technology (including IT), health and mathematics. Programs in arts, physical education, gym, theater, music, sports, social studies, or other skill-based classes should be electives supplementing, not replacing the required courses.

Each of these rights is something simple that every person should be able to enjoy. If we are truly a developed society, we need to take the time to understand that everyone has the right to achieve these principles, but they do not have the privilege of someone else paying for them. The system should make these as accessible as possible to everyone, but people must understand that they must work to better themselves to obtain access to these things.

International Lobbying for Access

Information is the key element of accessibility to spot and derivative trades; however, governments' still have methods to block or inhibit the use of these systems. The more we ensure that governments do not block access the more people will be able to use these systems. Building more access for people means giving them the access that they need (not always the access they want). Since this is an inherent individual right of a human being, governments should do what they can to facilitate this.

As noted above, governments block trade because they want to control people. Free people do not need the government's permission to help to conduct their lives; therefore, they can be more critical of a government. When a government controls aspects of a person's life, then they can make those aspects more difficult if the person "gets out of line." This is a useful tool to ensure that people comply and do what the government wants them to do.

The crypto community needs to work with people in countries that are stifling the rights of people to ensure that these rights are always growing. If a country is violating people's human rights and the western democracies will not do anything, the crypto community has the ability to exercise sanctions of its own. Ships can be chartered to move grain to poorer countries, cutting off shipping for corrupt countries looking to export goods. Banking can be encouraged to limit business with a country, or banks can be blacklisted by the community. While the cancel culture is a problem in the world today, it can be turned into a valuable tool to ensure that countries comply with international standards, set by the crypto community, not the UN.

The UN was created to represent the rich in each country in a world forum. This is where you use the campus meme asking someone to prove you wrong. If Greta Thunberg and her parents were not millionaires, she never would have given her complaining speech at the UN. The UN is not, nor has it ever been for the regular people of the world. The Crypto community brings together the rich and the poor into a forum where the poor can compete with the rich if they work together. Voices for everyone in the community are important and if we lobby for everyone to have access, then we have the ability to improve the world.

Chapter 20: Accessibility to Review Trade Policies and Trade Confirmations

One of the most important parts of industry regulation is ensuring that the rights of traders and users are protected. While many of the conversations around regulation focus on the government setting rules for different types of traders, the community needs to understand that community and industry regulation is more effective than wrought government regulation. The community and the industry will always be able to adjust to the changes in the environment faster than the government. For the community and industry to be effective, however, there needs to be good information on how the system is working.

The first issue that needs to be restarted is that a trade is a contract. Understanding that each trade is an individual contract allows us to set the parameters for trading and usage under the current law. Next, there is a basic right for traders and users to know how the systems on which they are trading work. This includes blockchain systems, exchange systems, and banking systems. These are the foundational items, without which traders are unable to make informed decisions and thus the transactions are in question.

There is also a right for the users and the investors to know how the coins are managed. The tokenomics of given crypto are important. Understanding tokenomics further helps a user or investor of a currency make an educated decision. Underlying the tokenomics, are the strategies that a crypto use for storage (wallets), the burn policy (Dead or black), and the staking policy (1st and 2nd Wave). Finally, we need to look at how the community can better educate traders to ensure that they are better able to trade their currency.

Overall, the rights of the trader are paramount to the system. Without the trader's rights being defined, the system itself is in flux. If we wait till regulators set the rules for trader and user rights, then the dream of the DeFi system breaks down. Centralized governments can make the laws, but the rights are inherent in the system. Users and investors need to work together to ensure that the rights are enumerated to ensure that governments do not centralize the system.

Knowledge and Contracts

Heralded American screenwriter Dalton Trumbo once said, "A good businessman never makes a contract unless he is sure that he can carry it through, yet every fool is willing to sign a marriage contract without considering whether he can live up to it or not."[234] When we look at the idea of a contract, so many people are willing to sign the contract without understanding how the contract works. It is in understanding the basics of contract law which enables it to be so robust. Once a community understands that there are industry best practices for contracts and that trades are basic contracts; it becomes much easier to explain why we do not need new laws around crypto- the laws already exist, we just need to acknowledge them.

Contracts are built with a bargained-for exchange of detriments.[235] Unfortunately, the law does not always look at the benefit gained by people in the contracting process, choosing instead to look at the elements that are given up by the parties. This mutual exchange of detriments is the payment that defines the contract.[236] In crypto trades (and derivative trades) the parties each choose to give something up. The seller gives up their rights to the crypto (derivatives) that they currently hold. The buyer gives up their right to the surety that they give to the other party (generally currency of some type). Once both parties have given up what they have agreed to give up, then the contract is complete. These are very simple contracts. So simple that they happen millions of times each day.

For there to be a bargained-for exchange of mutual detriments, both parties need to know or imply that they know, they have something that is being given up. In the case of cryptos, people need to know the worth of the crypto they are trading (in some sense). This does not mean that they

---

[234] AZ Quotes (2021). "Dalton Trumbo" at https://www.azquotes.com/quote/645962.

[235] Wexlaw (2021) at https://www.law.cornell.edu/wex/contract.

[236]

have to have an actual valuation of the crypto, just that they know the object they have indeed had worth. The more educated the person is on the worth, the more valid the contract. Courts have a long history of giving the benefit of the doubt to someone who is a less skilled trader, putting a higher burden on the party with more knowledge. When both parties are at the same level of knowledge (or the same level of access to knowledge), then the courts tend to treat them as equals (regardless of the level of the knowledge).

When dealing with a community the likes of crypto, the community needs to ensure that everyone has access to the basic information that they need to make educated trade decisions. Many believe that if the government regulates, the exchange of information will lead to a system like the public school system. The government will insist on "proven standards" for information before it can be considered a necessity. In many cases, the crypto landscape is changing so quickly that by the time the government conducts a 2-year study on a given topic, the subject of the study is no longer relevant in the system. Therefore, the information is more effective if it evolves from the community rather than handed down from on high.

The underlying concept of a bargained-for exchange between two parties who have access to information is that a uniform contract is unconscionable.[237] Just like the old movies where you see people taking advantage of people who own land with resources, people who prey on uninformed traders are despicable. However, when the community provides information to everyone (generally for free), then it is the person who willingly chooses to stay uninformed that is the problem. Pity should not be given to those who choose to stay ignorant.

The Trumbo quite brings forward a salient point, do not be too quick to enter into a life-changing contract. We live in a society where we "sign" click-through agreements without even looking at them. Do we know what we are agreeing to? Just like needing to look at what we sign, we need to look at what we trade and understand it. Crypto trades are simple,

---

[237] *Id.*

therefore even the layperson should understand what they are doing. The more education that we put on the market, however, the more that layperson can become a savvy trader to have more of an advantage.

Right to know how Platforms Work

Another bit of information that is essential to the success of the market is that users have a right to know how platforms work.[238] This does not have to be a thesis on the innermost functions of any system, but there needs to be a standard across the industry of how blockchain, exchanges, and DeFi platforms work. The sooner that the industry agrees that this is a "right" of the users and traders, the sooner we can check this off the list of things that the government does not need to interfere with. The crypto-community has the ability to educate each member who wants to be educated, it just lies with the person who needs to learn to choose to become an informed trader on the market.

One of the key elements that people need to understand is the blockchain system itself. Similar to a botnet where a reserved bit of processing space does a specific action working in collaboration with other reserved spaces to combine the actions into a functional aggregate, the smart contracts and smart contract overlays for the system need to be accessible for review.[239] By and large, the only people who are going to look at the specific coding of a block in the chain are auditing agencies and people who are looking to fork off of that specific chain. However, there is a need for the blockchain to be public enough that a potential user or investor can look at how the chain functions. Even more important is the "what" of the blockchain, rather than the "how."

Creators of coins and tokens should include the purpose of their coins in their White Paper.[240] While the person reading the White Paper does not need to know "how" the system works with the expertise of a coding

---

[238] Riley, Bryan & Kin, Anthony (2015). "Freedom to trade: A guide for Policymakers." Heritage Foundation at https://www.heritage.org/trade/report/freedom-trade-guide-policymakers.
[239] *Id.*
[240] Foleon, Supra.

professional, the Paper should be written simply enough that the reader can see "what" the coin or token does. Is it for a niche market? Is it for business transactions? Is it a general token? Is it a global exchange token? The answers to any of these questions can be yes or no, but they need to be defined so that users and investors have the ability to make an educated decision about their involvement with crypto.

Next, exchanges also have a duty to inform their clients how their process works. To be fair, the major exchanges of the world are well ahead of the game in this area. Educated traders can generally glean from the exchange websites the basic trading patterns and formulas that are needed to make an educated trade. The problem becomes when an uneducated trader enters the market. While it is true that it is the responsibility of the trader to develop their knowledge, the exchange will find itself in a better position when they provide free education to their traders.

One of the best examples of this is Coinbase.[241] Coinbase has a program that incentivizes people to learn about the currencies that they are trading. Further, Coinbase has training on trading and staking that any member can access at any time.[242] Even with the incentivized lessons (lessons where you earn currency), there is the ability for users to "go back" and look at past lessons to learn what coins are doing, why they are on the exchange, and how they can be traded more effectively on the platform. If other platforms were to follow suit, this would greatly increase the skill of the trading community and push out the need for more government regulation.

Finally, the DeFi banking system needs to educate people on how their systems work. Of the three, this may be the most difficult because each DeFi system tends to be proprietary. Like blockchain, DeFi banking will likely need to be more open source and allow for hard and soft forks in how the system works. While unique ideas are important to the brand, it is also important that individuals understand how the banking system works to

---

[241] Coinbase.com.

[242] *Id.*

be more effective.

Simple disclosure should be the industry standard in DeFi banking.[243] Banks should not be forced to give out all their code (it would make hacks too easy). They should be able to give a "cocktail party" explanation of how their model works and why it is more effective than central banking. Even a simple explanation will allow traders to be more savvy and allow the system to evolve.

While these are all simple things that the system should do, we cannot clamor for the government to regulate them as things that the system must do. The more relaxed the system is, the more the community will be able to control it. This is the heart and soul of the DeFi model, which should be something that we strive for. The more active the community is in asking for these standards, the less we need the governments of the world to interject.

The Right to Know How Currencies are Managed (Tokenomics)

The management of a currency is vital to its success. One of the oddest things that were seen in the crypto 2nd Wave was currencies that did not release any information, they just dropped their coins on the market and let them sink or swim. The majority of these coins just made a windfall for the creator, with no backing, and then went on the market and had market value alone (with no information the transitional value is impossible for the market to determine), these "junk coins" created the failed fiat currency equivalent in the crypto space.

When we look at the release of a new coin, there are certain elements that the community needs to demand. The first element is the need to know how many coins there are (or can be). Too many coins are released on the market without telling people the number of coins until someone researches it. Almost every crypto has a max number of coins, it is a

[243] Padmanabhan, Arun (2021). "Explained: How Defi Could one day liberate finance." The Economic Times (India) https://economictimes.indiatimes.com/tech/trendspotting/explained-how-defi-could-one-day-liberate-finance/articleshow/87511218.cms

function of the system. Therefore, why not insist that before a coin can be traded and listed that the creator disclose this number. This is not requiring anyone to say who has the coins, it is simply asking to know the number of coins or tokens in the system.

Once the baseline is established of how many coins are in a system, then the public should demand the right to know how the coins are distributed. Once again, this does not mean that everyone that owns the crypto needs to be outed, only that there is a plan of how the coins were released into the wild. How many of the coins/tokens stay with the creator? How many were given to partners? How many will be in the ICO? How many will be donated? All of these questions help investors and users assess the value of the crypto. Once again, the specific people who hold the coin can be kept private, the distribution is the part that the valuation system needs to know.

After coins have entered the market, it is vital that the system know how the crypto will be managed. There are two basic models for this, hands-on or hands-off. A hands-off model allows the DeFi system to be the most flexible. When the creator allows the model to be hands-off, they are allowing the system to define the parameters of the coin or token, the system will evolve based on market forces. These coins tend to grow and develop quickly but are static because the controller would need to change the coin coding to make any "modernizations" of the coin, which can diminish faith in the coin.

The hands-on model tends to cause some fear in DeFi circles. The measure of centralization for a hands-on coin is whether the coin is controlled by a human or by a computer. If the changes to the coin are controlled by an AI, it tends to follow the DeFi model much more closely. Conversely, if a person is calling all the shots (like the burn rate) the system is disrupted by human error which can break down the system. As a general rule, cryptos should be pushed toward AI management systems whenever possible (built on the blockchain if possible).

A question that any savvy investor should ask is whether the coin has a reserve.[244] Many cryptos use the creator holdings as a reserve. This is not a true reserve. Any real reserve should be held by a third-party company that can manage the reserve. The controller can (sometimes should) own the company holding the reserve, but the reserve should be separate from the holdings of the creator.

Once a reserve is established, it is important to ask whether the reserve is active or static. A static reserve is a reserve that is kept in the coin. This is a portion of the coin that is kept out of the ecosystem for injections when the system is becoming unstable. The benefit of a static reserve is that they have a set valuation and will only change when they are used. Eventually, any static reserve will be used up. On the other hand, an active reserve takes the reserve coins and places them in a market. This allows the coin's value to be increased via exchange of the coin. The value of the reserve should always be growing (if managed properly), and a small portion of the reserve should be static in nature. The advantage of this system is the coin is growing in value all the time. The disadvantage is a lapse in the market can cause a dip in the value.

Finally, educated investors should look at the burn program of the coin. The burn program is the system of increasing the value of the coin through manipulation of the supply. Burns can be general, which is an acute burn controlled by the coins controller, or standing, which is a constant tax for system management. In general, the standing burn is a more effective model as the general burn breaks down the DeFi philosophy. With a standing burn, the more digitization of the system the better. Each human choice makes the system less stable, therefore the more AI involved the better for the ecosystem.

When looking at coins, cryptos that follow these rules tend to be the most stable and have the highest growth potential. The more the community

---

[244] Locke, Taylor (2021). "Future of Money' Economists says the end of cash is coming- Here's what could replace it." MakeIt (CNBC) at https://www.cnbc.com/2021/11/11/predictions-for-future-of-money-cbdcs-stablecoins-cryptocurrency.html.

and the industry insists on these standards, the sooner the system will be able to function effectively. Effective systems result in steady currencies for trade and growth rates for investment, the best of both worlds.

Right to Know burn and Storage Procedures

When looking at the storage and burn procedures for a coin, it is important that these procedures are well thought out.[245] While it is possible for 3rd Wave coins to adjust these procedures without adjusting the coding of the smart contract overlay, it is still best for crypto to have these elements planned out in advance.[246] This means that if the crypto is following the program in their White Paper, they tend to be a more stable currency than those that are using a system of general burns to manage their value.

When looking at the burn policy, look for coins with heavy AI influence on how the burns are handled. If the burn is constantly monitored based on the trading volume and price, which act as a stimulus for the AI to change the burn rate, then the system is dynamic and is working to help the user and the investor. When the system is static (once again a standing burn) you have a reasonable system that allows you to speculate on how the coin will work. This is good for investors but can be difficult for users. The worst model is a model where you see the creator or controller of the coin doing random changes to the standing burn rate.[247] This minimizes the ability of the community to adjust to these changes and should be avoided as much as possible.

The storage policy of the crypto is a very volatile market. Some argue that coins should be stored by the owners. Others say coins should be stored by exchanges. Still, others want banks for crypto. Which is best? Whichever you are comfortable with. Some people insist on having a wallet and the

---

[245] Rieff, Nathan (2022). "Cryptocurrency burning." Investopedia at https://www.investopedia.com/tech/cryptocurrency-burning-can-it-manage-inflation/.

[246] Daly, Lyle (2021). "What is Cryptocurrency burning" The Motley Fool at https://www.fool.com/investing/stock-market/market-sectors/financials/cryptocurrency-stocks/coin-burn/.

[247] *Id.*

key for their coins. If they want to maintain this level of risk, then that is what is best for them. The downside of this is that they need to shift coins to the exchange anytime they would like to trade it. There are also people (like me) who leave most of their coins on active exchanges. This allows you the ability to trade your coin quite readily, however, you do not have control of the key and are unable to shift the system into "cold storage." DeFi banks are also an option. These may be best for the people who want the hands-off approach, allowing the bank to work with your crypto to increase your holding (like a savings account).

The final big question in this area is whether the coin has a staking policy. Staking is a process where you put some of your coin in the hands of someone else to maintain the coin. Generally, the holder pays you "interest" on the coin being kept in one place.[248] Similar to a CD, you put your coin in for a steady rate. Generally, this is a lower rate than you could get on the open market, but like DeFi bank holdings, you do not have to directly manage the crypto.

The burn, storage, and staking policies of a coin are important to investors. Different types of investors have different needs. The Market needs to adjust to these needs. Some people are hands-on, some people are hands-off. Once you realize your style, you can make an informed decision on how you want your money managed.

Educated Traders Make Better Trades

Within an industry as dependent on information as the crypto industry, it behooves the community to educate themselves to the best level possible.[249] Different traders have different thresholds, you need to find your threshold to ensure that you are ready to trade. Every person should make every effort to increase their knowledge of the system before their commit their hard-earned currency to the system. In a DeFi world, you do you; those who stay true to themselves will often do the best.

---

[248] Rieff, Supra.

[249] The Better Traders at https://www.thebettertraders.com/?r_done=1.

The community needs to maintain the knowledge is power ideology of crypto. The biggest change that we need to make is ensuring that the community understands that it needs to stay in a place of individual empowerment. Knowledge is not a depletable resource. The more we give knowledge to other members of the community, the more powerful the community becomes. Hoarding basic information helps no one, but spreading this information helps everyone.

Being part of the digital world, nothing is stopping the community from making information available to everyone. The websites are there, the space is there, all that it takes are individuals, exchanges, and DeFi banks putting the information up on their sites. Not only does this make the community better by sharing the information, but it also makes the website better by increasing the volume of traffic going to the website.

For those in the community who are more ambitious, the community always needs trainers to help people with information. If you enter this space; remember, you will make more money by selling to millions for a little than you will make selling to dozens for a lot. Low-cost training to bring new people into the community increases the size of the community. Helping them become educated traders helps the community become more powerful.

The final access point that we need to look at is access to past trades. The community needs to know the amount of each trade so that the present market value of crypto can be accurate. This does not mean that we need to know each time who made the trade. The DeFi community needs to maintain a level of privacy while still maintaining the level of information needed. This is a balancing act, but a balancing act that the community has the ability to do.

Chapter 21: General Risk Disclosures Related to use and Trading on a Platform or with a Currency and Proper Protections for Coin/Token Issuer

Many investors do not read the terms of conditions or the end user license agreement or any of the terms that they accept before accepting the clickwrap agreement, in anticipation to embark on their new product or tech. In fact, *Komodo* found that "in a previous study, only 9% of people read the terms of service. For the younger generation in the 18 to 34-year-old group, that number fell to an astonishing 3%."[250] While tedious and sometimes hard to understand if not in plain English, they are there for a reason and worth understanding fully before engaging a platform.[251]

Further, *Investopedia* states that "full disclosure is the U.S. Securities and Exchange Commission's (SEC) requirement that publicly traded companies release and provide for the free exchange of all material facts that are relevant to their ongoing business operations."[252] The disclosure of the information is imperative for crypto transactions because crypto traders cannot make informed decisions about cryptocurrency without having the information about the transaction. Information breeds security, security breeds a more efficient system.

Definition of Risk Disclosures

Risk disclosures act as an important guide when using a product or tech. To understand a product, it is important to fully grasp a company's risk disclosures.

Risk Tolerance

It is also important to understand your personal risk tolerance. According to *Investopedia*,

---

[250] https://www.komando.com/security-privacy/read-terms-of-service/786502/#:~:text=In%20a%20previous%20study%2C%20only%209%25%20of%20people,that%20the%20documents%20are%20too%20long%20and%20complicated.

[251] *Id.*

[252] Investopedia Citing https://www.sec.gov/pdf/annrep02/ar02fulldisc.pdf.

Risk tolerance is the degree of variability in investment returns that an investor is willing to withstand in their financial planning. Risk tolerance is an important part of investing, particularly having a realistic understanding of your ease to stomach market highs and lows lest you panic sell.[253]

Young investors may often have the gift of time to tolerate greater risk than their older counterparts. Those with a higher net worth and more disposable income can generally take greater risks with their investments, and likely make a change in economics.

Greater risk tolerance is often synonymous with equities and equity funds and ETFs, while lower risk tolerance is often associated with bonds, bond funds, and ETFs.[254]

Risk tolerance quantifies how much of a loss an investor is willing to endure within market plays. It looks at how much market risk—stock volatility, stock market swings, economic or political events, regulatory, or interest rate changes—an investor can tolerate, considering that all of these factors might cause their portfolio to slide. A person's age, investment goals, income, and comfort level are factors in their risk tolerance. Someone with higher risk tolerance, is willing to risk more money for the possibility of better returns than a conservative investor, who has lower tolerance. A person with moderate risk tolerance sits in the balance between an aggressive and conservative investor.

Understanding Risk Tolerance

Risk tolerance assessments for investors include risk-related surveys or questionnaires. Investors may also want to review historical worst-case returns for different asset classes to get an idea of how much money you would feel comfortable losing if your investments have a bad year or bad series of years. Other factors affecting risk tolerance are the timeframe of your investments,

[253] *Id.*
[254] *Id.*

your future earning capacity, and the presence of other assets such as a home, pension, Social Security, or an inheritance. In general, you can take greater risk with investable assets when you have other, more stable sources of funds available.

Risk tolerance is different from risk capacity, which refers to the minimum amount of risk an investor has to tolerate in order to reach their investment goals, relative to their time frame and income.

Aggressive investors tend to be market-savvy. A deep understanding of securities and their propensities allows such individuals and institutional investors to purchase highly volatile instruments, such as small-company stocks that can plummet to zero or options contracts that can expire without use. While maintaining a base of riskless securities, aggressive investors reach for maximum returns with maximum risk.

Moderate investors accept some risk to the principal but adopt a balanced approach with intermediate-term time horizons of five to 10 years. Combining large-company mutual funds with less volatile bonds and riskless securities, moderate investors often pursue a 50/50 structure. A typical strategy might involve investing half of the portfolio in a dividend-paying, growth fund.

Conservative investors are willing to accept little to no volatility in their investment portfolios. Often, retirees who have spent decades building a nest egg are unwilling to allow any type of risk to their principal. A conservative investor targets vehicles that are guaranteed and highly liquid. Risk-averse individuals opt for bank certificates of deposit (CDs), money markets, or U.S. Treasuries for income and preservation of capital.[255] Additionally, all investments have risks associated with them.[256]

---

[255] Twin, Alexandra (2020). "Risk Tolerance." Investopedia at https://www.investopedia.com/terms/r/risktolerance.asp.
[256] *Id.*

For example, investors in equities run the risk that the market as a whole could decline, dragging otherwise healthy stocks with it. Bond investors could see their income get chipped away by rising inflation. Both types of investors could experience a changing legal and regulatory requirement that could detrimentally impact their portfolios. Many times, an investor will assume one type of risk in the effort of avoiding another. For instance, an investor may have fled the volatile market for the safety of fixed income, only to be left on the sidelines should the market experience a significant rebound.

While risk is unavoidable, it can be managed. Diversification is one powerful tool in managing risk in a portfolio; a balanced portfolio distributes the various types of risk over a basket of securities. Maintaining a relationship with a knowledgeable Advisor is another way to lessen the impact of risk; your Advisor can help you in the security selection process, and will help you monitor your portfolio's performance.[257]

In late 2021, the Office of the Comptroller of the Currency issued a statement outlining a "coordinated and timely clarity to promote safety and soundness, consumer protection, and compliance with applicable law." Agencies discussed and analyzed crypto-assets called "policy sprints."

These sprints sought to:

1. Develop a common vocabulary;
2. "Identify and assessing key risks, including risks relating to safety and soundness, consumer protection, and compliance with applicable law;
3. Consider legal permissibility related to potential crypto-asset activities conducted by banking organizations; and

[257] TIC (2020). "Risk Disclosures." The Investment Center at https://www.investmentctr.com/client/disclosures/risk-disclosures.

4. Analyze the applicability of existing regulations and guidance and identifying areas requiring clarification."[258]

Risk Disclosure Example

As of late 2021, *Currency.com's* cryptocurrency risk disclosures include:

> There are several risks associated with cryptocurrencies and cryptocurrency trading. By accessing and using the Services, you hereby represent and warrant that you have read the following Cryptocurrency Risk Disclosures.[259]
>
> *Unique Features of Cryptocurrencies.*
>
> Cryptocurrencies are not yet legal currency in the United States, and therefore fiat currency. The price of cryptocurrencies is based on the agreement of the parties to a transaction, which does not have to based on the market value of the cryptocurrency at the time of the transaction.
>
> 1.) Price Volatility. -The price of a cryptocurrency is based on the perceived value of the cryptocurrency and is subject to changes in sentiment, which make these products highly volatile. Certain cryptocurrencies have experienced daily price volatility of more than 20%. Therefore, there is a high volatility risk, and holders may suffer large losses.
>
> 2.) Valuation and Liquidity. -Cryptocurrencies can be traded through privately negotiated transactions and numerous cryptocurrency exchanges and intermediaries around the world, each with its own pricing mechanism and/or order book. The lack of a centralized pricing source poses a variety of valuation challenges. In addition, the dispersed liquidity may pose challenges for market participants trying to exit a position, particularly during periods of stress.

---

[258] Morrison Foerster (2020) New Strides in Crypto-Asset Regulation." MOFO At https://www.mofo.com/resources/insights/211206-new-strides-crypto-asset-regulation.html?utm_source=Mondaq&utm_medium=syndication&utm_campaign=LinkedIn-integration.

[259] *Id.*

3.) Cybersecurity. -The cybersecurity risks of cryptocurrencies and related "wallets" or spot exchanges include hacking vulnerabilities and a risk that publicly distributed ledgers may not be immutable. A cybersecurity event could result in a substantial, immediate, and irreversible loss for market participants that trade cryptocurrencies. Even a minor cybersecurity event in a cryptocurrency is likely to result in downward price pressure on that product and potentially other cryptocurrencies.

4.) Opaque Spot Market. -Cryptocurrency balances are generally maintained as an address on the blockchain and are accessed through private keys, which may be held by a market participant or a custodian. Although cryptocurrency transactions are typically publicly available on a blockchain or distributed ledger, the public address does not identify the controller, owner, or holder of the private key. Unlike bank and brokerage accounts, cryptocurrency exchanges and custodians that hold cryptocurrencies do not always identify the owner. The opaque underlying or spot market poses asset verification challenges for market participants, regulators, and auditors and gives rise to an increased risk of manipulation and fraud, including the potential for Ponzi schemes, bucket shops, and pump and dump schemes, which may undermine market confidence in a cryptocurrency and negatively impact its price.

5.) Cryptocurrency Exchanges, Intermediaries, and Custodians. -Cryptocurrency exchanges, as well as other intermediaries, custodians, and vendors used to facilitate cryptocurrency transactions, are relatively new and largely unregulated in most jurisdictions. The opaque underlying spot market and lack of regulatory oversight create a risk that a cryptocurrency exchange may not hold sufficient cryptocurrencies and funds to satisfy its obligations and that such deficiency may not be easily identified or discovered. In addition, many cryptocurrency exchanges have experienced significant outages, downtime and transaction processing delays, flash crashes, and may have a higher level of operational risk than regulated futures or securities exchanges. It may be difficult or even impossible to identify and/or locate the issuer of cryptocurrency, the trading platform, wallet provider, or intermediary, especially in a cross-border situation where it may also be difficult to determine which laws may be applicable. Thus, if a holder has a claim, it might be difficult to sue the issuer or the wallet provider and enforce a title.

6.) Regulatory Landscape. -Cryptocurrencies currently face an uncertain regulatory landscape in many jurisdictions. In addition, many cryptocurrency derivatives are regulated by the provisions of national and supra-national (i.e., EU) securities legislation; moreover, some state securities regulators have cautioned that many initial coin offerings are likely to fall within the definition of a security and subject to their respective securities laws. One or more jurisdictions may, in the future, adopt laws, regulations, or directives that affect cryptocurrency networks and their users. Such laws, regulations, or directives may impact the price of cryptocurrencies and their acceptance by users, merchants, and service providers.

7.) Technology. -The relatively new and rapidly evolving technology underlying cryptocurrencies introduces unique risks. For example, a unique private key is required to access, use or transfer a cryptocurrency on a blockchain or distributed ledger. The loss, theft, or destruction of a private key may result in an irreversible loss of cryptocurrency associated with this private key. The ability to participate in forks could also have implications for investors. For example, a market participant holding a cryptocurrency position through a cryptocurrency exchange may be adversely impacted if the exchange does not allow its customers to participate in a fork that creates a new product.

8.) Transaction Fees. -Many cryptocurrencies allow market participants to offer miners (i.e., parties that process transactions and record them on a blockchain or distributed ledger) a fee. While not mandatory, a fee is generally necessary to ensure that a transaction is promptly recorded on a blockchain or distributed ledger. The amounts of these fees are subject to market forces and it is possible that the fees could increase substantially during a period of stress. In addition, cryptocurrency exchanges, wallet providers, and other custodians may charge high fees relative to custodians in many other financial markets.

9.) Risk of a partial or total loss of the invested amount. - Information regarding any specific cryptocurrency may be missing, inaccurate, incomplete, and unclear with respect to the project and its risks. Documents may be highly technical and require sophisticated knowledge to understand the characteristics of the cryptocurrency and/or the project.

10.) Risk of insufficient information disclosure. -Information regarding any specific cryptocurrency may be missing, inaccurate, incomplete, and unclear with respect to the project and its risks. Documents may be highly technical and require sophisticated knowledge to understand the characteristics of the cryptocurrency and/or the project.

11.) Project risk. -In many projects, the value and stability of the cryptocurrency largely depend on the skill and diligence of the project team behind the cryptocurrency or the ICO. The project underlying an ICO might not be realized, which would ultimately make the cryptocurrency worthless.[260]

Indeed, the above are terms extracted from an actual, current agreement for edification purposes.

---

[260] https://currency.com/cryptocurrency-risk-disclosures.

Get Clarity

There are websites designed specifically to make this information as clear as possible. "Terms of Service; did not Read (ToS;DR)" is one such website that attempts to rate and break down the Terms of Service from various companies and websites.[261]

That fine print we generally gloss over in favor of commencing a new journey right away? Try not only to read it, but ensure that you understand it and if not, get help from those who do. The internet has been classified as a human right by the United Nations. At the very least - use it for understanding.

Conclusion

Risk disclosures may seem like something that the crypto community does not have to think about in the general system of the crypto marketplace, but the disclosures are very important to be sure that the system is functioning normally. One of the best attributes of the cryptosystem is that people are working together to validate the system with smart contracts and AI. Legitimate language is very easy to spot for a community, so is illegitimate language. When these disclosures are out in the open, someone will catch the scams and someone will challenge them.

When the community demands proper disclosures, only true scammers are harmed. The users have more information. The sellers have more protection and the exchanges are can properly arbitrate the settlement of disputes between their clients. In this scenario, everyone wins but the scammers, so you can see why the politicians are mad about good risk disclosures.

---

[261] https://tosdr.org

Chapter 22: Minimum Capital Requirements

One of the outstanding myths of the cryptoverse is that crypto does not have any inherent value. For someone who does not understand the blockchain, it can be difficult to explain to a person how the system works. Crypto actually has four different types of valuation: Transitional (Chapter 31), Transactional (Chapter 32), Market (Chapter 33), and Inherent (Chapter 34). While not every coin has each of these types of valuation, each coin will have at least two of the valuation methods to ensure that the coin is stable on the market.

In this Chapter, we discuss the need for a unified system of valuation. There are many firms and companies out there who have their own valuation method, generally one that favors their favorite type of coin or token; however, as the crypto economy evolves the valuation needs to be simplified and standardized so that everyone is working from the sale set of rules.[262] While this discussion always allows for the evolution of the system, the system must be built on a strong foundation for it to stand.

The first level of valuation is transitional value. This is the value-added to the process through the active use of the blockchain. Through smart contracts and smart contract overlays, the system has developed a method for tuning this value into currency. Once value begins to be acquired, the system needs to have some sort of reserve. Too often we see that "Junk coins" will tap out all of their value to make money off of the coin, thus eliminating the transitional value of the coin. This causes a coin to rely only on market value.

Once market value enters into the equation, we need to ensure that there is no market manipulation. Though this topic is covered in detail in Chapter 25, it is important to introduce it here to the conversation. As the market takes note of the usefulness of the coin, this is where the coin begins to acquire adopters, which can create transactional value. Transactional value

---

[262] Aaron, Brown (2021). "Is crypto really worth $3trillion dollars." Bloomberg at https://www.bloomberg.com/opinion/articles/2021-11-10/is-crypto-really-worth-3-trillion.

is very different from "cash-out" value which is a technique used by Junk Coins and central banks to decrease the overall value of a system. Cash value, however, is a legitimate type of valuation, measured by the actual value of the coin (the combined, adjusted amount of four valuations) with heavy weight given to the market value.[263]

When we look at the valuation of a coin, the company (or person) placing the coin in play should have some type of reserve to ensure that the coin has value. For many, this is a growth reserve, which starts small and grows, because the system does not start with a lot of money. In some cases, such as Stablecoin 1.0, the reserve will reflect the amount on a 1 for 1 basis, where the users can exchange their currency for fiat. In cases such as the Stablecoin 2.0, the value is linked to an entire portfolio and there is no ability to "draw" against the holdings, they are a permanent system to increase the value of the currency.[264]

The Need for A System of Valuation

Within the family of crypto users, there are some early adopters with a very strong libertarian streak. In their mind's eye, there is no need for a standardized system of valuation as each transaction should be based on the perceived value that each party places on the coin. This system does not work in the real world. Valuation is important because there needs to be some way to maintain and secure the system, knowing the value of the system is the first step in this process. Once the value is known, parts of the system (DeFi banks) can be insured. It is difficult to insure something where no one knows the value. Another reason that we need to know the value of the system is to prevent governments from "saying" what the value is. The market determines the value of the cryptosystem, when governments interject using Keynesian techniques, the system tends to fall

---

[263] The equations for this are complex and covered in an academic paper forthcoming.

[264] *Id.*

apart.[265]

Those that say there does not need to be a system of valuation are the pioneers who built the system. To them, each trade is an indicator of how much a currency is worth. Many of them became billionaires in this wild, wild west system and are unwilling to let that system change. Unfortunately, as more complex instruments become available for trading, people need to know the value of the underlying asset. This is no longer a "trading a goat for three dozen eggs" system, it is a highly organized modern trading system built on the backbone of blockchain. Value is inherent in the system; people should know the value of what they have.

Valuation gives people a way to secure the system on the exchanges and in the DeFi banks. If the system does not have a set value (only the perception of value), then the property rights of the users and holders are in question. If someone enters the system thinking it is a game, then there may not be the *mens rea* available to protect the assets of others. For the system to be protected, the participants in the system need to know the value of what they are holding.

Another group that needs to know the value of holdings is the insurance industry. As DeFi banks become more common around the world, mistakes will happen. Since a digital transaction is final once it is complete, banks do not have the same methods of moving money around to cover mistakes that they had in the past. This means that insurance will be more important in the future. Insurance companies will not ensure an asset that has no value, even no defined value. This means that it is very important that we know what the value of a given system is.

Additionally, governments hate a vacuum. If we do not assign value to cryptocurrencies, the governments of the world will. This is not action out of any benevolent intention, this is simply a fact that they need a value to tax us. The crypto community needs not only to value the currency so

[265] Kelleher, John (2021). "Why do bitcoins have value?" Investopedia at https://www.investopedia.com/ask/answers/100314/why-do-bitcoins-have-value.asp.

governments do not do it for them, but we also need to identify when a coin is profitable and when it is simply in transit. Otherwise, millions of traders will be liable for their transactions.

Starting with Transitional Value

In order to build value in a coin, the system needs to have a foundation. In the case of cryptocurrency, that valuation starts with the transitional value. Covered in detail in Chapter 31, the Transitional value is the use-value of the blockchain. This use-value (which is a common valuation model in the real world) allows crypto to begin building value. Once this value is established, it can be monetized. Rather than entering into the fiat world, the users in the crypto world allow the valuation to be done in crypto. This is where the transitional value begins.[266]

The concept of use-value is very important in finance. This is one of the problems that the field of economics seems to have, that the use-value can be just as high as the trade value of a good. In the case of crypto, people are using a block on the blockchain for something. Regardless of what the transaction is for, the block is providing a calculation (or part of a calculation). As this happens, the block increases the value of the data passing through it. The owner of the block "rents" this space to the user for a fraction of a second. Since the rental has value, the owner of the block is paid for their rental and the system builds value.

Use value happens all the time in the real world. Leases are one of the most common forms that we see. In a lease (car), the car lot still owns the car but the lessee has the right to use it for some time. The leaser is paid for the use of the car and the lessee then can use the vehicle for what they need. There are restrictions, you cannot destroy the property because it is not yours and will lead to a conversion claim, but you do have the right to use it properly during the time. This is the same thing that happens on the blockchain, just in a fraction of a second.

The amount that the owner of a block charges depends on the service

---

[266] *Id.*

being conducted. The amount is irrelevant for this discussion, what is important is that the owner does charge something. Once this money enters into the system, the system begins to build value. Monetization of this value is how modern crypto coins are built. While there are other models of initial valuation, this is the most common. As long as the owner keeps this money in reserve, they can then trade their coin/token on the market to increase the value.

Building A Reserve

One of the concepts that get many crypto coins in trouble is the idea of a reserve. The reserve can either be the value that is held back in the system, or some sort of Stablecoin system, but there needs to be some value in the coin itself. Many novice coin creators have failed with their coins because when they extract money for use of the chain, they collect the money and are on their way. There is nothing wrong with this model (it is staying in the fiat world), it just means that you cannot have an individual token. Strong currencies need strong reserves (after 1st Wave).[267] The faster creators understand this, the faster Stablecoin 2.0 will be adopted.

One of the easiest ways that reserves can be created is that some of the coins that are created are held back in the system, as a balancing tool. This is not the same as the creator having a person "stash," this is a designated amount of funds, often in cold storage, that is maintained to protect the stability of the system. Reserves should be between 10% and 30% of a system to ensure that if the system needs more liquidity people can "buy" these coins into the market, increasing the liquidity of the system but maintaining the value of the coin.

The second option for building a reserve is to participate in a Stablecoin system. Stablecoin 1.0 systems build value based on a direct relationship to a fiat currency. Stablecoin 1.1 systems build a reserve based on a single asset or family of assets. Both of these systems tend to have a value for

---

[267] Robbins, Christopher (2021). "How do you value digital assets?" Coindesk at https://www.coindesk.com/markets/2021/09/09/crypto-for-advisors-how-do-you-value-digital-assets/.

exchange ratio. Stablecoin 2.0 systems are based on a portfolio managed by a third-party actor. This system does not have a "1-for-1" ratio and trades within this system need to be on the open market to "cash-out" your holdings.

One of the biggest dangers is when a creator "cashes out" using the transitional value. In these cases, the money that is created by the system is immediately taken out by the creator. This is similar to a standard lease contract. This does make the creator short-term profits but means that there is no value in any coin/token created by their block. It is not a problem unless the creator tries to attach a junk coin to the system, then it becomes a scam.

The faster that coin creators accept the idea that we need to have some reserve for transitional value, the more quickly we will see people enter into the Stablecoin 2.0 system. As the system builds transitional value, the system can grow. Oddly, the valuation of a coin system is cyclical, first, it is transitional, then it moves to other methods, then eventually it will return to a balance of transitional and inherent value as these systems are constantly growing. Unlike the fiat system, which is constantly taking value out of the system, the Stablecoin systems ensure that value is always being maintained or grown in the system.

No Market Manipulation

Once a market is established for a coin, based on the value, the coin can be placed on an exchange. While the transitional value of a coin is constant (which grows in a predictable manner), the market value is based on the decisions of the people participating in a market. The decisions can be based on market patterns, or they can be based on people liking the name because of a specific event. The market is a very fickle manner of building value. Many coins make the mistake of putting the coin on the market early, this can be fatal as the market valuation can destroy any hope of transactional value.[268]

---

[268] *Id.*

Another danger of the market that people do not think about early is market manipulation. When a coin is in its infancy, it can have a value well below one US cent. In this case, whales can buy billions of these coins and hold them to see if there is movement. These purchases are not usually long-term purchases. Usually, when this happens, the whale's purchase creates a market rush for the asset, then the value increases. Once the value hits a particular point, the whale abandons the coin and the market drops again. Unscrupulous whales can repeat this process several times and collapse a coin before it has a chance to build value.

The market is a very dangerous place for a young coin, this is why many coins are choosing to work with systems to establish transactional value before they establish market value. In an ideal society, the ICO would be less than 15% of the total coin release as the other portions of the coin are either in reserve or already in use. The higher the use-value, the less relevant the market value is for normal users; it becomes a benchmark only for traders.

Traders will usually rely on patterns rather than any other valuation method. While the market will reflect the value of the coin in trade (because people will remove their asset from the system if they are not getting value for it), it does tend to move quite quickly and the patterns can drive the market price up and down.[269] This can be like an auction where you can find coins for a very low price on the market, or you can be overpaying when you get caught up in the hype of the trade.

On the other end of the spectrum is the situation when the market is reacting to something that has nothing to do with the value of the coin. Around Halloween 2021, Basic Attribute Token (BAT) had rapid growth in the market. This was followed a few days later by a rapid decline in value. People saw the ticker "BAT" and thought it was cool for Halloween. The rise and fall in value had nothing to do with the value of the coin, which is a very good coin, it was simply the whim of the market. This can be one of

[269] *Id.*

the most dangerous factors for a new coin on the market.

When working with a coin, always look at why it is moving in the market. Make sure that the growth is based on the activity of the coin (or the outside use of the coin). When you get caught up in a rush, like with BAT, you could find yourself holding the bag when the excitement fails. This is similar to following the tweets of celebrities, they can cause a momentary jump in price- but the market will usually correct fairly quickly for a valueless coin.

Building Transactional Value

A more reliable valuation method is the transactional value of a coin. Transactional value is based on three different valuation elements (among other things). The first is the number of users for the coin/token. These are the people who are using the coin for commerce, not just for investment. Next, is the number of companies that are using the coin. A company using a coin has a value related to how big the company is. This can be generalized as small, medium, and large. The last valuation in this category is the number of governments that are using the coin. Governments can rapidly increase the value of the coin when they adopt it.

The users of the crypto are important because if no one is using the crypto then the crypto is just a market phenomenon. Generally, the transitional value of the coin grows between $10, 000 and $50, 000 based on the holdings and volume of the trade. Users have the most potential to increase the value of crypto because there are more users than there are companies or governments. While most users only add around $10, 000 to the transactional value of the coin (this is the constant used for the simplified valuation method), the value can increase. This is why the transactional value is often higher than the simplified method.

Companies using the coin create an increased valuation of the crypto, but there are less so they do not account for as much of the value of a crypto. A small company increases the value of a crypto by about $250, 000.[270] A

[270] Small companies are less than 500 people.

medium-sized company increases the valuation of a crypto by approximately $1 Million.[271] A Large Company increases the value of a crypto by upwards of $10 Million.[272] While these numbers are much larger than the increase based on the user value, the sheer number of users can be a better sign for a currency.

Governments allowing a crypto to be used as legal tender are a massive boon for the system. Unfortunately, the valuation is mostly theoretical as few countries have adopted cryptos as legal tender. The best estimate of the value is the GDP of the country in relation to the number of users in the country. The more people in the country who adopt the crypto, the closer to the GDP the value is. This is a percentage basis and will be refined as more countries adopt cryptocurrencies.

The more that the system evolves, the more that these equations will be refined. Currently, there is difficulty distinguishing people who use the coin vs. the people who trade the coin. Company valuation is fairly steady, but there needs to be the biggest company category (based on value not on a number of people) because some major players change the value. The country value will also continue to evolve and refine to ensure that we are working off the best possible set of numbers.

Cash-out Value of Exchanges

One area that we need to watch as a community is that exchanges maintain enough funds on hand to cash out users who are working on the exchange. Sometimes exchanges are so focused on how many people are in the system, that they forget that people leave the system. Especially when there is a bear market or near the end of the year, people tend to pull their money out of the short-term markets. This can cause a run on the exchange, which can look bad for the community. Therefore, exchanges (and to a lesser extent, banks) need to have the proper funds on hand to ensure that they can pay people who want their money.[273]

---

[271] Medium Companies are between 501-2,500 people.

[272] Large Companies are above 2,500 people.

[273] Kelleher, Supra.

One of the big items that exchanges need to keep in mind is how much you can take out at a time. While setting withdrawal limits makes sense for smaller investors, when you have large investors working within the system, this can be a problem. A billionaire does not want to make thousands of $50, 000 withdrawals to get their money out of a system. A balance needs to be made to ensure people have access to their funds, but also that there are no large runs on the market.

When an exchange focuses on how many people are in the market, then they lose sight of how many people are leaving the market. The population of a market is always a market in itself. As long as the population value is growing, the system tends to be able to handle those who are leaving. Even when the system hits a plateau, the system is usually able to handle some people leaving. It is when the number of people in the market starts to decline where exchanges have problems.

Unlike the stock market, the crypto market has an added benefit. Cryptos are currency. In some cases, a person may have to either trade for the currency that they want or cash out in the currency that they have. The only real problem for the exchange is when a person wants to cash out in the form of fiat currency, this is where they have to have "cash on hand." In any other case, the exchange can just transfer the crypto held by the trader to their wallet. The best case is when the trader has a wallet with the actual exchange (or a linked bank.)

When the market turns south or near the end of the year will always be the worst times for the crypto exchanges. When the markets get bad, the paper hands pull up their stakes and make a run for it. This can cause a run as most paper hands want their money in fiat currency. Likewise, because of the incompetence of national governments and tax codes, many investors need to pull money out of their accounts because they have it stored in a method that the government considers "profit." This means that they need to take their money out to ensure that they have enough to cover the national fee on productive people.

Comparing Cash Value

Crypto will always have a relationship with cash value. Cash will until crypto is widely accepted by the "what is it worth?" question. We will eventually move past this (with GETs), but for now, this is a question we will answer time and time again. Fiat currency is the measuring stick, sometimes not worth as much as what it is measuring, but it is still there. When we set up systems, we need to know that this will always be a question; however, exchanges need to move to a system where you can value cryptos in other cryptos to see what the direct trade value is.[274]

Established currencies will always be used to measure what new currencies are worth. It is always a valuation ratio. We do it with fiat as well. How many loaves of bread is a dollar worth? How many Yen does it take to buy a car? What is the value of a plane in Pesos? The idea that there is a ratio of value between two assets is not a new idea, the way that we look at this relationship is something that we need to pay attention to.

Fiat currency is a measuring stick. There is a perceived value in the stick, which gives credence to the valuation obtained from the stick. The validity of this measurement depends on the stability of the measuring device. There is an old legend that there were fake monks in the Middle Ages who used their beads as a measuring device. They then buy in dry climates (the beads were wood), this would have the beads dried out when they purchased. Then they would sell in wet climates. The beads would swell and thus it would look like the beads were bigger meaning that they would look like they had more value. The same scam is done as fiat currencies change in value.

Conclusion

To ensure that the valuation of crypto is done as honestly as we can, we need to ensure that the ratio between individual currencies is always shown. This allows the traders to know what they are worth compared to each other, not just compared to fiat currency. The faster we adopt this as a general policy, the more established the crypto trading market will

---

[274] Some already do this.

become. The more people know the more confidence they can have in a system.

Once we establish that there is a variable system where everything is in relationship to everything else, we need to have rules that exchanges have enough funds on hand to cover normal withdrawals. If an exchange cannot cover a withdrawal (when a person converts their currency to fiat currency on the open market), it looks bad for the system. If a person has the stated amount of currency, then they should be able to access it. This is why converting to crypto cards is so important; it eliminates the need to rely on the traditional banking system.

Chapter 23: Avoiding Stablecoin 1.0 as a Template

In the beginning of cryptocurrency, Bitcoin existed with the transitional value being the only indicator for the value of the coin.[275] As the networks built on the blockchain of bitcoin increased, so too did the value of the technology underlie the coin. However, as the systems became more complex and moved into the real world from the digital world, the transitional value was quickly bowled under by the transactional value and the market value. OG investors scrambled for something looking like actual value, but there was nothing to be found. This is when Stablecoin 1.0 found its way onto the market.

Stablecoin 1.0 is the first iteration that cryptocurrency should be backed by something other than the transitional or market value of the coin. The idea that a currency should be backed by something has been around for time immemorial, it was only in the last 100 years that the failed experiment of fiat currency was tried. With this evolutionary dead-end of currency explored, now it is time for the industry to move to more dynamic models of holdings and staking to give crypto inherent value.

This Chapter attacks the problem of Stablecoin 1.0 at its root. However, before we uproot a broken system, we need to understand why the system was initially used in the first place. 3rd Wave cryptos would not exist without the pioneers who created Stablecoin 1.0.[276] When we look at the foundation on which modern crypto is built, it is impossible to avoid seeing the problems with Stablecoin 1.0, first among these is that it is linked to fiat currency.[277] As crypto is a way to move away from fiat currency, the idea that we should link our coins and tokens to the broken system seems silly.

The fact of the matter is that Stablecoin 1.0 is an outdated system. It was needed, but now it is time to move on. As a result, we need to look at global

---

[275] Bitcoin, www.bitcoin.org.

[276] Hayes, Adam (2021). "Stablecoin." Investopedia at https://www.investopedia.com/terms/s/stablecoin.asp.

[277] Coinbase (2021). "What is Stablecoin?" Coinbase at https://www.coinbase.com/learn/crypto-basics/what-is-a-stablecoin.

exchange tokens that are based on Stablecoin 2.0 to move the cryptocurrency system to the next level. This means at a very minimum that a coin should be based on a multi-currency reserve, if not a multivariate reserve. These complex reserves create more stability and allow the diversity of the system to hold the value of the ecosystem, regardless of the movement of one of the elements.

Stablecoin 1.0 had its place.[278] Now it is time for us to move away from this place. Just like the governments of the world need to move away from the Boomer politicians and allow Gen X and Gen Y to try to build a better world for our children, first Wave coins need to embrace the stability of Stablecoin 2.0 and move the entire industry toward the future.

The Necessity of Stablecoin 1.0

The Ford Model A was a concept that helped shape the world that we live in today. The first of Ford's models was not fast, it was not reliable, and it was not what the world needed. It was, however, what the industry needed as a proof of concept to make sure people understood the value of the automobile. People far and wide used this car, it had problems but was better than not having a car at all. This is the world that Stablecoin 1.0 entered into.

Stablecoin 1.0 entered into the world when the cryptocurrency world was based on a system similar to fiat currency.[279] While the Bitcoin model did limit the number of coins that could go into the system, it did not do anything to move beyond the "I say so" model of valuation.[280] Each validation on the blockchain has value, but the value is based on a bargained-for exchange. Bitcoin said what the value was and used it. When Ethereum and the other primary blockchains entered into the mix, they also used a fiat method of valuation which was simply fiat currency in the

[278] *Id.*
[279] Sahadi, Jeanne (2021). "How Stablecoin is different than other cryptocurrencies... and how it is not." CNN Business at https://www.cnn.com/2021/10/27/success/what-is-stablecoin-feseries/index.html.
[280] Hayes, Supra.

digital world. Investors saw this weakness and this is one of the reasons it took years for these currencies to build value.

When Stablecoin 1.0 entered the market, it entered parallel to other cryptos on the market. While the Stablecoins were not as exciting as some of the other alt-coins, they were a part of the system that added valuation to the matrix.[281] Crypto is, and will always be a knit ecosystem, that is the soul of DeFi. As Stablecoin entered the market, they created an anchor that could allow investors to see values in the ecosystem. While the speculators rallied to the "junk coin" markets, harkening back to the junk bond markets of the 1990s, the stability of the Stablecoin 1.0 model allowed the entire ecosystem to grow.

Stablecoin 1.0 is a proof of concept.[282] Not only does it show that inherent value can be added to coins, completing the four-part valuation model, but it also shows that stability in one sector of the industry can increase the stability in other sectors. Stablecoin 1.0 is the Model A of the system, now it is time to move past the Model A to the Model T, which is more reliable, safer, and has a little more flash to draw people in.

Dangers of Linking to Fiat Currency

Bitcoin was visionary in the same way that President Kennedy was visionary. Bitcoin saw the that currency fiat currency system run by the banking cartel could not last. Human influence over the market will always cause inefficiencies in the market, even as the people try to make the market better. The market is the market and it works best when it is allowed to operate. Bitcoin created a digital currency to allow people to step away from the central banking cartels, the banking cartels treated Bitcoin (and are treating crypto) the same way they treated Kennedy.

The reason fiat currency is failing is the same reason that every other fad in history has failed. People make things people want. People want them for a while and the market booms. Then people find the next big thing and

---

[281] *Id.*

[282] Coinbase, Supra.

the market starts to fail. The burgeoning rise of the "maker economy" was an indication that people were losing faith in the fiat system. People started building old skills again because society believed that society was going to collapse. If enough people believe this, it will happen. However, we were lucky (kind of) that COVID came around and stabilized the system with the tyranny of the medical field. The evils of COVID kept the system afloat until something better could be found. The better thing is 3rd Wave cryptos.

Governments have problems with money for the same reason that parents with spoiled children have problems with money, they give in to their whining kids. Governments tend to 'help' those that cry out the loudest. When people riot, governments give them what they want- even if it is only a small portion of the population that agrees with the rioters. The "squeaky wheel" theory is very ineffective and breaks down the market consolidating wealth and power in the hands of the very few. When the elite have most of the money (which they do now) the system cannot work, and it starts to show signs of collapse. Without a better system, we will follow the bust and boom cycle that we have seen in human history for the last 4, 000 years.

Physical currency had its place.[283] It continues to have a place. However, it cannot be the only place where we keep our wealth. As the digital age moves into its second (maybe third) decade, people need to realize that crypto is not replacing currency, it is simply making the currency more efficient for people around the world. Banks getting 5% because people need to use different currencies, agreed upon by banks, for exchange of international goods is not only silly, it is criminal. Society needs to move beyond the extortion of the banks to move toward a global exchange token that can be used to ease the exchange between multiple currencies.[284]

As fiat coins start to lose their value, the people who use the fiat coins need more fiat coins (and bills) to live their daily lives. 100 years ago we saw this

---

[283] Sahadi, Supra.

[284] Please note that one global currency is a bad idea, whether digital or physical.

in Pre-World War II Germany. In the 1980s we saw this in Tanzania. In the 1990s we saw this in Venezuela. In the 2000s, we watched China manipulate its currency to avoid this fate. In 2010, we saw the United States dollar lose value quickly. The world's fiat currencies are losing value, and all they are doing is printing more money to compensate. Even a 10-year-old child who collects sports cards will tell you, the more they print the less each one is worth. Unfortunately, those running the central banks do not listen to small children.

The central banks do not lose money on quantitative easing, the countries do. When the central bank prints out more money, it "loans" it to the government. The government pays much of it back with interest. This means that the central banks set the interest rates to hedge the losses they take when they print more money. It is a shell game, and we are the nuts who are getting shaken around in the cups. When we link to fiat currency, we are allowing the same people to shake us, though now they can just use our computers.

We need to bring the Internet of Things to an Economy of Things. The economy has always been interconnecting, but the connections were very difficult to master. With the digital world that we live in now, these "real world" things can be combined with the "Internet of Things" to ensure that things go where they need to go. Food shipments can be redirected to increase the dispersion of the foodstuffs and reduce spoilage. Fraud and criminal activity can be tracked more readily through proper records. RFID technology embedded in shipping containers not only benefits the ports, but also distribution networks around the world. By bringing advanced technology to the world, we can end wage slavery and move people toward a 30-hour workweek.

Outdated System

While linking crypto to a single fiat currency was by far the most popular method for creating a Stablecoin 1.0 system, it was not the only one. Several coins linked their coins to commodities or stocks to distinguish themselves from the crowd.[285] These coins are, in effect, Stablecoin 1.1. By expanding the scope of Stablecoin, these cryptos opened the world to the ideas that underpin Stablecoin 2.0. Like Stablecoin 1.0, Stablecoin 1.1 was a needed step to ensure that the system moved forward.[286]

Stablecoin 1.0 is outdated because there is a better system coming. Some many Stablecoin 1.0 coins are clinging to the old ways similar to how the ice truck industry fought against home refrigerators. As the systems around them evolve, outdated ideas need to change or they will fail. Most Stablecoin 1.0 coins can adapt their system to join a Stablecoin 2.0 system. While the direct 1-1 exchange will have to be discontinued, the coin can stay alive as its value will increases.

The truth of the matter is that linking to a single fiat currency or a single commodity puts the entire system at risk. Any currency or any commodity can fail. Ripple uses gold because gold has been an amazing hedge for all of human history (possibly the best Stablecoin 1.1 model); however, if there is a large amount of gold discovered, the value of gold will stagnate or even drop (the asteroid or more efficient ways to pull it out of soil). This will cause the system to drop. Diversity is a strength in all financial portfolios, crypto holdings are no different.

The other major drawback of Stablecoin 1.0 is the Disney Bucks problem. As we discuss elsewhere in the book, Disney Bucks were a concept where you could buy "Mickey Bucks" at the park to give to your kids to spend. If someone stole them, they were still lost- but the thief could only use them at the park, so they were worthless to steal. As fewer establishments in Disney accepted the Mickey Bucks, they became worthless in the parks as well.

Stablecoin has shown that we need a global exchange token. These tokens allow an ecosystem to form around a collective holding system, all the while taking away the banking cartel's ability to charge 5%-10% for a

---

[285] Hayes, Supra.

[286] Coinbase, Supra.

currency exchange on the global market. To buy a good, you should not have to buy a currency that the receiver will take, there should be an intermediary. Global exchange tokens take the 5-10% model down to approximately 1-2%.

The evolution of any system requires dead ends for the system to evolve. If we keep the dead ends functioning through artificial means, the more efficient systems will not rise to the top. Stablecoin 1.0 has served its purpose and the system has moved forward. Now it is time for the Stablecoin 1.0 cryptos to join with 3rd Wave cryptos to ensure that the system continues to evolve.

Multi-Currency Reserves (Stability)

For a system to be functional, it needs diversity. Mono-base systems will eventually fail because a mono-base system, by its very nature, resists change. When a system has a single source of stability, they fight to defend that source of stability, forcing other sources to move away. As a result, the system completely fails if that source breaks. Stablecoins that only have one source of stability are teetering on the top of a long post, with nothing to catch them should their post fail.

Diversity breeds stability because it allows for the system to evolve. Each mutation, each variable that changes allows the participants in the system to see what worked and what did not. Think of all the people who died because they tried new foods and found them to be poison. Think of where the world would be today if we all had to learn from our own mistakes- not learning from the mistakes of others. When the field becomes more diverse, some elements will succeed and others will fail. The more we spread the losses across several areas, the more effective we can be in identifying what works.

Many 1950s and 1960s babies grew up in the era when the dollar conquered the U.S.S.R. To these boomers, the dollar is a constant. With the dollar being a constant, they use it as a frame of reference. Gen X was the first generation since World War II that had to deal with the idea that the dollar is not a standard, it is just a more stable commodity. The reason it is so stable is because of the diversity of the United States economy. However, it is still a currency whose value changes about other currencies. To understand why fiat currency linking is so dangerous, we need to reject the fact that a dollar is always worth a dollar. We do this by looking at what today's dollar is worth compared to a dollar from years ago.

The dollar is always declining.[287] Therefore when you buy a US dollar coin, linked to the dollar, you are buying something that is losing value. Just like when you buy a car off a lot, the value drops as soon as the ink dries on the contract. It is the same thing with fiat currency-linked coins. As long as a country is printing more money, the coins linked to that currency will always be diluted. While currencies are a decent hedge against a volatile market, they are no replacement for a diverse portfolio.

Complexity increases diversity in a system. Each new part that comes to the system must be tested to see if it can function, then either accepted or rejected based on its functionality. In a business system, we cannot establish a need for something because we like the idea. Something must work or it needs to be rejected. We see this in countries around the world that adopt a nanny state policy because they "feel safer," yet become shocked when the nanny state commits some atrocity. Remember, people accepted the Nazis because they thought they would protect them, and many Germans were shocked when they became some of the worst bad guys in history. The same story repeated itself in Russia, Iran, Iraq, China, Cambodia, and dozens of other countries around the world- all in the span of one century.

Multi-Currency Reserves (Size)

The final area that needs to be discussed is the idea of size in the context of a single currency-linked system. When crypto decides to link to a specific currency, the value of that crypto is locked into the maximum value of the currency in question. The existence of two pools of wealth drawing from the same system diminishes the value of the system. In effect, Stablecoin 1.0 currencies force their own value to diminish because they are cutting

[287] Us Debt Clock. Debtclock.org.

the value of the linked currency by the amount of coin that they are putting into the market. Just because it is sitting in an account somewhere does not mean that it is not in existence.

Any economic system has a present value. The present value of an economic system is the value of the resources, labor, and currency-related to that system. The world economic system has value also. Most experts put the present value of the system at $1.4 quadrillion USD.[288] As more people are born around the world, their labor adds to the value. As new resources are discovered that also adds to the value. However, unless there is a major technological boom, there will not be massive growth in that value. Every crypto ecosystem is part of this system- unless we add value to the system, we are taking value away from the system (there is no zero-sum gain).

This creates the problem that when a coin comes into existence and does not add value to the system, then the coin actually takes value away from the system. Because of most politicians' primitive understanding of how valuation works, this is one of the chief worries of the Boomer politicos. While this is one of the dangers of there being too many coins, we must realize that if the market rejects "junk coins" then the system will always be building value. Large Stablecoin systems are a major drag on the current economic system because they are little more than an avatar of the actual value they mimic. The industry needs to ensure that coins have a plan to add value to the system.

While it seems like valueless coins are the end of the problem, they are not. Junk coins spawn more junk coins. When a creator realizes that they can enter something into a system with no value and no stake, all income from the project goes to the creators. This is one of the chief reasons that you should not invest in a coin that has no proof of stake. When you invest in a junk coin you are simply hoping that you can ride the pump and get

---

[288] Desjardins, Jeff (2020). "All of the worlds wealth in one visualization." Visual Capitalist https://www.visualcapitalist.com/all-of-the-worlds-wealth-in-one-visualization/. Crypto has increased this exponentially.

out before the dump.

Stablecoin 1.0 is the fiat system with a protective step. The coin acts as a buffer to prevent the fiat currency from collapsing. This is why many governments are so eager to force Stablecoin 1.0 on the crypto market, it keeps the money flowing into their pockets. Stablecoin 2.0 provides a similar hedge for the fiat currency, but because it is so diverse, it also prevents the system itself from falling into depression. Any country that works with a Stablecoin 2.0 system that is sufficiently diverse is basically depression proof and will have a difficult time falling into recession as well. Stablecoin 1.0 cannot add value to the system, it can only slow the bleed.

Conclusion

Avoiding the pitfalls of Stablecoin 1.0 is like retiring a hero from a community. Stablecoin 1.0 saved crypto, though most modern cryptos are not willing to admit that. Without the proof of concept that Stablecoin 1.0 established, Stablecoin 2.0 (and Stablecoin 1.1) would never have been possible. They proved what was needed for the world to accept crypto, and we need to recognize those coins for their contribution. However, just because they are heroes does not mean that we need to keep following their example. Heroes can make mistakes too and we must learn from those mistakes.

The more widely Stablecoin 2.0 is adopted around the world, the more stable the global economy. For developing countries with internet access, this is a Godsend. Stablecoin 2.0 allows nations to have a digital legal tender in addition to their current legal tender, which is more effective than 1st Wave cryptos which have no inherent value. The people of the world can effectively become the bank of the world as the system evolves.

We do not reject Stablecoin 1.0 because it was a bad idea. We accept the role that it had in the history of crypto. Now we need to accept the systems that arose from its progress to make the world a better place. Stablecoin 2.0 is a child of Stablecoin 1.0, the coins that are clinging to Stablecoin 1.0 need to be proud of their descendants and move into the modern era.

Part II

Section II

Introduction to Part II: Section II- Criminal and Laundering Protections

One of the strongest claims that governments have to regulate the crypto markets is the idea that crypto markets make it easy for criminals and money launderers to move money around. In all actuality, every crypto transaction is recorded; therefore, if the community cooperates with the governments of the world to prevent crime, such as money laundering, illegal arms trades, sex trade, and fraud, crypto can actually make the world a safer place. While physical money can only be tracked through serial numbers and inking, crypto can be tracked across cyberspace.

Chapter 24 of this section looks at the cooperation needed between platforms and the governments that they serve. Public and private systems cooperating to ensure stability for the system is vital to ensure that the system continues to develop in a way that benefits everyone. However, it is also vital that we ensure that members of the community have due process when their information is accessed. There should be no carte blanche for governments to invade the private lives of community members just because they are invested in crypto. Once a person is caught breaking the law (and is tried in court and convicted), there needs to be a registry that prevents them from accessing the community resources. To have a stronger crypto community that is not overly regulated we need to understand some cooperation with the governments of the world is needed.

Chapter 25 looks in a direction that is mutually beneficial for the community and the governments, preventing market manipulation. Stable markets require controls to ensure that the corrupt do not break the system. While governments often claim that this area is their exclusive right, in the crypto community this duty falls squarely on the backs of the exchanges. To do this, the community must have a clear definition of market manipulation. Once manipulation is defined, we turn our attention to how manipulation relates to anti-trust issues. Rather than governments creating new laws to oversee this area, the current anti-trust laws in most developed states will suffice. Similar to anti-trust issues, manipulation by whales can also be a problem that must be addressed. Like whales, the modern media has moved beyond being an information source to a source that has been manipulating information about crypto. The crypto community has responded by developing a robust system of crypto journals that have pushed back against corruption. The biggest threat to the crypto community is the system of central banks that controls a large portion of the world government, their influence and market manipulation has been troublesome to the community. If these types of manipulation are restricted by the community, in collaboration with the government, then we have the ability to move the system forward.

Chapter 26 focuses on non-discrimination policies. As governments around the world get involved with crypto trading, it becomes important that governments do not discriminate against currencies or users within their system. One of the biggest threats that the crypto community is seeing around trading is discrimination against a currency based on the nationality of its creators. Countries have enmity between them and we cannot allow this enmity to unbalance the global market. Likewise, governments should not pick winners. If a coin is a valid coin, then the government should allow the coin to be traded in its economy. Governments should also not favor coins that are in a rivalry with another coin, this can unbalance the trade. While digitally it is difficult for governments to discriminate based on race, creed, sex, religion, or ethnicity- bigots always find a way. We need to ensure that everyone has access to crypto trading. Finally, we need to ensure that institutions are not set up to discriminate against any group of people or the field of crypto in general. The more egalitarian we can be in the crypto community, the better we can help the world leave bigotry behind.

Chapter 27 discusses how governments need to cooperate with the crypto community to ensure that money laundering is not taking place. Cooperation is a two-way street. For the crypto community to make the moves needed to support governments (from Chapter 24) the governments of the world need to let the crypto communities know who the bad actors are. This includes the elimination of the "plea deal" in matters involving international fraud in currency. As we educate people about the threat of money laundering, we can then let people how assets are used to launder money. The more people are educated, the less they will be worried. Crypto itself helps with this by triangulating currency exchanges, when combined with the digital record- governments and the crypto community can work together to prevent crime.

Crime will always be a threat where money is involved. The more the community works with the government while maintaining its independence, the better the community will be able to deal with the problems that it faces on a daily basis. The crypto community is an evolving ecosystem and crime is cancer on that system. The government wants to over-regulate, effectively bombarding it with radiation. The community can avoid this by using preventative measures to stop the cancer of crime from growing within it. Healthy living for the community keeps the government away.

Chapter 24: Cooperation Between Platforms and Governments for Information Exchange

One sad fact that we need to face as a crypto community is that "the tax man cometh." Governments, as long as they exist, are never going to let something as valuable as the crypto market go without being taxed. The longer that the community bickers about the government's "right" to tax us, the longer that the community is going to look like desperados looking for a quick buck.[289] The governments of the world have an inherent duty to follow tax laws. The countries of the world that are still using regressive income taxes to punish innovation and work, have a duty to their people to tax those making money within the state. The crypto community needs to accept this fact, and then begin the world of getting rid of income taxes and moving toward a fair (sales) tax.[290]

For the crypto community to be the global citizen that it needs to be, the community needs to start working with the government as equals. This does not mean that the community should kowtow to the whims of uninformed government officials, however, it simply means that the crypto community should do what it needs to do as a good community. Next, there is a need to look at the different types of information that are entering the market. Not all information is equal and the government does not have a carte blanche to access any type of information at their whim.

One of the most important parts of the relationship between the crypto community and the government is due process. Individuals within the community have certain human rights that governments must respect. If these rights are not respected, the community should help people get those rights in the country in which they live. However, if a bad actor is convicted in a court allowing the rights of the community, then the

---

[289] Governments do not have any inherent rights.

[290] Income taxes are the most regressive form of tax because they are punishing people who are trying to change their lot in life. Sales taxes are more effective because people can choose how much they want to pay in tax, if you want a luxury item, then pay more in taxes. *See* Smithmyer, Christopher (2012). The Realistic Republican. Amazon.

community must blacklist that bad actor.

Working with the government is a process of give and take. The community should work to be as friendly with the governments of the world as it can be, without violating the rights of the members of the community. This means that the community requires free access to information about trials and arrests made around crypto issues. Secret deals, closed-door courts, and sealed documents should be banned- and the crypto community should fight to prevent these from being allowed in any crypto-compliant country!

The Need for Cooperation

People expect their governments to protect them. The crypto community exists in a state beyond any one single government but works within all crypto-compliant governments. This means that the crypto community needs to recognize that a government has a job to do and that we need to be part of the system that helps the government do its job. Now when a government violates the trust of the community, we need to use the courts and other methods to defend the rights of the community; however, when a government is simply performing its duty, the community has a duty of its own to help protect the greater good.

In protecting the greater good, the community cannot sacrifice the rights of its members to make a good impression. Like Socrates said, “Democracy is the worst form of government because it is the rule of the mob.” Just because people are afraid does not mean that the right of their neighbors should be voided. Each of us is required to not only look out for our own rights but also the rights of those around us. As one person loses a portion of their rights, the community loses a portion of its rights. Eventually, governments will try to abuse every right, if we do not defend the ones that we do not care about, the power to fight back may not be there when they come after rights we do care about.

When we are working with the government, the crypto community needs to remember that one of the most active professions in the community is lawyers. Just because you are trading crypto does not mean that you are giving up any of your rights. You still have the right to defend your rights in court. Since the crypto community is international, there is the ability to sue for civil issues in the court whose jurisdiction fits the case best. This means that we should be forum shopping. With criminal issues, remember that the case will likely be tried in the country in which the crime took place- or where the actor is a citizen. Keep this in mind if you work in any of the grey areas of the system.

Lobbying is another powerful tool which can help the crypto community work with the government. Very few laws are set in stone. Most laws can be changed by the governments who instituted them. To empower the crypto community, the crypto community needs to work with lobbying groups to ensure that laws enacted are not in violation of the rights of crypto users (the crypto bill of rights). This means that crypto users should make it a habit of donating small amounts of money to crypto lobbying groups, light Green Wallet. When these lobbying groups have the funds to defend the rights of the community, countries will then pass laws that are more helpful to the community.

One inalienable truth is that the people of this world have the ability to be equals. If the community enters into a relationship with governments acting like the governments have universal control, then they will have universal control. The crypto community needs to respect the government but not bow down to the government. The community is a viable community of its own, bringing people around the world together. Rather than be treated like a corporation, beholden to a government, it should expect to be treated like the UN- except the crypto community does not welcome the corruption of the rogue nations.

Tracking Information

When it comes to information that we should share with the government, we need to understand the conditions in which the sharing should take place. The government does not have an unabridged right to access any information.[291] There must be a reason that the government needs the information, and they must follow the due process of the law to access that information. In all cases, a person or company has the right to be safe in their person, papers, and property. To pierce that veil, the government must provide a good reason, lest tyranny run the global market.

One of the primary sources of information that government may need access to is trade confirmations. Trade confirmations are a set of information that allows someone to see when trade was initiated and completed. When it comes to this type of information, governments should have full access. Why? Because everyone should have full access. An exchange should put up the value and type of every trade that is entering the market to allow the market price to be as current as possible. The reason that the government should have access to this is that it should be public information. One caveat, however, is that the parties to the transaction should still have their anonymity without due process of the law.

Another type of information that a government may want access to is who holds the rights to specific digital accounts. Unlike trade confirmations, this information should be private. Exchanges should maintain this type of information, preventing anonymous accounts from trading on the open market; however, this information should be protected information-information available only with a valid warrant. Governments should need to present a warrant from a court before the names associated with accounts should be released. Additionally, the holder of the account should be notified that the name has been given out at the same time that the government is given the name of the account. This still allows the government to free the account, but also allows the account holder to challenge the seizure in court.

What types of currency are being traded by an account is also information

---

[291] World Justice Project (2018) at https://worldjusticeproject.org/sites/default/files/files/introduction_key_findings.pdf.

that a government may want to know. Once again this is a type of information that should be public on the trading forums. Who owns the account is still protected, but what is being traded should be public information? The reason for this is because we need to know this information to see how currencies are moving. The amount and value of the currency directly relate to the volume and valuation of the currency. Both the government and the community should be able to see if someone is selling currency undervalue for manipulation purposes.

The international exchange of currency is information that governments will be interested in. Depending on the country, the government may have legal access to this information. International trade is an odd item in any constitution. Governments do not have jurisdiction beyond their borders; therefore, they SHOULD only have access to information about items coming into their country. Outgoing items should be the private information of the owner. However, many counties still have a legal claim to information about international trades, and this information should be provided after due process has been served.

One area of information that should be fought tooth and nail by the community is the government's claim that they have a "right" to know the ownership of given coins. Coins are a currency, and thus are papers and are an inalienable human right. The community should always fight any general activity for a government to create a "list" of coin holders, or to offer a bill of attainder against any individual without a court case. This is one of the information systems that the crypto community should be most concerned with sharing.

Governments tend to like the idea of a unilateral exchange of information between denizens of their jurisdiction. In most developed nations in the world, this type of unilateral forfeiture of information is a violation of human rights. Just because a government wants something does not mean that it needs to be handed over immediately. While the documentation may be required to be handed over, the information request must follow due course and due process. Anything less is tyranny against the masses.

Due Process

As noted in the appendix, the crypto community believes in the inalienable rights of human beings. To this effect, there are some due process rights that every member of the community should demand in any country that calls itself crypto compliant. Countries that violate these rights should have community sanctions placed against them. Key among these rights for due process are:

1.) Right to Know what the Crime/Tort was- Every Terran in the world has the right to know of what crime they are accused of before any criminal or civil proceeding may move forward. This requires a formal declaration of what the crime is, that cannot be amended during the course of the hearing.
2.) Right to Appear Before a Court (before a seizure is finalized)- Every Terran citizen has the right to appear before the court to argue their case. This includes the grand jury process. Information, at no time after the warrant, is issued, shall there be an ex parte appearance at court where the representation of the defendant is not present.
3.) Right to a Lawyer- Every Terran citizen has the right to an attorney, of their choice, whether the person is licensed in the jurisdiction or any jurisdiction. No person can be forced to represent another person, should a person pick a lawyer who declines to represent them, then the person must pick another lawyer. If it is found that the government influenced the lawyer's choice not to represent the person, then the case against the person is dismissed.
4.) Right to see a Warrant before the information is turned over Every Terran citizen has the right to see a warrant before any information is turned over, civil or criminal. A warrant must be issued by a judge, in a jurisdiction that has subject matter and personal jurisdiction over the person, issued only upon just cause.
5.) Right to a Public Trial- All cases involving crypto shall be public trials, broadcast via the internet so the community can watch.
6.) Right to a Speedy Trial- The initial hearing after an arrest must take place within 48 hours of the arrest, or the defendant must be released and charges dropped. If the arrest takes place in another jurisdiction, the initial hearing must take place within 48 hours of

the person arriving in the nation where the case will be heard, or else the person is released. All trials are limited to two weeks long for a maximum time frame.

7.) Right to an Appeal- Every person has the right to an appeal for violation of the law. This hearing can be either done through briefs or in person, at the discretion of the court up to matters of 500, 000K and the choice of the defendant for matters over 500, 000K.[292] Appeals must take place within two months of the finalization of the initial case. The defendant may ask for an extension of up to two months.
8.) Right to Confront the Accuser Publicly- Every Terran citizen has the right to call the accuser to testify. If the accuser cannot testify, because of foul play, this is information that can be entered against the defendant in the trial. The jury is the arbiter of what foul play is.
9.) Ban on Plea Deals on Crypto related Matters- No matter related to the exchange of crypto may result in a plea deal for any Terran citizen. All accusations must go to a public trial.
10.) Ban on Double Jeopardy- No person can be tried for any case which they have already been tried for. Once a cause is dismissed or an acquittal is reached, the party is free to go on that matter. By caveat, any case involving the abuse of children may be re-opened on new information and does not fall under the double jeopardy rule.

These rights are inalienable, which means every person has them. "Whether the best person in the world or the worst person in the world," we should fight to ensure that these rights are granted in every Terran nation.

Blacklisting Criminals

When working with the government, the crypto community must also do its part to deal with criminals. Unfortunately, because of the function of the law, some criminals can move their assets to places where governments cannot reach them. To be good global actors, cryptosystems

---

[292] K is a representation of the KIROS global exchange token.

should work with governments to punish bad actors, including, but not limited to, preventing them from using the crypto market as a place to store ill-gotten gains.

Before any compliance with a government order can be conducted, the bad actor must be convicted.[293] Accounts can be frozen, but should not be seized without a conviction of the courts. This means that the exchanges or DeFi banks should keep the currency in trust until the case is over. If there is a conviction, the account should be turned over to the government, less a 10% fee for maintaining the account. If there is not a conviction, then the funds should be returned to the owner.

The crypto community should also reject the cancel culture. Accounts should not be frozen or attacked because someone is not liked. Accounts, even for unpopular people, should be maintained until due process has been served. This will ensure that the system will be secure and that people will not be singled out by the market for attacks. Cancel culture is very dangerous as it is one of the tactics that central banks tried to use to undermine the value of the currency.

The community should enforce a ban on the creation of coins by a bad actor. Any person who is convicted of a crime relating to the creation or exchange (not taxation) of a cryptocurrency should not be allowed to create new coins and put them on an exchange. This type of rule creates a standing punishment for someone who has violated the community rules. This ban is permeant and should stand for the remainder of the bad actor's life.

Additionally, once a person is convicted of a bad action relating to crypto, the accounts of that person are frozen until three years after that person has served their time.[294] This freezing does not go into effect if the government seizes all of the accounts. If only a portion is seized, then the freezing of the accounts should stand. The interest from the frozen

---

[293] *Id.*
[294] *Id.*

accounts (if staked) should be maintained and kept by the exchange or DeFi bank in which the accounts are held. Any interest value over 500, 000 K per year should be placed in a Stablecoin 2.0 system of the choice of the exchange.

The community can make the crypto space a place where bad actors do not want to participate. Unlike the art and currency markets, the crypto market is a live market with its own internal controls. Working with governments discourages criminals from entering space in the first place. Stopping bad actors from creating currency helps keep them from repeating. Freezing accounts places a community punishment (set forth in the terms) for those who take away trust from the community. The stronger the community response to bad actors, the fewer governments will have to interfere in internal operations.

Building a Better Community Through Empowering the Community

One of the mantras of the crypto community is that knowledge is power. For the community to enter discussions with the governments on equal footing, the community must know what its rights are, especially in the jurisdiction in which a member of the community lives. To this end, we need to be our own best teachers. We need to work together to ensure that members of the community know what their rights are and how to claim those rights.

One of the first steps of this process is ensuring that people know what their rights are.[295] Civics has been removed from many schools and replaced with social studies. Students are being taught what social activists want rights to be, not what rights are. People need to have access to their rights and how they are important to their lives. This means that the community needs to start putting out podcasts looking at the rights in specific jurisdictions. Anyone anywhere should be able to find out what their rights are through free webcasts.

---

[295] National Lawyers Guild (2021). "Know your rights." NLG at https://www.nlg.org/know-your-rights/.

Knowing how to protect your rights is just as important as knowing what your rights are. Let the community of crypto users and traders be a powerful voice in global crypto rights issues. For us to have proper crypto rights, everyone needs to have proper human rights. This means that we need to help people understand how to protect their rights once they know what they are. This goes double for the idea that the community should know whom the government is holding for accused crypto crimes. The ability of governments to "black site" Terran citizens needs to be ended. Any arrest needs to be made public as soon as the accused is in any government facility.

It should also be a matter of public record the accusations against any citizen.[296] Once a person is arrested, they should be told what their crime is, and so should the community. This also goes for people who are being held as "a person of interest" which is a term used by the government to interrogate a citizen without a formal arrest (which in many countries activates their rights as an accused). If you are forced to come to a police station to answer questions, you should be told why you are there and the detainment should be made public.[297] Governments have no right to take people off the streets in secret, that is how tyranny is born.

Finally, the community needs to work together for a set of punishments for particular crimes. Mandatory sentencing is the only fair way for crimes to be punished. Juries and courts giving lower or higher sentences should need to state mitigating or aggravating circumstances. The use of "ranges of years" only gives undue power to the courts. If a person commits a crime, then they should serve a set time. Yes, there are factors which allow it to be reduced or increased, but the base rate should always be known. This is the only way for the system to ever be fair.

Conclusion

When the crypto community works with the government, then we have the ability to make the crypto community more mainstream. However, the

---

[296] World Justice Project, Supra.

[297] *Id.*

community needs to realize that this is no reason to give up all their rights in a given situation. The community must work to balance cooperation for the common good with protecting the members of the community. This process will develop through time and we must work together to make sure the development is well thought out.

We must realize that citizens control the government, not the other way around. This means that the community needs to enter the discussion as an equal, not as a servant. This will allow the people of the world to enforce their inalienable human rights, backed by the support of billions of crypto traders around the world. Governments cannot be allowed to abuse their people or people from other countries, crypto gives the community the ability to enforce these rights against the government.

Chapter 25: Preventing Market Manipulation

When we are looking at government regulation, there are some reasons why the government should enforce the current laws on the books. The one clear area where this is imperative is preventing market manipulation. Market manipulation can decrease confidence in the market and is prevented by already existing regulations on the market. If the government was more aggressive in preventing manipulations, then the market would be free to ebb and flow as needed.

In this Chapter, we look first at market manipulation. Without a good understanding of a subject, it is hard to have an educated opinion on it. Therefore, politicians may seem incompetent; they are required to have opinions on everything, but they often required to know very little. Second, we look at the problems of anti-trust issues and insider trading. These are two of the biggest issues that can fail the market in its infancy (we also see problems with existing monopolies attacking cryptocurrency).

Whales are another issue that the market needs to look at, while we discuss whales in detail in Chapter 35, we introduce this issue here so it can be on your mind during other Chapters. Whales are both a boon and a bust for a market. On one hand, they increase the volume of trade and money in the system, on the other hand, they can cause the market to collapse in one fell swoop. Just as problematic as the whales are the members of the media and celebrities. Unlike whales (who generally trade on educated moves), the media and celebrities talk about the coin as experts when... we can just say their qualifications are in question.

Manipulation by banks is another problem that we are seeing in the crypto market. Central banks have been manipulating currency for the last 100 years, the idea that they would manipulate a new currency should not come as a surprise. The reasons why central banks are failing should be front and foremost in the minds of crypto traders; the central banks have had their turn, now they need to pass into history. The community must come together to ensure that manipulation is ended and that the system can grow in a stable manner for the good of all traders.

What is Market Manipulation?

The concept of manipulation is simple, I want to make more so I will do things that benefit me. We all manipulate the market to our benefit; the goal of preventing market manipulation is that we eliminate undue market manipulation and that my friends are a horse of a different color. Undue market manipulation is using some technique or method that is illegal to move the market in your favor. This can be moving the market up to ensure your spot trades grow. This can also be moving the market down so that you see greater value in your shorts. Either way, you are exploiting the market to ensure that you illegally receive greater gains and this is problematic.

Many times, market manipulations are scams. These are the snake oil salesmen of the system, the people entering the market using an unfounded idea to dump coins on the market, make their millions, and then disappear into the ether of the internet. The same people who run chain letters and pyramid schemes have entered onto the market, and they have brought the same models of scamming with them. Always be wary of any coin that forces you to get other people to join you. A good coin should build a network without forcing you to bring people in, if you are forced to bring your friends and neighbors or else leave them behind you have found a scam or a cult.

Anyone can be a person manipulating the market. In most cases, the people manipulating the market will know what they are doing. In some cases, we see people manipulating the market without any concept of what is going on, we call them politicians. All kidding aside, politicians are one of the biggest groups that manipulate the market. If you do not believe me, look no further than the politicians who became millionaires after vaccine makers were given immunity.[298] Now, these criminals want to

---

[298] DeChalus, Camilia et al. (2021). "As the pandemic raged, at least 75 lawmakers bought and sold stocks in companies that make COVID-19 Vaccines, treatments, and tests." Business Insider at https://www.businessinsider.com/lawmakers-bought-sold-covid-19-related-stocks-during-pandemic-2021-12.

lecture the crypto community on how to do our business.

Methods for manipulation vary but fall into three categories, information, misinformation, and anti-trust issues. Once you start to deal with these major issues, you then are left only with the scammers and other small-time criminals. Exchanges and banks are developing methods to deal with these groups, therefore, if you keep your trades with the decentralized exchanges and banks, you can do pretty well (just use the better exchanges).

Manipulation and Anti-Trust Issues

Trust in the market is one thing, but trusts in a market are an entirely different animal. A trust is a group that is manipulating a market using a series of agreements to build a system excluding others. Trust methods can include region granting, price-fixing, anti-labor methods, oligopoly, and tacking. In the United States, illegal trusts are prohibited under the Sherman Anti-Trust Act and the Clayton Anti-Trust Act.[299] In other counties, the laws vary.

Most trusts are problems because they are set up as a monopoly. Monopolies are a system where one group or company has control over an entire industry. The government ignores that it is the monopoly on the use of lawful force (unless a constitution recognizes people's rights to defend themselves). Monopolies have been around for centuries but really came into their own in the 1920s. The breaking up of the monopolies, along with the creation of the federal reserve and central banks, and war, were the big reasons for the global depression of the 1930s. All of the major monopolies were broken up, and a new monopoly around the central banks was created.

Oligopolies are another type of monopoly. Rather than having control of the industry through controlling all of the sales and production, a company can manipulate the market by having control through purchasing all of the goods from a market. Generally, this is done through being a middleman,

---

[299] Cite Sherman and Clayton

which causes a company to be a monopoly and an oligopoly. In this case, a company buys all the goods, then has control over who they are sold to. Oligopolies are harder to break up as the resulting monopoly is seen as a legal monopoly (better process and better prices), so the oligopoly is usually overlooked.

When we bring this formula down to the microcosm, we see one of the major market manipulators of our time, insider trading. Insider trading is the process of a person having knowledge about the movement of an asset without that information being known to the public.[300] The trader then uses this information to make a beneficial trade before the information becomes available to the public, making money off of others. This can be devastating to the market because it reduces investor confidence.

Manipulation and Whale Issues

Whales are another type of investor that can disrupt the patterns of the market. The difficult aspect of whales is that they are only doing what every other trader is doing, they just do more of it. A whale is a trader who deals with massive amounts of a stock or a currency, to the point that their trades move the market on their own. When a whale makes a normal trade, this is not a problem- however, some whales realize the Waves that they make and this is where there is a problem.

Whales, in general, are a good force on the market. Whales bring a lot of money to the market. While the majority of the market is made up of individual traders, the plurality of the market is strongly dominated by the whales on the market. The whales also bring a lot of volume to the market. One large trade can move a stock or currency from level 1 to level 3 if it is big enough. This puts the stock or currency on the watch lists and gets people trading.

When whales become a problem is when their trades cause a bear market. One big trade can flood the market with a stock or crypto. This means that the price is going to drop. Responsible Whales make their purchases in big

---

[300] Cite Insider Trading

blocks but sell in small blocks. Even if they sell in 30 small blocks of the same amount, it can prevent the market from looking like they are abandoning ship. When whales are responsible the market tends to grow, however, when they manipulate the market, it can collapse very quickly.[301]

For the market to succeed, we need to treat the whales fairly. Whales have every right to trade as much on the market as they want. However, other traders on the market should be able to be protected too. Some exchanges limit sales amounts in a single trade. This seems to be a good way to allow the whales to get rid of stock they do not want, but still prevent whales from manipulating the market. When the market comes up with fair exchanges like these, then everyone has the opportunity to make money, and everyone is protected.

Manipulation and Media Issues

Global media is a major problem currently. The rise of neo-yellow journalism is becoming a problem for countries around the world. From the outright false stories in the USA and the UK to the media blackout of the COVID protests in Australia, to the outright censorship in China about the abuses in Hong Kong, the media has failed its mandate. The governments of the world should be doing everything that they can to ensure a free press that presents facts to people (not opinions). However, we have seen in the current age of neo-yellow journalism that politicians and journalists have intermarried to the point that the mainstream media (both liberal and conservative) is just no longer reliable. The time has come that media companies need to be broken up (under antitrust laws) and required to be non-profit and responsible for stories they know to be patently false.

Another group that we see spreading false information is celebrities. In some cases, they are spreading false information because they are ignorant, sometimes they are doing it because it benefits them, in other cases, they are even being paid to spread false information. One of the biggest questions is, “Why do people even care what celebrities think?”

---

[301] Big Whale Sells article

Dumb kids we can understand being drawn in by the mystique of being rich and famous, but adults should know better. Just because someone plays a smart person on TV does not mean that we should believe them![302]

The media and celebrities manipulate the market by interjecting misinformation into the market. People who are listening to them are following the advice of idiots gambling with millions of dollars that they have as discretionary money. Most traders are trading with their savings to invest in the future. People are playing on two different levels. Listening to the rich who are just gambling, is like taking your life savings and dropping it on black in roulette because some starlet is wearing a black dress. While it may pay off sometimes, most of the time you will lose your own shirt. Bad information on the market can cause a lot of people a lot of pain, but it is the people's duty to deal with this.[303]

One group that seems to be dealing with this is Grift coin.[304] Their model is using the crypto market to generate funds to pay lawyers to go after people who are spreading false information about given coins. The group seems to have a decent following on Facebook and seems to be growing in size. If the group does well, it is excellent that the community is finally starting to rally around its legal rights around the world.

When looking at famous people who are commenting on the market, always gauge who you are listening to. Just because someone works for a news agency does not mean that they are an expert. Also, just because a person is not a professional trader does not mean that they do not know what they are talking about. Elon Musk seems to have a pretty good financial head on his shoulders. So, each trader is responsible for who they are getting their advice from. Just remember, if a system is called a system, it is probably a scam or everyone would be doing it.

---

[302] This goes doubly because smart people who are actually claimed to be "smart" have really lowered the standard of what smart means.

[303] Unless the celebrities say they are giving finical advice, then they can be looked at under finical laws.

[304] Grift Coin CITE

Manipulation by central Banks

Central banks are the antithesis of DeFi currency. Central banks have been one of the biggest voices against the adoption of cryptocurrency since its inception. They have argued that it is "nothing from nothing," "illegal currency," "scams," and "an opiate for the masses." Each time they have made these claims, the community has risen above them. However, we can never forget that central banks are not the friends of crypto. Each time a central bank adopts crypto, we need to be leery as to what they are doing.

The models used by centralized banking and DeFi banking are fundamentally opposite. While they provide some of the same services, they are doing things the opposite way. Central banks are a centralized repository for the wealth of nations, ignoring the needs of the people that make up that nation. DeFi banks are depositories for the wealth of the people, ignoring the actions of the government. This is why when central banks look as if they are supporting crypto, the community should always be looking for the wolf in sheep's clothing.

One of the greatest threats that we see in the central banks is when they act like a whale. In many cases, the banks act in a way that is the opposite of how a good-intentioned whale should act. Rather than buying in big blocks and selling in small blocks (which grows the market), central banks buy in small blocks then dump the currency in large blocks. This causes a problem as it makes the market look like a selloff. While this does not kill the market, it stifles growth, which allows interest to eat people's fiat currency reserve that is not in play.

One of the best ways that the crypto community can hedge against central banks is to invest crypto in the exchanges and DeFi banks (such as XX).[305] DeFi banks allow the system to grow away from the influence of central banks. Also, DeFi banks are offering higher interest rates (the kind of rates banks used to offer). This allows the community to set up its own finance system which is not trying to undermine the success of the crypto

---

[305] DeFi banks like Citreon are working to create a decentralized, stable backbone for the crypto finance industry.

marketplace.

Ending Manipulation to Allow Markets to Stabilize

By way of concluding this Chapter, there are some areas where the crypto community needs to grow. One of the key areas is for users and creators to associate within the market. Associations give the individuals in the market the ability to voice their opinions as a chorus rather than as a single voice. The louder the chorus, the more likely the governments of the world are to heed our call to just enforce the current laws. The more the community works together, the more chance we can make in the market.

We also need a unified approach to dealing with whales across the cryptoverse. Whales are our friends when they are functioning as traders in the markets. Whales are not our friends when they are functioning as market manipulators. The more we concentrate on this idea, the better we will be off. Exchanges and DeFi banks need methodologies for whales to buy in big blocks, but then create a method for structured selloffs that they can put big blocks on the market without the big block causing a major sell-off. It is a difficult balancing act, but one that we need for a more stable market.

Dealing with media is an easy solution, we make our own. There are already several great crypto news outlets on the market. We need to empower these news agencies to ensure that they are providing us with the information that we need. Even though many of them are run by specific crypto groups, they are still better than the mainstream media. If we frequent the best outlets in the system, the others will up their game so that people use them. The community needs to talk amongst itself and ensure that we are getting the best, up-to-date news on the market about crypto.

To deal with central banks, we have a more difficult problem. The only way for central banks to not be a threat to the crypto community is to let them fade into history. The more the community works together to ensure that businesses accept all crypto (with the conversions to their chosen crypto via the card system they use) the better it will be for the whole system. Why use fiat currency when you can use crypto. The world will be a better place when the only reason that you need to convert to fiat currency is because of taxes and yard sales.

Chapter 26: Non-Discrimination Policies

"[T]o interpret everything in terms of politics is suicidal. It is the source of most modern confusion. The crisis finds its roots elsewhere; it is a crisis of culture, a crisis of the heart and the intelligence."[306]

Maurice Girodias, a French publisher, wrote this as part of the forward of Valerie Solanas' S.C.U.M. Manifesto (1967) and while intended for different purposes, this could arguably be considered holding true in these circumstances. With cryptocurrency thinking outside of the box through our heart and intellect, we also must find new ways to utilize it for our various benefits.

Similarly, most of us are familiar with the popular phrase in the novel Animal Farm, by George Orwell that "all animals are equal, but some animals are more equal than others."[307] Here, the potential for governmental hypocrisy is acknowledged through this quotation under the facade of citizen equality, while only a small percentage actually enjoy benefits and power:

> It is important to note that eliminating discrimination does not mean removing judgment from the system. As in any marketplace of ideas, we need to take the good and leave the bad. The trick to doing this properly is not to allow our biases to dictate what is *acceptable*. We need to enter the marketplace in an egalitarian fashion, judging people only on their contributions to the system. When we look at the system, we need to take a system-agnostic pathway and look at each change with new eyes and see if it will work in the system. If it would make the system better, but cannot work in the present system, then we need to look at how we can make the system better to accommodate the new ideas.[308]

Subject matter and personal discrimination must be abolished from

---

306 Maurice Girodias (1968). Maurice Girodias. Publisher's house ppXiii.
307 Orwell, George (1945) Animal Farm. Penguin New York.
308 Ingber, Stanley (1984). "The Marketplace of Ideas: A Legitimizing Myth." Duke Law Journal at https://www.jstor.org/stable/1372344.

cyberspace. Subject matter discrimination or when someone or an organization in power takes opportunities away from another because they do not like or understand the new concept. With regulators chomping at the bit to regulate the crypto space we must ask the (sic) single question "Why?" The answer is one of the themes of this Chapter, looking at how the government's ignorance of the system is the reason that the government wants to discriminate against the system.

Personal discrimination is the other specter that haunts areas of cyberspace. Since crypto arose from the digital world, trolls moved into the system with those who want to make a better world. While trolls challenging ideas is a good thing, when they attack people because of an immutable trait they become (sic) something that we do not want in the field. Crypto has the ability to make the world a better place, one of the ways it can do this is by ending personal discrimination.

Definition

For the purposes of cryptocurrency, the concept of non-discrimination policies is to ensure that everyone in the world is treated fairly and has access to the same services including cyber security and general crypto investing.[309] Any industry in this century has some form of boilerplate terminology stating something along the lines of:

"Said organization has a policy of equal opportunity and does not discriminate in the terms, conditions, or privileges of employment on account of race, age, color, sex, national origin, physical or mental disability, or religion or otherwise as may be prohibited by federal and state law."

Harassment or intimidation of a client, staff person, or guest because of that person's race, age, color, sex, national origin, physical or mental disability, or religion is specifically prohibited and may be grounds for termination. Harassment and intimidation include abusive, foul, or threatening language or behavior.

---

[309] Hayes, *supra*.

Modern organizations are committed to maintaining a workplace that is free of any such harassment and will not tolerate discrimination against staff members, volunteers or agency clients. Issues of discriminatory treatment, harassment, or intimidation on any of these bases should immediately be reported and, if substantiated, prompt action will be taken. Yet it still happens regularly.

CoinDesk writes that "one of the founders of Ethereum, Vitalik Buterin, considered "non-discrimination and non-censorship" one of the key principles behind Ethereum's design."[310] In the same CoinDesk article, a question is pondered:

"Are cryptocurrencies sought out of distrust in fiat currencies or regulated finance?" Then follows with an argument "that a clarifying regulatory and supervisory framework for cryptocurrency markets may be beneficial for the industry in a context where cryptocurrencies are being targeted by less-educated investors and adoption is becoming widespread."

Not Discriminating Based on Nationality

One of the greatest dangers in the crypto market is that governments will start to favor crypto from their own countries. While protecting industries originating in their own nation can be a good system, converting that mentality to a global crypto can be dangerous. For crypto to work on the international stage, the market of ideas must be in play.[311] When a country focuses on a crypto that is created within its system, it is breaking down the marketplace of ideas and reducing the efficacy of the system. Market agnosticism is the only way that the system can truly become a global system.

The FreeMarkets demands that ideas be given the opportunity to succeed or the opportunity to fail. Oddly enough, it is the opportunity to fail that is

---

[310] Auer, Raphael & Terecero-Lucas, David (2021). "What Drives Crypto Users? Distrust of the System or Speculation?" CoinDesk at https://www.coindesk.com/policy/2021/10/26/what-drives-crypto-users-distrust-of-the-system-or-speculation/.

[311] Stanley, supra.

more important. When governments of the world "prop up" cryptos that have no remaining function (we assume that they had a function to start), the system suffers as a value from viable coins is drawn into these zombie coins. this also creates a problem where, when a government realizes that a coin is a lost cause, the system collapses when the government pulls its support; reducing the faith in the system.

The marketplace of ideas is the most efficient way for evolution in the system to take place. Governments that cling to the idea that failed fiat systems still work are no better than people denying evolution, gravity, or proclaiming that the earth is flat. Science demands that ideas be challenged and those bad ideas discarded, it is time that society discards the fiat currency system.

The heart and soul of this problem go back to the Orwell quote, "All animals are equal, it is just some animals are more equal."[312] In the case of countries manipulating cryptos, "All cryptos are equal, it is just our cryptos are more equal." This process of putting a nation's full faith and credit on the scales of the marketplace can break the balance of the coins in the cryptoverse, even if just in that particular nation. This is why market agnosticism is so important.

Not Discriminating Based on Token/Coin

Another common problem that we see is the government's discrimination based on coins. The world was excited when El Salvador chose to allow Bitcoin to be legal tender.[313] While embracing crypto was a great idea, the idea to select on crypto (especially bitcoin) was folly. For the cryptoverse to work properly, the adoption of coins should be multilateral, not specific, this allows for the market to adapt as the market changes. The use of select exchanges, and all the coins that they allow on them, is more efficient for a replacement of legal tender.

---

[312] Orwell, Supra.

[313] Editor (2021). "El Salvador President Says It's 'Game Over' for Fiat Currency." NASDAQ at https://www.nasdaq.com/articles/el-salvador-president-says-its-game-over-for-fiat-currency.

The choice of El Salvador to use bitcoin was monumental.[314] While not a major world economy, El Salvador was the first nation to accept crypto as legal tender. This allowed the world to see that crypto was able to be used, specifically as a proof of concept. Overall, the experiment has been quite successful. Millions of people in the country have adopted the system as El Salvador moves forward into the digital age.

Though the move to adopt bitcoin was monumental, there are severe problems with how it was adopted. First of all, the coins are massive. People are conducting everyday transactions in ten-thousandths of a coin. Second, the currency they chose, while the biggest in the world, is un-staked. This is problematic as there may, someday, be a bitcoin crash because the transitional value of the coin cannot sustain the market value. Finally, limiting the legal tender to one area of the cryptoverse limits the ability of the country to pivot. Changing direction in the digital world is important, and El Salvador has both feet planted securely in bitcoin.

The "better way" to deal with this problem is to adopt a group of exchanges, rather than a single provider. The soul of cryptocurrency is the decentralized nature of the system. Choosing one piece and making it central is counter viewing the methodology of crypto. Selecting several exchanges and DeFi banks allows the people of the country to use whatever crypto those systems support, then it can be converted into the crypto that the business wants. Like the money changes at the airports, when the exchanges are allowed to make these transactions possible, anyone can use any supported currency that they want to make business easier. IF countries following in El Salvador's footsteps of accepting crypto adopt these policies, then the world can be crypto compliant almost overnight (there is a lag for updating software in business.)!

Not Discriminating on Race, Creed, Sex, Religion, or Ethnicity

Oh, the eyes of the woke when they realize that cancel culture is just another manifestation of racism and discrimination on the market. 100 years ago, people were banned based on race, their feelings on marriage,

---

[314] *Id.*

and what religion they followed. In 2022, people are banned based on their race, their feelings on marriage, and what religion they follow. Bigotry is always and will always be evil. Until society realized that the only acceptable form of judgment is on "what people do" not "who people are" we will always have problems in society.

Discrimination, on its own, is not a bad thing. We discriminate when we take one bottle of milk over another bottle of milk in the store. We discriminate when we pick one movie over another. We discriminate when we choose which shoe to put on first. Discrimination and judgment are normal parts of making choices. The area where discrimination becomes problematic is when we made decisions based on illogical metrics. This is when we see discrimination that actually hurts people.

Discrimination on race, creed, sex, religion, or ethnicity has no place in the crypto market. Society has moved beyond this type of bigotry, and the digital community cannot allow the system to backslide. This is why the "woke" movement is so dangerous, it is simply the racism of the early 20th century rebranded as "progressiveness." Each person is equal (no Orwellian quote here). It is our actions that distinguish us. Who we are born is much less important than the choices we make, and those that want to base their hate on how a person was born are the problem in this world?

That being said, discrimination on what people do is completely legit. Pedophiles should be executed or sent to jail for life if they touch a kid- no argument. Criminals who commit fraud should be banned from access to any financial platform or position of trust for the rest of their lives- no argument. As humans, there is no problem in discriminating against people who do bad things for bad reasons (and we also have to discriminate by looking at people "who do bad things for good reasons and good things for bad reasons"), but this should be our focus in making choices, not who people are born as.[315]

---

[315] We also need to quite "re-justifying" bad actors. Just because someone is in a bad situation does not mean that they are "born that way." Bad conditions can lead to bad choices, but they are still bad choices. Giving people a free pass for

Not Discriminating on Systematic Issues

One of the greatest problems we see in society is mob rule. Plato said that "democracy is the lowest form of government."[316] The reason for this is that the prejudice of the mob can make its way into the institutions of a government. Those crying for "pure democracy" do not understand that it is the democracy of the past that created the "systematic racism" that they are crying out against. The only way for the system to correct is by allowing people a voice in politics, economics, and the community. Crypto is a pathway to all three.

The infiltration of prejudice into systematic institutions is because "equity" replaces "egalitarianism" in hiring. The best candidate for a job should always be the person hired. This should be done regardless of race, creed, religion, sex, or ethnicity. However, humans have a natural bias, that bias built its way into companies until the government decided that it needed to step in. As a result, the ham-handed nature of the government forced people to hire based on the selfsame categories that they were decrying.[317]

Ironically, it was "pure democracy" that caused these problems. Originally, people were hiring people based on discriminatory policies. They were doing this across the country, so the majority rule was discrimination (this happened in other countries as well). People realized that this was a bad idea, and rather than fixing the problem, they turned to the government

---

Their actions because of how they were raised is problematic. Even worse is when we use a condition a person has as an excuse for why they "should be allowed" to act out. Everyone makes choices, if they make bad choices (illegal) then they should face justice, not have someone give them a pass because they had a hard time so they can give someone else (who is not a bad actor) a harder life.

[316] Illing, Sean (2016). "The People's Tyrant: What Plato can teach us about Donald Trump." Vox at https://www.vox.com/policy-and-politics/2016/11/7/13512960/donald-trump-plato-democracy-tyranny-fascism-2016-elections. Illig's analysis is shaded wrongfully, but the initial aspect of Plato's analysis is correct. Any politician elected by popular vote can be a tyrant, which is why a republic where the representatives elect a chief executive who has extremely restricted powers is more efficient than any democracy. LGB.

[317] Wexlaw at https://www.law.cornell.edu/wex/affirmative_action,

for regulation. The government, in its normal inept way, used the same criteria, just changed the weighting. This resulted in more discrimination and angry people. As the government attempted to regulate this (this time through the courts) they codified that "All people are equal, just some people are more equal than others" through standards of discrimination review, and the entire system became a shell game.

The only way for the system to be corrected is by giving people a voice. Crypto gives people a voice in their politics and it allows people to donate to candidates that they support. Crypto gives people economic power, moving away from the central banking cartels. Finally crypto gives people community power, as the wealth of the world is not centered on Wallstreet, it is centered on the main street.[318]

Conclusion

Do not ever let someone tell you not to judge, that is a bad idea. Smart people tell you not to judge on unfair standards because people will use those same standards to judge you.[319] Judgment and discernment are some of the reasons why humans are successful in life. Lower animals do not have the same ability to make decisions that we have, and thus they do not do as well as we do. As we watch the chimpanzees and apes make war, we realize that society develops as we learn to control our choices.[320] It is now our time to control our discrimination.

Crypto can be the nexus that brings us past the discrimination that has hampered humanity for the last thousand years. If we are to thrive as a civilization and reach out to the stars, then our choices must be based on fact and reality- not bygone myths of the superiority of one group over another. We are a human race and a Terran people. Turning our attention

---

[318] Which is odd that Elizabeth Warren, who uses the "Wallstreet, not Mainstreet" comment all the time hates cryptos. Maybe she wants the money moved from Wallstreet to her street.

[319] Mattew 7:1.

[320] Neld, David (2021). "Chimps and Gorillas Seen Going to War in the Wild for the First Time." Science Alert at https://www.sciencealert.com/scientists-just-caught-chimps-and-gorillas-going-to-war-in-the-wild-for-the-first-time.

from things as inconsequential as skin color and birthplace is vital for our success. Let us turn our choices toward the criminals that prey on our communities, the politicians who prey on our dreams, and the banks that prey on our wealth. Dealing with these areas of corruption will be much more effective than hating someone because they have a better tan, a different ancestor, or hope their voices are heard by a deity who may be different than ours.

Diversity is our strength; we need to realize that. Discrimination based on silly things is silly in the digital world. Silliness gets us nowhere. The system of crypto needs to welcome all good actors and reject all bad actors. Just like you cannot judge a book by its cover (except this book because our cover is awesome), you cannot judge a person before you see their work product. Everyone deserves a chance-Trust but verify.

Chapter 27: Internal Compliance to Ensure that Money Laundering is Not Taking Place

Internal compliance is often referred to as self-regulation in the crypto world. For those purposes, this book interchanges the two terms. The juxtaposition of the two terms is due to the way the system handles the terminology. As government regulators attempt to move more regulations into the industry, the targets for the industry to comply with are continually shifted. By merging the terminology in the lexicon of the field, we limit one of the tools that corrupt regulators use to force outside views on the industry.

> International Organization of Securities Commissions (IOSCO) has defined a set of elements that comprise self-regulation.[321] These include transparency and accountability, contractual relationships, and coordination, and information sharing. Additionally, Within the context of cryptocurrencies, self-regulation is the establishment of guidelines, industry organizations, and a code of conduct for market participants to operate businesses within the ecosystem. Those guidelines can span a broad spectrum, from knowing your customers (KYC) to maintaining transparency to ensuring security against hacks.[322]

The interjections by governments and other regulatory bodies work as excellent suggestions; however, these rules need to be brought into effect by the industry (across jurisdictions) for them to be effective.

Government regulatory agencies can offer more oversight for self-regulation agencies. For example, major rules promulgated by NFA (the National Futures Association) are approved by the CFTC.[323] At the same time, NFA has the authority to audit and regulate non-clearing futures Clearing Merchants (FCMs).[324] These were spelled out in a recent

---

[321] See IOSCO.
[322] *Id.*
[323] *Id.*
[324] Hayes, Supra.

document. With the new prospects of regulation for cryptocurrency by government agencies, many also fear the freedom that investors found from crypto's self-regulatory beginnings may be at risk. Regulation, however, "might offer a way out for exchanges to clean up their act."[325] The supposition is that legitimate exchanges are not acting in the best interest of their customers, which is not true. As we have seen in 2021, the good exchanges thrived on the market whereas the bad exchanges started to fade away.

Money Laundering

The SEC (in the United States) has a cryptocurrency working group, which include economists and technologists and consult in order to predict the future directions of digital currencies.[326] "The basic concept of money laundering revolves around transforming dirty money into clean money or in a more formal way, money laundering is the process of making a large amount of money generated through illegal activity appear to have earned through legitimate sources."[327] Unfortunately for the SEC analysis, there is more complexity to money laundering than the simple, first year of college, explanation to the senate.

If we turn to the digital community we find

> Money laundering is generally accomplished through currency exchanges, wire transfers, smurfing, and shell companies. Moreover, globalization and digitalization have expanded the capabilities of money launderers, making it more difficult to identify the source of the transaction. Online banking, P2P services, money exchange businesses, and now cryptocurrency have made it difficult to detect the illegal transfer of money.

One of the key factors of modern money laundering is that the system

---

[325] *Id.*

[326] Sharma, Rakesh (2019). "SEC Chair Testified About Cryptocurrency Regulation Before Senate." Investopedia at https://www.investopedia.com/news/no-surprises-sec-and-cftc-chairs-congressional-testimony-cryptocurrency-regulation/.

[327] *Id.*

needs to be untraceable, this is not present in crypto as transactions are validated by multiple sources and preserved in transaction records on the blockchain.

In the early years of crypto, statements like the following from "The Chain" may have been true, "[Cryptocurrency] has its pros but it has also led to an increase in fraudulent activities in the financial industry. To launder money through cryptocurrency, criminals open up an online account with a digital currency exchange that also accepts fiat currency from conventional bank accounts. Then they cleanse their illegal assets by moving them into the system. Money is moved from one crypto exchange to another with an untraceable trail due to the anonymity factor. They obscure the origin of the cryptocurrency and once that is done then they integrate the currency into the legal financial system. Criminals also use cryptocurrency to launder money from theft and gambling."[328]

Scams and gambling will always be present, but laundering money is much easier (and less traceable) through processes such as earl world art and lobbying. The criminal element will always be an element in every space, but crypto seems to dilute that threat as money launderers do not want a set of transaction records leading right back to them

The Use of Assets to Money Launder

To understand why the accusation of money laundering is such a problem, the community needs to understand how money laundering works. In money laundering, a criminal has "dirty money," the amount is irrelevant. Because of current government interference in personal finance, one of the side effects is that when a large amount of money comes into your possession, the government feels entitled to know how you got the money. This leaves criminals with a quandary, "How do I convert my ill-gotten gains into legitimate income without the government auditing me."

By and large, the most common way for criminals to do this is to bribe

---

[328] Efron, James (2020). "Video KYC- A Digital Solution for Digital Currency." Chain at https://vocal.media/theChain/video-kyc-a-digital-solution-for-digital-currency.

government officials. Around the world, there are those in power who will take a cut to make the money look legitimate. In some countries is this done through lobbying, some countries this is done through nepotism, and in some countries is still the old "cash handoff" method. One must question whether the "cash handoff" method or the lobbying method was more civilized, in many cases the lobbying method is worse because it seems to have the inherent legitimization of corruption.

When someone cannot find a corrupt politician or they simply do not want to pay what the politician is asking, then they "clean the money" some other way. The most common way to do this is through a cash business. A cash business is a business where most of the payments are made via fiat currency, rather than a digital transaction such as a credit card or a debit card. The reason for this is that the cash creates limited records in regard to the other methods. When a person pays cash then the only record is the receipt, no bank record or credit card statement is ever created. This allows the customer to "overpay" and allows the money to move through the business's system. The money then shows up on the books, no one ever sees what was "bought" with the money, and the criminals can then declare their ill-gotten gains on their taxes.

As you can see, there are many problems with this when crypto is involved. First, there are transaction records for each transaction converting crypto to fiat currency. This limits the criminal to use their ill-gotten gains to purchase things via crypto (not entirely a problem). If they attempt to "wash" the money, the source accounts and the destination accounts are part of the transaction record (regardless of the system that they are on). This allows forensic investigators to "follow the money." For those criminals that are dumb enough to use legitimate exchanges, their identities (or the identities of their scapegoats) must be registered with government regulators. This means that they can be tracked down quite easily. It is almost as if governments are accusing crypto companies of being compliant with money laundering to push money launderers into the space so that they can catch the launderers and attack crypto all in one fell swoop (like governments did with gambling, marijuana, alcohol, and various other elements).

Triangulation of Information

An added level of security is the triangulation of the system. Not only are transactions validated by the sender and the receiver, but they are also validated by the system. While this may seem like a minor issue to most people (who used banks to validate transactions all the time), this can be a problem for the criminal element. Criminals tend not to trust people outside their group. Now players add new transactions. The only way that this would work for criminals is if there is a movie-style criminal DeFi bank.

First, criminals tend to distrust everyone, even each other. When large amounts of money are transferred, they like the money to be cleaned money so they can use bank validation systems. When dirty money is transferred, there is a lot of counting and looking over each other's shoulders in the process. Without faith in the system, the system needs more complex validation measures. Criminal enterprises have created methods in the traditional market to validate transactions and increase "honesty."

When a system changes, such as the crypto market, there is always a time for the market to be tested to see if it is secure and confidential. Without question, the crypto market is secure; however, the market is not confidential in the traditional sense. Not only does a third-party AI confirm all transactions (which most criminals can accept as computers are not squealers), but the transaction record is available for all people to see. This enables the world to look in on their dealings, something that criminals really do not like.

The only solution for this problem (for the criminals) is for the creation of a criminal DeFi bank. While this would be effective for the purposes of the criminals, the nature of the institution would quickly spread across the cryptoverse. A criminal bank is only useful if criminals and corrupt government officials know that it is a criminal institution. If regular people know this, they can effectively "cancel" the bank by forcing exchanges and other banks to refuse transaction requests. Rather than all of the rigmarole of new government regulations, the system can protect the system by force of the community.

The digital record and preventing crime

The greatest asset that we have in the cryptoverse is the digital record. No matter how much congressional committees and government regulators around the world accuse the system of being corrupt, we can show the digital record to show that the system is agnostic to the intent of the users. The system is neutral in all transactions, as long as the smart contract is written properly, all legal transactions (in the eyes of the contract) are complete, all illegal actions are rejected.

This brings up a unique quandary for governments around the world. If the system is, for all intents and purposes incorruptible, then it means that the bad actors fall into another category, the users. Since every user is a citizen of a country around the world, and any laws being broken originate in those countries, then it is the duty of the countries to deal with this problem- under existing law. The places the burden of action squarely on the shoulders of the governments of the world, and their attempt to regulate the industry is simply an effort to shirk this responsibility.

New regulations in this space do nothing. Governments are already not enforcing money laundering laws in cyberspace (whether intentionally or unintentionally). If they enforced those laws, then the system would work even more smoothly. Money laundering is a crime. Theft is a crime. Fraud is a crime. If the governments were willing to work with the cryptoverse, then these bad actors could be arrested and removed from the system. Until the government deals with its lack of enforcement of current laws in spaces it does understand, then it has no business making new laws in a space that it does not understand.[329]

---

[329] Friedmann, Rebecca (2021). "Unpacking the Government's Cryptocurrency Regulatory and Enforcement Agenda." JDSupra at https://www.jdsupra.com/legalnews/unpacking-the-government-s-1312122/.

Part II: Section III

Security Issues

Introduction to Part II Section III

Security is one of those issues that will be ever-present within the space of cryptocurrency. People see the billions of bits of data flying back and forth as an easy target for manipulation and theft. The truth of the matter is that crypto is one of the most secure assets on the market today. Because of the validation process in each transaction, people are actually more secure in crypto transactions than they are at their regular bank. The difficulty in crypto, therefore, is because of the human element. This is the element where most security breaches happen- this is also the easiest to sure up.

When we are looking at security requirements for the system, the current system of laws gives us a good framework. While the community should establish its own laws, we should not disallow the past from helping us make a better system. As a result, we need to build with the knowledge of what has come before us, so that we can be prepared for what lies ahead of us. To that end, we need to learn that each trader needs to work to ensure that the system is as secure as possible. That means learning how to keep their passwords, keys, and wallets secure.

When we look at how to manage our digital assets, we need to realize that there are institutions that will be needed to protect assets. Chief among these institutions are the DeFi banks and the exchanges where you go to work with your crypto. As the system evolves these systems are going to offer new, secure instruments to improve our access to the community. Exchanges will offer more derivatives. Banks will offer Cds, Bonds, and Cold Storage. Each of these products must be secure and each of us must work to help maintain the security.

The biggest movement that we need to see in the security of our cryptocurrency is redundant access paths to the system. Any person should be able to access their wealth when they need it. While it may not always be instant, there needs to be a path where a person can start the process. Maintenance windows are one of the biggest challenges in this area; however, by linking banks and exchanges with Global Exchange Tokens (GETs), we can close those windows of time when we cannot access our crypto. The more we interconnect through spiderweb bridging, the better the system will be.

Though security is not one of those areas that everyone wants to talk about, it is an area that we need to talk about. In the following three Chapters, we build the case for each type of security needed. This is not a "how-to" guide for security (which often turn out to be "how-to" guides for bank robbers); this is simply an explanation of how we can build the best system. The experts in security will be able to build on the backbone that already exists, we just need to make sure that the regulators do not prevent them from protecting our assets.

Chapter 28: Security Requirements

When you build, it is often most important that you check out the zoning for your area. Once upon a time, you could build whatever you wanted however you wanted and no one would say a thing about it. Those days are over. Governments have created the landscape in which we need to operate via contract law, at least until there is some virtual sovereignty. This means that we need to be aware of the world around us as the community makes its new security rules. Right now, we have good security; however, security is only as good as the next hacker. That means that we need to build the system constantly to ensure that virtual wealth stays in our real accounts.

In this Chapter, we are going to look at the security landscape that currently exists. Military encryption, bank encryption, video game encryption, each have their own level of security. Understanding which type of security measures your system has (or your banking system) can help you understand how tedious it will be to access your account and how hard it will be for others to access your accounts. These are the systems that are in place under the government regime, this is where we start building.

Next, we take a moment to talk about being better than the best. Having the best current security can often be the difference between being the target and being left alone. Just like the guy who has a pistol on his hip will not be the first target for a robber, a company with good security protocol will be an unlikely target for hackers. As a community, we need to be the guy with a self-defense AR-10 walking around.[330] We want the world to know that the crypto community stands behind its members and that attacking one part of the system is attacking all parts of the system.

Beyond working together to ensure that the standards are set, we also need to work together to ensure that the standards are met. New coins, tokens, banks, and exchanges will always be entering the market. As they

[330] I chose an AR 10 here because we all know that they are 5 ARs safer than an AR 15.

enter into the market, we need to ensure that they are meeting or beating the current security levels for the industry. Only then can we be assured that the system will continue to grow.

Security should not be a scary thing for the crypto community, it should be something that we understand is a necessity and are willing to work to build. The more we do as a community to ensure that the security is there, the less involvement we will see from the government. We all know that the government will be the biggest retarding factor for the system; let up hope that we can do a good enough job to keep them from infringing on the market.

Government Security Measures

Cybersecurity is one of those elements where you have many people looking at the best type of security and saying why their type of security is better. The most common terms that you will hear when dealing with cyber security are bank-level encryption, military-level encryption, and game level encryption. Military level encryption is an advanced encryption standard that uses 256-bit encryption.[331] Banks also use an AES 256 model as the base encryption level; however, banks usually add another level of security on top of the AES 256 model to increase the stability.[332] Gaming industry encryption is an advanced form of bank-level security. They also use the enhanced AES 256 systems that the banks are using for purchase modeling but also add other portal systems to protect the system. Gaming level security can also have a portal to get into the network, a portal to get into the game, and a portal to get into guilds/clans, each having 64–256-bit security. In most cases, it is harder to hack your younger brother's game system clan than it is to hack a basic military system.

When we look at the crypto markets, many of them are based on the gamer model of security. The underlying AES system is a 256 system. Many

[331] Scott, Benjamin (2020). "Military Grade Encryption." Nord Pass at https://nordpass.com/blog/military-grade-encryption-explained/.
[332] Alarm New England (2021). "How Safe is Bank Level Encryption?" ANE at https://www.alarmnewengland.com/blog/bank-level-encryption.

systems allow you to put a biometric scan from your device on top of this system. When wallets are involved an additional level of encryption is entered on the top of the system. In many cases, this is a dual-factor authentication with two parties holding independent keys. The owner of the account generally has a password, functioning as the initial key, then the bank or exchange has the wallet key, which functions as the second key. Some groups have higher-level security, structured groups within your own account, which would, in turn, have another 256-bit encryption on them.

When looking at what the government dictates, you have five levels of security. These are network security, which entails the physical, technical, and administrative security of a system.[333] Endpoint security, which would be firewalls on the systems you use (which operate in the background of your devices, hopefully).[334] Cloud Security, which deals with exchange protocols.[335] Application security, which is the actual system that you are using.[336] Finally, there is identity security linking your access to the human element- which can be the biggest weakness of all in a cybersecurity system.[337]

Further, we are seeing great advancements in security, moving beyond simple encryption to smart security. Systems such as the CMMC framework are allowing companies to enhance their security well beyond what is currently in use today.[338] New integrative models (along with personnel training) can enable a system to have a much higher level of security than has been used for the last few years.

---

[333] Sail Point (2021). "Five types of cyber security" Sail Point at https://www.sailpoint.com/identity-library/five-types-of-cybersecurity/?gclid=CjwKCAiAzrWOBhBjEiwAq85QZ9KZ4FrWKHeSbzuyiowep_FMp5I086JukhbqzvHjVlkyexJpkgSWcxoC-IgQAvD_BwE.

[334] *Id.*

[335] *Id.*

[336] *Id.*

[337] *Id.*

[338] Horan, Martin (2020). "The levels of cybersecurity maturity Model Certification." CMMC at https://www.ftptoday.com/blog/levels-cmmc.

Unified Security

While the government sets the current standards for best practices in the system, the crypto community has the best minds in the world working as part of the system. Best practices simply are not good enough for the future of all wealth in the world and metaverse. This means that the current best practices are just a baseline, we need to do better because we can do better. Each time a new great mind joins the crypto community, there is the potential that the security and the system itself can get better.

One of the best assets that the crypto community has for the development of a better security system is the development of spiderweb bridging. Being able to securely link different platforms through systems design, not code allows for the system to have multiple operating systems. For a hacker to breach the access, they either have to breach the code of each system or break down the system itself. Therefore, the simple nature of spiderweb bridging is so important. The more simple a system is, the harder it is to hack.

When looking at enhancing security features for a system, the first breach that we need to look at is the people in the system. The community of crypto users needs to realize that they are the greatest weakness of the system. Why would a hacker spend months trying to hack top-level encryption, when they can simply send a fishing email and get a person's password to get access to the system. The human element is the greatest strength of the system but also the greatest weakness.

This is why the community must work together to educate members of the community about the different scams out there. One person giving a scammer access to a system can compromise the whole system. One worker at a DeFi bank can give access to a system too. This is why new and novice users need to be trained in protocols on how to keep others away from your data. When all of us have data saved on our devices, our lives are vulnerable to someone just picking up our devices. Make sure to take care of your system.

Beyond this, we need the community to keep everyone appraised of what is going on. New viruses, new worms, and new scams will always be coming out. The faster the community can respond to these elements, the better. We need to have a network that creates both a whitelist and blacklist of security protocols to ensure that the system is as secure as it can be.

Better than Best Practices

Working together means another thing; that we need to accept the tedium of proper security when we are working within the community. The faster the community accepts this, the faster the system will be secure. We all hate entering our passwords to get into something, we hate it, even more, when we have to authenticate the system; however, we all need to understand that this is keeping our wealth secure. The more levels of protection we use, the better we can be.

While the standard 256-bit encryption is a great way to start a system, we need to have a little more than that to be better than the best practices. One of the best ways to help with this is by having a code on all your devices. Even if you have a computer that sits at your home, it is good to have the financial section of your system behind a password. This goes double for when you have your financial setup on your phone. Anytime someone can access your system easily, it takes them one step closer to accessing your wealth.

If you have a device that allows you to set up facial recognition, then consider it. I know there were issues with ladies not being able to access their phones because they have their makeup on or guys not being able to access their phones when they shave, but suck it up, people. Be less vain, be proud of who you are. Keep one look. If you care about your wealth, then this should be a small price to pay for an extra level of security.

Biometrics are also available on some devices. While the early-level biometrics was a little sketchy, the modern versions of them seem to work quite well. If you have the option to set up biometrics on your device, it is a good idea to do it. This makes it harder for other people to access and prevents accidental exposure to hackers.

Finally, do not be an idiot with your password. The times of it being fun to have "12345" are over. It is no longer what an idiot would have on his luggage, it is what an idiot has on his computer. Make sure that your password has capital letters, lowercase letters, some numbers, and some symbols. Generally, you want to avoid names and birthdays. Also, keep your password access questions close, do not participate in internet games where you say what your first car is, that is usually an access question.

Security is the Heart of Faith in the System

Faith in the system is what keeps it a free system. When people are not whining about the system, the government does not need to get involved with the system. It is when there is a problem that people start to ask their representatives for protection. The community has the ability to protect itself, we need to make sure that we work together to realize this.

Take the time to talk to people in your groups about security. If you are in a trading group, homeowners association, or any other group, have a security guy or gal come in to talk. Usually, they are not very expensive and can give you a wealth of knowledge in a half-hour speech. We spend so much money buying state-of-the-art systems, then locking them down with passwords like "Sex123" or "Money2021$$$$." Even worse is when people put passwords on Post-it on their computer. These are security no-nos that can lose you all your investments.

When having a security consultant come in to talk to you, make sure that they talk about emails and jump drives. Emails are a great way for a hacker to get into your network. Once link that you click on can be a virus coming into your system. Another link can be you giving them access to change data on the system. Always beware of what is going on through your emails.

Jump drives are another source of an information breach. When you plug a zip drive into your computer, it exchanges data with your computer. It is just like having sex with a stranger when you allow someone to put an unverified drive into your computer. This can drop a virus or steal information at a very quick rate. Remember, we built the jump drives to transfer data quickly, hackers can allow them to access your system very quickly too.

You are the first line of defense in a system. Learn about your system and how to protect it. Yes, some of the steps are tedious and boring, but they keep you safe. You can pay the best security in the world to back up your system, but if you are not working on the front end to make sure that the system is functioning, then you may as well post the key to your digital wallet on a billboard in Times Square.

Chapter 29: Management of Crypto Holding Agencies (Wallet and Keys)

When it comes to the management of a person's personal wealth, people tend to get a little picky. They want universal access to their money, and they want it now. One of the problems with this is that security means giving up some of your access. People need to have faith in the systems in which they place their money, the crypto institutions need to earn this faith from the people. The sooner we allow this system to function properly, the faster this system can move to the next level.

The biggest problem facing many institutions right now is the key and wallet myth. So many OG investors are spouting this myth acting like the banks and brokerages they use to give them instant access to their money, they do not. No financial institution works on a system without some validation. To dispel this myth, people need to realize that security means giving up some of their "ease of access" to their wealth. This can be something as simple as accepting the maintenance window each week, or something as complex as four-level security.

Going hand in hand with the security of the system, people need to have faith in the institutions that they are using. As a community, we need to build exchange and DeFi systems that people can believe in. Otherwise, the system will stagnate. Institutions, for their part, need to earn the confidence of the people who use them. This will allow more people to use the system and allow a bright crypto future for all users.

The lock and the key have always been very important parts of any financial system. With crypto, we are not changing this model. There will always be bad people out there who want to take what they did not earn; good security helps us prevent that. Each step we take towards better security is a step towards a better cryptoverse, and this is one of the best reasons governments will have to not regulate an already successful market.

The Key and Wallet Myth

Stop me if you heard this one, "If you do not have the key to your account, you really do not own the account." This is one of the most common myths that we see in the cryptoverse about how holdings are done. This falsehood is problematic on so many levels, it is very difficult to understand where to begin. When someone says this to you, try not to argue with them. They have already shown that they do not know what they are talking about and should not be in the field of finance, just give them an economics book (or this book) and send them on their way.[339]

In the real world, you do not have access to your money unless it is in your pocket. In some cases, your money will be at home, in other cases, it will be on a credit card, but usually, you do not have immediate access to your wealth. If you have your money in a bank, then you rely on them to hold the key. If your wealth is in your paycheck, you need the person who cashes the check. Each of these people has their own validation and security policies. We are beholden to them to access our wealth.

When you have your crypto stored in an exchange or a bank, then you want them to hold one of the keys. This dual-factor authentication is an extra level of security that can allow you peace of mind. Just like a nuclear key, you want two people to have it. In this way, if you make a mistake, there is still one level of defense to ensure that you can save your money. As we have noted, one mistake in crypto can be deadly, as a transaction once completed cannot be revoked.

When someone challenges you with the idea that "not holding the key means you do not have ownership of your account," it is hard to convince them otherwise. These people do not understand the concept of account ownership. 100 years ago, these would be the same people storing their money in a mattress in their house, then crying when the house caught fire. Banks have been around so that there can be a second level of validation for an account. In the crypto world, DeFi banks and exchanges have assumed this mantle. You cannot expect extra security then complain when the security does its job.

---

[339] If you do give them this book, make sure to get another one for your shelf.

Security Means Giving up Some Access.

As a discipline, security is the process of giving up some access for better protection. When you place security on your house, you give up speed of access for better protection. When you secure your computer, you do the same thing. Locking your car, chaining/caging your pet, even accepting police in the world, all mean giving up a modicum of access for a pound of peace of mind. Now any community needs to know where to draw the line, but it is a line that must be drawn for the success of society.

One of the easiest examples of security is the multi-level security of your home. Let's start with the most basic level of security, the walls. Walls have been a valuable part of security since the dawn of time. Walls keep animals out, keep the heat (or cool) in, and protect us from the weather. They are generally a good thing. In modern homes, there are different levels of walls depending on where you live. In good communities, they are made of drywall and siding, in more dangerous communities they can be made of concrete. The level of security you need is based on what is inside and who is outside. In the digital world, we have walls. These are the basic system elements that keep people out. These are "dumb" defenses, nothing fancy, they are just there to stop others.

At some point in history, people realized that it is easier to get into a place if it had a door on it. Door are holes in walls with some covering, for those of you who do not know that. In the computer world, we generally call these "portals" or "logins." These are simply access points through the wall through which traffic flows. Portals do not care who comes in, nor does a login (as long as you have a password). Therefore, portals would just be a door, and logins would be a door with a guy standing there asking for IDs.

As security evolved, the need for the guy at the door diminished (though was not eliminated). When locks were created, a person could control who entered into and out of their home with a small device. This device was only as full proof as to the person who was using it. If you gave away your key, then someone else can get in. In the digital world, this is your key or password. Unlike the guy who just validates if you are allowed in or out, the key and password also validate what you are allowed to do in the system.

Homes evolved even more to have private security. Private security has the ability to place more protection on your home. You have windows, they protect them. You have other doors, you protect them. These can be active or passive systems. Active systems have a person who is looking at what is going on within your system. Passive systems use mechanical (or code) to ensure that only those who are supposed to use the system are using it. In the digital world, this can be the blockchain confirming transactions (passive), or a dedicated specialist who works with you on your account (active).

As each level of security grew, we gave up a little access. Walls made it harder to get into our places than the open world. When we made doors to fix that, it became easier, but then others could get in. Therefore, humans created locks to make this easier. Locks had keys, which gave up a little access but it was a good tradeoff. Eventually, we created methods to protect other access points. In the digital world, each access point, and each level needs protection. This means that you need to have some way of getting in. If we want our wealth to be safe, we need to accept a little bit of security.

People Need to Have Faith In institutions

Just like any other institutions, people need to have faith in crypto institution. People make a conscious decision on whether a system's security meets their needs. We do this through two methods, record and what we see. The record is what the world tells us the security is worth. The visual is what we see going on in the system. Combined, they allow a person to make an educated decision on what is a good system and what is not.

One of the first elements that you need to understand about faith is that there needs to be enough good that we can see to give us confidence in what we cannot see. People who are system agnostic tend to say that no system is secure because there is always some hypothetical boogeyman that is lurking in the shadows. Likewise, there are people who will accept any security without any proof. This simulates the real world, where atheists do not believe in anything and zealots will believe everything. Faith is a balance of taking what you see and believing what you cannot, based on logical deduction.

Validation is one of the important elements of faith in a community. If we see others around us that know a system is good and can explain why it is a good idea. Learning from the mistakes of others is always less expensive than making the mistake on your own. Having a good community that can tell you when something is working and when something is not working will allow you to improve a system more quickly.

Looking for problems on your own is also something that should not be outsourced. While you cannot live in a world where you simply let hypotheticals keep you locked in your house, there is a need to work within a system to be better. If you were worried about getting COVID, then you had several options. The first was to hide from the world. This was effective, but many of these people still got sick. The second option gave you more freedom but had more risk- that was wearing a mask. The third option gave you the most freedom but also was problematic. The vaccine was effective (letting someone else set up your immune system), but it did not work as well as the natural immunity from getting the diseases. Therefore, millions of people with the vaccine got Delta and Omicron because we have not learned to program the human system as well as nature can.

Faith is a system that should not be given blindly, but we should also not be obstinate in looking at a system thinking of everything that could go wrong, however unlikely. This is one of the reasons that we use banks to store our wealth. They think of the most common things that may affect us, they have insurance for the rest. This creates a more stable system and moves the world forward; we can do the same with the cryptoverse and the metaverse.

Institutions need to Earn this Faith

On the side of the institutions, they need to earn the faith that we give them. We cannot live in a world where we give blind faith in authority because people tell us to, that is how we ended up with government fiat. Institutions need to publish guidelines to let us know where our funds are and how they are being used. These same institutions need to let us know how we will access our funds and our wealth. The more information that the institutions give to the people, the more the people can make educated decisions to use the system.

Blind faith has led us down the primrose path to the central banking cartels. When looking at good religion, you need to look at whether they give you the choice to be faithful or not. Many would argue that Bad religions say, "do this, or I will kill you." Good religions say, "do this because you love God." Finance works the same way. If a government says "this is valuable because we say it is valuable, challenge us and you go to jail." That tends to be a bad system. Good economic systems say, "We agree this has value, and accept challenges to it."

The better the information provided by the system, the better the system will be. Institutions can help educate the people using their products, this will allow the system to grow based on an educated mass. Rather than follow the government system of indoctrination, people should be challenging the system to be better all the time. Each new idea that enters the system is not a threat, it is simply a development in the system.

The crypto community is a team working together for a better system while we all make income off of the development. Bringing strong institutions like banks and exchanges into the mix allows the system to bring in new people. New people mean new money. New money means new growth. We get bigger through being better, and institutions keeping people informed on how the system works helps us get better.

Chapter 30 Multiple Access Paths (Preventing Lockouts)

One of the lead problems that people see with cryptocurrency is the inability to access their accounts during updates and lockdowns. For some reason, central banks tell people that if they cannot access their monies 24 hours a day, that they are somehow being cheated. This is odd because the reserve banks do not operate 24-hours a day, most of them are limited to an 8-hour day. Meanwhile, crypto exchanges and DeFi banks are known for only having one hour a day or one hour a week set aside for maintenance (basically to keep the banks up to date). While this myth is one that banks are spreading, there is the issue of access to wealth that needs to be discussed to see the future of crypto.

This Chapter first looks at why people need unrestricted access to their wealth. The banking industry has always been a little shady in its ability to have several people own the same piece of currency at once. While the blockchain prevents this from being a problem in crypto, it is still something that is on people's minds. This is why access is such an important factor in a field that is changing as rapidly as crypto.

The two primary methods of accessing crypto wealth are through the exchange and the DeFi banks. When you have a wallet, you are accessing it through the chain- so this is like money you have stored at home. When looking at these two parallel systems, you will see that the main issues are withdrawals, moving of the money, storage solutions, and card usage. Because they are handled differently in each medium, they will be discussed separately; however, because they are the same, in theory, they have a huge upside of being integrated.

The Chapter concludes with a discussion of how banks and exchanges can work together to increase the access people have to their accounts. While in the future maintenance periods may be shortened, they will always be there- so there will always be a time when it is difficult to make large trades; however, as the system evolves people will still have access to their accounts- just through different means. Building a more robust system of access can help alleviate the concerns of the naysayers and increase faith in the system.

The Need for People to Access Their Wealth

Throughout history exchanges and banks have a storied history of people not being able to access their wealth. Stock exchanges have one of the worst histories because people treat them like they are a static investment. They are not. When the market drops, people "want to get their money out" of the market. The money they are talking about is the gains that they have made over the course of their time in the market. The bad news is that the stocks that they are holding are only what another person will pay for them. The reason that this is different in the crypto (non NFT) market is that the crypto has value on its own (if you are using a Stablecoin model). Whereas the stock can drop to zero, the crypto should only be able to drop to the transitional value or the inherent value, whichever is higher.

Banks also have some problems. In most civilized countries, a bank only needs to have cash on hand to cover 10% of the deposits at the bank.[340] In some western countries, banks only need to have enough cash on hand to cover the anticipated transactions of the day (which could be much lower).[341] This means that if there is a run on the bank, you best be within that first 10% (3% in the United States). The banks do not keep all of their deposits in the bank because the money is active (that is one of the ways banks make money). This means that if a lot of people want their money, many of them will be out of luck.

The DeFi banks can solve most of these problems. First of all, your currency (which is held in an active account) should always be held in the cyberspace of the bank. Whether a bank keeps a portion of this in cold storage (an air-gapped system) or not is part of the bank's style, but active accounts should be available for withdrawal (digitally). When a bank holds some of its reserves in standard accounts, the bank is using this money to make more money, so that is how you earn your interest rate. Most banks can pull this out quickly (with a penalty) if you need your money now, but it is rarely advisable as your earnings will be affected. The digital age gives people

---

[340] Staff (2021). "How Much do Banks Keep on Hand" Go Banking rates at https://www.gobankingrates.com/category/banking/banks/.
[341] *Id.*

more access to their money, which is something that the central banks never evolved to do.

Access to Accounts Through Exchanges

Exchanges and banks are the most popular place for people to store their active accounts. While wallets are nice for convenience (Chapter 29), exchanges give you the flexibility to trade your currency and keep your portfolio rising. Most exchanges have a limit on how much money you can withdraw in a day (which you have an affirmative duty to read in the contract). In most cases, this amount is enough to cover anything that someone is looking to pay for "in cash." For larger transfers, you will likely need the account to be converted to cash or a GET and then the funds can be wired to the destination. This allows for withdrawing money at any time outside of the maintenance window.

Another popular area of how people move crypto in exchanges is moving the crypto to another exchange or a bank. Sometimes people move currency because they like the deal at the other exchange better. Sometimes the currency is moved because they want to convert it to a currency not handled on the original exchange. Regardless of the reason, it should always be easy for the owner of the currency to move their funds to another system. Sometimes this will have a validation period (just like traditional banks) while the exchange checks the credential of both the account holder and the other bank. As this takes place over some time, the maintenance windows generally have little effect on this.

The ease of accessing your funds often turns to the question of whether you have the funds inactive accounts or cold accounts. In an active account, the money is actively being used by the user in the exchange. This means that the funds can be bought and sold at any time by the user. Active accounts are the easiest to access because you simply convert the crypto to the form that you want it and either transfer it to a bank account from which you can withdraw it or you transfer it directly to your digital wallet. Cold storage accounts may have an access time, a time that you need to wait to get your currency. This is because they must be transferred from an air gapped computer back onto the system. Because these are done in batches, it makes takes time.

Crypto cards are being offered by some exchanges. While not as widely accepted as bank crypto cards. These are another great way to access your account. Because the accounts are settled periodically, the maintenance window is not a problem in this scenario. This gives users better access to use their funds when they see fit, as opposed to just trading their funds. As more major credit card companies get involved with crypto, these cards will be more useful around the world.

Finally, trading is one of the most important aspects of crypto. Maintenance windows are devastating to trades because this is a time when you cannot access your coins. As a result, some people question the validity of the currency. Think about it, if you were not allowed to look at your money in the bank because they were having repairs (or were closed for the night) would you overreact? Of course not, we expect some limits to our access so that we can assure the security of our funds. This system is no different in crypto.

Access to Accounts Through Banks

Banks also have withdrawal policies; though they tend to be more advantageous to the user than the exchanges. When you look at a bank for withdrawals, they are set up to do this (exchanges just hope that you put more money in). As a result, the banks allow you to withdraw your funds much more readily. In the crypto world, most of this is done through compliant ATMs.[342] When you are looking at a larger withdrawal, you are likely going to have to have the funds wired to a local physical bank for currency to be handed to you. This can take more time. If you are simply moving funds to your wallet, this is almost instantaneous.

As with exchanges, when you move to another bank or an exchange, you can expect some delay. Banks, like exchanges, need to validate your credentials and the other organization's credentials before they can allow

342 Frankenfield, Jake (2021). "Bitcoin Atm" Investopedia at https://www.investopedia.com/terms/b/bitcoin-atm.asp.

your funds to be transferred. Unlike traditional fiat currency, once the transfer is complete it cannot be undone. This means that the DeFi banks need to take special care to make sure that everything is done correctly. This also means that you need to make sure everything is done correctly on your end too.

DeFi banks have other options not present on exchanges. DeFi banks allow you to put money into savings accounts (a type of staking), CDs (another type of staking), or hold them inactive accounts. In an active account, you would use the crypto just like in a debit card or checking account. In a savings account, you have access to your account at any time, but the interest rate tends to be quite low, comparatively. When you place your funds in a staked account (CD) the rates tend to be higher, but you must keep your money in the account for a set period of time. If you take the money out, you generally lose all of the interest (sometimes even a bit of the principle).

DeFi banks have the advantage of working with larger credit card issuers. This allows them to have cards that are accepted more places and have better perks. These also have the best access to your funds because they are accessible 24 hours a day. Some cards even allow you to have cash forwards on your accounts, which are an effective way to withdraw money (though can have withdrawal rates. Banks cards tend to be more useful than exchange cards, so always keep this in mind if you are choosing where to "stake" money.

Banks and Exchanges Working Together

As the spiderweb bridges become more robust across the system, the ability for DeFi banks and exchanges to work together increases. Regardless of the currency, the Global Exchange Tokens that power the spiderweb bridging of the system are giving banks and exchanges the ability to build new relationships, giving people dual access to their funds. Whereas the bank or exchanges maintenance window could keep you from getting your assets, with dual access unless both times line up you will have 24-hour access.

This not only makes accessing your funds easier, but it also allows for there to be a better, stronger network. Banks can only do so much. The same can be said for exchanges. When they are able to work together, then they become more than the sum of their parts. The relationship that they build will help the crypto marketplace expand into new areas- which will increase the utility and value for all users.

Redundant access to accounts is also important. Banks and exchanges can draw from the same accounts, as the accounts are confirmed immediately when the transactions are placed. This is why settlement of account timestamps is so important. Banks and exchanges need to see, in real-time, how much money is in any account. Settlement at the requested order ensures that account holders do not "double draw" the account, either through error or malfeasance.

The ability of exchanges and DeFi banks to work together while remaining separate is key to the decentralized nature of the system. With central banking cartels controlling nearly everything in the regular world of finance, the new molding in the cryptoverse allows for users to break away from the old system. The more the control of the system is spread around, especially to the users, the more the system will be able to evolve with the needs of the users. Banks and changes working together helps the users have more access to their funds, which means they have more control over their funds.

Another benefit of bilateral agreements between the banks and the exchanges is that there is increased faith in the system. Too often faith is lost when people cannot get what they want when they want it. By working together, the banks can work with the exchanges to make sure that people have access to their crypto at any time. The more access people have, the more faith they will have in the system. While there will always be people who do not understand why they have to wait- people who understand the system will realize that banks and exchanges have to validate complex transactions. However, this is not a big deal with 95% of all crypto exchanges being simple transactions.

The final major benefit of banks and exchanges working together is the triangulation of resources. In a regular transfer, the fund is validated by the user and the bank OR the user and the exchange. When the banks and exchanges are working together, the transfer is validated by all three parties. While this may not seem like a lot, one more set of processors looking at the validity of the transaction (possibly even using a different method) can find a lot of mistakes before they are unable to be fixed. By diversifying the system, we can increase security. More security means more trust in the system.

Conclusion Part II Section III

Security issues are always going to be a major part of the crypto banking industry. People who do not want to do the work to make their own money will always try to steal money from those who are willing to do the work. The community must come together to ensure that they can protect what they have built. One of the ways that the crypto community can do this is by ensuring that we have security standards.

This starts by ensuring that all DeFi banks and changes follow a set of guidelines for security. Most governments have set these requirements for regular banks, it falls of the community to ensure that we exceed these best practices. The best practices for the digital world should always be higher than those for the normal world. The more we work together to ensure these standards are met, the faster the community will develop and bring in new investors. Without security, we do not have the ability to trust the system, without trust people will not use the system.

When speaking about security, we need to make sure that people know the difference between access and ownership. Too often, people spread the myth that "If you do not have the key, you do not have the account." 100 years ago, this may have been true, but do you hold the keys to your current bank? Security means giving up some access. As we move into the 3rd Wave of crypto, people need to have faith in the institutions that are protecting crypto. Institutions need to earn this faith. The system becomes better as more people use it, increased faith in the system will increase use in the system.

The more groups work together in this industry, the more powerful this industry will become. Many different paths all working to make the system better means that more and more of the paths will be successful. We do not always have to be competing to make things work better. Elements like security are things that we can all agree are necessary. We need links between banks and exchanges. We need stronger networks. We need redundant access to our funds. Most of all, we need to keep away from the failed models of central banking.

Overall, security is going to be one of the big issues for the crypto industry. There will always be threats. As long as the community insists that we continually evolve the system, we can stay ahead of those threats. The crypto community is the future, and to be the future we must keep up with the dreams of the present. This is the only way we can all be successful.

Conclusion Part II

As the cryptosystem evolves, we need to have faith in the structures that protect the system. Honest banks and exchanges are not enough for the system to flourish, we need to have codified systems of development that have been created by the community. If we do not build our own set of rules, the governments of the world will ham-handedly assign regulations to us. Whether they work or not is not the problem of the government, they see it as our problem.

The first element that we need to ensure is market protection. There should be one primary market regulator for the market. This should be a body made up of users, exchanges, and DeFi banks. When the government tries to create a system to manage a system that they do not understand. The community has an understanding of the system; therefore, the community should be the arbiter of the system. This authority should be spread around as much as possible to maintain the decentralized nature of the system.

We also need to ensure that the policies governing tokens, settlements, trades, and information remain at the hands of the users. If 2020 and 2021 taught us anything it is the governments will hide information that makes them look bad to ensure control over the people and the economy. We cannot allow the self-governance of the system to have the same problem. Access to community information needs to be free. We also need to ensure that we cannot have people "sealing" information to protect their own interests. Within the community, nothing beyond the smart contract overlays should be "seal" or "proprietary."

One area where the community must work with governments is the prevention of crime. Until the government gives up its monopoly on the use of legal force and force of law, the community must rely on the governments of the world to imprison criminals. All we can do as a community is ban them from participating, it is difficult to get our funds back. The ability to cooperate in this area allows us to keep the system secure.

Our own security needs to be paramount to ensure that we do not need to overly rely on government help. The more help the government gives, the more control they will want. The more that we establish strong protocols in the market, the less we will need the interference of the government. Crypto is meant to be decentralized. In order to maintain this vision, all must participate in the system to ensure that every voice is heard and every idea is headed. The market should deem what is a good and bad idea, not necessarily a system of bureaucrats in an office somewhere.

Part III

Stabilization Mechanisms, Derivatives, and The Metaverse

Only in understanding can we have stabilization.

Thus, Wisdom is better than Knowledge.

Part III

Section 1: Stabilization of the System

Introduction to Part III: Section 1

One of the fundamental advancements that we are seeing in the cryptonomics space is the hybrid valuation of coins and tokens. When crypto first began, the only method for valuation of a cryptocurrency was the valuation that the market placed on it. This was not because the other types of valuation were not present, rather it was because the market value of the coin was the preliminary determinant of whether the coin was worth anything or not.

Once people began to show an interest in cryptocurrency, and started to learn about it, the system started to correct itself. People learned that the first type of value crypto has is not market value, but transitional value. This is the value that the crypto gains from being part of a block on the blockchain (Chapter 31). Between the block itself, the smart contract, and the contract overlays, the crypto has an inherent value in the transaction that can be measured.

As cryptocurrencies evolved, people soon could use them for more than simple crypto-based exchanges. As more groups accepted them in the market, the crypto increased in value because of the transactional value. The transactional value (Chapter 32) is the value embedded in the coin by each trade of the coin for a good in the real or virtual world. This "worth" value allowed the coin to move past the simple stages of coin-for-coin transactions to being used to pay for goods and services.

The market value of a coin has been ever present in the system (Chapter 33). As coins develop more worth, the system becomes more sophisticated and complex. Whereas many early coins gained market value as a novelty (like NFTs are now), the sophistication of the markets has made coins have real value on the market that can now be traded. Not only are the coins being spot traded on the market, but we are seeing derivative markets forming in the industry.

With the beginning of the third Wave of cryptocurrencies, we are seeing the fourth part of the valuation equation start to take form in the shape of inherent value. Early cryptos had the other three forms of valuation in some form of measure, but it was not until Stablecoin 1.0 began that there was inherent value in the coin. Stablecoin 1.0 operates off of the grade school type mentality that if "I pay a dollar for the coin then I should be able to get a dollar back for it." If only that was the rule during the 1990s heyday of arbitrage, many would be rich; the idea that you can invest in something and it keeps a static relative value is problematic for both users and investors. If you are an investor and allow a coin that is linked to a failing currency to continually lose value, then you are not a very good investor. If you are a user that buys a coin (and pays the fees to buy it), just to use it the same way you would use the currency, then you are doing something very shady or Disney would have made a lot of money off you in the 1990s.[343]

Stablecoin 2.0 change the inherent value modeling by using hybrid holding systems managed by a decentralized third-party corporation across a family of currencies. This allowed for a "stake" to be created, which in theory would continually rise and trade on the market, all the while keeping one coin or token from controlling the entire ecosystem. Through a system of diversified subsidiaries, the value of the fund is known, but the allotment is proprietary to prevent manipulation of the inherent value of the coin.

Chapter 35 looks at one of the "touchier" subjects when it comes to market stabilization, anti-whale technology. Crypto has to walk a thin line between keeping the big investors happy and ensuring that whales do not negatively disrupt the market. There are several methods that can be used to deal with this problem and we examine the most popular ones in turn.

Chapters 36 and 37 look at the methods for stabilizing a coin launch in its early levels. Chapter 36 discusses the methods and management of an Initial Coin Offering (ICO). How crypto puts itself onto the market can

---

[343] In the 1990s Disney issued "Mickey Bucks" park currency that could only be used in the park. Things in the park were the same price with the Mickey Bucks but some places would not accept them even in the park. When you left the park, they were just a novelty.

determine the success or failure of the crypto. Whether the crypto decides to go with a general launch or a tiered launch, this is a time that takes a great amount of planning. Another consideration during the early phases is the standing burn rate and the starter burn. Starter burns are burns where the burn rate is set high to keep the focus on the ICO trading to allow the ecosystem to form (Chapter 36). Standing burn rates are part of a 3rd Wave system called burn and earn, where the coin is constantly being taken out and returned to the system to keep the value rising.

Finally, this section takes on one of the biggest problems in the crypto ecosystem, Dead Wallets. Dead wallets are a broken throwback to the beginning of the second Wave which is dangerous to the stability of the system. The primary problem comes from the idea that they are not actually "dead." Someone can always get the key to the wallet and dump the coin on the market for fun or profit. Chapter 38 looks at how to improve the system with active wallets to help the ecosystem move forward.

Overall, management of the valuation system is an important first step to ensuring that the entire ecosystem is efficient and effective as it evolves. The more we work together to ensure that this system moves forward, the more we can place spot values that accurately reflect the resilience and the promise of the crypto system, now and in the years to come.

Chapter 31: Transitional Value

Transitional value is properly called the root of all crypto value.[344] Anytime that you enter a new product onto the market, there has to be some value added to the market for the item to be worth anything. Now, as history has shown us, the valuation by the market can be as varied as there are people in the world. Sometimes a product will be introduced that has such a high utility that everyone needs to have it to use.[345] Sometimes, something will be such a "flex" that everyone wants one, even if they have to have a knock off of it. Still, other times, we have people racing to buy something on the market where no one has any idea why they are buying it. The market runs on the will of the mob, and many people have lost and made fortunes betting on the will of the mob.

Cryptocurrency started with an idea. The idea was a decentralized currency that could not be manipulated by the banking cartels and the governments and would allow for peer-to-peer transfers of wealth around the world. While this is a great idea, it is an idea that capitalists have been spouting since the writing of "Wealth of Nations."[346] The reason why Bitcoin was successful in its offering is that rather than just talking about value, Bitcoin added value to the system.

When Bitcoin was created, blockchain was just getting its start. Now, all that blockchain represents is the legalization of the old hacking tool of a botnet.[347] Blockchain uses a series of hubs in an order only known to the chain (each hub is a block) to do calculations. The calculations are done in a way that allows complex transactions and equations to be calculated by using many small computers rather than a single supercomputer. Technology has been around since the internet, but blockchain has done it

---

[344] Bender, Jan Philip, Buchardi, Kaj, & Shepherd, Neil (2019). "Capturing the value of blockchain." BCG at https://www.bcg.com/publications/2019/capturing-blockchain-value.
[345] *Id.*
[346] Smith, Adam (2014, 1776). "Wealth of Nations" New York Penguin.
[347] Kapersky (2021). "What is a botnet." Kepersky at https://usa.kaspersky.com/resource-center/threats/botnet-attacks.

legally.

Bitcoin saw the value in each block on the chain.[348] When data moves through the chain, the chain adds value to the data. The old joke is that the transition changes "data" to "data." (If you pronounced the words differently then you are probably a computer nerd or old). Data (with the short "a" sound) is pre-computational information.[349] Data (with the long "A" sound) is post-calculation information. Whoever came up with this brilliant idea should be shot, but the fact is that the transition of data to data has value. Bitcoin found a way to monetize that value and the digital currency era was born.

This Chapter explains how the value is added to the system. The best way to do this is through analogy, which is what section one will look at. Section two of this Chapter looks at how the block is used in its given form, and how the natural movement has been monetized. The monetization, which is often seen in the smart contract, makes up the bulk of section three of this Chapter.

Section four of this Chapter is an explanation of the "use value" system to the OG investors. Too often we hear "There is no value in cryptocurrency." That is akin to saying that there is no value to borrowing someone's tool, the value is that it would cost you more to do it another way (if it could be done). Section five expounds on this looking at how to establish value within a non-ownership model. This is not promoting a system where no one owns the system, that would not work, this only demonstrates why a non-owner system is more efficient for most transactions because not everyone needs to manage their own ecosystem. This also discusses how a third-party ownership system is more humane because it will not be manipulated by the stakeholders.

---

[348] Dematteo, Megan (2021). "Bitcoin Doubled its value in 2021. Here's a look at its price over the years." NextAdvisor at https://time.com/nextadvisor/investing/cryptocurrency/bitcoin-price-history/.
[349] *Id.*

The analogy of the Highway

Likely everyone reading this book has traveled on a toll road at some point in their life. Toll roads are one of those nasty little features that we have in most free societies that show us how "free" is relative. In all honesty, fees and tolls are one of the "most fair" ways that a government can raise revenue to keep the services that they provide running. If you use something, then you pay for it. If you do not use something, then you do not pay for it. Ironically, the people who use it are the ones who tend to be complaining- and this is what we hear a lot about toll roads.

I have a friend who hates the Florida turnpike. Something you hear from him at least once a year is, "why do we have to keep paying for a road that we paid for 20 years ago?" Since it is fun, we always bait him with, "Well, if you hate the tolls, then why do you use it?" The answer is always either "because it is a better road..." or "because it is faster..." To which we always reply, "why is it better/faster?" The answer to this is why tolls and fees are so important in societies.

Tolls allow the system to be maintained.[350] Yes, somewhere there is a person who is likely making money off of the tolls, but very rarely does the entire toll go to that person. Usually, there is a vast network of employees, tradespeople, and other workers whom the fees go to pay. Therefore, the question becomes "why should not the person use it to pay those people?" Taxes are the most common reply to this question. In the example of the Florida Turnpike, taxes subsidize the private company that runs the pike (to keep the cost down), but the tolls are what allow the repairs to be done much, much faster than FDOT does repairs on the state-operated roads. When you travel on the turnpike, you are paying the company that runs it for the privilege of using that road, and in return, they keep the road in better shape than the other roads so people enjoy using it. One tire not lost to a pothole can cover a year's fees for the pike, so it is usually worth

---

[350] IBTTA (2021). "Toll Talking Points- The Importance and Benefits of Tolling." IBTTA at https://www.ibtta.org/sites/default/files/documents/MAF/Talking%20Points_2017.pdf.

it.

This is how the blockchain works. For each company, the government, or each person to run their own blockchain is silly.[351] Not only does the company have to build the chain, maintain it, and pay all the fees- but once the chain is built, then it is a bias chain and it is not decentralized. If someone wants to attack the company, then they do not have to attack the blocks- just take down the whole chain. Integrated blockchains, like Bitcoin and Ethereum, and others allow companies to work on their chain (for a toll) and have the best of both worlds. They can do their transactions on a secure system, but they do not have to maintain the whole system. Bringing down one of the high transaction chains would be difficult and would probably hurt hackers too, so this is avoided. With the creation of spiderweb bridging, coins such as KIROS are allowing companies to perform trades on multiple chains and then bring their material back to their preferred chain through GET.

Just like where you do not own the turnpike when you are on it, you are only renting the piece that you are on at any given moment, when you are on a block you are only using that block for the time it takes your transaction or calculation to be validated. You do not own the block, but the block is working for you. When you pay your gas fee (which helps give value to the coin), you are paying the block for its service. Blocks are just AI employees doing the work for you, the person who owns the AI is like the owner of consulting service. You pay them and they keep the employees doing a good job (through upgrades, training, and reviews.)

Use of the Block in its given Form

When it comes to using a block in a blockchain, you have to look at what type of block you want to use and what kind of transaction you are doing. The more complex the transaction, the more data will be used to validate the transaction.[352] The same can be said for complex calculations. As a

[351] Zhang, Zhong (2019). "Too Many Blockchains." Medium at https://medium.com/@maxzz/too-many-blockchains-637241f607d7.

[352] Infra.

company, if you are moving into the blockchain space, you should work with a consultant to find the right chain for you. Each coin has its own chain, and each chain has its own smart contracts and overlays.

The simplest use for a blockchain is transactional validation.[353] When this happens the block uses its memory space to validate the owner, the transaction, and the receiver. The blocks do not care who these people are and how it is transferred, they just want to make sure that the coin exists and that it is transferred from the current owner to the receiver.[354] If you are a company that is modern and using open crypto systems, like crypto.com or a Binance card, then you likely do not care which type of crypto is being used. Your account will be credited (or debited) the coins transferred and they will come/go where they need to be. All you are looking for is that the transaction is validated.

In a more complex situation, or if you are using an archaic one-crypto system, you may find that you are paying more in fees to validate that crypto is the type of crypto you want or that the transaction is doing what you need it to do. In this case (if your archaic system works with a modern system), then the original coin is converted to a GET, then the GET is converted to the type of coin that you want. If you are an intermediary in the system, then the coin you just collected is converted to a GET and then the GET is converted to the type of coin that you are sending it too. In an archaic system, the coin may be changed to a GET and then changed back into the same type of coin. This can result in fees of 3% being charged up to 10 times in a given transaction.[355] This suppresses the value of crypto not because the exchanges or chains are greedy, but because many people

---

[353] Euromoney (2021). How does a transaction get into blockchain?" Euromoney at https://www.euromoney.com/learning/blockchain-explained/how-transactions-get-into-the-blockchain.

[354] *Id.*

[355] Nover, Scott (2021). "The failed effort to buy the Us constitution could cost more than $1.5 Million in crypto fees." Quartz At https://qz.com/2093357/constitutiondao-may-pay-1-5-million-in-ethereum-gas-fees/.

are operating on an archaic system.

When you use a modern system, you accept whatever type of coin is traded on the exchange that you are using for the transaction (assuming you are not going wallet to wallet, but account to account). In this scenario, you accept the coin (with its minimal transfer fee) and have it in your account. If for some reason you do not want to be holding that particular type of coin, you simply trade it on the exchange for fiat currency or another coin (once again a small fee). Using a modern system can lower your fees from above 20% in complex transactions to under 4% just by accepting multiple cryptos.

Use of Smart Contracts

To understand how 2nd and 3rd Wave cryptos work, you need to understand what a smart contract is. A smart contract, simply put, is "a program stored on a blockchain that runs when certain conditions are met."[356] This is the dumb (or not so dumb) AI that ensures that transactions are validated and that computations are run.[357] Without getting into the complex protocols, these are the cashiers of the new digital world (among other jobs).

Smart contracts only do what they are programmed to do. This means when a company is picking a blockchain that they need to look at what the smart contract options are and how they will interact with the task that they need to be done.[358] A transactional smart contract will do you little good if you need a computational smart contract, so you need to know what you are doing when you get involved with the blockchain. Usually, there are dozens of consultants out there that will help you get what you

---

[356] IBM (2022). "Smart Contracts Defined" IBM at https://www.ibm.com/topics/smart-contracts. Full definition "Smart contracts are simply programs stored on a blockchain that run when predetermined conditions are met. They typically are used to automate the execution of an agreement so that all participants can be immediately certain of the outcome, without any intermediary's involvement or time loss. They can also automate a workflow, triggering the next action when conditions are met."

[357] Nover, *Supra*.

[358] *Id*.

need.

Some companies work with the blockchain to build smart contracts as needed. This can be an effective strategy to get your work done more quickly within the block. Since blocks only have a limited amount of memory, they can only do so many computations at a time (this is why Ethereum can be slow). When companies work with the chain, they can make the contract more efficient, thus they need less memory to complete the project.

The Value of Using the Tool

One of the most enduring myths around cryptocurrency is that it has no value, or that the creator of the coin can shut off the utility of the coin with no recourse.[359] Both of these statements are false. Cryptocurrency has always been a contract. Just like the dollar bill (or other currency in your wallet) is a contract with a government that this bill has the credit of the nation riding on it, the value of crypto is built on that same type of contract. You have a coin; it has a value. Whether it is market value, inherent value, transactional value, or transitional value depends on the type of coin and what you are using it for, but each coin has transactional value.

The coin's value is derived from one of the four categories of value. Now, this is a choice that the user needs to make. Just like in the real world, if you go out and buy a useless currency, you will find yourself holding useless francs in the age of the Euro. Cryptocurrency is a developed market, so you need to make sure that you have the level of sophistication necessary to trade/use. All cryptocurrencies have some type of value, however, not all cryptocurrencies have equal value.

The second myth is a little more difficult to understand. The creator of a

---

[359] Gupta, Sumit (2020). "Bitcoin has no Intrinsic value' Then what gives bitcoin value?" Authority at https://aithority.com/guest-authors/bitcoin-has-no-intrinsic-value-then-what-gives-bitcoin-value/.

currency may or may not have the ability to shut the coin down.[360] This depends on how their chain is set up, how the smart contracts are made, and whether there are any complex overlays. Generally, major exchanges will not list a new coin that can have the "rug pulled out from under it." This being said, there are several 2nd generation coins that need to be watched because this ability is out there. Now it is unlikely that the creators will do this, but it is always a possibility (or that they are hacked).

Third-Wave cryptos tend to be "too decentralized" to do this.[361] Technically, the system could abandon the support for the coin, but the coin would still be present. Further, if a company did drop the support for the coin, then the amount in the reserve fund (the non-coin reserve) could be legally used to compensate the people holding the coin for their losses (or the company could be turned over to the holders). Make sure that you look at the contracts and White Papers for coins before you invest in them. An informed investor tends to keep their money longer than an ill-informed investor.

How to Establish Value with the Non-Ownership Model?

To put the myth of "something you do not own has no value" to bed, for good. It is time that the crypto community points out that most things in people's lives they do not have full control over. We live in a "rental society." A rental society is a system where people are convinced that they are better off using credit and renting than they are accumulating wealth. While some things are better to be rented, most things are better when you actually own them. However, to suggest that crypto is worthless because the transitional value is based on the rental of digital space is just silly.

---

[360] Jones, Kelly (2021). "No, the government can't shut down cryptocurrency." ABC at https://www.abc10.com/article/money/no-the-government-cant-shut-down-cryptocurrency/536-4358c9a4-e974-479f-8939-9d7ea208d59e.

[361] Federal Reserve Bank of Cleveland (2019). "Bitcoins Decentralized Decision Structure." At FED https://www.clevelandfed.org/en/newsroom-and-events/publications/economic-commentary/2019-economic-commentaries/ec-201912-bitcoin-decentralized-network.aspx.

Reason 1: The fees have already been paid for the rental.

The main reason many people do not understand the value of the digital rental related to cryptocurrency is that they do not understand the fee has already been paid. Once a coin is mined or a token is minted, the fee has been paid to the system. This means that there is money in the system. If you are looking at a coin with a Stablecoin 1.0 or a Stablecoin 2.0 system, then there is an identifiable value in the system. Once people understand this, they can see why the Stablecoin 2.0 market is redefining the system.

Reason 2: People have been Renting things for years.

A lot of people think that a system based on rentals is not sustainable. These people are still living in the 70s, so if you see wide lapels, stay away from those investors. Rental systems are what most of the major cities in the world are built on. People rent apartments from corporations, who rent buildings from other corporations, who rent authority from their shareholders, who pay the government taxes every year to use land that they own. Now which is sillier, a company paying chain money to do a transaction, where the money paid is converted to coin- or renting land, from someone renting land, from someone renting land, from someone who owns the lands as long as they pay the government taxes on something they already own? I hope most people will trust the first system

Reason 3: Crypto has more value than Fiat Currency.

Fiat currency is like your parents giving you a note you can use for food when you complete your chores. It has value only because they say so, and your labor has been converted to their "say so." Conversely, crypto has inherent value (if it is Stablecoin 1.0 or 2.0), it has a market value (if it is on an exchange), it has transitional value (all coins have this), and it has transactional value (if it is on an exchange with a card). If you are worried about the coin, avoid the coins that do not have those types of value!

Conclusion

Transitional value is the simplest form of value, but it is the form of value that gives the coin its intrinsic value. Regardless of how you look at coins, they are always building value as long as they have some relation to the chain. There are "junk" coins, but that is an investor's job to avoid them. Stick to coins that have a strong transactional value and you can ensure that your coin will be there and will flow with the market.

Do not let people convince you that transitional value is not important. Every business, every nation, every person runs on transitional value. Your bank account is only worth what is in that account at a given time. The amount of the money in your wallet is only what the state says it is worth at any given time. With crypto, the value is what the market says it is. As long as the internet is being used and blockchains are being used, the coins will have some value. This is more than can be said for fiat currency, do not believe me- try to go to a money exchange with confederate dollars.

Chapter 32: Transactional Value

The second leg of the value analysis of crypto is the transactional value. Unless a coin/token has some use in the world, whether the real world or the metaverse, it is not that useful. Therefore, one of the best ways to increase the total value of a coin is to increase the transactional value of a coin. One of the best examples that we have seen of this was the announcement that Tesla was going to accept Dogecoin to buy products.[362] Within minutes of the announcement, Doge had rallied nearly 25% helping the coin move back above the $0.20 level.

The problem that many coins and tokens in the crypto space are finding right now is the greed of their systems. The crypto ecosystem is an interconnected platform.[363] This means that as one coin grows the ecosystem grows. Now the platform is still in its primordial stages. Some evolutionary forks are not working out and are destined for extinction. However, one of the constants is that for the ecosystem to be successful, the ecosystem needs to celebrate its advancements. The use of a currency by a major company is a boon for the whole ecosystem. Each time a company, like Tesla, adopts a currency (or all cryptocurrencies) the proof of concept for the crypto ecosystem becomes better defined.[364]

The development of transactional value is shifting the purely digital transitional value into the real world. While the digital age is fast adapting to the world, there are OG elements that are holding back advancement. Until those elements see that crypto has real-world value to complement its digital world value, the system will not become universal. As such,

---

[362] Beals, Monique (2021). "Musk: Tesla to accept cryptocurrency dogecoin for merchandise." The Hill at https://thehill.com/policy/finance/585687-musk-tesla-to-accept-cryptocurrency-dogecoin.

[363] Bitcoinist (2021). "By combining cross chain and oracle together, PLUG chain connects the world." Bitcoinist at https://bitcoinist.com/by-combining-cross-chain-and-oracle-together-plug-chain-interconnects-blockchain-with-the-real-world/ (very good example of the movement between 2nd Wave [code based] and 3rd Wave [hybrid] methods, where a company worked with purely code rather than extending a spiderweb bridge.

[364] *Id.*

transactional value and actual value are heavily weighted in the analysis of the true value of a coin or token.

This Chapter starts off by looking at the right to contract. If you are supporting the cryptocurrency movement, one of the underlying philosophies is that every person in the world has a right to contract. Part of that right is the right to exchange. To establish this right, a user needs to have an understanding of the types of contracts. This Chapter discusses the differences between a unilateral contract and a bilateral contract. Both of these contract formats are important in the crypto space.

The actual valuation of the trading system is also important in how cryptocurrencies function. If a currency is adopted by one "mom and pop" shop, it helps a little. If a cryptocurrency is adopted by Walmart, then it helps a lot. However, giants like Tesla and Walmart can only do so much, cryptocurrencies being adopted by main street USA is one of the biggest goals of the system (and the business districts around the world.[365] Chapter 32 concludes by looking at how to build a more robust trade system through cryptos working together. Building a space where the currency has a chance to take root and lead the world to a new level of economic success.

Upon completion of this Chapter, you should have a better understanding of how contracts and crypto work together to become a basis for an exchange system. Moving beyond the fiat system requires that the competent consumer understand that there are other ways to value objects than a single type of currency defined by region. Objects, thoughts, and actions have value- the valuation of these realities needs to be derivative of the market value and the present need. Setting the value to a single currency excludes billions from being able to enjoy the freedoms that the digital age should bring with it. Crypto diversity allows for the world to find this equilibrium.

---

[365] *Id.*

The Right to Contract

Every human being has the right to contract.[366] One of the greatest calamities of history is the backward idea that one person has the right to another person's thoughts, labor, or inspiration. For years, governments and corporations have tried to minimize this right and force people to work on the terms of the elite. In the 1990s and 2000s, we saw pushback from the other side. Socialist ideology became a vouge in western democracies and radicals (along with unions) argued that it was the individual who should tell the corporation what their time was worth.[367] Both philosophies are asinine. The right to contract means that you have the right to compromise with other people to reach your goals, not that you have the right to tell others what they are worth (regardless of who you are).

The two elements here that society has failed to teach in schools is that people are not the center of the universe. No person is the most important person in the world but for mere moments in life. When a woman gives birth, when a leader makes peace, when a scientist makes a discovery, when a teacher teaches a child with a lesson, when you feed the hungry, clothe the poor, or house the homeless; when any person forgives another person, these are the moments when a person can be the most important person in the world. Unfortunately, the narcissism epidemic in the world community has taught people that they are the center of the universe all the time.[368]

A person has the right to be a person. A person also has the duty to work for what they need. The "you must do as your told philosophy" which we

---

[366] Bernstien, David (2008). "Freedom of Contract." George Mason University School of Law at https://www.law.gmu.edu/assets/files/publications/working_papers/08-51%20Freedom%20of%20Contract.pdf.

[367] *Id.*

[368] Twenge, Jean & Campbell W. Keith (2010). The Narcissism Epidemic: Living in the age of entitlement. Atria Books at https://www.amazon.com/Narcissism-Epidemic-Living-Age-Entitlement/dp/1416575995/ref=sr_1_2?keywords=the+narcissism+epidemic+the+narcissism+epidemic&qid=1639570777&sr=8-2.

saw on display during the COVID crisis, is one of the greatest human rights abuses of recent human history. Likewise, the "living my best life" philosophy where people say "work to live, but do not live to work," forces people into lives of false success, having moments of happiness controlled by a majority of their time worrying about how to pay their bills. Society is always a pendulum, the 80s were all about corporate hegemony and the 2000s were all about personal feudalism, we need to bring the pendulum back to the center where people have worth but they understand that worth is only realized by how they help others in society.[369]

The right to contract is quite simple. No person should be forced (without due process of the law) to do something that they do not want to do. However, society is not responsible to ensure the survival of a person who chooses not to do enough to get by in life. Society has a duty to protect the security of people, specifically the security to make a living and acquire their needs; but society does not have to support a person who will not work. This means working for survival is a decision that every person needs to make. There are, of course, caveats to this idea. Children need to have support to get to the point that they can contribute (and society is better off if it gives them the opportunity for education). The elderly and infirmed also should have special care from society. The able-bodied person who has the opportunity to support themselves but will not do so, because they do not feel the work they can do "suits" them, however, some critics may believe should be allowed to fail.

The right to contract is based on the concept of freewill. If you follow one of the Abrahamic religions, you understand freewill is a funny thing.[370] Under these philosophies, the world is based on the love of the creator. Without freewill, love is nothing. A person must choose to love someone and it cannot be forced, lest it not be love. To love other people in this world, and love society- you need to believe in the right to contract. A person who is forced to work because that is what they are told to do will

---

[369] Smithmyer, Christopher (2014). Quadralectics. Dobbs and Brodeur, available at Nova Southeastern Library.
[370] *Id.*

always be a slave to a system. A person who is working in a position based on the choices that they made during the course of their lives, however, likely accepts that is a free person. Not everyone makes the choices to have the job that they want, high school parties, sleeping in, addiction to substances, all of these actions can take away from your success. Society, however, cannot insulate a person from their choices.

To be short, the most important part of the right to contract is the right to contract with yourself. Too often the world thinks that people fail because they were dumb enough to make a deal with the devil; in all reality, the devil knows that it is much more destructive when a person breaks a deal with themselves. Evil reigns when good people do nothing, but failure becomes the norm when people lie to themselves and do not work to be the best people they can be because they want to "live their best life."

Unilateral Contracts

The first type of contract that is relevant in the crypto world is the unilateral contract. Since most of the creation process of crypto is based on unilateral contacts, this idea is underpinning most of the cryptocurrency ecosystem. A unilateral contract is "a contract created by an offer that can only be accepted by performance."[371] In the crypto world, I will pay for transactional verification that can only be accepted by the actual transactional verification. This is bringing real-world money into the system.

Unilateral contracts are very important within the contract space. While a large portion of the economy is built around promises for promises, the fundamental bedrock of the economy is based around one action, in particular, payment. Payment is the ultimate resolution of millions of unilateral contracts each day. When you pay your bills, that month's contract is completed. When you go to a store and pay for goods, that payment is the completion of the negotiation. If you are working with a college to get a degree, you culminate your education receiving your "payment" for your hard work (your degree). When you get to the end of

[371] Wexlaw at https://www.law.cornell.edu/wex/unilateral_contract.

the week, your boss gives you your payment (usually a week after the work is done because of pay finance).

Payment under the unilateral model is very important for the success of any ecosystem. When people learn contract law in law school, regardless of the country, most of the lessons are on breach, performance, repudiation, and other "in course" elements of the contract. In reality, most contract law cases revolve around these issues; however, the vast majority of contracts that are created are fulfilled and complete without problems.

When we look at the transactional value in the cryptocurrency ecosystem, the completion of unilateral contracts is one of the most important issues that we can look at.[372] The completion itself is neither here nor there; however, the exact moment of completion is a question that must be answered. Payment is complete when the payment is received by the payee and the services are rendered to the payer. The contract is not complete until the promised action is complete. This means that the contract can still be active after payment is received, thus there needs to be some sort of holding system within the ecosystem to ensure the viability of the contract, because in crypto once a coin is moved to a new wallet, it belongs to the new owner.

Bilateral Contracts.

When it comes to the right to contract, another group of common contracts are bilateral contracts. A bilateral contract is "A bilateral contract is a contract in which both parties exchange promises to preform. One party's promise serves as consideration for the promise of the other. As a result, each party is an obligor on that party's own promise and an oblige on the other's promise."[373] While this seems to be much more complex than a unilateral contract, it is simply "if you do this for me, I will do that for you."

---

[372] *Id.*

[373] Cornell Law at https://www.law.cornell.edu/wex/bilateral_contract.

Most bilateral contracts are nearly as exciting as unilateral contracts. They are simply paying for service contracts. "If you do this for me, I will then pay you..." amounts to a person promising to pay if another person promises to do something. Once again, these are standard contracts that are completed by the millions every day without problems. It is only the very few contracts where we see problems that cause things to go to court. This is why we need more education on how to make efficient contracts that go to fruition rather than worrying about the 1% that fail.

In the crypto world, bilateral contracts are generally more based on the derivatives market. While any contract can technically be turned into a bilateral agreement with payment being reserved until after the work is done, the majority of bilateral agreements within the system itself are going to be complex financial instruments. The goal here in a decentralized system is to ensure that people are allowed to create these complex instruments. Overregulation prevents innovation. While innovation is disruptive, it is how the system evolves.

Valuation of Trade Systems

One ever-present question within the system is "how the addition of a system that adds transactional value to a crypto ecosystem should be valued?" There are three elements that should determine the value added to the system:

1.) The Volume of Trade;[374]
2.) The Utility of The Trade;[375]
3.) The Conception of the Trade.[376]

Each of these is important to how the trade should affect the system. Each of these has its own ins and outs that the crypto ecosystem will have to define.

---

[374] Twin, Alexandria (2021). "6 Factors that influence exchange rates." Investopedia at https://www.investopedia.com/trading/factors-influence-exchange-rates/.
[375] *Id.*
[376] *Id.*

The volume of trade currently is the most important factor in how transactional value is calculated in the current ecosystem. The volume of trade is the amount of transactions each day that are conducted in the ecosystem or by a specific coin. The more that the coin is traded for goods, the more value that it has. This should not be confused with market volume, which is the amount that the coin is traded on the market. While market volume has a direct relationship to the market value of the coin, it does not affect the transactional value of the coin. When looking at the volume of trade, the value of the trade is not taken into consideration, only the number of transactions per day.

The utility of the trade is a much more complex calculation when working on the transactional value. How important the type of good being traded for the currency is vitally important to the valuation. The NFT market is an excellent example. NFTs are making up a respectable portion of trade in the digital exchange market. The volume is high, which adds to the value of the coins being used for the transaction. The utility of NFTs is currently low, however, which makes the NFT volume detrimental to the system rather than beneficial. If the advice in the derivatives Chapter is taken and derivatives are memorialized in NFTs, this could change the equation entirely and make NFTs a boon to the calculation. Another area that could vastly increase the valuation of a token or a coin is the commodity market. When coins are used in exchange for use goods or valuable goods, it increases the value of the coin quickly.[377]

Finally, there is the conceptual value of the exchange. This is a difficult criterion to measure because it is so vague. The people who are trading have the right to trade. The trade agreement that they come to can create the value of the coin. How many coins is a loaf of bread worth (or how many loaves of bread are worth a coin)? These questions move beyond the internet of things into the economy of things. When we tag the price of a coin or token to their conceptual value, rather than just a "pegging" to a currency, we see a functional shift in the valuation. This is where

[377] *Id.*

transactional value and actual value of a coin can be at odds because the conceptual value is dealing with the trades and the actual value is dealing with the stake.

Building a framework for a steady trade system

Cryptonomics is a difficult field because it is not a quasi-fictional field like economics.[378] In economics, the guidelines are set by a government and the exercises are within a controlled area. This leads to "definite" science (which is often wrong), but people can feel comfortable with it because the boundaries are defined. Cryptonomics, on the other hand, is open world. The rules of the environment change constantly because the environment changes constantly. Anyone learning about crypto has to be constantly learning because what you knew yesterday may not be what is true today.

This is why the framework, both industry and regulatory, is so important. While the sands of cryptonomics may always be shifting, the desert has to stay the same. Certain elements need to be in place to ensure that the transactional value is defined. The three key types (volume, utility, and conception) need to be defined and used as value indicators. If each currency is creating its own set of indicators, then the valuation will never be compatible across the spiderweb bridge. This will mean the system could collapse back to Wave 2 or even fiat.

In addition to a stabilized framework, crypto savants need to have constantly evolving literature on the subject of cryptonomics. The more the literature evolves, the closer it will be to reality. Without a good "canon," the system will not work efficiently. Transactional value is one of the defining features of an economic system. The more the industry allows the terminology to become uniform (with new stuff coming in all the time), the more stable the industry will be.

---

[378] Economics, in its modern state, has confirmation based on agreement, rather than observation. This is allowing the theory to supplant the actual validation of the process.

Chapter 33: Market Value

Entering the third different type of valuation, the market value of a cryptocurrency is something that most people tend to associate with the system. Simply put the market value is the value that the market assigns to a cryptocurrency. Since most of the use of cryptocurrency in the current market is the trading of the currencies on the market, market value is the primary method of valuation of cryptocurrencies from the first and second Waves.[379] Now that the world has entered the stage of Stablecoin 2.0, we are seeing that the inherent value of the coin tends to join the transactional value and the market value as the key indicators of value.

This Chapter looks at the market for what it is, a place of exchange for currencies, cryptos, and commodities.[380] "To understand the market value of an asset, one must first understand the functions of the market." Market dynamics are one of the critical factors that indicate whether crypto is making a run, or whether the crypto is just reacting to the market. Underlying the complexities of the market there is the simple concept of the bargained for exchange. Every move that the market makes is dependent on the agreements reached by the participants in the market.

The market is not a calculating monolith. however. Many changes in the market are dependent on the movement of the communities within the market. Traders dictate the value of any asset on the market, and traders are humans and computers combined. This deadly combination can cause the market to move in unpredictable ways as the mob and the AI interact in unexplained ways.

Next, the efforts of the creators and the holders of the coins can affect the stability of the currency. There are times when the amount of currency expands (such as a mining boom), these can cause the amount of coin to grow (growing the size of the market) while the value of the coin sees a correction. Conversely, we can also see efforts to diminish the amount of

---

[379] KIROS Whitepaper.

[380] Frankenfield, James (2021). "Cryptocurrency." Investopedia at https://www.investopedia.com/terms/c/cryptocurrency.asp.

currency, causing the value to rise as assets are removed from the system. These two elements that occur within the dynamics of the market allow the system to evolve and have major effects on the market valuation.

Finally, regulatory and industry moves to secure the stability of the market can actually cause the market to react as the news hits the traders. Even the best-intentioned government actions can cause a coin or token to lose value if the community does not believe that the move is in the right direction. Even if the community feels that the move is in the right direction, there can still be a tank in the value as the community rejects over-regulation by the industry or the government.

The market is a fickle system for managing wealth, but it tends to be an honest method for valuation. A wise man once said that nothing has value until someone gives it value. This is doubly true for cryptocurrencies. The market is one of the key indicators that tell the community what the coin is worth; likewise, the community's reaction to the market's valuation of the coin gives the market an idea of where the value of the coin is going. When you add derivatives into the mix, you can see a pattern of where the value is, where the value was, and where the community thinks that the value is going. This is why the market value is seen as one of the strongest indicators of actual value.

The concept of the Market

The idea of a stock market is based on the idea of a classic market.[381] In the concept of a classic market, people would take their goods to a location, announce a price that they wanted for their goods, and then if someone came to them with the price, they would sell their goods. If the seller could not find a person to sell the goods to, then they had the option of taking their goods home with them or lowering their price. The price where the single type of good was purchased was known as the market value. This price was the daily aggregate of what the sellers wanted, what the buyers wanted, and where they met in the middle to make sure that that they

---

[381] Kenton, Will (2021). "Market" Investopedia at https://www.investopedia.com/terms/m/market.asp.

made the sale. Modern markets are still operating on this concept as buyers and sellers meet at the market (exchanges) to do business on a variety of things.

The seller in any market scenario is the catalyst for the process. Regardless of how many buyers there are in a marketplace for a determined good, if there is not a seller that has the ability to sell, then there will be no goods to sell. Once you find a seller that has the ability to sell, you need to find a seller that is willing to sell. While the ability to sell is a determinative variable, the willingness to sell is a dependent variable. A seller's willingness to sell depends on the price that they are willing to get. Any seller entering the market generally has a Best hoped price and a worst acceptable price which creates the range that they are willing to accept. Now any savvy seller will not advertise their lowest price, many will not even announce where the price is that they hope to get at the top end. This allows for the gamesmanship of the market to begin.

On the other end of the spectrum is the buyer. Now buyers are dependent on there being a seller for the system to work; however, there must also be a buyer who is able to purchase the goods. If there is no one in the marketplace with the funds to pay what the seller is asking, then the goods will go unsold. This is the determinative variable. The dependent variable is how much the buyer is willing to pay. Just like the seller, the buyer will enter the market with a low number of what they are willing to pay, a higher number of what they are able to pay, and the range in between is the area where they can find a settlement.

The third player that makes the modern market work is the exchange. The exchange is a system that matches buyers and sellers with overlapping ranges together to enable the sale. Because of the natural complexities of the market, sometimes the buyers and sellers will never meet and be able to ask/tell each other what they are willing to buy/sell for. This is an inefficiency that causes the market to misrepresent the value of a good. The exchange acts as an intermediary between groups of buyers and sellers to ensure that when there is a match to be made the people who can make the match speak to each other.

The interesting thing about the modern market is that people can see what the buying and selling are going for on the market. Each time a purchase is made, the purchase amount is listed on the exchange. This is the spot rate for the good. The spot rate is the determinative factor that identifies the price of the good at that moment. When using the market to calculate the actual value of the good, you need to look at the spot rate and the average spot rate for the day.

Bargained for Exchange

All trading is based on the bargained for exchange. So, when the market is wide open and there is a high demand and low supply there will be bargaining and bidding.[382] When there is low demand and a large supply there will also be a system of bidding that allows for the market rate to adjust the need to the supply, or the demand to the need. When this happens the volume of trades seems to be lower, but the importance to the price of the asset is much higher. This is the point where cryptos really show their vulnerability to the market. When there is low trading volume the price can drop very quickly.

When there is a high demand and low supply, the value of the asset goes up.[383] The reason for this is that the people who need the asset are willing to pay more so that they can get the asset. This often divides the people who need the asset from the investors because the investors can wait for the price to go down, while those in need are forced to deal with the inflated price. These types of rallies can sometimes lead to an opportunity to "short" stocks or cryptos. A short can happen when traders see the price run-up and believe that there is an impending decline.

Shorting crypto is the process of borrowing crypto from another seller and selling the coin with the expectation that the coin is going to drop in value. Under this paradigm, you borrow while the price is high and then sell the

---

[382] *See* *https://www.shsu.edu/klett/ELEMENTS%20OF%20CONSIDERATION%20ch%2012.htm*.

[383] *Id.*

coin. You then wait (within the timeframe of the deal) and buy back the coin at a lower rate, returning it to the owner (minus a fee) and pocket the difference in the decline. This can be a very daunting prospect as it can bankrupt a trader if the coin goes up in value and forces the trader to buy the coin at a higher rate to pay back the exchange.

An example of this could be seen on December 12th, 2021.[384] Elon Musk tweeted that Tesla was going to begin accepting Dogecoin for its products.[385] The market reacted with the price of Doge going up 21% in a few hours, raising the value about its actual value.[386] Someone who saw this movement could "borrow" coin on an accepting exchange, sell the coin. Then if they would wait till Tuesday, the coin had dropped approximately 5%. While this was not a major movement for the coin. If the purchase was big enough, the short could make a fair bit of cash on the 5% drop.[387]

Now change the facts a little. Our shorter is not going to do the same thing on Sunday, but rather than what actually happened in the market of the price correcting, if that the price continued to rise as the community rallied around the coin (maybe they were going to buy Tesla's). If the coin rises in value, the shorter still has to buy back coin to pay off the short (before the deadline), this means that if the coin goes up 10% in value, the shorter has to come up with that extra 10%. To add insult to injury, the shorter will still have to pay the fee to the exchange for allowing the short. This is why shorts are dangerous.

The opposite of a rally caused by a shortage is a crash caused by an excess in the system. When there is more of crypto on the market than there are people who want the crypto, the price starts to drop. This can often cause

---

[384] Browne, Ryan (2021). "Dogecoin spikes mor than 20% after Elon Musk says Tesla will accept it as Payment for Merch." CNBC at https://www.cnbc.com/2021/12/14/dogecoin-price-surges-after-elon-musk-tweet-about-tesla-merch.html.

[385] *Id.*

[386] *Id.*

[387] *Id.*

the crypto to drop very quickly until it reaches its support line. A support line is an area on the chart where there are a lot of bids at a rate lower than the market rate which will take a long time to fill. The support line acts as a floor, and savvy investors can buy the dip- even when there is little interest in the crypto. This "buying the dip" can often turn the fortunes of crypto as people see others making the move and follow suit. These negotiations are essential for the market to keep moving, even if the negotiators never meet each other in person.

Community Hype and Valuation

Like stocks, cryptos can be heavily affected by community hype and valuation.[388] Since many of the traders on the crypto markets are "new" money, they sometimes play loose and fast with the money buying hypes. NFTs are one of the areas where this happens. Likewise, celebrities and regulators can cause a movement in the market when they put out information about the coin/token (whether it is correct or not). These movements are usually a surprise and are hard to follow. Another interesting factor is that since the market is not highly regulated, rating agencies can cause the market to move- even markets that they are participating in, which makes rating agencies suspect in the crypto world. Serious crypto traders need to be watching the trends across the digital universe to see what is causing the market to move and deciding whether it is a correction or whether the is actual movement in the system.

One of the most unsettling things about the crypto market is new crypto millionaires flexing on the market.[389] They do this by buying up meme coins, buying NFTs, or even buying a coin because they like the name of the coin on any given day. When they make these moves, the market tends to react as lemmings tend to follow what they feel are indicators. This lemming reaction can cause crypto to skyrocket with little underlying value in the coin. When "junk" coins do this, the whale can pull the rug out from under investors and take a sizable chunk of the equity to become even richer.

---

[388] Vigna, Infra.

[389] Infra.

Celebrities and regulators are another factor that can cause a stock or crypto to move quickly and unpredictably. While whales need to have the capital to make these moves happen, celebrities and regulators only have to have enough social capital to get people moving. Even when they are wrong, a celebrity or regulator can say something that gets people buying or selling, often for no other reason than the regulator mentioning a coin. In one congressional hearing, a congressman in the United States mentioned the Mongoose coin, a coin that did not exist. Within an hour, the coin was created and had gone up in value by 3000%![390] The moral of this story is that people can be stupid, especially when they listen to stupid people.

One of the most alarming influencers of market value is rating agencies. Agencies that rate the value of a coin (private or government) and participate in the market are no better than fiat currencies. There is no one that I know who does not understand how the federal reserve and the banking cartels make money. The announced monetary policy then move the interest rates in a direction that allows them to collect more because of the policy they just announced. When they are still not making enough money, they tell the government that they need to print more money (and they keep a percentage of it). This is the same thing that rating agencies on cryptos are making money, rate something a strong buy (after you have bought a fair amount of coin) then sell the coin as the market goes up. The only way they get caught is if they hit on the same coin too often or sell when the coin reaches the top. As long as they sell in the middle and are happy with reasonable gains, they get away scot-free.

Efforts to expand the currency

There are times when there will be an effort to expand the currency. In these cases, the creators of the currency will release some of the reserves into the market or will offload some of the holdings of the creator. In

[390] NDTV (2021). "US Congressman's Joke During Hearing Leads to Creation of New 'Mongoose Coin." NDTV at https://www.ndtv.com/business/us-congressman-mocks-about-mongoose-coin-it-exists-now-with-m-cap-in-millions-2649905.

general, these moves will cause the value of each coin to go down, while still maintaining the value of the ecosystem. This can be dangerous to the system because many will see it as someone "cashing out."[391]

Regardless of the market's feelings on owners cashing out, the owner will eventually sell some of their coin on the market to actually make money on their coin. The question that arises during these times is whether the owner is cashing out almost all of their holdings or if the owner is just taking out some of their equity. Taking out some of their equity should be normalized. No one expects a creator to make a billion-cap coin and not make some money out of it. The danger comes when an owner sells almost all of their coin; this can be seen as cashing out and a loss of faith in the coin.

The release of reserves should also be a well-structured plan. Reserves are used to stabilize the amount of coin in play at any time. Reserves will eventually be fed into the system as the system grows. Just dumping the reserves into the system, without a plan, can cause the value of a coin to the tank. Reserves should be released gradually or with a like amount of income to ensure that they increase the viability of the system.

Regardless of how many coins come into the system, there has to be a plan for it. If you see coins coming into the system, check the White Paper for the coin. If this was a planned release, then you should not worry (may consider buying some of the new coins) and enjoy the growth when the correction takes place. If you see a large number of coins coming into the system with no rhyme or reason, it may be a signal to bail on the coin and find another place that is more secure to store your money.

Efforts to diminish the currency

One of the unique efforts of cryptocurrency, especially in the third Wave is the effort to remove currency that is in play from the system. Governments do not take currency out of the system often because the higher the

---

[391] Vigna, Paul (2021). "Crypto and its many fees." WSJ at https://www.wsj.com/articles/crypto-and-its-many-fees-what-to-know-about-the-hidden-costs-of-digital-currency-11639825202.

amount of currency, the more that they bring in through the tax system. This system of inflation forces people to increase wages, increase spending, and devalue the currency (all of which bring more money to the government and the central bank). Cryptocurrency has gone through an evolutionary process of maintaining the system, and the 3rd Wave system seems to be an improvement on the already viable methods of the 1st and 2nd Waves.

In the 1st Wave of cryptonomics, the amount of the supply was defined by the coin's creator.[392] When the coin was created, there was only a finite amount created or creatable. This meant that the coin would only ever have so many coins (for Bitcoin it is 21 million). This method kept inflation from being a problem. One of the reasons that inflation was not a problem was because as new coins were minted, the work was being done on the blockchain and the transactional value was increased to need of the ecosystem.

The 2nd Wave cryptocurrencies evolved this system even more.[393] The alt-coins followed the same model as the 1st Wave, with a limited number of coins minted; however, they also added a twist. During certain times they had coins "burned" to remove them from the system. These coins were sent to a dead wallet, allegedly to never be heard from again. However, on Nov. 19th, 2021, one of these dead wallets reactivated and dropped $2 billion Bitcoin onto the market, which caused the price to drop. This is why the 2nd Wave system is a little suspect.

The third Wave system is using a deflationary model to make the system go around. Rather than just trying to maintain value in a system where the fiat currency is collapsing, the 3rd Wave coins, especially the coins participating in Stablecoin 2.0, are increasing the value of the coin through deflation. Oddly enough, when banks titled inflation and deflation, they

---

392 Mcclure, Ben (2021). "How the burn rate is a key factor in a company's stability." Investopedia at https://www.investopedia.com/articles/fundamental/04/022504.asp.
393 CFI Supra.

made it seem like inflation was a good thing and deflation was a bad thing. Well for the banks it generally was. Inflation decreases the value of money, which means that the money held in savings accounts at 1% interest would lose money when the inflation rate was 3%.[394] If you were saving with a bank, you would have less money when you took it out than when you put it in (in the real world). This forced people and banks to put money into bonds and other projects that could make more money, forcing people to spend money- not save it.

A deflationary system allows people to make money through the exchange. As the coin is used by people, a portion of the coin is burned.[395] This coin that is burned is not destroyed, like in the 2nd Wave, but re-entered into the system. The re-entry into the system is not a direct re-entry. A portion is given to holders of the coin, the ensure that the move does not lower their stake. A portion is used to purchase more assets for the ecosystem. Finally, a portion is used for donations and lobbying to ensure that the ecosystem stays viable. The whole process recycles about 1% of the coin each year giving it a growth rate of 4% against a declining fiat currency at 3%.[396]

Ensuring That the Market is Practical and Protected

The market is like any other system in the world. It can function on its own, but it needs to be protected and not interfered with. While these seem like two competing ideas, they actually work very well together. The market will stabilize itself. When exchanges attempt to stop trading on a given asset (unless fraud is detected) generally they are protecting their growth rate. The market will have declines and rallies, and they need to be allowed to happen. Likewise, the market must also be protected from scammers. This is the only area where the government should get involved with the system when someone commits a crime.

---

[394] *Id.*

[395] *Id.*

[396] This is a very simplified analysis, the growth rate can actually be nearing 25% against the fiat currency in a given year, across each coin in the system.

Too often we see the exchanges and government try to protect the market from itself.[397] Most of the time, when they interject, they cause more problems than they solve. The government is heavy-handed in an area that needs finesse to make things work. When an exchange tries to manipulate a currency, they tend to cause the community to lose faith in the agnostic nature of the system. Either way, there can be problems created by people who are haphazardly trying to solve a problem.

When it comes to government interference in the market, there is only two times when a government should interject into the market: when they are buying and when they are arresting criminals. The crypto market needs to understand that the government is not needed to regulate how the market functions. Since it is decentralized, the bad exchanges will fail and the good exchanges will succeed. IF the government wants to protect investors, offer classes on how to spot a good exchange, and make exchanges have insurance against failures. The community also must acknowledge that when there is a crime, we need to turn the data over to the government (this includes tax evasion). While the community exists on its own, it still exists under the laws of nation-states and needs to follow those laws that do not violate human rights.

Conclusion

The market valuation will always be one of the major valuation factors for the crypto ecosystem. While the Stablecoin 2.0 system is pushing the boundaries of how the coins are valued, the market will still have its place in identifying the base value for the coin.[398] As members of the crypto community, we need to ensure that the market is allowed to function in its proper manner and not to turn the government every time something happens that we do not like. Investing has risks and investors need to accept those risks.

---

[397] NYU Dispatch (2021). "Can the Government regulate cryptocurrency." NYU at https://wp.nyu.edu/dispatch/can-the-government-regulate-cryptocurrency/.
[398] Frankenfield, Supra.

Chapter 34: Inherent Value

One of the best features that has been brought by the 3rd Wave of cryptocurrencies is the instillation of inherent value separate from the normal Stablecoin 1.0 model. Under the original model, which was started under the 2nd Wave, a coin would be pegged to a currency or a commodity and then the trading value of that coin would hover around that value as the commodity or currency moved. This was an effective stopgap measure to prevent the losses that were prevalent in "junk" coins with no staking, but attaching the value of a coin to a fiat currency does not help you gain value and really is just a "trendy" way of maintaining value in the coin.

The other method, attaching a coin value to the value of a commodity is slightly more effective, but still is simply using the coin or the token as a proxy for the other item. If a coin is attached to gold, why not just hold gold for value? The security of the gold is still there, and the gold is actually in your hands, rather than in the hands of the creators. This method had the right idea, helping the coin be attached to something other than the fiat currency, but the scope of the attachment was just not broad enough.

In this Chapter, we look at how all coins moving forward and is staked, should participate in a diversified staking process

. While a coin can have an internal staking process, this is contrary to the decentralized ideals of the cryptocurrency market. The first section of the Chapter looks at the different methods that are available for valuation. Understanding how rating agencies are going to look at the valuation helps one understand how the value is reached.

Next, this Chapter discusses the different types of assets that can be used to grow or maintain value within a system. While a system does not need to have all of the assets present, the more that are present the stronger the portfolio will be. These assets are:

1.) Currency;
2.) Cryptocurrency;
3.) Precious Metals;

4.) Bonds;
5.) Property;
6.) Stocks, Derivatives, and Companies.

Once we have discussed each of these, the Chapter then talks about how they can all be combined together to form one ecosystem.

Methods for Valuation

Unfortunately, the market does not let cryptocurrencies just "say" what they want to be worth, like the fiat currency system. In the market economy, the currency has to have a value that others can see for the coin to be useful on the market. As noted in the last few Chapters, this means that a coin must have transitional value, which is the value that comes from the blockchain, to even be a cryptocurrency (that is not a junk currency). The more translational value the coin has, the easier it will be for the coin to be successful at getting onto an exchange; however, transitional value has the lowest value for determining the actual value of crypto once it is mature.

The next value that we tend to see when we look at the actual value of the crypto is the market value. Once the coin moves from the basic transitional value to the market value it steps outside the control of the creators and places its fate at the hands of the whims of the market. For most coins, this is a good thing. When a creator says, "my coin is worth X..." people know that this is just a person trying to sell their product. However, once the market determines that the coin is, in fact, worth X, then the world can start trading the coin at X and watching it gain value. This initial market value of a coin is a benchmark, but market value returns to the equation later.[399]

When crypto is heavily traded, the good cryptos are accepted as currency in different markets. The different types of cryptos work differently in different markets. Some coins are designed for one specific market, other coins are general tokens that can be used for exchanges, still others are global exchange tokens that are used to trade for goods and even between

[399] Smithmyer & Jadoon (2022, Forthcoming) Valuation Matrix Article.

currencies. Each of these coins has different market indicators for their transactional value. For a niche coin, that can only be traded in certain areas, and adoption by one of the large companies in the space could increase the transactional value greatly; whereas, the acceptance by a major company outside of the space could actually dilute the worth of the coin. For general tokens, the size of the company is important, but the volume of trade conducted in the crypto is even more important. For GETs, everything comes down to the volume of trade added to the ecosystem for the transactional value to be increased. Each has its own place and each has its own valuation.

From transactional value, we return to the market. The more companies that are trading a token or coin, the better the market will react to the crypto. This means that while a company outside of the niche market accepting a coin may decrease its transactional value, it may still increase the total actual value of the coin because the market value of the coin may increase. Once the market value of the coin increases, this is when coins start to look at how they are staked and how the staking process needs to come into effect.

The reason holdings and stakes are so important is because of the give inherent value to the coin. The system owns things, those things have value, therefore the system has value. Since the coin is the representation of the ecosystem, this means that the coin has value. Now what type of value the ecosystem has determined how the actual value of the coin is determined. Linked coins, like Stablecoin 1.0, tend to be stuck at a value relative to a fiat currency rather than have growth potential. Stablecoin 2.0 coins have diversified portfolios that allow them to grow with the market and avoid the inflation that kills fiat currency.

When you combine all four types of valuation, the currency can pose an actual value. Who determines the actual value depends on who you trust? If you are not a trusting person, you can do all the calculations yourself with the publicly available information. This gives you knowledge of how the coin should be valued. If you do not have the time to do that for every coin or token you trade, you can look at one of the larger valuation sites. Some people even look to gurus and creators looking for the "next big thing." What you do is up to you and how much time you spend putting into the system tells you how much you may get out.

Currency

Right now, in the world, fiat currency is king. Even those that are using crypto everywhere that they possibly can are still beholden to the fiat currency for many aspects of their daily lives. With more and more companies issuing "crypto cards," those of us who want to fully embrace the digital age can move part of our portfolio to crypto, but even the biggest Stablecoin 2.0 groups still have some cash in the portfolio to keep the portfolio ultra-liquid.

Managing a capital account with money in it is usually quite simple in the eyes of most people. You hold the money, if crypto or stock runs, you buy, and if something drops you convert it back into currency. This type of thinking is still in the 1980s when fiat currencies were a "stable" economic structure. Be very clear, when portfolios hold currency in a static pattern, they are simply allowing inflation to eat away at their stake.

A currency portfolio always needs to be moving. Some people would equate the action to a money market with a few extra steps. Instead of looking for arbitrage simply with the different currencies around the world, the computers the portfolio uses should look for arbitrage between exchanges for currencies, cryptos, and even derivatives. By constantly having your currency making money by finding and triangulating areas where trades can be made to increase the value of the holdings (exploiting them till they are corrected) the average growth rate can be as high as 0.5% daily.

The currency will always be something that is easy to identify in a portfolio, therefore you should look at what the currency holdings of a Stablecoin 2.0 system are. The more diverse the currency holdings the better, which means that when a currency inflates, they can move away from it and when it gains relative value, they can move the gaining currency. While currency markets will never be "big money" (unless countries leave the EU again), they are a great hedge against inflation in a single currency.

Cryptocurrency

While this does seem like common sense, cryptocurrency portfolios should have some cryptocurrency in them. If they do not, then they are not showing confidence in the market.[400] These accounts should be in a constant state of turnover as currencies are added and dropped as they gain value. Just because a currency is a member of the family does not mean that the portfolio will hold that currency (though it will have reserves). Any coin that is dropping should be converted to a coin that is gaining, and when coins demonstrate that they are making a run, then there should be a big buy.

AI computers should make most of the choices for given crypto trade. This allows emotion to be removed from the equation.[401] With thousands of cryptos on dozens of exchanges, there are always opportunities for arbitrage in the system. This will allow the portfolio to constantly grow in value to build the value of the ecosystem. Since the crypto market is growing so rapidly, this will be one of the fastest-growing aspects of the portfolio.

It should be noted that the entire portfolio should not be cryptocurrency. Crypto is an aggressive asset that can, as a group, all lose value at the same time (like the week of Dec 10th 2021).[402] This means that the market takes a double hit if you see a coin that is on the portfolio and a member of the group drop in value. When several of the coins from the group follow the same pattern, it can be a major problem. This is why only a portion of the portfolio should be in crypto (the whole point of Stablecoin 2.0 is to keep a portfolio stable.

---

[400] Haar, Ryan (2021). "Why do bitcoins have value?" Next Advisor at https://time.com/nextadvisor/investing/cryptocurrency/why-do-bitcoins-have-value/.

[401] *Id.*

[402] *Id.*

Precious Metals

Some advisors say that precious metals should be a big part of your portfolio, some say that you should stay away from precious metals. When you are looking at building the actual value of a coin, precious metals can be useful. Precious metal will always have a value; therefore, they fall into the "safe" category for investment. People have been predicting that gold and silver were going to run for years, they still have not. They are undervalued and should move up in the market, but it has not happened yet.

When looking at precious metals, look at what will be precious not what is precious now. Too many people focus on gold and silver (which have great value). But metals that are needed for the space race and metal that are needs to increase the size and accessibility of the metaverse will explode in the next few years. As cryptos grow, these metals also grow. Make sure that you have some of them in your portfolio.

When looking at valuation, always check to see how much of the metal the portfolio owns and how much it owns on paper. It is estimated that the fiat currency system has oversold the world gold reserves buy up to double. This means that many people "own" gold that does not exist. As long as no one calls all of the ownership, this house of cards will fall, but if enough people call in their ownership there could be a financial collapse in fiat currency like the world has never seen. This is why hedging in non-Stablecoin 1.0 crypto is so important.

Bonds

Bonds are a safe investment in most cases.[403] They have different levels, government, municipal, corporate, with different risk levels, but generally a bond is a safe way to store money with an interest rate that matches the inflation rate. Bond investments do not increase the value of the portfolio much, but they do provide a level of stability that cannot be seen in any of

[403] Investor.gov (2021). Bonds. US gov at https://www.investor.gov/introduction-investing/investing-basics/investment-products/bonds-or-fixed-income-products/bonds.

the other models.

Government bonds are the safest bonds to invest in.[404] Most governments are so worried about their made-up credit scores that they will print more money to pay off the bonds. Because of this, the bonds barely keep up with the interest rate. Since they do usually "just make the cut" they can be a good place to put money for a period of time. Since bonds can be traded on the secondary market, they can also be short-term hedges against volatile crypto markets.

Municipal bonds are also a good investment. Most of the time the state or federal government of an area will not let a bond issue fail, because the taxpayers will get mad.[405] This does happen sometimes, but it is an odd occurrence. Because of the added risk, there is a higher interest in municipal bonds (barely). This can be a more effective hedge against inflation and still be a safe investment.

Corporate bonds are a crapshoot. You need to know if the corporation is stable and if they can cover the bond issue. Most companies insure their bonds (because there is lawsuit potential if they do not) so you will usually get your money, it just might take longer. Corporate bonds tend to have the highest return rate of the three.

Overall, you would like to see all three kinds of bonds in your ecosystem's portfolio. All three are fairly safe options because the bond market has been boring since the 1990s when "junk bonds" were replaced with different stock options. Most bonds are safer, but you need to watch to make sure that your ecosystem is watching what the companies are doing (municipal and government bonds tend to be very safe). As noted, this is not a way to grow the ecosystem, just a way to keep things stable.

Stocks, Derivatives, and companies.

Major portfolios are going to have stocks, derivatives, and companies under their control. The bigger the crypto family is, the more holdings in

---

[404] *Id.*
[405] *Id.*

this area they should have.[406] There are two reasons why a crypto ecosystem portfolio would want to have stocks, derivatives, and companies. The first is because they are a growth industry, so the portfolio will grow. The second is because a portfolio should gain voting control of companies to make sure that they accept as many cryptos as reasonable.

Stocks are the safest bets for a crypto portfolio to build upon. Stocks maintain or grow value, and even the ones that lose value still have some value as long as they do not go bankrupt. They do not have as high of a growth level as cryptos, but they can fall into either the aggressive or moderate category, which is good for the growth side of the portfolio.

Derivatives are a great way to hedge your stock ownership.[407] A portfolio should trade derivatives and be very leery about buying them in the initial offering. The play on the derivative market should be in and out moves, staying away from long-term holdings.[408] When they do acquire a strong derivative near the execution date, they should execute the derivative as long as it is in the black. The goal of this derivative is constant growth, not meteoric growth.

Buying companies is an end-stage level for the portfolio. Once a portfolio acquires a company, it should be moved to a management firm that deals with the day-to-day systems. Big Stablecoin 2.0 systems, like *The Wallet Group*, will have subsidiaries dedicated to the management of the firm's holdings. This allows for the companies to become producing entities on the portfolio, rather than just dividends or trading fodder.

Bringing it all together

Once you see the systems that all come together, then you have a better

---

[406] Hall, Mary (2021). "How Companies use derivatives to hedge risk." Investopedia at https://www.investopedia.com/trading/using-derivatives-to-hedge-risk/.

[407] Capital.com (2017). "How companies are using derivatives to hedge." Capital.com at https://capital.com/how-companies-are-using-derivatives-to-hedge.

[408] *Id.*

ability to create an actual value for crypto. With a Stablecoin 2.0 system, you need to look at how the portfolio is managed and divided among the coins. Systems with joint voting power in the system are preferable to systems with deviated voting power. While the larger currencies should have a little larger voice, they should not dominate the conversation.

Most Stablecoin 2.0 portfolios will be semi-private, this means that the distribution across the assets will be announced, but the actual assets being held will be closely kept. This is to prevent the portfolio from becoming an independent benchmark, which can affect the valuation of the coins therein (positive but is still creates a conflict of interest). A strong inherent value of a coin will surpass the market value as the key indicator of the coin's actual value.

Chapter 35: Anti-Whale Technology

One of the most dangerous things to a crypto market is when a whale dumps billions of units of coin in a single sale. This can either be a liquidation of the whale's assets or the whale can just be manipulating the market to increase the size of its share. Either way, when we see a whale do this in the crypto world, it is not just the coin that is being traded that is being affected but the entire market. Since many coins and tokens are linked, a major drop in one coin or token can cause a ripple effect.

This Chapter looks at some of the ways that cryptocurrency can limit the effects that whales can have on the market at any given moment. We start by looking at the big question, "What is a Whale?" Sometimes the most difficult situation can be defining what a whale is and is not so we can set up anti-whaling technology. Operating from the position that whales are dangerous, we next look at why account locking is dangerous, not just for whale accounts but for any account in general. This leads to the discussion of why some of the more complex methods of whale management, such as time limits and limit-limits are also hard on the market, along with being hard on the evolution of the coin. Next, we take a moment to look at high initial burn limits. While these are only preventative in the ICO phase, they can be very effective in the fledgling period of a coin or token to manage its viability. One of the best methods of managing the coin flow is to manage a high reserve. Too often coin creators want to put as many coins on the market as possible to increase initial profits, having a high return slows the profit rate but can help control whales. On the same page, having an international reserve, that is getting a country to buy a portion of the coin, can also be a good tool.

Overall, whales will make or break a coin. Designers need to make sure that when they create the coin parts are in place to ensure that whales do not manipulate the coin, all the while making sure that a coin is an appealing place for the whales to invest their money. It is a dangerous dance for a young coin, but those who learn the steps can make a coin that will see promising returns.

What is a Whale?

When you enter into any crypto forum, it will not be long before you see the term whale thrown around by the denizens of cyberspace. Whether they use the term correctly or not, almost every major move in the crypto world is going to be underscored by a move a whale made. The most common thing to see in the summer of 2021, when many of the young alt-coins were seeing the 1000%+ runs, was that the "Dogefather," Elon Musk, had said something positive or negative about cryptocurrency. As recently as December 12th, Musk's tweets about crypto not out performing fiat currency have caused massive selloffs by paper hands.[409]

Elon is just one of the many people around the world considered to be whale. Mr. Musk has the disadvantage of being known (or advantage to some) by being known by his real name. Many whales in the crypto space are only known by their chat handles. There is a wide variety of how whales act throughout the crypto ecosystem. Some of the whales like to keep to themselves, with the ripples they make barely breaking the surface as they buy and sell large quantiles of coin in a reputable way. Others take pride in manipulating the form of the market by making large sales all at once so that there is a drop that they can then capitalize on.[410] Either way, the whales are a force to be reckoned with across the blockchain and the crypto valuation.

But that does not answer the question, what is a whale? A whale is a person who has bought or is holding a large portion of coin or token. The amount of the coin that needs to be held to be considered a whale is a largely debated topic. In some coins, whales will hold over 10% of a coin. In other circumstances, the whale may only own a small percentage of the coin but can still move the coins because of their influence and how they wield their position. The amount is not nearly as problematic as the power that the

---

[409] Time (2021). "Person of the Year." Time at https://time.com/person-of-the-year-2021-elon-musk/.

[410] Shumba, Camomile (2021). "A Crypto Whale scooped up 50 billion Shiba inus as the meme coin slumped this week." Business Insider at https://markets.businessinsider.com/news/currencies/crypto-whale-50-billion-shiba-inu-meme-coin-fell-bitcoin-2021-12.

whales hold, which is why anti-whaling technology is so important.

As early as the beginning of the second Wave of cryptocurrencies, alt-coins started to look into anti-whaling technologies. At the beginning of the Wave, the technologies were timid and more "suggestions" than actual policies that had teeth. When new coins and tokens were challenging the thrones of Ethereum and Bitcoin, they were taking money from whoever would sponsor them- regardless of how the money came in. This mirrored the early 1800s when anyone who called themselves a railroad could get money from the United States government. Cryptos were desperate; however, now that the market has stabilized a little the cryptos need to keep whales in check. Make no mistake, whales are still treated well- but there are some methods to keep them from manipulating the market.

Why Locking is a Dangerous Practice?

One of the most primitive methods of dealing with whales is a practice called locking. In some situations, creators of coins keep enough power over their coins that they can stop trading on their coins should a market manipulation be seen. This practice prevents large shareholders from dumping their coin when the markets turn south. It is effective in keeping the whales locked into the coin through a downturn, but generally, it locks everyone into the coin as well. This practice is very dangerous, not just for the coin but also for the industry, as people lose faith when they cannot trade their coin during a downturn.

While this has always been frowned upon, many of the exchanges suggested that they would no longer allow coins to do this after the SQUIDCOIN collapse in 2021. With the success of the new show, Squid Game on Netflix, a meme coin had a skyrocketing success rate, jumping thousands of percentage points in mere days. The coin led many of the charts and seemed to be more popular than some of the dominant meme coins, SHIB and DOGE.[411] This seemed to be a safe investment for many,

---

[411] Cook, Scott (2021). "Squid Coin: An ending scam or a rising phenomenon." Cryptonewsz at https://www.cryptonewsz.com/squid-coin-an-ending-scam-or-a-rising-phenomenon/.

and many joined the coin near the end of October. This coin even outpaced BAT (a legitimate coin that ran because of the Halloween holiday) by a great amount.[412]

On November 1st, however, the people who invested in BAT were celebrating the day after Halloween while the Squid traders were crying in horror. The coin dropped from a high of $2,861.80 US down to $0.0007926 in only five minutes.[413] To make matters worse, the anti-whale technology of locking was used and people who had their life saving tied up in the coin could not sell as they watched their value drop to below a penny. The designers (who were not locked out) ran away with millions while the people who invested in the coin were devastated.[414]

Locking technology is a dangerous way to ensure that whales do not manipulate the coin. Regardless of the intention, whether legitimate or hostile like the SQUID coin, the locking should be banned. People have a right to contract for their coin, it would be akin to someone (not a government) locking your accounts because they do not agree with what you are doing. Even when a government does this, it is a violation of a person's human rights. Expediency does not legitimize abuse. Only via due process should a person's accounts be seized in any free nation. This is why locking should be banned outright on major crypto exchanges.

Time Limits and Limit-Limits

Two concepts that arise out of the same family of ideas are time limits and limit-limits. Both of these mechanisms are used to ensure that someone does not move too much money too fast, while still maintaining the individual's freedom to trade their coins. While still one of the more oppressive methods that a coin or exchange can use to ensure that there are no mass selloffs of coins (no one is worried about mass buyouts for

---

[412] *Id.*

[413] Cheng, Amy (2021). "Squid Game' inspired cryptocurrency that soared by 23 million percent now worthless after apparent scam." The Washington Post at https://www.washingtonpost.com/world/2021/11/02/squid-game-crypto-rug-pull/.

[414] *Id.*

some reason), it is much more useful and humane than the lockout method.

A time limit block is something that is used to prevent someone from moving too much coin in a small period of time. Markets can be manipulated if a person puts a large number of coins up for sale, well under the market rate, and allows the market to adjust to the rate. Often, the algorithms used by exchanges will move the "close" trades first, which allows the market to start to trend downward quite quickly. The sales are often made at an average slightly higher than the amount of the offer, which results in a collapse of the market and the coin being traded at a higher rate. Even worse, a large sell-off well under the market value can cause the coin value to drop without the actual coin in the offer being sold. Market hawks can watch the market, see a big lowball sale, and try to beat the sale. Herein the algorithm can work against the market as the person can drop the cost without ever selling a coin.

Why would a person want to do this? Because it allows them to average down the value of their coin. If they are going to buy a large chunk of the coin, they can put up what they have on the market for sale at a depressing rate, wait for the price to drop (whether they sell or not), then buy more coin at the lower rate very quickly. This can cause gains in market share by as much as 20% of the current holdings. Time limits limit the number of coins/tokens that can be traded during a given time, which makes whales take longer to sell-off. This is still dangerous because when there is a legitimate sell-off, it makes it hard for large holders to move. This is why some exchanges have "smart" algorithms that look at what the market is doing before they allow the trade.[415]

Limit-limits look at limiting the other end of the spectrum. While time limits limit the amount of coin that a person can dump in a period of time, limit-

---

[415] As evil as it is, it seems it is legal in the United States. *See* Doherty, Kathrine and Massa, Annie (2021). "Robinhood, Citadel Win Dismissal of Meme-Stock Lawsuit." Bloomberg at https://www.bloomberg.com/news/articles/2021-11-18/robinhood-citadel-securities-get-meme-stock-lawsuit-dismissed.

limits limit the amount of coin that a person can trade in a single transaction. While this is not as effective as lockouts or time limits, it is much more human and protects the market better than the previous models. This allows a person to trade, just perhaps not as fast as they may like.

A limit-limit sets a limit on the trade amount. Unless an exchange has a limit on the number of trades that you can do during a period of time, the person can make as many small trades as possible. Each of these trades would have a maximum amount, but you could not do it all in one fell swoop. The effect of this is that a person can get rid of all of their stock, but they cannot "signal" a crash which causes a false crash. This is an effective way to manage how people can disperse large amounts of a coin. Some are limited as high a 0.01% of the coin in circulation, some are more aggressive at 0.00001% of the token in circulation. Regardless, it limits the amount that you can trade in a single transaction so that there are no "whale" signals manipulating the board.

Both time limits and limit-limits have their place on the market. Whether they become popular or not depends on how the coins that use these methodologies are received on the market. Personally, buying a large number of coins with the potential for a lockout or a time limit is a little frightening, however, we do not buy to manipulate the market. The limit-limit seems to be a fair compromise in letting the whales be whales and still maintaining the viability of the market.

High Burn Periods

NOTE: that this method of anti-whaling is only viable during a ICO and the period right after the ICO. Any coin with a high burn rate outside of the ICO should be avoided.

High burn periods may seem like something that no one would like when you are dealing with a coin. A high burn rate can be as low as 5% or as high as 20%, depending on how the coin is being launched. The concept behind a high burn rate at the ICO is to prevent trading of the coin too early. Giveaway holders and early buyers can thank the launch of a coin if they drop what they were given (bought for cheap) before the ICO can get a significant number of coins on the market. If the market tanks, the ICO can tank and the only coins being traded on the market are the ones that were given away. Worse, the ICO acts as a resistance line keeping the coin deflated and away from the ICO amount. It can be bad news all around. This is why high burns can be useful if they are used correctly.

Single ICO coins sometimes keep the burn rate high at the beginning to ensure that the ICO is complete before people start trading the coins, this can show a "lack of faith" in the coin as they want people to hold for a period of time before they sell. In a single burn ICO, anything over 5% is suspect. The 5% is enough to keep people from trading the coin too quickly around the ICO (the burn is Waved for the initial purchase). This allows the ecosystem to stabilize before the rate drops (or raises) too quickly and allows the coin to establish itself on the market.

When you are looking at tiered ICOs, be leery of coins that do not have a burn rate mechanism to protect the value of the coin. In a tiered ICO, the creators release packets of coins at ascending values to find the market value of a coin. Generally done in groups of 5-10 tiers, the coin creators release a portion of the coin at a rate then determine the value of the next tier based on how fast the present tier is selling out. If it sells out quickly, then the rate needs to be raised quickly. If it sells out slowly, then it needs to be raised slowly. If it does not sell out, well then the price is too high and it needs to be lowered. The burn rate should also be tiered based on the length of the release. In the case of a 10-tear release plan, a burn rate could start at 15% and drop one percent for each tear as it is released. Then when it hits the final tier, the rate is dropped to its constant burn rate (generally between 0-2% and the trading can occur naturally. (The 2% burn rate is only for Stablecoin 2.0 coins if there is a burn rate on a non-Stablecoin 2.0 coin be warry about it).

Many people are nervous around high burn rate coins, for good reason. Their trading is severely curtailed during the initial release by the burn rate. This is beneficial to the system, and if you are a user or a holder, this can highly benefit you. The goal of this is to keep whales and day traders from tanking the value of a viable coin to buy in lower than the ICO and increase their holdings illicitly. Generally, if the high burn rate lasts longer than the ICO, then you are looking at a scam, so you have to do your due diligence.

High stability Reserves

Reserves have been a constant with economic policy since currency became a "thing." A country or issuer of a currency needs to have a reserve amount of the currency to use for operations and to ensure that there is enough of the currency circulating. While it is highly unlikely, one person or a cabal of people could, in theory, come to acquire most of the currency, allowing them to artificially inflate the price or deflate the price. Ironically, this is one of the things that cryptocurrency sought to avoid but has become a problem in some tokens.

One of the reasons that we see reserves as a problem with some cryptocurrencies is because creators conflate personal "stashes" with reserves. A stash is a coin that you can sell onto the market to make money for creating the coin. This is a good thing as it incentivizes the creators to create a good coin. In many first and second-Wave cryptos, creators often kept 30-50% of the coin as a stash/reserve for the coin. This led to situations where creators "found" more coins after the market had gained stability through trading. The massive amounts that were maintained by one person allow for "rug pulls" and dumps by the creators which can be devastating.

The third Wave of cryptos has improved upon this mode slightly. Major third Wave cryptos, such as KIROS, have limited ownership of the creators to 12-15% of the total token.[416] Further, the coin that is shared with partners and early investors is limited to about 7% of the token. Additionally, KIROS in particular assessed over 50% of the token to reserves (approximately 23% to active reserves and 23% to international reserves. This creates a system where the reserves are active, but they are not being actively traded on the market- which increases the value of the ecosystem

[416] KIROS White Paper

while still maintaining liquidity (10-20%).[417]

The additional benefit of massive token reserves is that the price of the token can be stabilized through a coin release. While there are many ways to release the reserve token (warrants being the best option), when a reserve token (or group of reserve tokens) is released, they should go, at least partially, to the holders of the token (unless released through a warrant where the buyer adds money to the ecosystem to get a newly released token). This ensures that, while the value of each token drops slightly, the net value of the holders will increase as they will receive more coins to balance out the losses from the reduction in value. In a perfect release, there will be a net-zero gain; however, strong coins often error on the side of the users and make sure that the users gain value.

Having an International Reserve

Another new feature of the third Wave of crypto is the international reserve. "In 2021, El Salvador became the first country to accept Bitcoin as legal tender."[418] While selecting one coin over the whole of crypto as a coin may have been a mistake, the concept of having crypto as a primary or secondary legal tender may take hold, especially in the 3rd world.[419]

The specific appeal of cryptocurrencies to third world countries comes from the fact that it is not controlled by the government. Since the crypto is controlled by the market (or at worst with Stablecoin 1.0 cryptos a third party), corrupt governments cannot manipulate the currency to affect the market. The governments are getting out of the currency printing business and allowing reputable companies on international exchanges to do that for them. This may prove to be a winning strategy.

In the United States, it costs about $0.02 to create a penny, $0.07 to create

---

[417] *Id.*

[418] El Salvador, Supra.

[419] We are using 3rd world in its proper context here, not just a "poor country." 1st world countries are western democracies/republics, 2nd world countries are socialist and communist states, and 3rd world countries are countries that have hybrid systems wrought with corruption.

a nickel and dollars cost more than they are worth to print.[420] Countries do not pay anything to print cryptocurrencies, and they can buy it at face value or less to have a national reserve (to make sure that there is liquidity in the government). Bitcoin's massive worth and limited supply may not be the "coin of the future" for exchange, as it will likely be regulated to investments. Global Exchange Tokens (GET) look to be something that can be used much more easily, can be exchanged for any crypto coin or token, and have a system of price regulations that should keep them reasonable for decades (if not longer). Plus, once one moves past the usable phase, a token based on the token can be issued (2.0 if you will) to keep the ecosystem and increase the number of tokens as the human population increases.

Strong 3rd Wave cryptos are built around the concept of international reserves. This is a reserve of coins that is only touched if a country wants to buy coins for its national reserve (they can also be used for mega-companies). In a trillion-coin system, purchases are regulated to more than a billion coins. This ensures that the buyouts increase the size of the ecosystem holdings and add worth to the coin. Even when a large international reserve is depleted, which should take decades, the amount of the ecosystem is strengthened and the loss of reserves is replaced with a strong gain in the inherent value of the token or coin.

Conclusion

The war against whales is a difficult war to fight, because you want the whales to be successful for the good of the coin. This means that the system needs to try to seek a balance with the groups of investors that bring the most money to the coin. Only time will tell if a coin has chosen the right balance or has shifted itself in favor of the whales or in favor of the smaller holders. While this choice is made while the coin is being created, failures in this choice can be offset by adopting a strong smart

---

[420] Unser, Mike (2021). "Penny costs 1.76 cents to make in 2020…" Coinnews.net at https://www.coinnews.net/2021/02/23/penny-costs-1-76-cents-to-make-in-2020-nickel-costs-7-42-cents-us-mint-realizes-549-9m-in-seigniorage/.

contract overlay.

Our recommendation in this book is that exchanges stay away from lockouts. If a person wants to sell their coin, and they can find a buyer, then it is their right to contract that coin away. Time limits are better than lockouts but are still problematic from a contract's point of view. Limit-limits are annoying for large transfers, but are likely the most humane way that you can limit the sales of a good without limiting a person's ability to get out from under a bad coin.

One of the best ways that crypto can hedge against whales is to ensure that there are ample reserves. Reserves controlled by the sponsoring entity are the best, reserves that are held by national governments as a hedge for using the currency as a secondary legal tender are a close second. The more involved the reserve is in increasing the value of the ecosystem the better. The biggest mistake crypto can make is to allow its entire reserve to sit in a dead wallet doing nothing and not growing the system.

Chapter 36: Initial Coin Offering Management and Protections

One of the lead killers of new tokens is how they get their tokens to market. While this is not as big of a problem for coins (because most coins need some sort of mining), this can be something that kills a token with high potential. One of the reasons that many tokens face this problem is because they look at the problem of "how" wrong. Each token needs to have a set of goals that it needs to reach, and when the creators of the coin allow the "how it is been done" to dictate how they should do it, they tend to find themselves living someone else's dream. This is the digital age and each token is an experimental laboratory of how the financial system can be better. This Chapter talks about some of the best practices, but these practices will always be evolving with the distribution of each new coin.

This Chapter is an overview of the current best practices for releasing a coin through an initial coin offering (ICO). Of all the Chapters of the book, this is likely to be the one that gets upgraded with each new edition. Token creators need to get the coins to market, but they also need to remember that the ICO is not the only way that coins will get in the hands of investors (read the derivatives section for more methods). However, most investors expect an ICO for a coin, if for nothing more than setting the price for the coin to trade on the market.

This Chapter starts off by looking at the simplest form of an ICO, a general ICO. A general ICO is when a company releases the coins all at once at a set price. This allows the market to accept the price (where all of the coins are bought) or to reject the price (where coins are still setting around). We then move on to the idea of a tiered ICO. A tiered ICO is a modern form of ICO where the coins are released in pre-selected amounts at either pre-selected or market-derived prices, and each tier cannot start until the tier before it is complete. These are the two primary forms of ICOs.

This Chapter also takes the time to look at some of the protections that are recommended for protecting your ICO. One of these methods is a starter burn system. This is where there is a burn percentage set during the ICO, so that day traders cannot buy then sell the coin lower to short the coin. Another method for protecting your ICO is to ensure that your ICO is concurrent with other distribution techniques. While some coins have been successful with a single distribution technique; the more diverse your distribution model is, the better off your coin will be.

The Chapter concludes with a discussion of gamification of the release of the coin. This is the digital age and people want new ways to acquire goods. One of the hottest methods on the market is the gamification of the system. This gamification allows for people to do something other than pay money (watch videos, fill out surveys, play a game) to win the tokens and get them out into the system. While this method does not increase the value of the ecosystem as quickly as the ICO, it can be an effective way to increase your dispersal without having to drop your price.

The important thing to remember as you read this Chapter is that you always need to be thinking of ways that other people have not thought of to make your coin unique. While the best practices outlined herein will help you get a strong start, the piece that can take you from a successful coin to the next major release is the creativity of the system. Think about what people want, then think about how you can increase the value of the ecosystem by meeting that need. The better connection you have with your intended audience the better chance that your method will work and you can move your coin to the elite level.

A General ICO

Most modern tokens that are currently on the market have entered the market through a general ICO (if they used an ICO). The ICO model mirrors an IPO for a stock offering, which is the way that things have been done for years. The IPO model is effective, so effective that an entire industry has arisen around that model. It is no shock that many of the same players in the IPO industry are trying to dictate the format of the ICO industry. To allow this to happen sets a dangerous standard.

The people who are involved in the IPO industry have a goal in mind, to make money. The easiest way to make money is to continue to use working patterns (for them) to ensure that you do not have pay for new training, new systems, or consultants for new ideas. One of the reasons that the cryptocurrency system was created was to get out from under problems like this. IPOs are a centralized system, which have been controlled by the same major companies for the last century. Cryptocurrency is designed to remove that "middleman" from the equation so that the creators of the currency can deal directly with their community.

The simplest form of an ICO is when the creator releases the coins directly on a low-level exchange. This is one of the least profitable ways in which a coin can be released, but for many coins with a limited following, this is the only method that they have. Generally, the coin creates a wallet on the exchange (separate from their own wallet, lest they make a mistake) and dumps a portion of the coin on the market. Generally, in this model, the creator has to sell the coin at a deep discount less than its transitional value because people need to be incentivized to buy it. As the tokens take hold, the value of the coin rises. These are the tokens that you see start at a millionth of a cent. Tokens can be successful in this model, but the ecosystem suffers as the stabilizing holdings of the system cannot profit from the discounted tokens.

The next method that is marginally more successful is to pitch your coin to one of the more major exchanges. This can be either a major exchange or a mid-level exchange with a little more organization and a lot more customers. In this model, the creator will likely be able to sell the initial coin at a value near the working value of the coin, but the platform will take a small portion of the profits for platform fees and for overseeing the ICO. Depending on the platform, these fees and percentages can be negotiated. The ecosystem under this model tends to do a lot better because more money is flowing into the holding system which allows for a better ecosystem start.[421] The better you do with your secondary distribution techniques, the better chance you will have of working with one of the larger systems.

The best practice is to have a company, like *Black Wallet*, oversee your

---

[421] All examples in this Chapter are assuming that a token is using a 3rd Wave stablecoin 2.0 model.

release. In this case, you will not only have the opportunity to work with the partner network of the company that you choose, but you will also be entered into an already developed ecosystem. While the "inherent value" valuation becomes more complex, the hybrid joint relationship with the surety in the system allows for all coins in the system to enjoy the value. If you are accepted into a strong Stablecoin 2.0 system, then the value of your coin should be closer to the aggregate value upon release than the transitional value. This can be the difference between two to even three decimal places in the initial release and can make the world of difference over the first year of operation of the token.

If you choose to go with a general ICO, make sure that you know what you are doing. While a general ICO is much simpler than a tiered ICO, there is little room for failure. One wrong choice (or worse yet, one bad keystroke) and all your work could go down the drain.[422] Larger programs and companies can make this easier as they oversee the release and can ensure a higher level of quality control as the coin enters the market.

A Tiered ICO

The methodology that seems to have taken hold in the 3rd Wave of cryptocurrency is the tiered ICO. In a tiered ICO, the coin is released in batches, generally in rapid succession with each batch being more expensive than the batch before it.[423] The reason that many tokens are doing this is that the system was well designed. The faster the coin sells out in a lower-level dictates how fast the coin will be listed (and for how much) in the next tier. This allows for the token to be assured (if it has value) that the value should find the actual value of the coin and plateau at that point (or a little above).

The most common models of tiered ICOs are 5-tier and 10-tier. Both are effective and the number of tiers is generally dictated by the number of tokens that will be released. Under 500 billion tokens and you should

---

[422] BBC (2021). "Bored Ape NFT Accidentally Sells for $3, 000 instead of $300, 000." BBC at https://www.bbc.com/news/technology-59638565.
[423] KIROS White Paper.

probably work with a 5-tier system. Over 500 billion and you would be looking at a 10-tier system. Other than sheer volume, the reason for the number of tiers is at the discretion of the creator and the exchange that they are releasing the coins on.

Another consideration that must be looked at by the creators of the coin is how they want to release the coins within the tiers. There are three common options, each has its own benefits and drawbacks. These options are:

1.) Equal Release;
2.) Equitable Release;
3.) Pre-Planned Release.

Regardless of the method that is chosen, a creator should have some reason for choosing each one of these. Equal releases tend to be more effective in smaller offerings, while equitable releases and pre-planned releases tend to be effective with larger token releases.

An equal release is just what it says, each tier is going to have an equal amount of coin. If you are doing a small exchange release with little computer support, this may be the best model for you to use. Likewise, if you have a smaller number of tokens, this tends to be simpler for your community to accept. In an equal release, you would announce the number of coins per tier, and how the valuation of the tier will be dictated (pre-planned, based on speed, or hybrid). Generally, for an equal release, you will also announce when each tier will become active. This model gives your community and your investors the best possible approach to buying the coin. One note of caution though, if you give out the tier values ahead of time, you may see day traders buy in to flip a tier 1 buy on tier 3 or 4.

Equitable releases are the middle of the road in how releases are let out. They are also the most complex. Equitable releases build the amount of the tier on the same model as the cost of the tier. This requires a computer or a very smart overseer to do (mainly because equitable releases are generally a rapid release model). In this model, the speed at which the previous tier sells out dictates not only the cost of the next tier but also the amount of the next tier. There are two schools of thought in this matter, the Ashe school dictates that in a tier where there is a fast selling of the coin, the next tier should have a smaller amount of coin. The theory behind this school of thought is that having a smaller amount of coin will allow the market to decide if this is the proper valuation of the coin, or whether the valuation should be raised to the next tier. This type of model is generally accompanied by a large increase in price (80%-140%). The Smithmyer school of thought follows a fast-selling tier with a large offering. This is to keep the price of the coin from artificially inflating. The theory behind this is that if the coin is underpriced, the large offering will sell out quickly also. If the coin is having a false rush, the larger offering will slow down the growth and allow for better analysis for the tertiary tier. This is often accompanied by a larger window for the three-level change (10%-240% depending on the speeds of release). Both schools of thought are effective, and both have been shown to be quite successful.

The third methodology of release is the pre-planned release. This is the most arbitrary methodology for release and should only be used when you have ruled out the other methods for some reason. In this model, you have a reason for why you are releasing the amounts at different levels at different tiers. The only way that this model has been seen to be successful is when it is in conjunction with large presentations. When you know how big your audience will be (in-room and digital), you can base the amount of coin you want to sell on that. This is a difficult way to market your coin, but can be effective if you have the right people.

Tiered releases are the best system for a healthy ecosystem. Because the tiers allow the market to adjust to the value of the coin, more money comes in at the high tiers to but build up value. The more complex the model, the more control you have over it; however, the more difficult it is to explain in your White Paper. As a result, the number of tiers should be based on your amount of coin and the way that the tiers are decided should be equal releases for small quantity tokens and equitable releases for large quantity tokens. This gives your community the most control, and allows the market to regulate itself before the open exchange begins.

Starter Burns for ICOs

One of the biggest threats for a small-cap token is when there is a whale who would like to manipulate the price of your ICO. This generally happens with general ICOs, but there is also the potential for this to happen with tiered ICO. In order to deal with this problem, the third Wave of cryptos has adopted a "starter burn" philosophy that is put in place to protect the releases. The philosophy behind the starter burn is that the coin is not actually "live" on the market until the ICO is over. This means that the sales rates of the token can be controlled during the interim to ensure the protection of the buyers.

When working with a starter burn, you need to clearly define the burn rate in your White Paper. The burn rate needs to be high enough that it protects the coin, but not so high that it is prohibitive of those who have bought the coin from trading should the coin rally. In most cases, the value should be between 10-20% in a 10 tier burn and 7-14% in a five-tier burn. The goal of the burn is not to bring money back into the "burn and earn system" but is designed to allow the market to dictate the rate of sales for the ICO.

For those doing a small-cap token offering, the best way to do the starter burn with the equal release is to note the date of the start of the ICO (tier 1) and the date of the end of the ICO (tier 5). The starter burn rate will be in effect from the beginning of the release until the end of tier 5 (usually an hour is given for the system to do upgrades after the end of the burn period). At the end of the burn period, the starter burn should be reduced to the standing burn that is used in the contract overlays system. If no burn and earn system is being used, then the burn rate should be dropped to zero. It is important that the burn contract overlay should still be in place, if there needs to be a burn on the token.

When you begin dealing with a 10-tier equitable release program, the burn rate management becomes more complex. One option is to treat it like the starter burn for a 5-tier model, which can be effective. The burn rate on non-ICO sales stays at the same high rate until the process is over. This allows the ecosystem to be fully funded (and sometimes even valued) before the secondary market sales begin in earnest (some may sell early depending on the growth rate). Another option is a declining burn rate for the coin. If the model is 10-tier, the rate can be set at 15% (as an example). Each time a new tier is reached, the burn rate is reduced by 1% until the last tier is sold and the burn rate is lowered to the standing burn rate. This allows the market to dictate the rate, but also allows the market to start to develop under the growing system of value. Some investors will want to buy in at tier 1 and be gone by tier 5. This arguable form of scalping is legal and cannot be prohibited; they just need to be aware that they likely will be losing a percentage off the top in the transaction. This will also help keep people holding until the market stabilizes.

Tiered releases can have PR problems because of the starter burn rate. Day traders and scalpers who do not read the White Paper will complain about the rate. However, as long as you have the rate in the White Paper and it is announced with the genesis of each tier, you should be protected (make sure your platform allows this but most major platforms will). The burn rate for the starter burn should go right to the reserve, or it can go to a charity. Charity can be a great way to deal with the PR problem. A reply such as:

> *It was announced that all tokens burned during the starter burn would be donated to St. Jude's children's hospital at the beginning of each tier and in the white pages, we want to thank each of the community members that helped us donate XXXX coins to the children with childhood diseases. You have made their lives infinitely better.*

Not only do you get to make the world a better place, but you also get your coin into the medical system AND get to tweak the nose of the scalpers and day traders.

Ensuring that the ICO is concurrent with other Distribution Techniques

When you are setting up your ICO, you need to be cognizant that there are other techniques for distributing your coin onto the market. These other techniques can have more tokens involved with them than the general ICO. It is important to understand that you need to present how you are doing this in a White Paper and ensure that your community knows what is going on. Some of the other areas are:

1.) Tokens to your team;
2.) Tokens to family and friends;
3.) Tokens to direct investors;
4.) Tokens to Partners;
5.) Donations;
6.) Miscellaneous programs.

How you distribute the tokens is not as important as the fact that you let your community know how you are distributing the tokens. Having a "dump" of tokens that are not listed on the white pages can lower faith in your token within the community.

The tokens that are provided to your team are an important part of the process. The creator of a coin and the people who worked hard to get the coin off the ground deserve to be compensated for their work. The difficulty that many coin creators face is that they believe that this is "shady" and they need to hide the coin that they give to their team. DO NOT HIDE IT. Anyone who understands how the crypto market works understands that a creator is not going to do all this for free. There are hundreds of thousands of dollars that go into creating a top-level coin. Even garbage tokens cost thousands of dollars to create. The key rule here is that you tell your community how it is being distributed in the White Paper and only give out a reasonable amount. The total amount for the team should be somewhere around 10-20%.

Next, there are the giveaways that go to people who supported the project but did not actually do work for the project. Once again, some creators feel guilty about giving this type of token away. Do not feel guilty, families support you while you build your coin. What you need to remember, is that just like members of the team, you need to ensure that you have listed all the tokens that will be given to family and friends in the distribution (the amounts not who they go to). Also, and this is very important, do not hide coins for yourself in this category. This is a great way to get caught and lose the faith of your community. Keep this rate under 5%.

Tokens to direct investors are another important area. These are the people who are putting actual equity into the coin, not the sweat equity of the above groups. How much you sell to direct investors is up to you. Make sure that you do not sell out your reserves and you do not sell out all the coins. Direct investors without an ICO will make the coin very difficult to get on a major market. The major market wants to see that you have a lot of holders; however, they also want to make their pound of flesh for putting the coin out there. This rate should be listed in the White Paper and is at the discretion of the creator.

One way to avoid the fees associated with your ICO is to offer coins to the platform. The platform may accept them, it may not. Regardless, if you offer it, you should have some blocked out in the White Paper for this purpose. Remember, these are not investors, they are simply the platform that will carry your coin. The total amount you give out to this group should be no more than 5-10%. If you have the luxury of using multiple platforms, ensure that you "pay" each platform according to its size.

Donations can be an interesting tool to get your token on the market. Besides the fact that this helps you be, not just look like a good person, it also helps the coin get into all those nooks and crannies in the economy that you will never be able to penetrate through ICOs and other investments strategies. The more intrinsic your coin, the better the coin will be accepted. Donations can be a great way to get this done (just make sure that the donations are legal where you live). Also, you generally want to keep this under 20% of your coin as it only adds to the transactional value of your coin, not the actual value of your coin.

Finally, make sure you account for the miscellaneous costs of your coins being distributed. No matter how smart you are, the world is changing so fast that there will be elements that you do not see coming. Set some tokens aside for that. Whether you need to sell them to pay taxes or are going to drop them back in the reserve, or even give them to the cancer kids, make sure that you understand there will be things that you do not see coming and that if you do not set some coins aside for it you may be paying out of pocket.

Gamification and ICO Release

Gamification of your coin can be a great way to not only get your coin on the market, but also get people interested in your coin.[424] If you have been watching the growth of the metaverse, you are seeing the metaverse coins (MANA, etc.) exploding in value because people are using them to buy nothing. This is an interesting change in the valuation model from 2021, in 2021 the transactional value had to be an exchange for something that existed. In the year 2022, the exchange can be something exists only in augmented or virtual reality. This makes valuation here very tricky.

The value of the gamification cannot be understated and this is something where coins have seen some success in their path. Whether the coins gain value from applet games, which allow users to watch videos for progress or coins, or whether the token has a casino that is legal in a jurisdiction to win (or lose) coins, gamification is part of the ecosystem. There are millions of games and airdrops out there to research but you should be aware that they exist.

An airdrop is a system where a person gets a coin (or coins) just for being at a location at a given time. These airdrops can be too virtual or real-world locations, but the person has to have a presence (or avatar) there to participate. In the airdrop system, the person can go to an app to receive the coins/tokens, or the coins/tokens can be added to the person's account just for being there. This is a great way to get coins out there and generate interest, but it does not increase the inherent value of the ecosystem.

Gambling can be another method for getting the coin out there, but you need to make sure that the casino is legal in the area where people are using the coin. Because of VPNs, geofenced casinos can be circumvented. This can be coupled with many major exchanges that will not allow coins that have their own casinos (though casinos through a subsidiary are allowed) to operate on their platform. Make sure that you check the rules

[424] Blockium (2018). "Gamification of Coins." Blockium at https://medium.com/@Blockium/gamification-of-coins-simplifying-cryptocurrency-trading-d5a9ce46f965.

of the system to make sure this is legal and allowed.

Conclusion

As you enter into your ICO decisions or look at the ICO decisions of a coin that you are thinking of investing in, check to make sure that this is not a one-trick pony. Many tokens rely on the ICO because it is “easy money” but they find out that the “easy money” is not as easy, nor as abundant as they think that it is. The more quickly you build the system around the ICO, the more effective that the ICO will be.

One reason that a system around your ICO is important is that people want what other people have. If investors and charitable organizations have a token, other investors will want it. This is true especially if someone famous is using your token or coin in their life. The tweet of a celebrity can make a coin jump 10, 000% even if the celebrity does not know what the coin does or how it works.

ICO should not be the only way that a coin is going into a market. For some successful third-Wave coins, they make up only a small percentage of the way that the money is going into the market. Think to yourself how to get the most funding into the ecosystem. This is why working with a professional company can be more productive than simply going it on your own.

Chapter 37: Standing Burn Rates

How you burn your coins can define you as a cryptocurrency. Some coins and tokens refuse to have coordinated burns, this means that any burn done is by the community and is a voluntary shifting of the coin into a dead wallet (bad idea). So far, most of these efforts have been scams where someone has people donate to a "dead wallet" which is just an active wallet where they can move their funds away from the "hot wallet" to personal wallets of the people involved in the scam. The second class involves a coin creating its own dead wallet. These programs tend to be more legitimate, but can be problematic as there is a possibility of a massive wallet (where people know the wallet address) being hacked because someone only needs the key. This system tends to have "conditional burns" where coins are burnt at the discretion of the creators.

The third class, the class that we look at in this Chapter, is standing burn systems. A standing burn is a percentage of each transaction that is removed to an active *Black Wallet* and is used to increase the viability of the ecosystem. While most of these systems are dictated by associated third-party companies, they should have at least one level of separation between the use of the burned coins/token and the creator of the coin/token. The best systems have multiple coins/tokens involved with the ecosystem to ensure that there is constant growth.

This Chapter looks at what a standing burn is and how it functions within an ecosystem. As noted in Chapter 38, dead wallets are useless to the ecosystem and are liability the longer that they exist. Even "air gapped" dead wallets are a liability as the person owning the air-gapped servers have access to the dead coin. A nightmare scenario is a massive dead wallet being dropped on the market at once (as happened on Nov 19th, 2021). The next question to be answered is why a coin/token should have a standing burn. This, of course, is followed by the question of how to build a fair and balanced standing burn rate.

One of the key questions that crypto users have is whether the person in charge of the burn rate should have a "draw" off of a burned coin. In most cases, they should be rewarded for their actions, but their "draw" should be a very small percentage of the burned coin. The next question is what to do with the burned coins, since this book takes the position that dead wallets are a bad idea, there needs to be a distribution plan for the coins. Finally, this Chapter concludes with a discussion of how burned coins can be equitably distributed among the holders, users, and investors within an ecosystem or whether the coin should be used for other purposes.

What is a Standing Burn?

No, this is not the place for a long-standing "Yo Mamma" joke. A standing burn is a system that is in place, overlaying the smart contract that removes a portion of each transaction from the system for a period of time. Before anyone freaks out, credit cards have been doing this for years with funds transfers. With a credit card, you usually see a 3-5% fee removed by the card for each transaction (usually paid by the seller) which goes directly to the bank (they do not even act as if they have benevolent motives). This fee is even worse on international exchanges where it can be anywhere from 4-10% depending on if you switch back to your own currency for payment. Therefore, if a coin/token is asking for a 1-3% burn, you are saving between 1 and 12% over what a credit card would be doing.[425]

A standing burn should always go to a specific wallet, which is active. This is merely a holding wallet until the burn reaches a "critical mass." The critical mass is a pre-determined amount of coin that is in the wallet before it disperses the funds through a system. The filling rate of the burn wallet should always be closely held so people cannot "play the system" on the dispersal. When critical mass is achieved, the wallet moves the coin/token in the wallet to other wallets that oversee the dispersal procedure. Ideally, each of the wallets to which the burn is dispersed will be controlled by a different entity with shared governance.

The burn itself is a fairly simple piece of code. Each transaction sends a portion of that transaction to the burn wallet. Anyone who is using the smart contract overlay knows that this is happening, and it operates like a credit card fee. Unlike a credit card fee, half comes from the buyer and half

[425] Infra.

comes from the seller (though the seller can eat the whole cost, it works out the same either way). Once the transaction is complete, the seller has their coin, the buyer has whatever they have bought, and the burn wallet has the coin.

Why have a Standing Burn?

One of the big questions that the market faces is why to have a standing burn, especially if it is not going to a dead wallet. Unfortunately, many people have been indoctrinated that a dead wallet actually helps their holdings. It does not. The more you use your coin, the more you contribute to the dead wallet. That means that a person who is investing in the long term can watch their value raise as other people pay into the dead wallet to increase their value. Since dead wallet burns tend to have higher (or longer) burn rates than standing burns, active people tend to see less of a return on their money. However, with a standing burn, the increase in value is exponentially larger than the increase in value from a dead wallet, so while long-term investors still get the best of both worlds, everyone else sees more improvement in the standing burn model.

Now, what should a standing burn system do with the coins? Well, the goal of a standing burn system is to keep the coins active. While most of the mechanisms for using the coins are proprietary, the standing rule is that the burned funds should always be used for something that benefits the system. The coins/tokens should never go back fully into the reserve since that would simply be a dead wallet with extra steps. Coins/tokens should also not fully go to the creator, at that point it is a scam (though the overseer of the burn should have a small draw.

Another reason that a system should have a standing draw is the deflation of the coin. Inflation is the enemy of cryptocurrencies and even with non-mine coins, there is a risk of slight inflation based on the currency that they are most linked to. However, a standing burn is constantly taking coins out of circulation and entering them back into the system through several means (warrants, investment, or user drops). Any of these means can help the coin stabilize in value so that it has constant growth but the growth is manageable.

If the standing burn rate is active, which means that it can be moved by the controller. Controlled rates should have a small window of where the burn rate can go, no more than 2% of a swing, but it can be used as a controlled rate for reducing large swings in the currency.[426] If a currency is taking a nosedive, the burn rate can be increased to encourage people to hold. If the currency is taking a run, the burn rate can be lowered to encourage outside investors to buy currency and become part of the eco-system. While not a speed limit, per se, it can be a useful tool to manage growth.

Building a Proper Burn Rate

One of the biggest problems that crypto can face is setting up their burn rate in a way that has some meaning, but still is fair to their users. In many cases, new crypto creators try to keep the burn rate as small as possible to facilitate the trade of the coin/token. While this can look good for the users, holders, and investors, it can have a minimal effect on the efficacy of the burn system. Sometimes creators try to set up the burn rate to be too large, which results in a retardation of the growth of coin/token. This is truly a Goldilocks situation, where you need things to be not "too hot," not "too cold" but just right for growth.

The first danger that a new creator may face is setting the burn rate too low. While it may, at first, look like it benefits the traders to have the interest rate very low (lower than 0.01%) negligible burn rates do not have the necessary effect to stabilize a market. Now if the swing of the rate is 1% to -1% then the rate could, in theory, be less than 0.01% and still be useful; however, if you are working on a positive burn rate at all times (which is recommended because a negative burn rate can be abused) then you need to be sure that it has an effect. While a small burn rate (lower than 0.01%) can create a large burn wallet during times of high exchange, the ratio is still too small for it to be highly effective.

The next danger that a new creator may face is getting too greedy with a burn rate. Standing burn rates of over 3% are credit card level rates. Especially when you are working in conjunction with a crypto card, that

[426] KIROS White Paper.

means that while an investor is only facing a 3% burn on each trade, a user is facing a loss of 6% each time! Large rates styme trade of a coin, which will always be a bad thing unless you are attempting to keep outside traders from using your coin.

The next common error that we are seeing with third-Wave cryptos is too high of a swing rate. Swing rates have shown to be an effective alternative to general or conditional burns. With a swing rate, a third-party consultant can set the rate of the burn between two pre-designed points. When the markets are up, the rate can be set low to encourage trading. When the markets go down, the rate should be raised to protect the investment of the holders. Either way, if the swing is too great it can make the coin more volatile.

Using an AI to control the swing is also a good tool, though it may get confusing when the coin growth rate is near 0.00%. A computer can react to changes much faster than a person can, and they can be "on duty" 24 hours a day. This allows the burn to move at the right pace and still ensure that the burn rate is fair to the holders, users, and investors. The AI should be controlled by someone other than the lead shareholder of the company or the lead coin/token holder.

The burn rate is the method that a coin/token can use to maintain the stability of the ecosystem while continually helping the ecosystem to grow. However, unless the burn rate is set at the proper rate for the coin, it can stifle the growth of the system. While AI is the best option, if a human factor is needed, then the human should be as decentralized from the system as possible. It is always best to ensure that the human element is not benefited by the burn rate.

The Owners/Controllers Burn Draws

One of the ethical questions that arise from the question of standing burns is whether the person controlling the burn should be compensated for their work. Unless there is an extraordinarily rare set of circumstances, the answer is always yes, they should be compensated. Additionally, there is the question of whether an owner should be compensated for the designer of the burn rate. This is slightly less well defined, but as with all types of work, a person should be properly compensated. Regardless of the ethical discussion, the amount that a person is compensated should be but a small portion of the burn rate to ensure that the ecosystem continues to grow.

One of the easiest answers that we will look at in this section is what to do about controller draws when the draws are controlled by an AI. In most cases, the programmer of the AI will be compensated upfront for the design of the AI, and as such the programmer has already received their pound of flesh. The AI, until we have a system where AIs have rights, does not need compensation, therefore, there is no question of how they should manage the draw. There is the question of whether an AI can "donate" what it would have gotten to the research of better AIs to allow the system to function better. If a crypto developer was so included, this should be between 0.25% and 1% of the burn rate.

Moving on to the situation where you have a human controlling the burn rate, the human needs to be compensated. In fact, since crypto is traded 24 hours a day, the team of humans that run the burn rate need to be compensated. No one should be expected to do a job without being compensated. To be fair to the team, the compensation for the team should be no more than 2% of the burn rate. If the coin is lightly traded, then the monitoring is light work. If the coin is heavily traded, then the extra income will be a bonus to the controllers.

The next question is whether the designer of the crypto should be compensated from the burn rate. While the authors are split on this, this author believes that the designer should be compensated, but not more than 1% of the total burn rate. This allows for residual growth of the allocation of the designer while still keeping the lion's share of the burn rate moving through the smart wallet process. If the owner does take a draw, the draw should be clearly defined in the white pages so that all of the users of the coin know what the rate is. If there is a reason for the rate to be better than 1%, it should be a very good reason.

Distribution of Burned Coins

Once the coins have landed in the burn wallet, someone has to know what to do with them. Like a dead wallet, a burn wallet is a popular tool for hackers as it is a semi-monitored wallet with a static pattern.[427] The good news is that the smart contract overlay code can have the wallet address for the burn wallet redacted (or have a passthrough wallet that is always dumping the currency to another wallet). This will allow the wallet to be more secure but will still provide transparency for the regulators and exchanges to see what is going on. Even better, use an established burn system, like the *Black Wallet* system, which can move your burns into a general ecosystem that is even harder to penetrate.

The first element of the burned coins to be resolved is the draws. Always pay your workers first and ensure that their compensation relates to the work that they have done. Whether you give them the full burn, allow the burn to go to the company and then the company pays the salary, or whether there is a constant rate of pay, this money should always come out first. Never leverage your workers to impress your investors.

The second element that needs to be looked at is the return to investors. Does your company use a burn and earn system? Does it use a re-issue system? Does it use some other novel system (hybrid airdrops or gamification)? Regardless of the system that is used, how is the currency, if any, that is returned properly returned? Also, you need to look at how much is returned. Do you return all of it or a percentage? Each of these is an important consideration and should be looked at (another reason why an established system like *Black Wallet* is effective).

Another concern that strong crypto keeps in mind is whether the coin should be used in an active wallet (we recommend Blue Wallet or Red Wallet). An active wallet re-circulates the coin, but sells them to get something in return. Most often it is stock or a commodity, but there are other considerations. This is one of the more complex elements of the burn

---

[427] Alexandria (2021). "Burned/Burn." Alexandria at https://coinmarketcap.com/alexandria/glossary/burned.

design, and should be left to the professionals if at all possible.

Finally, will a portion of the coin/token be donated to charity or used to lobby for stronger laws protecting the crypto space? Either of these is a noble endeavor, and if you have disclosed this in your white pages, there is no problem doing this. Make sure that the percentage that you will be distributing is well known ahead of time to ensure that your community knows where their burns are going!

Ensuring Equitable distribution Among Stakeholders

If you are using a system that gives back to the stakeholders, then you need to make sure that your system is equitable and disclosed in the white pages. Burn and earn systems are very effective, however, if you do not administer them right, you can end up facing problems in court. The way to protect yourself from this, other than using a professional service like *Black Wallet*, is to make sure that the distribution pattern is listed in the White Paper.

When you list a distribution model in the White Paper, make sure that you follow it. As a coin grows, it may be tempting to change up your pattern. This is why the professionals are useful, they do not care about the volume, they only care about the thresholds. Stepping outside the model that you listed in the White Paper can be very dangerous from a legal standpoint as the White Paper is the "known consent" that the stakeholders use when they are deciding to use your coin.

All models we recommend use partner organizations for the distribution of the coin. Individual distributions through a crypto matrix are possible, but they can be difficult and costly. When you use a partner organization, they can access who is holding your coin and make the distributions based on the holder's status. This makes it easier to distribute, regardless of which model you use. If you use a professional service, they will generally list the partner exchanges that they use in their burn and earn system.

The first model that you can use is an equitable distribution of the burn and earn coins/tokens. In an equitable distribution, you look at how many coins are held on a specific platform (or group of platforms) and the burned coins that are being re-issued to the stakeholders are divided by the ratio of holdings to the platforms. The platforms then distribute (less a fee usually) the coins to the stakeholders based on what % of the coins they hold on the platforms. This allows people to earn more if they hold more. It highly benefits investors and can make a coin grow faster.

An equal distribution model is a much simpler model, but it benefits users and holders more. In this model, you spread the coins across all partner organizations equally. Once they have received the coin, they spread it across coin holders in the system equally. Regardless of whether you hold 1 coin or 1 billion coins, you still get the same number of coins. This system helps the smaller holders of the coin become larger holders; however, this can lead to gamification and people "competing for the coins."

Regardless of how you choose to distribute the coin, you want to make sure that the distribution is done in a way that benefits your community. The more power you give to your community, the more the community will stay with you (basically you are paying them to stay with you). This can make a coin much more stable as community members want to keep a stake in something that they believe in.

Conclusion

However you approach burn rates, you need to keep in mind that the goal is always to increase the viability of the ecosystem. An ecosystem needs to be fed to grow, and sometimes we see cryptos as something that we can keep taking from and expecting them to thrive. The gravy train will only last so long if you do not keep putting back into the system. A burn and earn structure is a great way to do this.

It is highly recommended that you work with a professional group if you choose to take this route. Individual cryptos creating their own burn and earn system may seem like novelties, but their ecosystem can only grow so quickly with limited volume. Major providers, like *Black Wallet*, allow for multiple currencies to enhance the ecosystem and empower the community. They also take away some of the burden of making the calculated decisions to manage the funds. *The Wallet Group* also allows for a decentralization of the management of the funds, single crypto burn and earns simply feed the goals of the creators, whereas highly developed multi-level system build for the future of the industry.

Chapter 38: Eliminating Dead Wallets

Dead Wallets are a popular buzzword in the world of cryptocurrency. While the "wallet" part of the name is correct, the "dead" part makes this a misnomer. If you want to know why this naming "arrangement" is such a danger to the field, look no further than November 2019, when a wallet, thought to be dead, activated and dumped $2 Billion U.S. in Bitcoin into the market, causing a major slide in the price of the coin.[428] Dealing with dead wallets is one of the first stages in stabilizing the market for cryptocurrencies.

Why? Dead wallets thrive on the myth that the blockchain cannot be hacked.[429] Ironically, the blockchain is a legalized version of the 2000s hacking botnets. To suggest that something that was built on the idea of using a hacker tool to hack individual computers could not be hacked is almost laughable. Anything on a non-airlocked computer can be hacked. Even airlocked computers are vulnerable if someone can make it to the physical point. The idea that a dead wallet is invincible is just an OG ploy to convince people that it is something it is not.

What is a Dead wallet?

Before we get into the discussion of why dead wallets are a bad thing, it is important to discuss what a dead wallet is. Dead wallets are a fictional black hole into which overproduced currency is dumped to artificially inflate the value of the remaining currency. This key idea has several flaws, which we tear apart in this Chapter, however the essence of the dead wallet is of vital importance to the evolution of the cryptocurrency ecosystem.

In its purest form, a dead wallet is a wallet created for the purpose of destroying coins. The creator of the wallet builds it, posts its address, and

---

[428] Wilson, Tom (2021). "Cryptocurrencies tumble as coronavirus variant shakes market." Reuters at https://www.reuters.com/markets/currencies/bitcoin-tumbles-coronavirus-variant-sees-riskier-assets-dumped-2021-11-26/.

[429] Luthrus, Infra.

then allows people to dump money in the wallet to "destroy" currency. The theory behind the dead wallet is that people will do this to increase the value of the other currency that they hold.[430] Dead wallets are suspect, however, in that the creator of the wallet has the key for the wallet. So dead wallets tend to have a history of springing back to life when they hit a certain amount of crypto.

As for the utility of a dead wallet, think of a guy sitting along the road holding a cardboard sign. This can be a homeless person or a person in a business suit, the status of the person does not matter. What matters is that the person is someone that you do not know. On his (or her as the gender here is irrelevant, as it usually is) sign, it states "If everyone gives me 1% of their money and I destroy it, the value of all of your money will be worth more." This is a true statement, generally the increase would be 1/1000 more than the burn rate. There are several suspect problems with this sign.

First of all, this person is a stranger. You do not know them. Just like most dead wallets on the internet, the operator of this benevolent program is random. Now, in our example, the guy holding the sign could become internet famous, just like dead wallet owners, but that internet fame does not translate to trustworthiness. Just because a person is recognized does not mean that they have your best interests in mind. Look at the Chairman of the Federal Reserve and even the President of the United States, they are both super famous and do not give a damn about you, only their handlers. Placing your trust in something just because the person is famous is like getting marriage counseling from one of the *Kardashians* or *Desperate Housewives*.

Next, the premise of the program is suspect, "if everyone gives me 1%..." There is no way that every holder is going to give 1% of their coin to someone they do not know. Firstly, there will be people who are not dumb enough to give their hard-earned coin to strangers. Regardless of your feelings on this, if even 1% of the population does not fall into this dubious

---

[430] *Id.*

scheme, then the increase fails to match the growth rate. If the growth rate at 100% is 1/1000th, then a 1% failure would result in a reduction by 1/100th or decrease the ratio of growth. While everyone else would gain approximately a little, the person who did not donate would see the only growth.

Additionally, there is the problem of the growth rate. If the currency has reserves, then the reserves will see the growth rate without donation. Suggesting that the system has a reserve of 15-20% it would reduce the efficacy of the scheme by an additional 20%. This means that the anemic growth rate would be lower than the amount that you donated. While some socialist "economists" are quick to point out that your later wages will be worth more too, so you will increase your net worth; this is conflating present value with the net present value of the system. When the net present value of the system is taken into account with the general rate, which is greater than the 1% or the 1/1000th of growth, so it will result in a net loss for most people.[431]

So who does benefit? Well, for starters the guy holding the sign. Very rarely does the dead wallet operate in a vacuum. The operator tends to take a reasonable fee for their services. This percentage further breaks down the "universal" gains of the community. This also shows that the owner of the system still has the key. For the guy along the street, this is not a big deal, but when it is a dead wallet where the owner(s) say that the key is destroyed, this is a problem.

The long and short of it is that a dead wallet is a hoax, at least in the form that was used during Wave 1 and Wave 2 of the crypto evolution. Yes, there are some dead wallets that did what they said they were going to do and destroyed the key, but even in those cases, there is a chance that someday someone, if even by dumb luck, find the key and have access to those "destroyed" funds. This will, as with the Bitcoin, example flood the

[431] O'Connell, Brian (2018). "What is Present Value and How is it Calculated?" The Street at https://www.thestreet.com/personal-finance/seo-what-is-present-value-14800837.

market and lower the value of all coins, not just the ones in the dead wallet.

Why are Dead Wallets Being Used?

One question you may have wondered is, "If dead wallets are such a scam in the worst case and broken system in the best case, then why are smart people around the globe still using them?" If you are asking this question, then you are on the right track. The answer, however, is quite simple. People are using dead wallets because people are resistant to change. Wave 3 of cryptocurrency brought with it *The Wallet Group* and the advent of *Black Wallet*, LTD, which is a more efficient system; however, there are still millions of people using dead wallets.

"But why did they use them in the first place?" Another good question. Dead wallets were a necessary mistake for the evolution of cryptocurrency.[432] Creators of coins sometimes make more coins that the system can support, the quadrillions of coins created by SHIB is a good example of this. Since SHIB was allegedly created as a joke, no one thought that it would ever boom the way it did. This resulted in a system that had potential but was in danger of failing because of the number of coins.[433] One of the equations that you are going to need to know in cryptocurrency (and stocks in general) is the relationship between volume and the number of coins/shares on the market. One hundred million trades in a day can seem like a big number for traders, but if there are quadrillions of coins/tokens in existence it is but a small fraction moving. This would be akin to getting excited about a mud puddle standing next to the Mississippi, Amazon, or Nile rivers. Volume is more important as a percentage than as a simple number.

So, we have these creators who messed up (well really, they did not) by creating too much currency. What to do? Any coin that is created can be

---

[432] Ram, Simina (2021). "How Dead Wallets can have an afterlife." Dailycoin.com at https://dailycoin.com/crypto-dead-wallet/ .

[433] Luthra, Evan (2020). "Dead Coins Wallets: the treasures of Atlantis or Zombie uprising." Cointelegraph.com at https://cointelegraph.com/news/dead-coins-and-wallets-the-treasures-of-atlantis-or-zombie-uprising (Great read, this guy called the problems on the market.

destroyed, using the code being validated- however, no crypto wants to do this (except for the Stablecoin 1.0 guys) because if a coin can be destroyed then any coins can be destroyed.[434] This lowers faith in the market. So how does one destroy something without destroying it? To answer this, crypto inventors looked at the great financial minds of New York and how they dealt with a similar problem.

At one point, New York could handle the trash that New York City created. We are talking about the actual refuse, not the New York Social scene. At one point, however, the city grew past the point where it could deal with the trash problem. Then someone had the genius idea that they would pay other states to take the trash. While this did take the trash out of the system, the trash was still out there causing problems for Pennsylvania, New Jersey, and other states. Not to mention, the people who had to deal with the trash were rarely the ones getting paid.

Crypto did basically the same thing. Using the dead wallets, crypto producers removed the coins from the system- even though they were still out there.[435] This process was an "out of sight, out of mind" model that allowed the coins to appear like there was less, but still maintain the validity of the coins. Just like New York and its trash, the dead wallets hid the problem, until people saw that the dead wallets could come back to life.

KIROS model of an Active Black Wallet

As the first true third Wave crypto, KIROS brought a novel solution to the problem of too many coins and not enough utility.[436] Rather than follow the traditional question of how to decrease the number of coins, KIROS and its system looked at the other end of the equation: how does one increase the utility of the coin. Now as you read about in the Stablecoin 2.0 section (Chapter 5), KIROS created a *Black Wallet* that was a depository.

---

434 Simona, *Supra.*

435

436 KIROS White Paper (This section is from the KIROS White Paper, paraphrased.).

Unlike the dead wallet models, which are like putting your money in a dump where no one is supposed to have access to them, KIROS places money into a recycling center.[437] The goal of this project was to ensure that the crypto that was disposed of (through the burn and earn mechanism) would be put back into the system, but would increase the value of the system when it was re-entered.[438] This allows the re-used coins to contribute to the value of the system again.

So how does this work? First of all, think of coins as money, not as an investment. When you look at it as an investment, then the system is not as apparent. When you look at it as money, the system makes more sense.[439] If you have money and place that money in a jar on your dresser, it does not gain value (it actually loses value due to inflation). So, if you have an amount of money what do you do with it? You invest it. To keep the model simple, we are going to say you put the money in a savings account. This account gives you 1% a year, whereas the jar on your dresser loses about 3% per year. It is a no-brainer to put the money in the bank, right?

Well, what if we found that you could put it into a managed account (money market, land trust, etc.) and gain 5% consistently? Which would be the better choice: the bank account or the managed account? Well, it depends on your level of risk, but most people would go for the managed account. Now how does this translate to crypto?

The dead wallets are destroying your money- which would be like throwing your money into a barrel and setting it on fire. Generally, we will accept that this is a bad idea. Putting your money in a jar is just like keeping crypto in any wallet. No gain, no loss other than inflation. Staking your crypto, placing it in cold storage to be counted as part of the reserve, can net you small returns, but not as much as if you had it in a managed account.

KIROS did not offer to manage the accounts of all of its holders, which

---

[437] *Id.*
[438] *Id.*
[439] *Id.*

perhaps it should have noted as the success of the model. KIROS took the money that was burned through the "burn and earn" system and placed it in an active wallet. This wallet returned a portion to the holders, users, and investors and then invested the majority of the rest in physical assets and stocks. By exchanging these coins for assets, the stake and holdings of the ecosystem increased, increasing the value of the coin. Each time a coin passes through the system, the value increases as the holdings of the system increase.

The benefits of an Active Wallet

There are three key benefits to an active wallet. The first benefit is faith in the system. When a coin is destroyed, faith is lost in the system; however, when the coin has recycled, the fidelity of the system stays in place. Second, there is constant growth. One of the key problems with fiat currency is that inflation saps the worth of the currency, only with a constant growth model can you expect the coin to retain or gain value. Third, it builds a community larger than the currency. *The Wallet Group* is open to allowing any currency to use its overlay if they manage the funds.

Faith in the system will always be a major component of ensuring the system stays viable. If the community loses faith in the system, they move to another coin. KIROS allows any cryptocurrency to participate in the system, which increases the value of the whole cryptocurrency community. Coins and tokens that join the system constantly gain in value, coins, and tokens that do not join still see growth as public confidence in the cryptosystem grows. It is a win for everyone, it is just that the coins that participate in the system are more stable and a better investment.

Growth will always be a defining factor of currency. Talk to an economist and they will tell you that a little bit of inflation is a good thing because it makes people invest rather than save their money. Then slap the economist because that benefits them and their bank masters, not the holders of the currency. The truth is that if we want to end poverty in the world, we want people to save some of their money. Let professionals invest the reserves through a cylindrical system. Yes, the rich will see some growth, but so will the people who live paycheck to paycheck. To the wealthy the increase will be but a small portion of their growth, it will mean a lot more to the middle and lower class. If wages remain standard and the value of currency grows, people will see better lifestyles without the minimum wage increase.

Finally, we need to see the community around currency. People only care what the currency in their wallet is worth when they are looking to buy something because the system does not reward people for the currency being successful. The Fed and other cartel banks want people to be worried about how they will spend the little they have, not how they can keep what they have and increase wealth. Schools teach that you need to replace a source of income to increase your wealth, any wealthy person will tell you that you need to keep earning your income and add to your income stream to increase your net worth. Active wallets help everyone by increasing their holdings while they do nothing but buying and spend the money that they earn.

Why Dead Wallets need to die with the second Wave of crypto

It is time for dead wallets to die out. They serve no purpose in the modern cryptosystem because idle money only increases inflation. Reserves should be active and coins that come off the market should be going right back into the market. Rather than "decreasing the number" active thinkers want to increase the utility of the coin. Dead wallets are an idea that is past their prime. The sooner they are taken off the market, the sooner the market can start to flourish.

However, why does the second Wave of crypto need to go away also? This is not a condemnation of any coin. All current coins on the market should stabilize and join the third Wave. The great thing about cryptocurrencies is that they can evolve with the system. The Active wallet is a "soft fork" that anyone can join in with. It is not a true soft fork, because if you do not accept it, then you do not get all the benefits of the active wallet, but it still has the potential to lift millions of people out of poverty around the world.

The dead wallet was a necessary evil in the growth of the cryptocurrency. It was the easy solution to a complex problem; however, the easy solution often leads to more problems. With the advent of smart *Black Wallets*, we have the ability to increase the value of the system as the system evolves. Further, it moves more holdings into secure positions, which increases the job stability around the world.[440] The more we work together, the more we can make the world a better place.

---

[440] One of the key values of *The Wallet Group* is to keep manufacturing jobs where they are an increase the demand around the world through active expansion. This allows people to keep the jobs they have, with a more humane pay scale and increase the number of jobs out there so more people can have better lives.

Part III: Section II:

Types of Derivatives

Introduction to Part III: Section II: Types of Derivatives

Derivatives are a complex subject when it comes to talking about cryptocurrency. Derivative trading brings to mind images from movies such as *Wall Street* and *Wolf of Wall Street*, the idea of unscrupulous traders taking advantage of innocent people by using techniques that regular people do not understand to make trades that only advantage the rich.[441] It makes for a good movie plot, but derivatives are just tools that trader can use to make more sophisticated traders. When people educate themselves about derivatives, then they have the ability to make more money, which is something that everyone should choose on a personal basis how to invest.

Chapter 40 opens this section by looking at the concept of options and how they work in a modern trading system. An option is a method for buying or selling a trade/crypto at a future time at a specific price. Chapter 41 looks at warrants, which are similar to options, but have a higher level of complexity because they are selling stock that does not exist yet, or cryptos that have not been released from the reserve yet. These allow companies access to market growth without the risk of working with a capital investment firm (the original crowdfunding). Options and warrants come from the same family of derivatives and are important as they allow investors to make "safe" moves to work towards future ownership.

Chapter 42 looks at futures, which are a defined option. Unlike options, when a person holds a future, they have but one date and one price to purchase the stock/crypto. Similar to a future, Chapter 43 looks at forwards. Forwards, are bilateral contracts between two parties (generally not transferable) that allow the party to purchase stock/crypto on a given date for a given amount. These are useful when the seller does not want the derivative to be traded. Chapter 43 looks into the complexities of stock swap derivatives where parties exchange one leg of the equity-based cash flows for a different leg of the fixed income cash flow. Chapter 43 also explains the difference between a swap (stock) and a swap (derivative).

---

[441] Wolf of Wall Street (2013).

This section concludes with Chapter 45, which looks at why derivatives are so important to the crypto market, especially in its early phases. Putting aside the billions of dollars that will be made through the derivative process, the market stabilization that will come from active derivative trading allows for the market to grow at a maintainable pace while the market becomes more sophisticated. Right now, the market is trading roman coins, we need to move the crypto market, for lack of a better term, into the digital age.

Chapter 39: What is a Derivative?

If you are old enough to remember Popeye the Sailor Man, then you may remember one of the returning characters in the story line, Mr. Wimpy.[442] As opposed as he would be by the modern "woke" culture, Mr. Wimpy was the irrelevant opposite of Popeye. In the stories, for those of you too young to remember, Popeye was a hard-working sailor how gained extra power through eating healthy (spinach).[443] This of course promoted healthy eating and involvement in the armed forces. Popeye's rival, often for his gal Olive Oil, was Bluto another tough guy.

On the sidelines of many of the stories was Mr. Wimpy. Wimpy had seemingly avoided military service and was a businessman. He was always on a quest to get hamburgers. He was chubby, passive, and very few of the elements that made you successful in the world were present in his character. His catchphrase was, "I will gladly pay you Tuesday for a hamburger today."[444] Wimpy was seen as a "sad sack" in the comic, but really was ahead of his time on the derivatives market.

Ok, so maybe Popeye was not trying to teach kids not to eat hamburgers and play in the derivatives market, but the idea still stands. Wimpy was trying to trade an action today for a promise of payment in the future, which, in its own way, is a derivative. Derivatives themselves are "complex financial contracts based on the value of an underlying asset, group of assets, or a benchmark."[445] This Chapter is a survey Chapter that unlocks the basic elements of derivatives in order to ensure a basic understanding as Chapters 40-44 explains the complexities of each type of option.

---

[442] Popeye fandom (2021). https://www.google.com/url?sa=t&rct=j&q=&esrc=s&source=web&cd=&cad=rja&uact=8&ved=2ahUKEwimoqq61Yf1AhWUp3IEHYiUDg4QFnoECAcQAQ&url=https%3A%2F%2Fpopeye.fandom.com%2Fwiki%2FJ._Wellington_Wimpy&usg=AOvVaw3j0PiZMO8WboYNu5AVJd6d.

[443] Though his smoking the pipe kind of gave mixed messages to the kids.

[444] *Id*.

[445] Birken, Emily Guy & Schmidt, John (assumably Jacob) (2021). "A Basic Guide to Financial Derivatives." *Forbes* at https://www.forbes.com/advisor/investing/derivatives/.

In this Chapter we look first at, "what is a derivative?" this lays an important foundation for understanding the system. One of the first things that a person needs to do when they enter a new system is to "de-mystify" it. Next, we explain why a derivative is so important for the market. While we looked over the topic briefly in Chapter 13, we now move into the specific elements of derivatives that are needed for the market to be successful. De-mystification and use value can make a market much easier to understand for those just getting involved with said market.

Next, this Chapter juxtaposes the use of derivatives in the stock market against the use of derivatives in the crypto markets. While the two markets are similar in nature, there are caveats in each market that make the trading of derivatives more complex in some areas and simpler in others. From this comparison, we then expand the discussion to look at how derivatives can be introduced into the crypto market without a negative disruption (they will of course be a market disruption). The Chapter concludes with a brief analysis of how the new complexity in the market will add sophistication to the system.

Derivatives are not a necessity in any market, they are a luxury. As with all luxuries, the market needs to show that it deserves to have the privilege. In order to do this in the crypto market, the market needs to show that it is willing to accept a more complex system of exchanges, in return, the market will receive a valuable stabilization factor and a method for serious traders to make billions of dollars as the market matures. The interplay between the decentralized nature of the crypto market and the necessity for centralized oversight of the derivatives market will be the defining factor of the next five years of cryptocurrency.

What is a Derivative?

As noted above, *Forbes* defines a derivative as, "complex financial contracts based on the value of an underlying asset, group of assets, or a benchmark."[446] While this is an excellent definition, sometimes definitions need a little bit of clarity for them to be effective. This means that to really understand what a derivative is, we need to take a moment to look at the parts of the definition. The more you understand the foundation, the more you will be able to understand the whole as you move through the system.[447]

First of all, a derivative is a complex financial contract. Unlike a spot trade, which can be summed up, "If you give me this, I will give you that;" a derivative involves a more complex formula, such as, "If I give you X right now, it will buy me the ability to buy Y for Z at/before the given time of A." This is still a bargain for exchange, it just adds other elements to the system. First of all, most derivatives are a purchased contract, which means that you are buying the option to do something in the future (except swaps). If you choose not to execute the option/warrant/future/forward, then the money you spent in the purchase of the derivative is wasted.[448]

Next, because this is a bilateral contract (promise for a promise), you still have obligations in the future that you must fulfill if you want to execute the contract.[449] The easiest way for a derivative (except a swap) to end is for the holder of the derivative to elect not to act upon the derivative. When this happens the derivative expires, the initial investment is wasted and both parties can move on. This happens more than one would think (mainly because the market did not move the way they initial buyer thought it would). The other way that the derivative may end is the holder executing the agreement. How that works is different for each type of derivative and will be discussed in the following Chapters.

---

[446] Birken, Emily Guy & Schmidt, John (assumably Jacob) (2021). "A Basic Guide to Financial Derivatives." *Forbes* at https://www.forbes.com/advisor/investing/derivatives/.

[447] *Id.*

[448] *Id.*

[449] Wexlaw (2021). Bilateral Contract. At https://www.google.com/url?sa=t&rct=j&q=&esrc=s&source=web&cd=&cad=rja&uact=8&ved=2ahUKEwi8sK7n1If1AhX4g3IEHbCMAhQQFnoECA0QAw&url=https%3A%2F%2Fwww.law.cornell.edu%2Fwex%2Fbilateral_contract&usg=AOvVaw3bond6tXy6_k88OYxv-3gV.

The reason we use the term "holder" instead of "buyer" is because most derivatives (except forwards) can be traded on the market.[450] Once a derivative is created, it becomes a security. Most derivatives can, at the discretion of the buyer, be put on an exchange and traded like you would trade stocks or cryptos. The value of the derivative fluctuates not only with the market, but with the predictions of how the market will fluctuate. When a holder buys a derivative, they then have the ability to resell it if it increases or decreases in value. At the end of the day, you are hoping that you are holding a derivative where you can buy (or sell) well away from the market to make an immediate flip (or hold the stock/crypto if it still rallying).

The second part of the definition is more complex "based on the value of an underlying asset, group of assets, or a benchmark."[451] All derivatives are based on other assets.[452] They are never a stand-alone asset. Most of the time, they involve the right to purchase another asset at a set price at a future time. As derivatives get more complex, they can relate to a group of assets or even a benchmarking system. The more complex the derivative, the higher the risk. The higher the risk, the higher the reward can be. Once again, you should only be investing with money you can afford to lose; however, when you are investing in derivatives, you need to understand you have a higher chance of losing your stake.

Why Derivatives are Important

Derivatives are important to the market because they give the market diversity. If people are just trading stocks, cryptos, and other assets, then the securities markets go flat because the movement is very small. Derivatives give people a chance to have a higher level of movement in a system, one that is not dependent on the current market but on the market at a future point. This allows for more money to move back and forth, allowing the market to keep a level of liquidity that is not present when a

---

[450] Murphey, Chris (2021). "Over the Counter." Invesopedia at https://www.investopedia.com/terms/o/otc.asp.

[451] *Birken, Emily, Guy & Schmidt, Jon (Supra).*

[452] Murphey, *Supra*.

stock or crypto is sitting at its present value. Basically, derivatives are a method for ensuring that traders in a given area have something to trade when the stock/crypto/commodity/bonds are not trading.[453]

The market is dependent on movement. Take even the most basic stock trading course and they will teach you that volume is the key to validity.[454] Small volume with great fluctuations in price does not indicate a rally/correction, it simply indicates the actions of a single buyer.[455] When you have high volume, even with the low moment the indicators are much more reliable because they are created by the aggregate.[456] Many a new trader has lost their shirt when they "see" a pattern on a low volume market, only to find that it was not a pattern at all, just a couple trades. The patterns they teach in different stock systems only where when there is the volume to support them.

So, what does this have to do with derivatives? A derivative increases the volume of trading in a specific market segment when the market is static. While people will trade derivatives in an active market (which increases the risk and the possible rewards), the "safest" derivatives are based on yearly patterns and periods of stability in the market. When people trade derivatives in a flat market, they are showing an indicator of where the market thinks the market will go. This generally causes the market to move, whether the market predicts where the market will go is another question entirely.

When we apply this system to the crypto market, we see that it can be very challenging. The crypto market tends to be quite volatile already.[457] This means that derivatives on the crypto market will almost always be on an

---

[453] MBN (2021). "Market Volume" MBN at https://marketbusinessnews.com/financial-glossary/market-volume-definition-example/.

[454] KIROS White Paper.

[455] *Id.*

[456] *Id.*

[457] PMC (2021). Cryptocurrency volatility markets." PMC at https://www.ncbi.nlm.nih.gov/pmc/articles/PMC8326316/.

active market. This makes the idea of crypto derivatives quite scary for the mutual fund and money market crowd. Before we move on, one point to note is that there is a reason that the mutual fund and money market guys tend to have business longer than options traders, it is a safer market. Mutual funds and money markets allow for people to make money over a long period of time (they are still derivatives). Options/futures/forwards/warrants all have the possibility of a higher return, but they also pose the risk of losing your stake.

Crypto allows for all of the options that you could trade on the stock market, but the calculations for crypto are different than the calculations for the stock market. Those companies that issue derivatives are going to base them on mortuary tables. Since the tables for cryptocurrencies are newer, the risk of the tables is greater. This means that the derivatives are going to be more expensive to purchase in the first place because of the risk. Remember, the companies that offer these derivatives are in the business to make money, they are not charities. Thus, not only will derivatives help the movement stabilize in the crypto space, it will also help build the record for traders in the future.

Use of Derivatives in the Stock Market

As noted above, derivatives keep the market moving. Speculation has always been a major part of how the market adjusted to movement in the future. As a result, it has become an important part of the market, even if some people have a hard time understanding it. Think of the stock market like a casino. No really, stocks are gambling. If the stock market is the slot machines of the casino, the derivatives are the table games. These are where more money is bet, and more rewards can be earned. However, remember more people go broke at the craps table than the slot machines (for this example crypto would be a lottery at the moment).

The stock market needs the derivatives systems for the same reason that casinos need the table games. It is not that the market makes more off the derivatives, casinos make more off the slots when they are full than they make off of table games (that is why there are more slots in a casino); however, they need the table games to draw people in (especially big spenders). If you ever walk into a casino where there are only slot machines, you see a bunch of quarter machines with bus trip grannies and welfare dads just hitting the buttons. If you walk into a full-scale casino with slot machines and table games, you see people playing the dollar machines and the penny machines (penny machines happen to have the best odds for the house) while whales are making a lot of noise at the tables. The tables draw the whales into the casino, the derivatives market draws the whales into the marketplace.

If you have a diversified portfolio, you are generally going to have someone run it for you (though this trend does not seem to stand true for millennials who seem to be losing their money without the help of advisors).[458] When people start to move into the derivatives market, they tend to either "go it on their own" or work with a group that buys the derivatives for them and then the rewards are split if it works out.

Derivatives are important to the market because they are the "wow" that brings people to the marketplace. When you hear of someone making millions on a stock trade, more often than not there was a derivative trade involved. To put things quite simply, 10, 000% increases in stocks tend to be a unicorn. However, they are a real thing in the crypto market and only time will tell how the crypto market will adjust to derivatives.[459]

Bringing Derivatives to the Crypto Markets

A lot of people are having conversations about whether we should bring derivatives to the crypto marketplace. This is the wrong question. Derivatives are already here in the crypto markets. They can be either legitimate (with a bonded company) or they can be back channel (people

---

[458] Lacurci, Gregg (2020). "Young Investors are going digital. Financial Advisors need to adapt with them." CNBC at https://www.cnbc.com/2020/10/14/millennials-gen-z-want-robo-advisors-and-digital-financial-advice.html.

[459] Langley, Karen (2021). "Wall Street Bets S&P 500 will say goodbye to outsized stock gains in 2022" Wall Street Journal at https://www.wsj.com/articles/wall-street-bets-s-p-500-will-say-goodbye-to-outsize-stock-gains-in-2022-11640514607.

on Pancake making handshake agreements), but derivatives are already being traded on the crypto marketplace. People asking if they should be there are already behind the times. The question that we must address in the present situation is how we should be integrating them into the marketplace to protect the investors.

Market integration is a very difficult subject in the crypto space. Since the goal of crypto is to be decentralized, derivatives pose a very nasty set of problems. First of all, in a decentralized market, who ensures that derivative issuers can cover the derivative. True, if they fail no one will deal with them in the future, but that does not protect the people who lose millions in derivatives that they thought they had. This means that there has to be some regulation on the insurances and capital that issuers need to have.

Another question around the decentralization is how does the market ensure that derivatives traded on the market are legitimate. Derivatives in the stock market need to be registered. This may not be as glaring of a problem as it seems to be on its face. Derivatives are securities, thus should be bound by present securities law. While this may limit the ability of derivatives to be traded on some of the younger exchanges, it provides the security and market confidence needed for the market to stabilize.

Why Complexity Adds Sophistication

Derivatives bring sophistication to the market because people have to make sure that they "want" to make the trade that they are getting involved with. If you buy a cryptocurrency and the crypto drops in value, you can sell what you have and get some of your money back. If you have a derivative and the market goes the opposite way, the amount that you spent on that security is lost to the ether. The danger of derivatives is not that you could lose more often, but that when you do lose you lose everything you have a bet. When new traders get involved with derivatives, they do not see this "whatever the opposite of a silver lining is."

New traders see the market as a way that they can play with money and not lose too much. If you do lose, then you can sell what you have left. You may lose some, but you still have something to bet again with. It takes a long time to go bankrupt in the spot trade market (unless you hit a bankruptcy). With derivatives this is not the case, a derivative either has value at its expiration or it does not, there is no middle ground. To be honest, the value of a derivative goes from potential value to present value very quickly on the execution date. If you find yourself holding a bad option, you are out all the money that you put in. This is where sophistication is found, when people actually are risking losing it all.

One of the best ways to make sure the adoption of derivatives goes smoothly is to ensure that the marketplace has the option to educate itself. The community has the ability to teach people about how options work. Every story of a teen getting involved with trading and going into debt or a grandmother losing her retirement nest egg needs to be punctuated with whether or not they took the time to learn what they were doing. If it was a scam, then treat it like it was a scam; but if the "victim" did not take the time to learn what they were doing, then it was their fault and they should have left it to people who knew what they were doing. It is a harsh reality, but people are responsible for their own investments- if you cannot handle the heat, then turn things over to an investment company.

Chapter 40: Options

When investing, it is good to have options, and when investing lots of money, it is good to have stock options. Options are one of the most common derivatives that exists on the market today. Most of the time when a person is talking about a derivative, they are talking about an option. These are entry level derivatives, but they are a very valuable tool to those who use them properly. If you want to know what you are talking about in the derivatives market, then it is best to study up on your options.

In this Chapter, we look at what an options contract is. The first part breaks down how an option contract works and the difference between American and European options. Next, we take the time to talk about the two different directions an option can go. If you think that the market is going to drop, then you want to make sure that you are buying a put option (sell option). If you think that the market is going to rally, then you want to make sure that you have a call option in the wings (buy option). Either way, it is important to know why options are useful and how they can help you be more successful in your trading endeavors.

This Chapter concludes with a discussion of how options relate to cryptocurrencies. Except warrants, options tend to have the most utility on the crypto market. Small bets on a rise or fall can create huge opportunities for you to swing trade a specific crypto and build your stake for future speculation. Be wary, there are also the opportunity to spread your option bets too thin, where you cannot execute the option to make the money, even if you have the right bet.

What are Options

In one of the most interesting coincidences in the English language, options are actually the option to buy or sell on or before a specific time on the market at a pre-agreed upon price. You should be able to see the utility of the option, if you think that the market is going to go up; then you buy an option that allows you to buy at the present price on a future date. Conversely, if you think that the market is going to tank, then you buy an option to allow you to sell your holdings at the current price at a future date. Both methods are a way that you can hedge your bets without putting your entire stake at risk, the only consideration is that you must have the funds to execute your option.

The first major point that you must understand is that options are a contract. You are not buying the stock, nor are you buying the right to own the stock presently, you are simply buying the right to buy or sell the stock to the issuer at a given time (depending on the type of option). Effectively, you are purchasing a contract for action at a future date. Many people, when they buy options, do not understand that you own nothing more than the contract when you buy the option. This leads people to be very disappointed if the option expires without execution.

Another mistake that people make involving options is that you are not buying the stock, you are buying the right to buy the stock (most people only get disappointed over the buy options here). When the option expires, you still have to have the funds to buy the stock at the price that is suggested. If you are correct, then you usually can buy the stock on the margin for immediate sale (though that can eat up your profits). Novice investors should be wary because large options can be a great investment, but only if you have the money (or the stock) to cover.

There are two major families of option contracts, European and American options. European options act like a future on the market (they are basically the same thing sans the amount you have to buy). In a European option, you have to buy/sell the stock on the expiration date of the contract. Now like all options, you have the right to buy UP TO the amount of the contract, but you do not have to buy the entirety of the contract (unlike a future). In the American edition, you can buy or sell the stock in the option up until the date of the execution.[460] This makes the American contract much more versatile, and more valuable on the secondary market.

What are Put Options

"Put options allow the holder to sell the asset at a state price within a

[460] Bank, *Infra*.

specific timeframe."[461] This option is pretty much what it says it is. You have the option to take stock that you currently own (or own on the date you chose to sell it) and sell it at an agreed upon rate to the issuer of the option. Effectively, this means that if you think that the market will collapse, you can buy a put option then wait till you think that the stock has hit the low point within the timeframe you have set, then sell stocks up to the amount of the stock to the issuer of the option at the agreed upon rate.[462]

When it comes to derivatives, put options are among the safest options that a person can buy. If your bet is correct, you have the option of going out and buying the stock at the depressed rate to sell to the issuer at the agreed upon rate. This means that you do not have to own the stock when the put option is created; as long as the market value is lower than the put value, you can buy the stock and immediately turn around and sell it at the agreed upon price.

Where things get really interesting is if you are very confident that the price of the stock is going to collapse, you can short a value of money on the stock at its current rate and use that short to leverage the purchase of the stocks to cover the option. This allows a person to cover a much larger option than they normally would be able to cover. This is also a very dangerous move because if the stock rises in value, you not only lose the option (which becomes worthless) but also have to cover the short.

Simple put options are a "safe" investment for people who are just getting into derivatives. You can buy a put on the market (it is generally easier than trying to find an issuer) and wait to see if your bet paid off. If at any time (in an American put) you see that the market is hitting the bottom of the range that you thought it would go into, you can buy the stock at that rate and execute the option.[463] This is a great way to make money when you

---

[461] Chen, James (2021). "Stock Options" Investopedia at https://www.investopedia.com/terms/s/stockoption.asp.
[462] *Id.*
[463] *Supra.*

are just starting to get involved with derivatives. Once again, it must be said that if the stock goes up, the put option is worthless at execution. The best action at that point is to sell the option on the market (if you can) before you are left holding the bag.

Call Options

Call options are the opposite of put options. In a call option, you purchase a contract that you will be able to buy a given stock at a given price up until a given date (or on a given date in a European option).[464] These options are bought when you believe that a stock or crypto is going to rise in price. Basically, they allow you to buy a crypto at the present price at some time in the future. Oddly, as they are not as "safe" as put options they are more popular on the market. People seem to understand call options much better than the put options. This is the "Mr. Wimpy" scenario, "I will gladly pay you for your stock on Tuesday if you give me the right to do so today." However, in this scenario, you have to pay for the privilege.

Call options can be very enticing to new investors. The option to buy a stock that you think will go up at the present price can seem like a deal made in heaven, but you need to remember that the issuers of these options are not just getting started in the market. Issuers can see many of the patterns that you will see in the market (pattern analysis for options is much more complex than simple stock pattern analysis). This means that the "good options" will tend to cost more.

Even if there is a good option on the market for a stock that you think will go up, the odds are that there will be someone on the market who will see the same thing you do and the market value of the option will go up. The closer you get to the expiration date, the less likely that there will be "fresh" options on the market.[465] Remember, the only reason that someone is selling their option on the market is that they think that they

---

[464] Personal Capital (2021). "Stock Options: What are they and how do they work?" Personal Capital at https://www.personalcapital.com/blog/investing-markets/how-stock-options-work/.

[465] *Id.*

can make more money on the sale of the option that they will be able to make on the execution of the option.

This means that options traders need to make a very important calculation. An options trader must take the time to see if the price that they are paying for the option and the price that they will have to pay to execute the option will be worth more than the value of the execution of the option on or before the execution date. No matter how good the option is, if the value of the execution is lower than the cost of the option and the cost of buying the stock in the option, then you will still lose money on the deal.

Another item that you need to take into consideration is the amount you can buy under the option. Small options can have small price tags, but the same equation still comes into effect.[466] If the cost of the execution and purchase of the option is greater than the returns for the execution of the option, then you will still lose money. While it is not a scam, it is an unethical practice, to list small options for high values hoping that people do not do the calculations right and purchase an option that cannot cover unless there is an epic failure of the market.

Call options are a great place to start if you are a little nervous about the derivatives market. Simply put you are buying a right to purchase stock at a given price up until a given date, which you can then "flip" on the market (or hold) to realize the greater profits. The purchase is just for the contract, as long as you remember that (and that you have to have the funds to execute the option) then you can do quite well for yourself on the options market.

Why are Options Useful?

While options may seem like an exciting way to get involved with stock, the truth is that this is one of the more boring markets out there. People have figured this market out pretty well, and while you can make a lot of money

[466] Bank, Eric (2018) "Where to report unrealized profit or loss from futures options." Pocket Sense at https://pocketsense.com/report-profit-loss-futures-options-7872529.html.

on options, the best options tend to be very expensive.[467] However, this is still a very strongly traded market. This poses the question of "why?"

The first reason why this is such a strongly traded market is the reason that we have already talked about, it is easy and it is "safer" than other derivative markets. With a put or call option, the money that you put out upfront is all that you will lose if you are wrong (though you can lose more if you are right and play your cards wrong). The purchase price of the option is all that you have to pay to get involved with the option, even if you are correct- if you do not have the money to execute the option at the end of the option (and cannot find a place to trade it) then you are only out the original purchase price. This makes it a very manageable derivative that people can understand.

The next reason that options are so popular is that they can be used as a hedge against movements in the market.[468] Depending on the rate at which you can acquire an option, you may be able to use them as a hedge on your investment. If you think that the rate is going to go up, you can spot invest a portion of your stake on the stock, then purchase an option at the present rate valid at some time in the future. When you see that the price is starting to rise on the stock, you can execute the option to "average down" your holdings before you sell. This makes people feel that they are doing better with their increase in value (on the budget line it looks better); however, it is simply two trades on the same stock where you do better in one.

This can also be done with put options, though it is much more difficult. When you have an option to sell stock at a given rate, if you invest in something spot and it goes down, the put option allows you to get out from under the stock without taking a huge loss.[469] This is not a money-making method, but a way to hedge your bet against a collapse of the market on a

---

[467] *Id.*
[468] *Infra.*
[469] Chen, James (2021). "Delta Hedging" Investopedia at https://www.investopedia.com/terms/d/deltahedging.asp.

spot investment to rise. If the spot rises, then you allow the put option to expire (or sell it on the market to recoup some of your loss). If the stock falls, then you can use the option to protect your investment to keep it from falling. This is the method that many of the "guarantee your stake will not decrease" investment firms use to protect your investment (and why their fees are so high).

Put and call options are a good way to get started in the derivatives market because they are "safer." You can always lose the money that you have invested in buying the contract, but you are never forced to execute that contract if it is not in your favor. Depending on your level of risk, you can either lose all the investment on the contract or you can lose a portion of what you invested depending on the route you go. How much you invest and where you invest it should always be done with the advice of professionals.

How do Options Relate to Crypto?

Options with crypto can be a goldmine in the present state of crypto. With the advent of third-Wave cryptos, the golden age of crypto is just beginning. What that means is that we are seeing major fluctuations in the values of cryptos, while the mortuary charts for the industry are still in their fledgling states. This means that some funds and some investment houses will be issuing options that may not be as well researched as a stock option may be.

If you had a call option on DOGE for purchase at the present rate from Monday, December 14, 2021, and you executed it on Tuesday, December 14, 2021, then you would have realized a 21% increase in just under 6 hours.[470] This would be a small increase when some cryptos move 1000% in the same amount of time.[471] The price and the length of time for the option would be a question that you have to assess about the risk you are

[470] Money Control (2021). "Top cryptocurrency news on Dec 14th: Markets in red as Bitcoin and Ethereum fall." Money Control at https://www.moneycontrol.com/news/business/cryptocurrency/top-cryptocurrency-news-on-december-13-7822661.html.

[471] *Id.*

willing to take, but there seems to be a big market for what is coming in the crypto space.

When you are looking at options, the three factors to keep in mind are the price of the option, the rate for which you can buy/sell the coin/token, and the length of time you have to execute the option. The longer the amount of time you have to execute the option, the better. This gives you more "options" in what you do with the coin. If it goes up quickly, you can execute or wait to see if it goes up more. If it rises slowly, you can sell the option on the open market to make money that way. More time always leaves you more options (on an American-style option).

Always make sure to look at the purchase value of the coin. When buying from an issuer, it will generally be the spot rate at the time of creation, when you buy on the open market it will likely still have been when the contract was originally created, this means that it could be higher or lower than the present spot rate. If it is higher, then the price of the option should be lower to purchase. If it is lower, the spot rate will almost always be a little higher than the present execution rate (this is where you can make a lot of money if you can find an "instant flip.")

Finally, look to see what the sale price of the contract is. If the sale price is too high, you may have a hard time making money on the trade. The lower the price, the fewer shares you have to buy/sell at a lower rate to make sure that you make money on the contract. Make sure that you do the math because many times they will look like a good trade but, you will find that you need a strong increase to make money on the trade.

Chapter 41: Warrants

Warrants are slightly more technical than options. The market also is a little more complex around warrants. The movement of the stock can dictate the value of the warrant, but a warrant is often seen as a static investment around the future offering of a stock (that does not already exist).[472] As a result, the warrants are not traded as actively on the market and they can, sometimes, be more difficult to acquire because of their very nature.[473]

The interesting turn of events here is that warrants may be more useful for cryptos than they are for stocks. Because of the interesting nature of crypto releases and crypto reserves, warrants may give companies and their users an interesting method for ensuring that they can distribute reserves in a fair and ecosystem enhancing way. Time will tell how they are accepted but the potential in this area is amazing.

This Chapter starts off by looking at the big question, what are warrants. As we have noted several times, understanding the foundation and the concept behind any type of security is important to ensure the success of the ecosystem. Next, we take a moment to look at how warrants are different from options. Even experienced traders tend to conflate warrants and options, understanding the differences is vital for understanding the market.

The next section of this Chapter takes a significant turn. Rather than simply use warrants for what they are, the crypto community has an option of using them the same way as something else from the digital age, crowdfunding. The similarities between the two systems can give the Millennial/Gen X backbone of the crypto community something familiar to attach to in the derivative community. On this same page, we look at how warrants provide crypto with protections from "vulture capitalism" usually conducted by capital investment firms that are looking to gain control of

[472] Divine, John (2020). "Stock Warrants: 101 an explainer." U.S. News at https://money.usnews.com/investing/investing-101/articles/stock-warrants-101-what-are-they-and-how-do-they-work.

[473] *Id.*

the security. The Chapter then ends, as all derivative Chapters do, looking at how warrants are useful for the crypto market.

Warrants, in the opinion of this author, have the highest upside to the crypto market.[474] They allow the market to grow its ecosystem and enhance its status while maintaining the decentralized vision of the coin. While the derivatives, by their very nature, are centralized, the warrant process allows the centralization to be diffused and allows the market to form around a viable security option, outside of the decentralized exchanges. It is truly the best of both worlds.

What are Warrants?

Let us start with the question, "What are Warrants?" To understand what warrants are, you must first understand the reason for warrants. A warrant is a method for a company to issue new stock, without depressing the value of the old stock.[475] The method for this is for investors to put money into the company through the warrant issue, which increases the value of the company based on the amount of stock issued through the warrant process.[476] In effect, the company creates new equity and assigns new stock the equity.

Companies that use warrants are protecting the corporate interests and the interests of the old investors. However, this does pose the question of why a new investor would participate in this process. If a new investor could purchase the old stock at the same price as the new stock, and maintain the present voting control, then why would they buy into the warrant. The answer to this question is based on how the warrants are offered. If a warrant was a one-day warrant, then they would be a poor investment, but a 3, 6 or 12 month warrant opens up a world of possibilities.

Warrants can be offered like options or like futures or options. The issuer determines whether the investor can activate the warrant at any time up

---

[474] Literally Chris Said this.

[475] Kavanagh, *Infra*.

[476] Divine, Supra.

until the execution date or on the execution date.[477] Most of the time, they will be akin to futures in that the execution is on the future date. The investor buys the warrant hoping that the company will increase in value during the interim between purchase and execution. This allows the investor to "flip" or "hold in a good position" the stock when they receive it at the execution date.

Both companies and investors benefit from the warrant process, so why are they not offered more often. The reason for that is simple, the company has to be growing.[478] The warrant cannot create artificial growth for a long period (though it can create a spike in company value).[479] The growth is simply a growth in capital reserves. If the capital reserves are held, then the company stagnates. This means that the company has to re-invest the money gained from the warrant/stock issuance. So, unless a company has a major capital project, the issuance of a warrant will likely stagnate the stock. This is why they are less common than they could be.

How do they differ from options?

One of the best test questions of an undergraduate investing class is an essay question on how warrants differ from options. The answer is quite simple. "Warrants can only be offered on a call style system, they cannot be 'sale warrants.' The other key difference is that while an option call purchases stock from the existing pool, a warrant issues newly created stock." In an introductory class, that is an A answer in two lines.

The longer answer is that warrants are a creative process, options are a recycled process. Both offer the investor the same call option to purchase stock at a lower rate hoping to sell it at a higher rate, but the warrant allows the company to grow and expand. Warrants have the potential to be excellent funding options for a company that is looking to expand a plant or build a facility in another country, which can be done, creating an independent capital reserve for the project without diluting the stock of

---

[477] *Id.*

[478] Kavanagh, Infra.

[479] *Id.*

the current investors.[480] It is a win-win for everyone involved.

The challenges to warrants are often based on two area: misconceptions and voting rights. The voting rights issue is a real issue for current stock holders.[481] They have the right to vote on each of their shares based on the number of shares present. When there is a warrant issued, the current stock holders lose some of that ratio to the new stocks. While most warrants are offered to current stock holders first, before they are opened to the market, it still can sit uncomfortably with people who have held the stock from the beginning.[482]

The other chief concern that torpedoes warrant offerings at stock meetings, especially virtual meetings where people are not present, is that people do not understand warrants. The company is not creating stock out of nothing, they are creating new stock to represent the investment of the new capital coming from the investors. People are buying into the company, not buying out the company. When novice investors see the idea that a company is going to re-release stock, they get the feeling that their stock will be devalued; however, this is not true (most of the time the opposite is true). The value for the new stock comes from the value input by the investors and the old investors get to share in the increase in general value as the new capital investment project increase the worth of the system.

Crowd Funding

One of the best analogies that we can make for the warrant process is crowdfunding of a project.[483] While not a direct analog, crowdfunding has many of the same elements that a warrant offering has. Both types of investment have the ability to create capital for a project. Both tend to

---

[480] Kavanagh, Robin (2021). "What are stock warrants and why do companies offer them?" Business Insider at https://www.businessinsider.com/stock-warrants.

[481] *Id.*

[482] *Id.*

[483] Smith, Time (2021). "Crowdfunding." Investopedia at https://www.investopedia.com/terms/c/crowdfunding.asp.

have "shared governance" elements that enable to investors return their money. Crowdfunding and warrants also both seem to form a community around the investment, which can help "publicly market" the effort.

For those of you who do not know what crowdfunding is, it is the process of a group of people coming together to help an idea get off the ground. Go Fund Me[484] is one of the biggest crowdfunding sites on the planet, followed by Kickstarter.[485] Either of these options allows you to put out a call for donors who will help your project get off the ground. Generally, the investors get a copy of a product or production in return for their investment.

Crowdfunding is an amazing tool for small projects to get the investors they need to succeed without relying on capital investment funds (next section). This allows the owners of the idea to maintain control while still promoting the idea across the board. There are some differences from warrants; however, in that warrants can be traded on the market where crowdfunding bonuses cannot (technically). Further, warrants give some shared governance while crowdfunding only has community shared governance.

Against Capital Investment Firms

One of the key reasons that warrants are so effective is that it gives a company an option that does not require loans or capital investment firms. Unfortunately, vulture firms exploit smaller companies to take over control of them when they invest (think Shark Tank). Warrants allow companies to

---

[484] Go Fund ME https://www.gofundme.com/?utm_source=google&utm_medium=cpc&utm_campaign=US_GoFundMe_EN_EM_Desktop&utm_content=gofundme&utm_term=gofundme_e_c_&gclid=Cj0KCQiAnuGNBhCPARIsACbnLzqoL1-KRWZ4YkVE0WOVEf9J77Ga44Whs7VhNceryO1WR6OjguLTijYaAqMREALw_wcB

[485] Kickstarter https://www.kickstarter.com/projects/synergicgames/harakiri-blades-of-honor?utm_medium=referral&utm_source=18.backer.camp&ref=e6qmyz&gclid=Cj0KCQiAnuGNBhCPARIsACbnLzp9Wm3JawwGi8irD-2oeu3q1Vb2Y3b5OrHg8opqt43XsrfX0e34x8IaAnswEALw_wcB.

"sell their idea" without putting their core ownership at risk.[486] Now, this only works for established companies (not many people buy warrants on a new company) but it can allow small companies who are expanding the capital they need to improve their situation.

Capital investment firms function in the same way that bank's function.[487] You need money, they give you money with strings attached. A bank will give you the money and you need to pay the money back with interest or else they seize the surety that you place against the loan or they put a lien against your business. The trouble with using banks is that you need to convince them your expansion project is a good idea. Even worse, if you already have a loan with the same bank, they may not be willing to give you another loan.

Capital investment firms tend to be more "forgiving" on ideas.[488] The capital investment firm will fund your idea for a portion of your company. They also expect that returns will be paid to them, however, whereas when you pay the bank back the money you borrowed you own your company free and clear, if a capital investment firm makes their money back, they still own the portion of the company that they bought.

One of the reasons that warrants are preferable to capital investment firms is that, while there are still other people who own a portion of your company, the ownership is spread across a group of people rather than just one company. Capital investment firms can also sell their shares in your company, tanking your stock (if you are a publicly held company), or they can sell their stock to someone whom you may not want to own stock. If they sell to your rival, it is hard to stay in business if you are giving part of your profits to someone you are competing against.

Generally, if you have the business record to offer warrants it is a better choice to offer the warrants than to enter into business with a capital

---

[486] Kenton, Will (2021). "Capital Investment." Investopedia at https://www.investopedia.com/terms/c/capital-investment.asp.
[487] *Id.*
[488] *Id.*

investment firm. They have their profits in their best interest (which means they do want you to make money), but sometimes their interests will not line up with yours. The more diversified you can keep outside control of your company the better. Warrants allow you to do this without breaking the bank.

Why Warrants are So Useful in Crypto

Whereas warrants are very valuable in stocks in their own right, warrants have the potential to ensure that cryptocurrencies can stabilize their launches more readily. Whereas options only come into play on existing coins/tokens, warrants can allow the companies to put their reserves into play while increasing the value of the ecosystem. This is a great way to ensure that anytime any coin/token from the reserve is entered into the market, that the ecosystem grows the match the launch.

The concept of ecosystem growth is very important to the launch of the Wave three cryptos. The ecosystem in which a crypto exists needs to have a value for the coin to be stable. While the system is based on the federal reserve model, where you have no right to access the stake, the coin has an inherent value because the stake is there. With active wallets, like those in *The Wallet Groups* systems, the constantly growing stake allows for the system to grow.

Specifically, on an active stake system, warrants pose the greatest potential for investors and for holders. When the system is an active system, the initial warrant value is set at the present value of the system when the warrant is issued. Because the growth of the system is a non-defined constant, the warrant will almost always (barring a market collapse) be worth more than the initial investment. This means that the initial holder of the warrant can make money calling the warrant in on the execution date, or using the constant growth rate as an engine to sell the warrant on the market.

The holders of the coin/token get the added benefit of knowing that the ecosystem will be growing, or the reserve will be staying the same- either maintains/increases the value of the system. Even though the purchase of the coins/tokens will be at lower the market rate on the date that the that the contract is executed, the Net Present Value of the purchase, within a relative time to the length of the warrant, should be, amid proper system management, 2x+ the value of the warrants an initial purchase.

Overall, warrants not only can replace a portion of an ICO to work as an initial outlay, but they can also help in ecosystem management by allowing a portion of the reserve to go into play with a value-to-value swap. This increases the vitality of the system, and allows new fuel for the burn and earn system to grow under the new release. This is also an amazing option for countries that want to buy a reserve for legal tender, as they can see how the crypto grows with only an initial outlay. If the value grows, execute the warrant. If the value does not grow, buy the crypto at the current rate.

Chapter 42: Futures

One of the most basic derivatives that are on the market today is the concept of futures.[489] A future is an obligation to buy or sell a stock at a future date for a future price. This is a derivative with very few bells or whistles, unlike an options, there is no wiggle room for the bet.[490] If you guess right, you are obligated to buy the amount for the given price at the given time. If you guess wrong, then your only hope is to sell the future on the open market, or else you need to buy (or sell) the asset at the agreed upon rate.[491]

Futures are a hardline bet on an asset. Once a future is created, someone needs to execute the future. Whoever is holding the future at the end of the time must either buy or sell the asset as agreed upon. This creates a system where you know what you are paying, you just do not know what you are buying (or selling). If the price of the asset goes up higher than the purchaser of the initial buy future planned, they can have a nice windfall coming their way (the same can be said for a sell future when the price drops more than expected). However, the holder of the future is still obligated to buy (or sell) the agreed upon amount, even if the movement is not favorable. This is the risk in the system.

While this may seem like a dangerous prospect it can have some benefits over an option. A future is a contractual obligation to do something, which means you know what you are going to have to do. If you change your mind at some point, you may be able to sell the future on the open market for more than you paid for it- if the price is going in the right direction. Since the future market is very speculative, many times a "bad" future can be sold and some of the initial cost recouped. Once the future is sold, the new holder is the one who has the financial obligation to buy or sell at the end of the cycle.[492]

---

[489] Schwab (2021). "Understanding Futures." At https://www.schwab.com/futures/what-are-futures.

[490] *Id.*

[491] Fernando, Jason (2021). "Futures." Investopedia at https://www.investopedia.com/terms/f/futures.asp.

[492] Nickolas, Steven (2021). "Call option v. Future Contract: What is the Difference." Investopedia at

Like any derivative, with futures, you are betting on movement that you see coming. One of the best strategies to use with futures is to look for long-term channels and bet on the move coming out of the channel. When you see an asset entering a channel on the upswing, there is a higher than average likelihood that you will see the asset leave the channel in the same direction. This can be a good time to bet on the up. Regardless of the strategy that you are using, when you see an asset that you believe will be up on a future date, you can use a future to bet on that date (assuming you can find someone to sell you the future).

The same basic rules apply for downturns. If you see a longer-term cup and handle forming, you can bet that the asset will fall to the bottom (or middle) of the cup. This allows you to have room for it to drop lower. While this is always a risk, it has a better than average chance of working out in the traditional market. The goal, of course, is to set the value of the future higher than the low so that you can sell at the higher price and make your money (remember, futures are not free). The same people who make a living on the short markets seem to do well on the sell futures markets.[493]

Futures benefit the market because they allow spot traders to see what the market is predicted to do. future traders are looking to make money, just like everyone else. This means that they are going to set their orders where they think the market will be. Get enough futures moving in a particular direction and the market tends to follow the futures market. While this is rarely a direct correlation, futures are one of the factors that affect the market and help bring stability to otherwise volatile sections of the market. As the crypto markets evolve, this can be a valuable tool for stability.

---

https://www.investopedia.com/ask/answers/072915/how-does-forward-contract-differ-call-option.asp.

[493] Fernando, Supra.

How do Futures Differ From Options?

Futures are a much less volatile market than stocks.[494] Because there is a lower margin requirement for futures trading, the futures market has greater leverage than other securities markets.[495] This means that when you combine the lower margin and the higher leverage aspect, you see the market become less volatile.[496] However, if you are a futures trader, this is what you want. When there are big swings in the market, you find that you are owing more money (or making less money) on your future bet. This means that a steady market where the value of the underlying asset stays the same allows futures traders to make more money than a widely fluctuating market.[497] This is where futures is different from the standard market.

When we look at how futures differ from options, the question becomes a little more complex.[498] Futures are an obligation to do something at a given time, options are simply an option to exercise a right.[499] This is a very different type of security in which to trade. In a future, the holding of the future is a commitment to purchase the asset at the agreed upon rate at the given time. This means, that you are obligated to purchase the good regardless of the movement of the good. On one hand, this is easier to budget for because you know the rate- however, at the end of the contract you have to purchase the good regardless of whether you want to or not.

With an option, you have the option to purchase (or sell) the security.[500] This gives you much more wiggle room in what you want to do. In the event that you made the wrong bet, you are simply out the value of the option. Unlike a future, where the holder is obligated to execute the contract; in

---

[494] Schwab, Supra.

[495] *Id.*

[496] Center for Futures Education, INC. (2021). "Futures are less volatile than stocks." CTR at https://www.thectr.com/article.php?article=volatility.

[497] *Id.*

[498] Schwab, Supra.

[499] *Id.*

[500] Fernando, Supra.

an options contract you can simply let the contract expire.[501] This makes the options markets much more open for speculation as there is no risk other than the purchase price of the option.

The lack of a choice when it comes to futures is a double-edged sword.[502] On one hand, options are nicer because you have the ability to choose if you want to buy or sell. This means that if you made the wrong call, you are not out as much money. However, this comes with a cost. Good options tend to cost more than good futures. With the stability of the future, you know what you will be investing when the time comes to execute the option. While you know that you are going to be doing this, it allows you to plan for the investment. This can help bring stability to your portfolio.

The big similarity between futures and options is that both can be sold on the open market. Once a future is created, it is a sellable security on the market until it is executed.[503] This means that many people who purchase a newly minted future will immediately try to sell that future on the market to make money in that way. While the big money that is made on futures is made off of the execution of a good future, the movement of futures on the market can allow others to make money spot trading the futures.

The value of a future increases or decreases due to its relation to the price of the market.[504] The more favorable the execution of the future looks, the more that the future will be for sale. The closer to the execution a future is, the more reliable it is. This means that the market is constantly changing and can be very profitable to move in and out of futures. This also means that resellers are going to try to get the amount of the future as close to the profit amount as possible without making it cost-prohibitive.

Why Futures are Useful for The Seller?

If you are the issuer of a future (the seller) then you have some advantages that you should be aware of. First and foremost, once you create the future

---

[501] *Id.*
[502] Schwab, Supra.
[503] Infra.
[504] Fernando, Supra.

and sell it to a buyer, then you know that your asset is going to be sold at a future date. This means that you have the ability to plan and budget around this known sale. For many companies and hedges, this is a vital part of ensuring that you have income during the 3rd quarter of a year. Sell a future in the first quarter and then know that the income is coming in in the 3rd. If the future is sold at a higher rate than the asset was purchased for, then you have made money and any gains or losses after that are the problems of the buyer.

Next, you know what income you will have for your asset. This allows you to move your assets around during the course of the future term to increase their value. While you will always have to have the assets to cover the future, the ability to sell and short the asset if there are major moves in the asset cannot be understated. As long as you have the ability to sell (or buy if the case may be) the underlying asset at the given time, you can still use the asset to make money during the term.

The sale of a future also allows you to be protected against future losses in the price (or gains in sell options). The price is locked in from the time that the future is created. As a seller, this is an "out of sight, out of mind moment." As long as you make money on the initial sale of the future, combined with the future sale of the asset, you are in the black. The best course, unless you are actively trading the asset, is to forget about the asset till the time to collect comes. This allows you to worry about other assets and how you can increase their value or holdings.

Futures allow a company to sell its vision of what its holdings are going to do. If they see movement, regardless of whether the movement is up or down, they have the ability to sell the future based on that movement. In the event that they are correct, this can give them a windfall in value that they may not have realized had they simply held the stock. Further, the initial sale price of the future can be a valuable receivable within the system.

Futures can also act as a hedge against future price drops. If you can sell a future at a current rate when you believe that the price is going to drop in the future, as long as you make money on the sale of the future along with the future sale of the asset, then you maintain a gain on the asset. While this can restrict your gains during a period of rapid growth, it acts as assured income regardless of the market. In some cases, a company can buy back the future (at a lower rate) then they will not have to sell (or buy) the asset in the future- and they can make the difference by "shorting" their own future.

Why Futures are Useful (for Buyer)?

If you are looking to buy a future, you are looking at a little more risk on the market. Whereas the seller of a future has a guaranteed payout at the end of the cycle, the buyer of a future needs to be sure of what they are doing. A future is a bet, just like any stock. Whereas a seller of a future is the house in the casino of the trade, the buyer is the person who is putting their money on the line for a possible beneficial future. Knowing your market patterns and how a market is likely to react is vital to try to move the odds, just a little bit, in your favor.

One of the big advantages for the buyer of a purchase future is that they will have access to buy a given asset at a given date. With the coming of the digital age and crypto, certain events during the year are starting to show patterns. This means that you are able to look at what is coming on the market and then able to make an educated guess based on that. If you guy the future soon enough, then you will be able to ensure that you can get the asset at the volume that you want.

Another benefit of a purchase of futures is that you have the ability to purchase the asset at a given price. Whereas a volume can be something important for large traders, a simple change in price can be a major boon for a smaller trader. If you see something that indicates a price increase, then sometimes the only way you can secure the margin that you need when you want it is to possess a future that will allow for a quick flip of the asset. This can open smaller traders to much larger market gains.

With sales futures, you have a unique opportunity to know what you will be selling your assets for (and how much you can sell). If you see a price drop coming, and you are a large holder of a given asset, then it behooves you to try to gain control of a favorable sell future. This can be a great way to limit your losses or even turn them into gains. While a sell futures may be expensive when the market is in a downturn, you can always look at the value of the asset to see if there is enough room to ensure that you still make money on the trade.

Holding a future can give you some modicum of protection from rapid moves in the market. While an option is safer to hold in this situation, a future can be more reliable over the long run. Once again, you know what you are getting at the end of the term. If the future looks to be of less value than you think it should be, you can always sell the future on the open market and attempt to secure an option with a more favorable rate (or even another future). This technique allows a trader to separate the value of the transaction from the value of the asset, which in the long run can increase your percentages.

Finally, if you have futures in a market, you regularly play, the futures in that market can be a valuable indicator of how the market is likely to move in the near future. Futures traders are in the game for the same reason all other types of traders are in the game. This means that they are going to be researching and assessing the movement of assets in the market. The futures market will generally indicate where an asset is moving better than the options market (remember people do not have to execute options so options can sometimes get crazy. Therefore, by looking at the futures market a savvy trader can get a glimpse into a possible future.

Why Futures are Useful in Crypto?

While stock rockstars have been using futures for a long time to ensure that the market does not get too volatile for them, futures are new to the crypto market and are still being felt out by crypto traders. With the speed that the crypto market changes, the large channels created by trading periods are difficult to predict.[505] This means that traders can have a hard time securing a future that makes any sense at the present time; however, any future bought on the crypto market can be invaluable in the near future.

As with anything in crypto, diversification is key. Being overly invested in spot trading is creating a wildly volatile crypto market. While this makes a fun market for small-cap speculators, it makes the market very dangerous for serious investors. It also stifles the growth of the market in the long term. The more diversified the trading technologies are in a given area, the more people may be interested in trading in that area. Diversity allows the modern crypto whales to mingle with the OG billionaires to bring crypto to the forefront of the modern market.

One of the holy grails of crypto is to get one of the G8 or G12 countries to invest in a crypto.[506] Right now the market is too dangerous for this to happen. However, with more diversification of the market, derivatives allow countries to get involved with crypto without purchasing the actual assets until they are mature. This means that the more we diversify the system, the more big players will be able to move in. Likewise, large companies are leery to move into the space; however, with more diversity they are more likely to take small risks.

Simple derivatives, like futures, also provide a valuable entry point for novice traders to enter the market. Futures are basically spot trades that you can buy and sell. Even the simplest trader has the ability to get involved with futures to hedge their portfolios against future losses (and guarantee gains). Just make sure that you have the assets to cover the future when it

---

[505] CME Group at https://www.cmegroup.com/trading/micro-bitcoin-futures.html?gclid=CjwKCAiAiKuOBhBQEiwAId_sK4hXiKKojMKfMzhEZTFZob7pV8LBY91tX0WHj2yTLxGdZ2W0NTSehBoCuVQQAvD_BwE&gclsrc=aw.ds.

[506] Tobias Adrian, Dong He, & Aditya Narain (2021). "Global Crypto Regulations Should be Comprehensive, Consistent, and Coordinated." IMF at https://blogs.imf.org/2021/12/09/global-crypto-regulation-should-be-comprehensive-consistent-and-coordinated/. Boo the IMF.

comes due, or you could find yourself losing assets that you did not invest.

Futures can also commit capital to the market ahead of time in a way that will help raise trust in the market. A future is a guaranteed trade. If it is at a price higher than the current market, it becomes a strong indicator that there will be higher level trades at a future date. Even when there is a bear market, this can be a good indicator or a reversal. Since people know that some trades are going to occur at a given point, it sets the top level of the candle in favor of the bulls. With sell futures, we can see restrictions that can slow down a rally, which can bring out the bears.

Futures, along with the other derivatives can also bolster the growth of Stablecoin 2.0. Stablecoin 2.0 systems can sell assets from the reserve at a guaranteed rate to ensure that the system grows. While this will bring lower growth than a spot trade at a potential higher rate, it will provide guaranteed income at the given date. Since the reserve is designed to increase in value, not speculate for massive growth in a time period, this is a safer measure to ensure that the ecosystem continues with a reasonable growth rate and that the holding system can continually recycle its holdings growing ever more rapidly.

Chapter 43: Forwards

Forwards are slightly more interesting than futures. Forwards tend to bridge the gap between futures and options, but they also have the unique aspect that they are unique between the parties that are trading them. Because of the customization features that are present in a forward, they are more likely to be used in the NFT markets than the traditional crypto exchanges. This makes them ideal for moving digital assets in the metaverse.

This Chapter provides a quick rundown of how forwards work on the traditional market and how they are foreseen to work within the crypto market. The first step in ensuring that a person is a savvy trader in this space is to help them understand what a forward is. Unlike a future, these are not likely to be traded on a centralized exchange, which means that they tend to be one-off events that are settled on a daily basis.[507] This Chapter also takes a moment to understand how forwards are different from futures because people who work in futures can tend to see forwards as the same thing, and they are not.

Next, one must understand why forwards are useful in a given market. These are a scapple whereas a future is a saw. Forwards can be highly customized to meet the given needs of both parties and a situation.[508] Futures are just a general instrument to move securities. Finally, this Chapter looks at how futures can be used within the crypto markets. This is one of the few areas of the book where we step away from fungible tokens and look at the wild west world of NFTs.

Overall, forwards have their place in the newly developing space of the crypto markets. Unlike options, warrants, futures, and swaps, the relationship between the market and forwards is still yet to be defined. The more developed the market becomes, the savvier the traders will become.

---

[507] Dhir, Rajeev (2021). "Forward Contract." Investopedia at https://www.investopedia.com/terms/f/forwardcontract.asp.

[508] CFI (2021). "What is a forward Contract." Corporate Finance Institute at https://corporatefinanceinstitute.com/resources/knowledge/finance/forward-contract/.

New ways to use old tools will become more apparent as the market develops.

What are Forwards?

Forwards are a customizable contract which allows the traders to define the asset, the amount, the payment method and the delivery date.[509] As the forward market evolves away from the stock market, more and more customizable mixtures will be available for traders to mold their agreement to meet their specific needs. As these are OTC trades, there is no need for exchanges to accept these agreements, meaning that the traders have more power over the trade.

One of the most useful aspects of the forward system is the ability to define the item (or items) to be traded. When looking at the NFT market, we see that the uniquity of the NFTs can be a challenge to the development of the market. When a person wants to trade on NFT, they can do so- but what if a person wants to trade an NFT in a non-traditional way. The spot rate market is not equipped to deal with this change. The forward market, however, is very well developed for this type of dealing, allowing the traders to define what they are trading and how they want to trade it.

Next, forwards allow the traders to set the amount of the trade. Since NFTs are a unique item, there cannot be a simple "1, 000" unit trade. In a NFT forward each unique NFT is defined in the trade and the traders can distinguish when each will be released to the buyer. This can allow a buyer to buy the rights to several NFTs but spread the payments over a period of time. This makes the instrument infinitely more useful than a spot trade and even more useful than an option.

The payment method is another interesting element of a forward that gives more flexibility for the crypto market. In a traditional forward the price is set in a given fiat currency. In the crypto market, this does not have to be the case. The sale can be for any type of crypto. The purchase may not even

---

[509] Lake, Rebecca (2019). "What is a forward contract and how do they work?" Smart Asset at https://smartasset.com/investing/forward-contract.

all be in the same type of crypto. We could see a trade for an NFT which amounts to 2 Bitcoin and 2 trillion SHIB as a viable trade within the forward space. This is the amazing flexibility of the variable market.

Finally, the delivery date is fully negotiable by the parties.[510] This means that parties can set the delivery and payment dates whenever they would like. In effect, some of the more complex elements of property law could be applied to a forward contract (life estate with a fee simple absolute remainder) and applied to an NFT. The unclear nature of how digital property works within the real property realm will be one of the most exciting developments of the next five years.

Customization is one of the elements that is driving the NFT market.[511] By adding a forward overlay onto the system, we could see a boom in the market that makes the 2021 boom look like a drop in the bucket. The more the market defines itself, the more stability we will see in regular cryptos and NFT trading. This will help the system become the system of the future.

How are Forwards different from Futures?

In the world of stock and commodity trading, forwards are very much like futures except that they give traders a little more wiggle room in building a trade. The defining of the assets to be traded allows the traders the ability to customize the trades more than in a futures. This allows futures and forwards to be very similar for the OG traders and often discussed in the same section of business textbooks.

This all changes when we enter into the world of crypto. Because of the diversity of cryptocurrency, and the unique aspect of NFTs traders have unlimited options in customizing their agreements. Different currencies, different delivery dates, different NFTs all lend themselves to a very open market on moving crypto assets around. While forwards are much more complicated in this space, they are also going to be much more profitable.

---

[510] Rajeer, Supra.

[511] Lake, Supra.

First of all, forwards are not traded on open exchanges.[512] This means that they are OTC trades and are usually closely held by the parties who create them. This means that once you create a forward, this is much more difficult to get rid of than a future. Once it is created, most of the time you will be stuck to fulfil your obligation when it comes due. The more complex the forward, the more difficult the execution is; however, because of the aspect of NFTs, this can also be spaced out over more time which can make it easier.

Next, forwards allow you more freedom to create the terms.[513] Forwards are simply a contract with bilateral promises at a future date. Other than this, the contract can be structured in any, legal, way that the parties want to have the contract started. This means that one forward will not look like other forwards. This can be a challenge on the legal end, but can be very exciting on the trading end.

In the crypto space, forwards and futures have a definite hard fork between them. How this fork will develop will be based on how the system evolves. At present, we can only speculate on how the markets will change as people find new ways to incorporate new elements into the forward space. This is one of the most exciting aspects of the crypto market.

Why Forwards are Useful for the Market?

As governments attempt to unlawfully regulate trade in the crypto space, forwards are one of the most difficult areas to regulate.[514] As each forward is unique, the traders have the ability to make the contract in whatever form that they want- including jurisdiction. Since the global precedent is to respect the valid choice of law clause in a private contract, this creates some very interesting opportunities for traders and countries as the market develops.

First of all, what is a choice of law clause? A choice of law clause is a section in a contract that tells the reader of the contract what jurisdiction the

[512] CFI, Supra.
[513] *Id.*
[514] Infra.

parties have agreed to have their disputes heard by.[515] Under global tradition, courts will respect a choice of law clause if it is written properly. This means that the parties must choose an area that has legal jurisdiction.[516] In the crypto space, there is a strong question of whether choice of law must be in a real-world jurisdiction or whether it can be in a virtual, more egalitarian jurisdiction.[517] While national courts will surely balk at the idea of virtual jurisdiction, with the expansion of mankind into space and the metaverse it becomes a real possibility that these virtual jurisdictions have more "rights" to hear a case than a traditional court.[518]

When choosing a choice of law clause for an forward it is important to know that there are two different elements of the law.[519] The first is the physical jurisdiction of the court.[520] This is the question that will become more dynamic as the metaverse expands.[521] If people create a social contract within the virtual space, do not those living people have more of a right to create a social contract than they have to be bound by people who died before the existence of the internet, especially when dealing with the virtual space? While this question cannot be answered now, and any court that directly tries to answer it without a convention of the people is beyond its scope, one settled aspect is that the choice of law needs to define what jurisdiction has physical jurisdiction over the parties to the case.[522]

Next, when choosing a "choice of law clause" you must also define the procedural law that you wish to use.[523] While parties can choose to have the case heard in one area, they must define whose procedures they are

---

[515] Rajeer, Supra.
[516] *Id.*
[517] Lake, Supra.
[518] CFI, Supra.
[519] Lake, Supra.
[520] West, Glen (2017). "Making sure you 'choice of law' clause chooses all the laws of the chosen jurisdiction." Harvard.edu at https://corpgov.law.harvard.edu/2017/09/18/making-sure-your-choice-of-law-clause-chooses-all-of-the-laws-of-the-chosen-jurisdiction/.
[521] Lake, Supra.
[522] Rajeer, Supra.
[523] *Id.*

going to use in order to have the case heard in an orderly manner.[524] In this case, most courts have ruled that parties can choose public or private law.[525] Since arbitration and mediation are private law mechanisms, there is no reason that they should not be able to be extended to the forward space. This should allow parties to choose digital jurisdictions for their choice of procedural law, if not the jurisdictional law as well.[526]

This mechanism alone could be a tool that allows traders from oppressive regimes that prevent crypto trading to have access to proper legal systems to enforce forward contracts. This could also create a "race to freedom" where countries attempt to give the most favorable system of laws in the forward crypto space to ensure that more cases are heard there (and taxed there). While this may be a challenge for many countries to accept, it is a right of contracting parties to choose the jurisdiction for civil case, if both parties agree and are from different nations.

Application of Forwards to the Crypto Markets

Even with all the complexities of the forward system, the application of the forward system to the crypto markets is not overly complex. Forwards should be treated as forwards have been treated since they were created. They are simply contracts that allow parties to set the terms of a futures exchange. Nothing more, nothing less. The more complex system becomes, the simpler the underlying premise needs to be. This makes for an efficient system.

One thing that the crypto community and the governments of the world need to understand is that forwards are the securities that are least able to be regulated. Because parties do not need to tell anyone else about a contract, the contract can stay secret.[527] This makes it very hard to regulate. Since 98% of contracts are fulfilled without breach, many contracts will be executed without anyone knowing the different. All that there will be is a record of the final transactions.

---

[524] Lake, Supra.
[525] Rajeer, Supra.
[526] CFI, Supra.
[527] Lake, Supra.

Chapter 44: Swaps

Swaps are the most complex of the derivatives that we look at in this book. Ironically, they are also the most related to a spot trade, which is simpler than any derivative. This full circle of trading looks at how the market is based on market forces, and we can never get beyond that while staying on the right path. Swaps are a complex, but "safer" type of derivative, which once you understand them, they do make sense- but wrapping your head around them can be tricky.

In this Chapter, we look at the key elements of how swaps work. Before we get into this, however, it is important to talk about what a stock swap is and how it is different from a derivative swap. Stock swaps are the basic form of the swap, which underpins the concept of a derivative swap. Once the stock swap is understood, it becomes easier to look at the derivative swaps and to build off of their system. The dichotomy between stock and derivative swaps is one of the reasons why this market (OTC) is so difficult to understand.

Next, someone working in this area needs to look at why someone would want to do a swap (rather than buy stock or other dividends). Swaps are a leveraged system of trading equity for defined value, but generally not in a currency format. These could be considered a foundational element of the crypto sciences as they are treating the asset not as the value itself, but "as the value of the asset being traded as an asset- thus they move to the opposite end of the spectrum from other derivatives."

Some experts in the field have questioned the utility of swaps in the crypto marketplace. Ironically, the value of the swap is not in the actual swap, but in the utility of the swap.[528] Going almost into the metaphysics of the stock and crypto markets, swaps have value because the relationship between the two markets which have swaps have value. Thus, the value of the swap is not in the value of the exchange but the value of the utility of the bridging of two universes. Swaps lift the market restriction of crypto/stock/ commodity without having to move through a traditional market exchange.

---

[528] McCaffrey, Infra.

Swaps expand the market beyond the simple planning of exchanging crypto for crypto or crypto for fiat currency. Swaps build the foundation for the underlying equity in commodities, stocks, crypto, and currency to be traded, directly in a decentralized manner. For those who say swaps will not work in crypto, one only has to look at the decentralized exchanges to see that the naysayers are wrong and swaps are as fundamental to crypto as the blockchain itself!

What is a Classic Stock Swap?

One reason why people get confused about swaps is that the term functions in two different ways within the world of stocks. The most common form of a swap is not the derivative swap which is more interesting to the crypto world, but the stock swap.[529] A stock swap is the trading of one group of stocks for another group of stocks so that the owners of each group of stocks now have equity in the venture of the other party.[530] Basically, I trade you part of my company and you give me part of your company so that we have shared interests.

Most often, you will see stock swaps in mergers.[531] Depending on the part of the world where the merger is going on, there may be need for government approval of the swap to ensure that the companies do not run afoul of anti-trust laws. Regardless, this is a more effective method of doing a merger than one company spending X dollars and the other company spending X dollars to buy shares off the market (which most still do). It allows companies to make the trade without other parties to the trade interfering with the system.

The exchange of equity in the company of another has been done for centuries. Rather than it just being an acquisition, sometimes it is an

---

[529]Elisabet Furio (2017). "Swaps: what are they and how they work." BBVA at https://www.bbva.com/en/swaps-what-they-are-and-how-they-work/.
[530] *Id.*
[531] CFI (2021). "What is a Swap." Corporate Finance Institute. At https://corporatefinanceinstitute.com/resources/knowledge/trading-investing/swap/.

informal peace between rival companies.[532] In ancient times, countries would send the children of leaders to live in another country as surety that they relation would stay positive between them. It is only fitting that companies, which are akin to the new nation-states in the digital frontier, would make these changes to make peace in a difficult market. You do not attack your opponent because you now are part of that opponent and your attacks hurt yourself.

This is also an excellent way for companies to balance equity in a trade.[533] Not all stock swaps are straight-up stock swaps, since they are customized contracts many times the parties will have to offer other assets to balance the deal. In a stock swap, the stock is the centerpiece for the trade while the other assets are simply tools for balancing the value. Just like when using a scale, you need to ensure that the trade is balanced for both parties.[534]

As noted, stock swaps are much simpler than derivative trades; however, it is important to understand the foundation of stock swaps before moving on to more complex types of swaps. As you move into the crypto space, you will see elements of these systems in the more straightforward derivatives, but once you understand the value of the swap derivatives, you will see that this concept underlays the whole system. Swaps may not have built the cryptoverse, but the theory underlying swaps is foundational to the cryptoverse that we see today.

What is a Swap (Derivatives)?

When we look at what a swap is as a derivative, it becomes more complex. A derivative swap is a "derivative contract in which one party exchanges or swaps the values or cash flows of one asset for another."[535] Generally, the variable asset of one leg of the swap is exchanged for a known value in the

---

[532] SoFi (2021). "A brief history of the stock market." Sofi Learn at https://www.sofi.com/learn/content/history-of-the-stock-market/.

[533] Furio, Supra.

[534] CFI, Supra.

[535] McCaffrey, Michael (2021). "An Introduction to Swaps." Investopedia at https://www.investopedia.com/articles/optioninvestor/07/swaps.asp.

other leg of the swap.[536] In effect, this allows parties to exchange a known value for a variable value, effectively letting one party speculate while the other party secures their risks. It is an effective method of extending exposure without overextending your risk.

Within the realm of speculation, having one value as a set value and one value as a variable value can be an effective way to move funds around.[537] For the party looking to minimize risks, the system is quite effective because, assuming they have access to a variable income stream, they are able to "trade" the results of that variable income stream for a known amount at a future time. Likewise, for a trader who would like to increase their risk (and increase their gains), they have the ability to get rid of a known value (which will not increase) and exchange it for a variable value (which they hope does increase). It is a win-win for both parties which is why this type of trade is so effective.[538]

One of the caveats of all types of swaps is that they are traded OTC.[539] This means that there is no secondary market for your swap. Generally, there is no way to trade a swap after it is created, because one party owns the specific rights to the income generated from the asset- so to trade a swap you would need to find someone with the same pool of assets as the original party that created the swap, which is no mean feat.[540]

The most common type of derivative swap is called a plain vanilla swap.[541] In this type of swap, a variable interest rate on a set of loans is traded for a fixed rate on a set of loans. This allows the holder of the variable rate to stabilize their holdings and the holder of the fixed-rate loans to open up the potential for more returns.[542] It is a fairly safe, fairly stable type of

---

[536] *Id.*
[537] *Id.*
[538] CFI, Supra.
[539] Furio, Supra.
[540] *Id.*
[541] Chen, James (2021). Plain Vanilla Swap. Investopedia at https://www.investopedia.com/terms/p/plain-vanilla-swap.asp.
[542] *Id.*

exchange that works best when the market is fairly steady (or setting within a channel).

Another type of swap, a type that is very closely related to crypto, is a currency swap.[543] In a currency swap "[there is] an exchange of interest- and sometimes principal—in one currency for the same in another currency."[544] The interest payments are exchanged at variable times during the contract (which can be defined by the party) allowing this to be a contract that can settle regularly (like forwards over futures.).

Swaps are a powerful derivative tool that can be used to stabilize your portfolio if you find yourself over-leveraged, but can also be an excellent tool to increase your exposure to speculation while still limiting your risk over the long term. Portfolios that properly manage swaps can be very effective in ensuring stable growth of the portfolio during the course of the swap system.

Why Swap Variable for Fixed Income?

For many who enter the world of swaps, the first question that many people ask is "why would anyone trade known value for potential value, when the known value is already in the black?" Most of the people asking this question are bankers and are risk adverse. If you are in a business where you are working to ensure constant growth throughout the development of a system, then you will always want to be on the variable for the fixed leg of the trade (meaning you get the fixed income). This is because most businesses want to see steady growth and are not willing to risk their stake on a potential gain. However, there are millions of people who speculate on the market, and those people want to make as much as they can as quickly as they can.[545]

For an active trader, it makes more sense to trade future value for future value if you want to increase your potential value without changing your

---

[543] Infra.
[544] Segal, Troy (2021). "Currency Swap Definition." Investopedia at https://www.investopedia.com/terms/c/currencyswap.asp.
[545] CFI, Supra.

foundational holdings.[546] In a swap, you can hold the note on a loan (the simplest type of swap). You know the payout of the interest on that loan. This number may not be in the range of growth that you want to see. Therefore, you seek out another entity that holds a variable rate loan. If you believe that the variable rate will rise, then it makes sense (and the other party is willing) to trade your guaranteed income for their potential variable income. The more that the rate grows, the more money that you make.

For those who question the validity of this idea, it is basically what you are doing when you make a spot trade in stock, however, here you are simply doing it in equity.[547] In the stock market you are taking money, something that you know has a value (though it is declining) and trade it for a stock (which you hope will grow in value). With swaps, you are doing the same thing, you are just not giving up the underlying asset. This means that you are only trading the interest rates (growth rate) on the stock. In this way, it is not much different from the opposite of a short in a stock market.

This allows large-scale traders to trade the values that they have on the market without changing the underlying assets in their portfolios. Since the interest value is all that is being traded, the underlying value stays the same- this means that the value of the portfolio is always going to rise (as long as the bet is correct).[548] If the rate goes up, the team that purchased the interest rates on the variable rate will make more money. Meanwhile, the team that purchased at the fixed rates can assure their client that their account is going to grow. Very rarely on a swap is the asset going to lose value, it simply is losing the interest-rate so you get less rather than getting more. This is why this is one of the safest methods of trading in stock.

Are Derivative Swaps Plausible in Crypto?

I apologize for having a section heading that looks like a question that someone on the finance committee of the United States House of

[546] McCaffrey, Supra.
[547] Furio, Supra.
[548] McCaffrey, Supra.

Representatives would ask an executive. First of all, currency swaps are the second most common type of swap on the market today. Translating these types of swaps to the crypto market is very simple and should be understandable for anyone who has any level of market savvy. While is likely why an institution with nearly 30 trillion dollars in debt cannot understand it.[549]

Swaps not only have a place in crypto, swaps are part of crypto. Every crypto trade that involves currencies other than fiat for crypto is a swap of sorts. You are moving one asset with the potential for growth to another asset with potential for growth. While these are the primitive stock style swaps, they are still swaps that make the market run. The extension of these types of swaps is not only foreseeable but also necessary as the DeFi market starts to make a move in the financial sector.

The amazing thing about the use of swaps on the crypto market is that swaps also bridge the space between the traditional stock market and the crypto market. While we are staring to see this in the primitive stages on certain exchanges, the ability to exchange crypto for stock is coming very soon. The introduction of Global Exchange Tokens (like KIROS) is making this pathway much easier. This allows everything to be done in two or three traders, rather than the four that the market currently needs. Each trade will act like a swap, but the exchange will be done immediately. Using advanced tokenomics to make this work will save traders (and platforms) billions in excess gas fees.

Global Exchange Tokens not only create a spiderweb bridge across different blockchains, but they also provide a spiderweb bridge that spans into the stock, commodity, bond, precious metals, grain, livestock, currency, and all other markets.[550] These allow traders to move from one market to the next, across mega exchanges, to ensure that people can trade in any area that they want. The addition of the GET also allows people to move from spot rates in these markets to derivative trades with little or no excess fees!

---

[549] Debt Clock at https://www.usdebtclock.org/.

[550] KIROS White Paper.

Making the Market More Robust

Swaps are not an instant payoff system like spot trades.[551] This is one of the elements that people need to accept when they enter into the swaps market (or swaps business as there is no real market for swaps). In a well-developed swap, you are trading reasonable interest payments over time for a one-time payout at the end of a contract you already hold. Steady versus immediate is one way that the market becomes more stabilized.[552]

All swaps are derivative elements. This means that generally you are trading interest, but you could be trading potential v. guaranteed growth. This means that the margins are shaper, but the potential for profit is more steady. While swaps are safer than most types of derivatives, one must realize that if they are trading on the margin, they can still get taken for a loop if they make the wrong move on a variable asset.

Once you are in a swap, you are in it till the end (unless you buy out the contract).[553] This means that if it takes a southward turn (or the underlying asset is voided), you could be in for a world of hurt. This is why many investors only do swaps with reputable companies on reputative assets. Volatile markets will offer bigger returns, but also bigger risks. *Caveat Emptor* should be the saying that guides a swap trader.

The key element of why swaps are needed in the crypto space is because they add a static element to a variable system.[554] The more complex the system, the more that the system needs anchors to keep the values within a stable range. If the system grows too fast, it becomes overleveraged. If the system declines too fast, then there is not faith in the market. Swaps allow for there to be a dual hedge, that when added to the other derivative (Warrants, Options, Forwards, Futures) makes for a much more stable

---

[551] McCaffrey Supra.

[552]Teri Geske (2021). "Swaps and other derivatives: Valuable tools of Instruments of the Devil." Investor Junkie at https://investorjunkie.com/investing/swaps-and-other-derivatives/.

[553] Furio, Supra.

[554] CFI, Supra.

system.

Chapter 45: Why Derivatives are so Important to the Market

Beyond the necessity for investors, derivatives are vital to the market for several other reasons. A complex market tends to have more elements that "prop up" the market than a simple market.[555] While everyone can understand how spot trades work, trends usually move the whole way through the market and can cause a single segment market to rally or fold on something as simple as a celebrity's tweet. Derivatives can act as a hedge against this, and that can make the crypto market (and other markets) more stable in the years to come.

One of the key reasons why derivatives are so important to the market is the diversity they bring.[556] When the market is trending down, derivatives (and shorts to some extent) act as a lifeline to ensure that the system does not completely collapse. The more elements in the system, the more likely it is that one of the elements will see a rise when the others are falling. This is why the current diversity of the crypto market is so important, each currency is a rung on the ladder that may save the market in a bear turn.

Another reason that derivatives are so important is that they give skittish people a way to own crypto without actually owning crypto. Anyone that was in the market of 2021 knows how annoying paper hands can be during the market. Paper hands cost real market players billions of dollars as a coin can die (or just fall out of public sight) because of weak players dropping out of the market. Derivatives place the trades in a system that allows everyone to have some success without having to actually "own" the crypto they are interested in.

Additionally, every time a new derivative is entered into the market, a new

---

[555] Battiston, Stefano et al (2013). "Complex Derivatives." Columbia Business School at https://www8.gsb.columbia.edu/faculty/jstiglitz/sites/jstiglitz/files/2013_complex_derivatives.pdf.

[556] Bindisha Sarang (2021). "Benefits of Diversity: A Coin-flip reveals better bitcoin alternatives." Business Standard at https://www.business-standard.com/article/pf/benefits-of-diversity-a-coin-flip-reveals-better-bitcoin-alternatives-121022500048_1.html.

predictor line can be added to the forecasts. While for most people this is clutter on their screen that they turn off, if you look at the indicator lines as a group, they tend to be a good predictive model. Just like the different lines on a storm forecast create an area that is likely to get slammed with a storm, multiple lines on a chart can help you figure out if the asset is going to rise or going to fall. In the end, more lines are a good thing.

Another great feature of the derivatives market is that some derivatives are never executed. Warrants and options may never be claimed, which means that the money put into these derivatives just feeds the system to increase value. This is one of the few ways that the market can have an influx of money without it being directly linked to the spot price of a given asset. While it is a shame for the trader who bought the option that was never realized, the whole of the market gets stronger with each unclaimed option or warrant.

The bottom line is that the more savvy the market is, the more savvy investors it is going to attract. While the spot market in crypto became a trillion-dollar industry, it is nothing to what the market will be as the complexities of the market become better defined.[557] This will enable people around the world to participate in the market in a way that they never before were able to. Even in tyrannical countries that are attacking the crypto markets, people can still get around the restrictions with VPN activity.

Overall, the more we bring to the market, the more the market has. When we bring more funds, the market grows. When we bring more options, the market grows. When we bring more ideas, the market grows. The only thing that reduces the size of a market is when there is excessive regulation and corruption in a market. These are things that governments are known very well for bringing to the market. The longer we can keep the market

---

[557] Locke, Taylor (2021). "From Bitcoin hitting $1 Trillion in market value to Elon Musk's dogecoin Tweet: 12 Key Crypto Moments from 2021." CNBC at https://www.cnbc.com/2021/12/27/12-key-moments-that-fueled-cryptos-record-growth-in-2021.html.

free, existing under the legal regime which has supported it for years, the longer it will continue to grow and challenge the fiat system of banking cartels.

Diversification is Key

If you are not tired of hearing that diversity is important to a portfolio, then you either are getting the concept or you will be sick of it by the end of the book. Diversity allows for parts of the market to be moving up while other parts of the market are moving down. This is the type of stability that investors and businesses alike. As long as the general trend of the market is going up, everyone can be happy. Yes, there will be those who are caught by the downward slopes, but they have the same opportunity to move with the people who are riding the rallies.

In the crypto market, we have a wild, wild west scenario.[558] The rules are up in the air because the governments of the world are not enforcing the laws that exist.[559] Crypto trading is the trading of currencies, which is allowed in almost every nation in the world. When a government puts restrictions on crypto trading, they are putting restrictions on the human right to contract with our peers. Even worse, when regulatory agencies hang "possible ideas" on market changes out there, it is like villains in the wild west hanging the bodies of innocent people they have killed out as a warning. Civilized nations stopped this practice over 1, 000 years ago-seemingly it is making a comeback in the digital form. The crypto community needs to work together to end this practice of "making an example of" people who do not support the rising tyranny.[560]

One of the great elements of a free market is that as the market evolves,

---

[558] Kuhn, Daniel (2021). "Gary Gensler Says crypto is 'wild west' others see pure capitalism." Coin Desk at https://www.coindesk.com/policy/2021/09/30/gary-gensler-says-crypto-is-a-wild-west-others-see-pure-capitalism/.

[559] *Id.*

[560]Lindsey Fitzharris (2011). "A Fate Worse than Death: Displaying Criminals Corpses." The Guardian at https://www.theguardian.com/science/blog/2011/nov/07/fate-worse-death-displaying-corpses.

there will be new instruments entering the market. The idea of global exchange tokens, Stablecoin 2.0 and even bitcoin was not present at the turn of the century, but now they are common tools in international trade. As we allow the system to evolve, people will find inspiration for new models and new things. This will allow them to expand the market even further in directions that we do not know. The brilliant thing about crypto is that older coins can join new movements with new smart contract overlays.

As these instruments enter the system, the system will become more stable. As noted above, each line that is added to a chart is a line, when done correctly, that can help the chart have a better predictive record. The better prediction, the tighter the margins. The tighter the margins, the more businesses will invest. While the wild west 1, 000% daily booms may start to become rarer, the number of people investing will rise- which means that more people are taking control of their destiny.

More instruments will create new exchanges also. Every time a new way of moving assets around is created, there will be a group that wants to trade in that fashion. Sometimes these markets will be small (the gem market), sometimes these markets will be massive (the grain market). When markets form, speculators will enter the market. This will help the market find a true market value for the asset. Therefore, new markets are needed, because the valuation of an asset is based on how people use it, and when the use is stifled the market is stifled.

All in all, the stability of the derivatives system is vital for the market to evolve into a fully tradable market. Battles on the spot trade market are exciting, but they are just the surface of a vast ocean of trading possibilities that will define the global economy for years to come. Each time we enter a new derivative on the market, we create another leg in the system. Each of these legs makes the market more stable and more able to support the volume of trade we are seeing. If we believe that the crypto market is part of the future, then we need to let this future evolve.

The Ability to Invest in Crypto without Owning Crypto

One of the biggest fears of most novice investors and OG investors alike is that crypto will just be a flash in the pan.[561] These people are ignoring the 10-year history where bitcoin developed from being worth less than a penny to a high of near $70, 000. Misinformation from mainstream news outlets is poisoning many people against the idea of owning crypto. One of the key reasons for this is that the owners and talking heads on these new stations are heavily leveraged in the current stock market. These "voices of a broken system" are convinced that the rise of the metaverse will destroy the dystopia that they have created and are profiting off of. I do not think that we are in any danger of new wealth destroying the corruption that the world has taken thousands of years to build (though hopefully we can chip away at it).

Derivatives help these fearful investors get in on the crypto market without getting in on the crypto market. Since derivatives are traditional securities, all of the market derivatives can be traded on classic markets. This way a person can buy a crypto future and then if it rises, sell the crypto future and take their profit. This means that they never will have to execute the future and actually end up owning any of the "scary" cryptos. For many, this distinction without a difference is enough to allow them to enter the market.

Ironically, this shell game that OG investors are using to "own crypto without owning it" is helping people learn about the market. People that are afraid of crypto will be watching their charts. They will be able to see that crypto is a real asset and as a real asset is worth trading. This can introduce new members to the community. Just like an atheist who comes to the faith can be a zealot, so too can OG investors who realize that crypto is a strong part of a portfolio can bring others to the community.

The more diverse the field of investors, the better off the market will be.

---

[561]Sam Shead (2021). "Bitcoin 'may not last that much longer' academic warns." CNBC at https://www.cnbc.com/2021/12/17/bitcoin-may-not-last-that-much-longer-academic-warns.html.

Everyone has something that they are good at. Programs, who built the crypto system, were good at the coding that helped crypto rise in efficiency above the banks. Early speculators were willing to take the risks to reap the rewards, and the rewards were far greater than many of them every imagined. Now that business professionals are getting involved with the crypto markets, they are allowing their understanding of security instruments to pioneer a new path into the future.

The final element that diversity brings to the market is new lobbying groups. If we are going to have a viable market, then there needs to be a committed group of individuals who are willing to fight for the rights of the community professionally. These are the people who work with governments and courts to ensure that the rights of the community are protected. While no one likes lobbyists, they are a necessary evil as the system develops.

Stabilization of the Market through New Predictive Models

If you have a stool with one leg, it is not very stable. When you add a second leg, it makes the stool more stable, but it is still not the best stool. With the addition of third, fourth, and fifth legs, the stool brings more stability to the table (usually literally). After the fifth leg, it makes sense to link the legs of the stool together. Each brace that we add that connects the system makes the stool stronger. While no piece (other than the seat) is more important than another, the more buttressing we do to a system, the stronger the system.

Each coin on the market is a leg in the system. Each line that they put on the charts helps the savvy trader see where the system is going. When we begin adding derivatives, we start to secure lines between the different currencies. This strengthens the relationships between the lines. When all is said and done, the more information we have on the system, the more we can understand how the system works. All in all, the most important element of the stool is the seat, the legs are merely support. When it comes to the market, you are the most important element and it is the information about the market that holes you up.

Before we go on, we need to address that the stability of the market is not something that is an oracle. Even the best charts can fail to be correct from time to time. The goal of having good predictive models is not to predict the future, it is just to give us better odds as we navigate the system. The more information we have, the better we can address the probability. This is why AI traders are starting to catch up with human traders in their success, they can simply crunch the numbers better than we can. However, when the market breaks from the patterns, the AI traders are the first to go into a tailspin.

The added level of protection that we are seeing in the crypto market is the idea of Stablecoin. Stablecoin 1.0 gave some surety to the market that was needed to help the market grow. While accounting for a small share of the market, this laboratory of an idea was enough to help people see that the future was in reserve wealth for the system, but not the 1 for 1 trade-off that the Stablecoin 1.0 model brought in. When the Stablecoin 1.1 entered the market moving away from fiat currency, it showed that fiat did have a limited place, but varied markets were more effective. With the advent of Stablecoin 2.0 in early 2022, the system stability can be supported by variable markets being traded outside the system to give a proxy for the system indicative value. This lets investors value the currency more accurately and allows the system to keep growing in wealth.

Dead Derivatives and Money Development

When watching government hearings, one of the most disheartening things to hear are elected officials complaining that some people lost money. While it is understandable that a group of people who often make more money (unless it is a politician taking a pay cut), they may be unable to grasp the idea of risk.[562] When people enter a market, they take a risk. This is why some people make money and some people do not make money.

When it comes to the addition of derivatives to the market, some people will make money and some people will lose money. This is the reality of the

[562] Other than Donald Trump who did not take a salary.

system. However, one area that does help the system regardless is that when a warrant or option is not claimed, there is still money that went into the system. Now when someone already in the system makes the investment, it is just money moving around. When someone who is outside of the system enters into the system, then new money is entered and the system becomes bigger.

This allows for growth in the ecosystem, even when the system is in a bear phase. People interjecting money to buy options, warrants, and even forwards can push money into the system even when it is down. While this only accounts for a few percentage points in the entire ecosystem, in a trillion-dollar ecosystem that is a lot of money! This is another reason why it is so important that other instruments be entered into the system.

This is another area where Stablecoin 2.0 helps the system. Stablecoin 2.0 offers options on funds that are in the ecosystem to bring monies into the system. As long as the option is greater than the purchase price of the good, the holding fund makes money. Stablecoin 2.0 only needs a 1-3% growth rate to be successful, so once those numbers are reached the system is growing. This means that the system can make an option that sets for the growth (in whatever time frame) and know that if the option is claimed it will continue to grow. If the option is not claimed, then the system still has the asset in reserve. It is a win-win for the system. (The system can also buy put options in given circumstances).

Savvy Investors in a savvy market

Everybody hates the NFL's celebration rules. It is more fun to watch a bunch of grown men who make a living playing a game dance poorly, than it is for anyone to act like it is serious business. The only people whose lives change for the better due to a game, are the players, the owners, and the bookies who run the numbers on the game. Everyone else spends money on cable to watch the game, buys jerseys of famous players, and may even lose a fortune to a bad bet. The game is much more fun when players at least look like they are having fun.

One good thing about the idiotic rule against celebration is, it deals with teaching people how to act around success. There is an old saying, "When you get to the endzone, act like you have been there before, even if you have not." There is a level of class that is needed in any system. Savvy players have class and you can tell that they are going to do well in the system. Trashy players overreact and cry like babies when something goes against them. It is the same with the market. If something goes your way, then act like that was the plan (but have fun with it). If things go south, you knew the risks- only gamble with what you can afford to lose.

The more complex the investment portfolio of a trader, the more they are able to keep stable in the market. The trader that makes 10% every year will make more over the course of a lifetime than a person who makes 100% all at once and squanders it. This is why derivatives and spot trades can be the best way to keep steady on a difficult market. The more knowledge that you have about the market, the more you will be able to manage these instruments.

Whereas a mob is always as dumb as its dumbest person, a community is as strong as its system. The crypto community needs to help others understand how derivatives work. If you like them, then trade them. If you do not like them, then let others trade them. There is no reason for the government to get involved with the system and bring everyone else to their (mob) level.

Conclusion Part III, Section II

Derivatives are a complex market for people to enter into, that is a fact. However, when we enter onto these types of markets, we can make the system better. Derivative, while quite lucrative, are the tortoise in the race of the tortoise and the hare fable. It is often hard to be an options trader or a futures trader because you are watching day traders make millions on savvy traders. However, it can be a relief when you see them lose that much money in the same amount of time while your returns are steadily growing.

Options, warrants, futures, forwards, and swaps are all great tools to empower your portfolio. Learn about them, choose the ones that you like, and then enter them into your portfolio. If you do not like a derivative, or do not understand it, do not trade in it. It is that simple. The more you know the more you can trade, but be wary, only trade what you know how to trade.

As we allow derivatives into the crypto market, they are not some scams to take money away from spot traders. They are simply another means of investing in the underlying asset. Derivatives are a rock that helps break the tides of the market when they are going the wrong way, and a quiet pool in the middle of a storm during a rally. They are more reserved tool for a more patient generation, the generation that is willing to make generational wealth in the metaverse.

Part III: Section III

Growth of the Metaverse

Introduction to Part III, Section III: Growth of the Metaverse

One of the most exciting new developments in the world of crypto is the metaverse. Stepping beyond the idea that digital rights are just currency and value, the Metaverse creates an entire system of property around the digital frontier and NFTs. Someone asked the question of why NFTs needed to be just artwork and documents.[563] Someone answered that they do not. This spawned the metaverse, a unification of VR, AR, and digital reality into a new frontier that people can explore from their devices on the internet of things.[564]

Within the metaverse, there are some questions that need to be answered. First and foremost is whether "real property" in the metaverse falls under traditional property law or copyright law.[565] Most people who are on the digital frontier believe that these pieces of digital property should be treated as property under the law, which means that property arrangements can be made around the asset. Governments want to use an archaic system of copyright and contract law to build a claim to sovereignty over the digital space. Unfortunately, the truth will always come out that the people own the digital space and a new social contract is being written day by day. The nation-state should not control the people, the people should control the nation-state.

Chapter 46 starts off this section by looking at what the metaverse is. Understanding the concept of the metaverse and why it is so important to the future is key to helping the system move towards the future. This means that we need to look at the reasons that people are interested in the metaverse. The interest directly leads to the question of why does the metaverse work, it works because the people are interested in it. The next

---

[563] Jordan, Harrison (2021). "No NFTs are not copyrights." Tech Crunch at https://techcrunch.com/2021/06/16/no-nfts-arent-copyrights/.

[564] Ng, Cindy (2021). "NFTs Permissions v. Share: Everything You Need to Know" Varonis at https://www.varonis.com/blog/ntfs-permissions-vs-share/.

[565] Natalia Karayaneve(2021). "NFTs work for digital art. They also work perfectly for real estate." *Forbes* at https://www.forbes.com/sites/nataliakarayaneva/2021/04/08/nfts-work-for-digital-art-they-also-work-perfectly-for-real-estate/?sh=2f5056b943f3.

big question many people have is who can participate in the metaverse. Quite simply, you are likely already participating in the system. The internet of things is directly tied to the metaverse and each device is a portal to a whole new world. This is the value of the metaverse, a new world people can explore and find new resources, skills, and centers for learning so that humanity can move forward.

Chapter 47 takes a look at the more "hard" concepts of the metaverse. How is trade protected in a space without government? Who is responsible to protect these property rights? Since we know that the government has failed at this 2000-year experiment of protecting the rights of the masses, we must now look at new methods to ensure that rights are protected. To do this we must answer what type of law will govern the metaverse. Some argue that it should be copyright and contract law. Most of these advocates are from the art industry or the government, the first because it is what they know and the second because of what they can tax. Digital realists are starting to realize that cyberspace is a new frontier and the digital frontier is not "ruled" by anyone. Shared governance and property rights under the concept of property law are vital to ensure that the system develops.

Chapter 48 looks at the existence of NFTs. If molecules are the stuff that makes up the real world, then NFTs are the stuff that makes up the metaverse. Each bit of digital land, each building, each concept in the multiverse that is the metaverse is a property that someone can own. How it will be owned really depends on how we treat NFTs in their infancy. While some are going to make the argument that the digital world belongs to everyone- those are usually the people who got in on the market late and want to feast off the labor of others.

Chapter 49 rounds out the section looking at how wealth can be created out of "nothing." The term that NFTs, the Metaverse, and crypto are nothing comes from government and central bank arguments that they have nothing backing them- all the while they are "peddling paper currency that is worth less than the paper that it is printed on."[566] The system is not creating value from nothing, it is creating value from the labor of the people who are building the system. Just like Napoleon thought the central US was worth very little, till industries American farmers made it the most valuable breadbasket in the world- industrious programmers are now building a better world in the digital space.

The Metaverse is the future, at least for a while. Those of us dealing in the crypto space need to know a little about it to ensure that we can work with its movement. The more we know about the system, the better we can make the system. Just like science, sociology, business, and law evolve, the cryptoverse will grow and continue to grow as we learn more about the system.

[566] According to the federal reserve it costs approximately between $0.062 and $0.112 to print notes (between $1 and $20) all that is backing those notes is the credit of the country, which is $29,377, 081500, 000. *See* Fed Reserve at https://www.federalreserve.gov/faqs/currency_12771.htm. *See Also* Usdebtclock.org.

Chapter 46: What is the Metaverse

The line between cyberspace and reality has always been a line that people tried to blur. The reality, that is the world that we physically live in, has a plethora of limitations that restrict our development as a species. These limitations have been challenges to creative minds throughout the ages. What if I could fly? What if space travel was as common as air travel? What if I had gills? These questions have sparked fantasy that made its way into fiction, but the real innovators overcame these puzzles. The Wright Brothers built the first plane.[567] Musk is planning on sending thousands of ships to Mars in the next thirty years.[568] Jacques Cousteau and Emile Gagnan invited the modern SCUBA regulator that allows people to "breath" underwater.[569] Innovation is inspired by imagination.

The innovation of the metaverse is no different, it is both the result of innovation and a catalyst of new ideas. The metaverse is the response to the question, "What if there was a world where anything is possible?" Creative minds from around the internet joined forces to create a system that was functional and viable for innovation and the exchange of ideas. An added result of the system was the inspiration of a world without bounds. Since the boundaries of the imagination are the elements that we can use as building blocks, the metaverse gives us a world with any block we can imagine. The ziggurat of creativity is now self-sustaining, any block we ever need is at our hands, so the bounds of imagination are now limitless.

This Chapter begins by looking at the key question on many people's minds, "What is the metaverse?" Explaining the system and how it works becomes

---

567 Smithsonian (2020). "The Wright Brothers Invent Airplane." Smithsonian at https://airandspace.si.edu/exhibitions/wright-brothers/online/fly/.

568 McFall-Johnsen, Morgan & Mosher, Dave (2020). Elon Musk says he plans to send 1 million people to Mars by 2050 by launching 3 Starship rockets every day and creating 'a lot of jobs' on the red planet." Business Insider at https://www.businessinsider.com/elon-musk-plans-1-million-people-to-mars-by-2050-2020-1

569 National Inventors Hall of Fame (2019). "**Jacques Cousteau** and Emile Gagnan." NIHF at https://www.invent.org/inductees/jacques-yves-cousteau.

vital for understanding the system itself. The next question, "Why are people interested in the Metaverse..." challenges some of our preconceptions of what people want- shoving freedom to the front and center of the debate once again.

What is the Metaverse?

Metaverse has been the hot topic of 2021 and has seen traditional and crypto-centric companies pivot to extract its success and hysteria.[570] We have seen one of the largest Web2 and social media companies in Facebook pivot their brand to Meta, as a sign of belief in the upcoming digitalized world.

The word metaverse has been a hot topic in the cryptocurrency and Web3 world, but actually, metaverse does not necessarily mean anything cryptocurrency.[571] The Metaverse in its actuality is not a particular type of technology, but rather it is reshaping how we interact with different types of technology.

As the shift from the real to the digital world happens, we are starting to see the early rise of virtual, augmented, and digital reality. With complex 3D emulated worlds, gamified mechanics, unlimited resources, and many components in a digital world, they are quickly becoming attractive for an average user to interact with. Whether this is harmful or not depends on your personal view on realism and human psychology, but there is no doubt that the shift to the digital world is and will continue happening.

The metaverse has already existed for many decades, think Tetris, Pacman, Google lens, Oculus, Zoom, Fortnite, Axie Infinity, Sandbox, and many more. These technologies and experiences form as a part of the growing

---

[570] Rane, Hitesh (2021). "Metaverse- The hot topic on the internet explained." The United Business Journal at https://theubj.com/tech/26224/metaverse-the-hot-topic-on-internet-explained/.

[571] CNBC (2021). "What is Web 3.0 and why is it significant." CNBC at https://www.cnbctv18.com/technology/what-is-web-30-and-why-is-it-significant-11826862.htm.

metaverse.

So, what is new? If the metaverse has already existed for many years and decades, why the hype? Good question and this is where the Web3 and cryptocurrency world comes in. In traditional games and experiences, the user was traditionally disconnected from the digital world and had a lack of stake. This was problematic, as your digital identity would never reflect your real identity. Thanks to NFTs and Web3, the digital economy has been unlocked in the metaverse. Meaning in the most simplistic sense, users can create, buy and sell goods. We'll dive into that later.

The metaverse is an ideology, it is a concept, it is a change in the human psyche, it is digitized social connections, it is a dystopian world and its immersive experiences. It is many things, but most importantly it is here. The trifecta of utility concludes with "Why does it work?," which looks at how the pieces of this digital world work together to move humanity to the next level.

This Chapter continues by looking at who can join the metaverse. Where the modern world is exclusionary (you are judged by who you are and what you can do) the metaverse is something else. In the metaverse, you are judged by what you may be able to do. This blurs the lines of reality and potential, which gives everyone a shot to be more than they can be in the real world. This leads to why the system will continue to have value, it is in expanding the human condition that we survive as a species- the metaverse is the greatest expansion (potential) the world has ever seen.

Is the Metaverse a utopia? Is the metaverse a dystopian hellscape of meme lords and popup ads? The answer to both questions is yes, the answer to both questions is no. The answer to both questions is maybe. We control what the metaverse is going to become. If we let governments interfere with its development, then we will be ushering in a new age of "woke" 1984, simply a cool graphic overlay on top of the present world. If we work together for a better world, then we have the ability to modernize the system and make the metaverse into what can be a utopia in cyberspace that helps us build a better real world.

Why are people interested?

As humans, we are an immensely curious species that have always enjoyed gamified experiences.[572] Perhaps you played Roblox, Fortnite, and Minecraft where you built your own worlds. Perhaps you used Facebook, Twitter, and Instagram to build a digital identity of yourself and connect with others all over the world. Perhaps you trekked around the GTA universe, building your character, buying your favorite car, and completing impossible missions. As humans, we often tend to want to escape our reality, which can seem quite dull and boring as compared to these digitized experiences.

As we spend more and more time online, we are becoming more desensitized to real-world connections and experiences. And why bother, right? When you can participate in digital worlds where there are no limitations, outside of the space-time continuum. You can be anyone you want to be, you can buy anything, you can connect with anybody, the opportunities are well and truly endless.

So perhaps the peaked interest in the metaverse has a dark undertone, with a dystopian virtual world, the population is seeking refuge from our real fallen world; troubled in war, evil, and violence. The metaverse is the real escape, it is the great escape.

Not only that, but it is imperative to note here that the rise of this meta-universe is made possible through breakthroughs in technology. The gap between the real and digital world is being bridged faster than ever. We have virtual headsets, we have immersive virtual reality, we have a digital economy. We are now able to explore all our 5 senses in the digital world (yes – it is happening) in a way that's never been done before. Companies like Meta (previously Facebook) are a testament that the future lies in these digital experiences. If one of the largest companies in the world is pivoting to extrapolate on the early success of the metaverse, then you

---

[572] Currin, Grant (2020). "Why are Humans so curious?" Life Sciences at https://www.livescience.com/why-are-humans-curious.html.

not only watch and pay attention. You participate.

Why does it work?

The world built on the internet quickly became a reality starting in the 21st century. But there were immediate limitations. For one, the digital world was disconnected from our physical world. We were there but we could not interact as freely. There were no cross-platform communications. You could not bring your GTA outfit/credits to your Minecraft World. You could not showcase and verify your Roblox character on your Twitter profile.

The world built on blockchain realizes this. With the rise of NFTs, users can create, sell and trade any collectible they want. The best thing about it all? It is completely interoperable, meaning those goods and items can be passed on any chain/world/platform that supports that particular chain. The metaverse now works because users are incentivized to participate, they are rewarded for their contribution, they are rewarded for their time, and perhaps for the first time; they are rewarded for their existence.

The digital fungibility of the blockchain makes it an excellent store of collectibles. Everything is verified, secure, and stored on the blockchain. Whether it is your digital land in Decentral and, the open world of Nifty Island, your animation you bought on OpenSea, your digital Gucci bag on Roblox, or your passport. The most important thing is, it is yours and it belongs to you. This ownership, reward mechanisms, social interactions, digital experiences, immersive realities, investable assets, and many more factors are why the metaverse is quickly becoming the 'hottest' topic currently.

Who can participate?

Everyone. The real world is discriminatory based on your geolocation, race, gender, religion, age, background, you name it. We are at all times limited in our experiences due to these numerous factors that govern us. Be in over-regulated constitutions, constrictive laws, and many times - just location. The metaverse built on decentralized and open applications aims to mitigate all of that.

The metaverse allows you and your friends to 'travel' place to place and experience different environments all while staying connected socially. Anyone, anywhere in the world can participate in a blockchain environment, own digital real estate, trade collectibles, communicate securely with each other, and even travel platforms from the platform while retaining your inventory. This is truly what makes the metaverse so exciting, the ability for anyone, anywhere in the world with an internet connection to participate in a growing digital world and economy.

The boundless nature of the Metaverse means there are no barriers, physical or otherwise. There are no limits to who can participate at the same time, the type of activities that can take place, and forms of discrimination. True accessibility can be achieved in some of these digital platforms, more so than those traditionally in the Web2 space.

Why it will continue to have value?

Gaming and entertainment are currently at the forefront of the metaverse, but this will soon change. The Metaverse could well and truly enable human and social connections, easier and cheaper than in the tangible world. But for now, the biggest beneficiaries of this new form of technology are those offering gaming and entertaining infrastructure.

Take Roblox and Axie Infinity, for example, both metaverse universes that are thriving due to their thriving marketplaces, some based on NFTs where users can buy, sell, or exchange items in return for tokens/cryptocurrencies.

The economies of the metaverse will behave differently to those of the traditional cryptocurrency market, as these tokens represent ownership and experiences as opposed to the store of value and investments. It comes as no surprise that NFT and Metaverse projects have seen a huge increase in valuations and token prices due to mainstream interest. This interest will continue to ensue as more traditional players enter the market and more experiences are created.

Blockchain-based currencies will allow all the assets inside the metaverse to be easily and securely created, exchanged, shared, and tracked, and also allow items to be seamlessly moved by its users across worlds or platforms. This interconnected nature of the metaverse will perhaps build some of the most complex and large spiderweb bridges of all time and will truly reshape how we view Web3 communities and social interactions.

The Metaverse is only just beginning and billions of people are set to enter and interact with it. While the majority still is left to the unknown, it is clear that metaverse, or whatever it will be named or called in the future, will be the topic for the coming decades. Are you ready, Player 1?

Chapter 47: Concept of Trade within the Metaverse

> Metaverse is the creation of permanent online environments. And that ship sailed a long, long time ago when the first online forums were created. These 'semi-permanent' environments evolved into living things. Rules and moderatos had to be implemented, and people got used, pretty fast, to exchange things – primarily ideas – via online recurrent interactions.[573]

And

"The consolidation of a global unified market, the automatization of supply chains, and the empowerment of a global culture."[574]

This last bit will be, perhaps, one of the trickiest ones: a global culture means that your products will need to appeal to people both in China and Germany at the same time. And although you will have things that will be "global" in this scenario, your marketing strategies will need to be finetuned to become efficient in all markets, regardless of the local culture. Because you will be competing against other traders, suppliers, and businesses from all over the world, that now, will be able to sell in any market on the planet.

The dreams of a world are only limited by the imaginations of those who live in it. Those that chose to may accept the world as it is, and do nothing to change the world for the better. Those who envision themselves as creators have the ability to change the world, solve problems and make the world a better place.[575] The metaverse is a world without form, which creators can now move through and build in the image of a perfect world

---

[573] Calvino, Frank (2021). "Will the Metaverse change Global Trade?" Cross Border Magazine at https://cross-border-magazine.com/metaverse-change-global-trade/#:~:text=To%20summarize%2C%20the%20metaverse%20will%20impact%20global%20trade,Faster%20speeds%20of%20delivery%20for%20goods%20and%20wares..

[574] *Id.*

[575] *Id.*

(in their minds). The bounds of the metaverse are only the amount of skill that you are willing to acquire and the imagination, hopes, and dreams that you will bring with you into the space.

Separation from Government Sovereignty

"Governments should take the future opportunity represented by the metaverse seriously. The metaverse will present entirely new ways, for example, to create employment, impart education, deliver healthcare, and plan urban spaces. It will be the next major labor organizing platform."[576] These are some of the key areas where the government should not have involvement. When the government gets involved in these areas, the interests of the politicians and their cronies pass up the interests of the people working in the space.

Unemployment is an interesting issue in the world with the metaverse. As new forms of human-AI interface become available, the ability for everyone to work and have self-determination. the days of differently-abled persons not being able to have self-determination and contribute a career to society will be over. The metaverse will allow people who previously could not support themselves to provide a valuable service to the community, even if only working for a few hours a day.

Education services will be enhanced as top-level educators can work with more students, allowing less qualified educators to act as teaching assistants to help students with problems. In a world where college students can have their classes taught by the top educators in the world, digitally, there is the need to have thousands of colleges around the world with major climate impacts and wasted tax dollars. Students can work online with their peers around the world (getting them ready for the digital environment) and have call centers of educators (working from home) who can answer questions when students do not understand. This would allow education to integrate around the world and have 24/7 access to professionals for students.

---

[576] Sudan, Supra.

Organization, both labor and politics is a very important human right. While unions are not a necessity in the metaverse, the ability for employees to speak to one another in an environment without the government or the owners of companies watching is essential. The metaverse provides this space, and if this space is "busted" then the participants can move to another place, then another till it becomes disadvantageous for the government or the management to chase them around.

These are just some of the areas that will be revolutionized by businesses entering into the metaverse. The service industry elements that do not need a person physically in the room with a person can convert to 24/7 virtually overnight in the virtual space. Employers can become truly global companies and the employees will not even need to leave their homes. The added bonus of integration is that this will help the dream of a 30-hour workweek become reality.

The Argument for Metaverse to be Under copyright/contract law

"The metaverse is a shared virtual 3D world, or worlds, that are interactive, immersive, and collaborative. Just as the physical universe is a collection of worlds that are connected in space, the metaverse can be thought of as a bunch of worlds, too."[577]

The argument for metaverse to be under property law

> The very nature of real estate makes it ideal for blockchain applications - it is immovable and easily findable by third parties with blockchain-based claims on it as collateral or otherwise. I previously covered the topic of why in many ways real estate already behaves as a digital asset.[578] Depending on the kind of real estate property (land, housing, commercial properties), there may be a need for a management company that will take care of maintenance, payments, and collection of rents. Still, the notion of

[577] https://blogs.nvidia.com/blog/2021/08/10/what-is-the-metaverse/

[578] Karayaneva, Natalia (2021). "Real Estate is becoming a digital asset: 5 Trends for the coming decade and the Coronavirus effect." *Forbes* at https://www.forbes.com/sites/nataliakarayaneva/2020/03/05/real-estate-digital-asset-trends-coronavirus/?sh=5025b4e35f63.

> "custody" as it applies to real property in the US is closer to an abstract function involving legal and accounting operations than the physical handling and warehousing required by movable personal property or commodities.[579]

Looking to what is best for the people of the world

People are moving differently now. People want more freedom in work. More creativity. More efficiency. Tech offering more leisure time in order to do this has been discussed for a long time, even in unlikely places like Valerie Solanas's S.C.U.M. Manifesto satire from the 1960s where she states,

> A completely automated society can be accomplished very simply and quickly once there is a public demand for it. The blueprints for it are already in existence, and its construction will only take a few weeks with millions of people working at it. Even though off the money system, everyone will be most happy to pitch in and get the automated society built; it will mark the beginning of a fantastic new era, and there will be a celebration atmosphere accompanying the construction.

While this 1970s quotation discusses a moneyless society and this book envisions a fiat, digital society, it is something to indeed ponder. Along with the author's vision of a quick turnaround, and the current level of interest cryptocurrency is generating, the manifesto might not entirely be satire after all. People have anticipated the times we are currently undergoing for a long while, and in schools of thought that many would never even considered.[580]

Similarly, many also dream of living as a "digital nomad" or a person who can work from anywhere in the world. Blockchain resolves this well. What with near secure payments online, you can get them anytime, anywhere.

---

[579] *Id.*

[580] Solanas, Valerie, *SCUM Manifesto* (Valerie Solanas, 1967), pp. 16–17 (self-published) (Northwestern Univ. copy) (hyphen surrounded by spaces after "SCUM" so in original).

Yet, do not get too comfortable, foregoing important work information needed just because your coins can be comfortably tracked or accessible through blockchain.

In fact, in the book, *Anywhere*, digital nomads are asked to consider that,

> You'll need to do your due diligence to reduce any liabilities. This includes having copies of written company consent regarding your plans to work remotely from several locations. Equally important is maintaining backups of your work efforts, software, systems (like computer drives), and more to cover yourself in the event of unforeseen circumstances.[581]

Thus, there is room to work and navigate freely through the use of crypto.

A better world means a new type of governance, the more shared that governance is the better

Governments also have a vested interest in the success of fiat money and allowing it to keep its hold on the financial world. As they issue the money, they hold the power to influence and control it - not to mention the ability to make more whenever they want. Look at the British Government, for example, they have made £435 billion through their quantitative easing program, to put that in perspective the market cap for all cryptocurrencies is currently £340 billion!

Governments cannot generally control cryptocurrencies; they can cause dips as we have seen this week with South Korea and China FUD, but this will just be a temporary blip as has been proven in the past. Cryptocurrencies also afford their users greater privacy and anonymity; some, such as DeepOnion, allow users to remain completely anonymous should they so wish. Governments do not like this; firstly they cannot tax what they cannot see, and secondly, they cannot control what they cannot stop. Should a government be unhappy about a citizen's actions they can

---

[581] Alli, Remi, et al. (2017), "Anywhere," June 20th 2017 by AND CO https://workspace.fiverr.com/blog/tax-and-legal-watch-outs-for-digital-nomads/

simply freeze their assets, they cannot do this with cryptocurrency.

Thus, the main reasons banks and governments may be hesitant with cryptocurrency is due to not having full control and possibly even the aspect of cryptocurrency being more efficient, secure, and private than traditional currency. Governments and banks appear to show how far the people have come and how big a threat the average person could become with these resources, allowing more protection of their assets. Yet, governments and banks may begin to understand that they have no option other than to accept cryptocurrency as part of the financial world, which could divide the banks and governments.[582] After all, money is not technically real; we just give our trust to it, which it seems more and more are willing to do for cryptocurrency. That is the power of cryptocurrency.

---

[582] Off the Cuff (2018). "What do banks and governments have to fear from cryptocurrency." Off the cuff at https://medium.com/@offthecuff/what-do-banks-and-governments-have-to-fear-from-cryptocurrency-82bb90b37c1d.

Chapter 48: NFTs

One of the topics that we have avoided in this book is the topic of NFTs, not because they are unimportant, but because NFTs are not currently being targeted for regulation in the same way as other traditional cryptos. NFTs are a major market right now, a market that only looks to get bigger as the metaverse expands. Whereas the major challenge to cryptos is coming from the legislatures of countries around the world, the major challenge to NFTs is coming from the courts.[583] As a result, we see another form of attack, from a separate set of dragons, which will affect this area in the near future. This is not a battle that we fight right now, this is a battle that we prepare for in the coming months.

NFTs have a utility that is completely different from the utility of crypto coins and tokens. Forged in the same way as other types of cryptos, the scarcity of NFTs (since they are nearly always a limited run of one) becomes an interesting dynamic that differs from other cryptos. It is in this dynamic that the NFT market changes direction and challenges other conventions of crypto-economics. As the field evolves, we learn more about the functionality of NFTs, which will illuminate some of the dynamics of the crypto world.

This Chapter begins with a discussion of what makes up an NFT. As you see, there are many similarities between an NFT and a crypto coin or token (more in common with tokens as the NFTs are a type of token). The key difference in this system is the difference between an NFT and a traditional fungible token. The unique nature of the NFT increases both the complexity of the system and the utility of the entity. This is the core of the NFT craze.

Beyond the "what" of the NFT craze is the "how." While they are an interesting footnote in this book, an NFT has no use to the world if it does not have utility. The first industry to make major inroads into the NFT field

---

[583] Staff (2021). "Art Collector's court case signals potential legal and contractual issues with NFTs." Pinsent Masons (Out-Law) at https://www.pinsentmasons.com/out-law/analysis/court-case-potential-legal-contractual-issues-nfts.

is the art industry. Art has been the top volume NFT area since the craze began. The second field which quickly followed the artists was the business community. This is where the landscape of NFTs began to become more systematic, which in turn led to more structured trades in this field. Other fields are starting to look at the utility of NFTs on the blockchain because of their immutable nature (in most cases). Law and politics are looking at how NFTs can be used to make both systems more stable and transparent to give more access to justice and voice to the people of the world.

NFTs present two core concepts. Data has value. Secure data has value. When we accept the first, we must accept the latter. As the cryptoverse expands, the secured transaction of data will become one of the largest commodities in the world. Currently, social media platforms broker in your unsecure data, giving people the rights over this data through the blockchain (not government-controlled Web 3.0) enables new levels of privacy around the world.

What is an NFT?

That which we do not understand is often the stuff of nightmares.[584] Fear is a component of the unknown, people are rarely afraid of what they know is coming (though they can be anxious), rather the fear of the unknown dominates our psyche.[585] When this translates from personal understanding to mob understanding, this can be devastating so something new is on the market. Whereas one person can make an intelligent and logical analysis of something, the mob is only as good as its dumbest person. In many cases, the dumbest people are the ones we elect to political office and watch in entertainment- therefore the panic monkeys have an undue ability to control the system.[586]

---

584 Breus, Michael (2014). "The Stuff of Disturbing Dreams." Psychology Today at https://www.psychologytoday.com/us/blog/sleep-newzzz/201402/the-stuff-disturbing-dreams.

585 *Id.*

586 *See Loosely* Staff (2020). Dumb as a Box of Hammers: Celebrities with Low IQs." Daily Care https://www.dailycare.com.au/good-living/life/dumb-as-a-box-of-hammers-celebrities-with-low-iqs. *See Also* Staff (2021). "The 10 dumbest

NFTs present a system that scares both celebrities and politicians. Some celebrities are nervous because of the new way that NFTs are handling art, that intellectual property may become a different system, and that royalties may be linked to the holder of the NFT rights, rather than contractual rights of a production. This could cause major production houses to limit exposure, paying celebrities (or athletes) for their time and removing residuals from the contracting process. Politicians either fear NFTs because they do not understand them (mostly), or because they do understand them and realize that information that is permanently on the blockchain cannot be suppressed easily in the modern era.

So, what is an NFT? An NFT is a "cryptographic asset on a blockchain with unique identification codes and metadata that distinguish them from each other."[587] Simply put, NFTs are single-issue tokens that cannot be traded as if they were all the same. Just like non-fungible goods in the real world are not "bulk" goods, NFTs are the single items of the cryptoverse. Regular tokens are fungible. Their code shows what they are, but does not care what each one is. NFTs are each unique, thus have a value all of their own.

The problem with NFTs is that there are many false definitions out there by sources often deemed to be reliable. *Forbes*, for instance, says NFTs are "a digital asset that represents real-world objects like art, music, in-game items, and videos."[588] This would be akin to saying that "all cars are Ford Mustangs." NFTs are digital assets, what they represent depends on the ideas of the creator. They do not have to have "real world" linked objects. The asset can be purely digital. It can also be a digital asset that resembles

---

Celebrities in Hollywood." SiFy.com at https://www.sify.com/movies/the-10-dumbest-celebrities-in-hollywood-imagegallery-movies-jdwmO5gabejsi.html. Please note that this is not agreeing that the articles representation of IQs are correct or even acknowledging the misconception that IQs in adults have any relevance.

587 Sharma, Rakesh (2021). Non-Fungible Token Definition. Investopedia at https://www.investopedia.com/non-fungible-tokens-nft-5115211.

588 Conti, Robyn &Schmidt, Joe (2021). "What you need to know about Non-Fungible Tokens (NFTs)." *Forbes* at https://www.forbes.com/advisor/investing/nft-non-fungible-token/.

but does not represent a real-world asset. A person can own the "White House" in a virtual space, such as Upland, but that does not mean that they own the real-world asset.

The interrelationship between the "Real" and the "Digital" is one of the aspects of the NFT market that so few people understand. While it is fairly concrete that the holder of the NFT owns a purely digital asset (like the virtual yacht) holds all rights to the object (including reproduction rights if they so choose), the question remains of who owns the virtual rights to the hybrid properties, which have aspects in both the real and the digital world. This is a question that is currently before the court and could present interesting conundrums to celebrities who release NFTs of songs whose copyrights are held by other people.

Difference between a Fungible Token and an NFT

With many people in the crypto space not understanding the difference between a token and a coin, adding the element of understanding the difference between an NFT and a token can make matters doubly hard. To see the difference, the legal concept of fungible and non-fungible needs to be made apparent. Once a person understands the difference between fungible and non-fungible, they can easily translate the difference into the token world. When a person can see this difference, they can understand why the investment styles of the two systems are different.

A fungible item is an item where all items with the same name have the same features. Grain, oil, metals by weight, even loose diamonds all are considered fungible items.[589] In the legal world, a fungible item is considered to be as good as any other item of the same type. One ton of grain is considered to be the same as another ton of grain of the same type. While different collections of fungible goods can be "graded," by and large they are just large collections of goods. This makes shipping and allocation easier. If someone owns a specific amount of a fungible good (at a specific grade), then any fulfillment of that specific amount at that grade fulfills the

[589] Kenton, Will (2021). "Fungible Goods." Investopedia at https://www.investopedia.com/terms/f/fungibles.asp.

order.

Non-fungible goods turn this aspect on their head. A fungible good is a specific item. Whereas Toyota Corollas are a fungible good (when outfitted with the same packages), Bob's Toyota Corolla is a non-fungible good, it has specific aspects (ownership by Bob) that make it different from others within the set. Fungible goods in society are the items that people want because of an identifying factor, not because the item itself has worth (most of the time). For instance, a piece of canvas with paint on it is worth about K3, whereas a piece of canvas with a Rembrandt on it can be priceless.

The differentiation between fungible and non-fungible translates directly into tokens. A fungible token (like SHIB INU) means that when you buy a token, you do not care which token you buy. Each token on the chain is represented, but its attributes are the same across the system. This means that one token is just the same as another token on the system. With an NFT, each token that is created is unique. There is only one of that token to buy, which means that you are buying that specific token.[590]

NFTs in the Art World

The first big player in the NFT world was the art world. Since the digital world is made up of imagery and data, the combination of imagery and data became the backbone of the metaverse. People did not want the digital world to be a text-based MMO, like GMUD, they wanted something that they could see and express themselves. As the digital world developed (mostly through the gaming world), items within the digital world became items with real-world value. Once it became accepted that they had real-world value, the system adapted that these individual items needed to have space. As blockchain became more utilized, more of the items were moved to the blockchain, NFTs were born.

[590] With the art craze, there have been several tokens that have series, these tokens are still unique, but the identifying attribute is the number within the series. These are still NFTs, but are more of a "poor man's" NFT (regardless of cost).

Digital designers create unique items for games, but soon the market realized that these were merely scratching the surface of what could be done with the system. The first recognized NFT was created by Kevin McCoy in 2014, called "Quantum."[591] "Quantum" is a pixilated graphic of a shape that pulses.[592] "This piece of art grew in value till it was sold for $1.4 million at Sotheby's auction house."[593] With this type of value arising out of something as simple as a picture on the blockchain, millions of people cashed in on art" talent" causing a craze where people would buy anything because it is an NFT, similar to the eBay craze which spawned the" Tedder Stick."

The NFT art market is just as legitimate as the real-world art market.[594] Right now we are seeing a boom, but there will inevitably be a correction as people will begin to distinguish between" good" NFTs and" Bad" NFTs. Who will decide which is good and which is bad is anyone's guess; but when it happens, some NFTs will rocket to the moon and some will bring out the bears in the market as the world has never seen?

NFTs In Business

In any space where there are artists willing to sell out, business is never far behind. As the NFT craze exploded, there were companies that quickly moved in to create millions of "Junk" NFTs (items with no artistic value and that were serialized). This allowed some artists to become millionaires while the companies promoting their art brought in billions. Operating off the idea that a slight change in a piece of art (like a lithograph in the real art world) could be sold as something new (which the real art world even avoided), these shysters moved into the market, threatening to dilute the market.

---

[591] Staff (2021). Where do NFTs actually come from? A Short history of Non-Fungible Tokens." Alt Press. Com at https://www.altpress.com/meta/history-of-nfts-non-funfible-tokens/.

[592] *Id.*

[593] *Id.*

[594] Take that as you may but research the CIA And the use of Art.

However, with the snake oil salespeople also came legitimate businesspeople. These businesspeople saw the worth of the NFT in the market. Rather than creating massive collections of Junk NFTs, these people created things that people wanted in the digital space. Want a fancy house? Someone will create that for you. Want a yacht? Someone will create that for you. Want a dog park where you and your creepy furry friends can entertain each other, there is some weird out there that will create that for you. Businesspeople saw that where there is demand, they could make money.

Business still has a lot of room for development in the NFT space. Everything in the metaverse can, theoretically, be an NFT. This means that new industries will crop up once we see what people want in the metaverse. Some of the things will be simple, things that anyone can create. Others will be quite complex, building systems that augment reality (AR). One of the key markets that look to develop is things that cannot exist in the real-world, this could be the biggest NFT market of all (Penrose stairs for instance).

NFTs in Law and Politics

The final area that we look at for NFTs is law and politics. While there is a plethora of other areas that NFTs will move into as the digital space expands, law and politics are the ones that may have the most effect on most people. It is in the law, and the creation of law, that civilization moves forward, when we look at how NFTs can work in this space, we can see how they may work in the future. Once again, this is one of the areas that the crypto community needs to empower through the ballot box.

The use of NFTs in the legal space has amazing potential. Wills, contracts, evidence, and claims are all being assigned a unique digital tag that can be publicly cataloged to ensure that people have access to the truth. This could be the first stage in preventing abominations of justice, like the sealing of the Maxwell case, from taking place, allowing the people in society to see who the criminals behind the criminals are.[595] However, it also allows for the evolution of regular legal cases, allowing each document to be memorialized in an unchangeable blockchain.

With politics, the system is even more useful. The petition, public, laws, and even the news can be locked in the blockchain so that future generations cannot "re-write" history. History should always be political, it should be offensive, and it should be the indicator of why we should do better. By memorializing these documents on the chain, and allowing for verification, the system can be more stable and allow people to see more of what those ruling them are doing- if they but take the time to look at the documents.

Secure Data Has Value in Itself

The key takeaway in this Chapter is that data has value in itself. If data has value, then secure data has value. The security of data for the future of humanity is imperative. How many historical records were lost in the Nazi purge of information? How many histories did Stalin and Mao destroy to make their communist fiction a para-reality? How much of the truth is being destroyed by universities and TV talking heads as we live our lives, the real truth is buried under whitewashed neo-realities that are "too offensive" for regular folks like you and me. Who determines the information that people should have, the social contract does not make us agree to remain ignorant- but we must remain diligent and prevent governments from putting blinders on us?

The more we know as a digital society, the more we can work together.

---

[595] Lampin, Tamar (2021). "Ghislaine Maxwell case details to 'sensational and impure' for public, judge says." New York Post. At https://nypost.com/2021/03/18/judge-says-ghislaine-maxwell-case-details-too-sensational-and-impure-for-public/.
Please not the entire record was not sealed (just the parts the public needed to see), *See Also* Curet, Monique (2021). "Judge in Ghislaine Maxwell Trial did not seal all evidence and proof" Tampa Bay Times (Citing PolitiFact, so take this as you may). At https://www.tampabay.com/news/nation-world/2022/01/04/judge-in-ghislaine-maxwell-trial-did-not-seal-all-evidence-and-proof/

This may negatively affect some people. Criminals, politicians, and other crooks should be held accountable in the digital age. While the government is needed to protect people and their property, it is not needed to tell us what we should and should not know. We each have the right to self-determination, but if we do not have access to information is it really informed self-determination. Allowing information to become NFTs and those NFTs to be publicly available will enable people to see the world around them in a new light. The only question is whether the light is too bright for some people.

Chapter 49: The Business of Creating Wealth Out of Nothing

Once we accept that the metaverse is something that is coming (or is already here), we need to look at how it is being used. Virtual spaces have a long history of being used for social and gaming measures, but the business aspect of the system has always been lagging. Why? Digital universes deal with many of the aspects that traditional businesses have a hard time with, so why do not more people use this space? The answer is customers. Until digital currency is normalized, it is difficult to draw people into this space. With the rapid growth of cryptocurrency, the metaverse is poised to have massive GDP growth.[596]

The first part of looking at this relationship is understanding how digital currency is deeply connected to the metaverse. On the first level, the metaverse is a collection of NFTs interconnected to create a series of worlds. The more that people create, the bigger the metaverse will become. Just like exploring the universe, exploring the metaverse will be one of the defining characteristics of humanity's next exploration. To explore this world, we need to be able to understand all that we are able to do there, and we are just scratching the surface right now.

Next, we need to look at why the new system needs new wealth. As we have noted repeatedly, the fiat system is failing. Some countries have even suggested abandoning this system for digital currency.[597] Why then would we encourage people to use fiat currencies, or cryptos directly linked to fiat currency, in the metaverse? That is just moving a broken system into a new, undefiled field. As members of the crypto community, we must work to ensure that working Stablecoin 2.0 currencies are the primary vehicle for economic growth in the metaverse. Stability will breed security.

The third issue that we must take up is how to make the metaverse more "business-friendly." The key element of that is getting customers to come

---

596 Digital Gross Production, the metaverse equivalent to GDP.

597 Hernandez, Ben (2021). "El Salvador's President Says it's 'Game Over' for Fiat Currency." Crypto Channel at https://www.etftrends.com/crypto-channel/el-salvador-president-says-its-game-over-for-fiat-currency/.

to the metaverse. When Las Vegas was founded, it was an oasis in the desert. It took years for the city to find its own entertainment hub that consistently brings people there for business. Similarly, entertainment and services will cause businesses to flock to the metaverse; however, we need to get customers using those services.

Metaverse valuation is one of the hottest topics on the market today. Unfortunately, most of the people valuing the metaverse are also people who are selling pieces of the metaverse. This is like a cryptocurrency being the only source of its present valuation (after the ICO). The community needs to look at different types of valuation (use-value, expansion value, meeting place value, etc.) to ensure that the system can be properly valued and that investors can see that the metaverse is one of the Waves of the future.

Finally, we need to look at where we have been to see where we are going. The metaverse is the future, but if we do not learn from our past, we will make the same mistakes that we have made throughout history. Is the social contract the same in the metaverse, or do new generations need to look at new reasons to work together? What elements of the old system worked and how can we use them in the new space? What elements of the old system did not work; how can we avoid them in the new space? By looking at our past, we have the ability to do better; now we have the choice before us, will we do better?

Digital Currency and the Metaverse

One thing that most people realize in the digital space is that a new system needs a new currency. This has been a truism in gaming for years, but now that business is moving into the space, they are falling into the same traps that gamers faced 20 years ago. Why? Because everyone thinks that they are smarter than the system. The system is not smart or dumb, it is a series of interactions that form patterns. When someone thinks that they can beat the system, they have to be able to not only beat the patterns, but beat all the people in the system who are relying on those patterns. While the mob is dumb and lets this happen, the community can be more prepared and preserve its ability to function.

There are also those who want to build a new world but are willing to allow the mistakes of the past to guide them, in a nefarious way. This new generation of robber barons knows the mistakes that people make when exploring frontiers, they have read the history books. These false prophets and snake oil salesmen are waiting in the digital space to make a quick buck and turn potential customers for the metaverse into doubters. The community needs to watch for these charlatans and do whatever the equivalent is of a virtual "tar and feathering".

Some elements of the present system, like racism, wokeness, systematic inequality, and government corruption are elements that everyone agrees need to be eliminated. The community can easily eliminate racism in the system, especially in systems where we are all participating based on avatars and our tags. Wokeness is problematic, because it convinces people to not challenge ideas that may offend other people. Ironically, racism and wokeness are part of the same systematic inequality coin. In the racist world, if you think differently or are different you are harassed. In the woke world, if you think differently or are different you get canceled. Same jerks, different sides of the aisle. To eliminate systematic inequality, we need to let the social contract work. Everyone does not have to be the same, but this is also not a carte blanche to do whatever you want. Government corruption likewise needs to be put in check. The metaverse does not need a big government to keep things running, only set systems to ensure that the mob does not take away from the individual and vice versa.

One of the primary elements that make the multiverse so appealing is that the power does not need to be consolidated at the top. While some social norms need to be followed (like eliminating theft, harassment, sex trafficking, underage abuse, or terrorism), each area of the metaverse can have its own set of morals. Conservatives can have their space; liberals can have theirs. Traditional value families can have their space, the LGBTQTIP community can have theirs. The metaverse is politically neutral, as long as you are not abusing someone else or attacking their property just go to your own corner.

Most important of all, the new system must ensure that everyone has a voice in the system. Shared governance is one of the most important elements of cryptocurrency, and it is one of the most important factors in the metaverse. This is one of the reasons that Meta moving into the metaverse so ham-handedly is frightening. Trying to control an area created to express freedom is the definition of tyrannical overreach, Facebook Stay in your lane censoring grandmothers for opinions that do not agree with your Globalist viewpoints. Let the users of the Metaverse make it a true Terran community.

New Reality Needs New Wealth

One of the most common phrases that are misquoted from the Bible is," Money is the root of all evil."[598] These people who are trying to say that scripture condemns money (mostly neo-liberal socialists on college campuses) attack those that use the money for good purposes; because, in their mind, that money must have been gotten in some fraudulent or abusive way. They say that all money is dishonest, shrouded in secrecy, and will only corrupt people.[599] This is ironic since they are purposefully leaving out the core point of the passage, "The LOVE OF money is the root of all evil."[600]

Wealth is not evil. Wealth tends to be a good thing for the world. It is from the wealth that we can feed our families, have homes, and secure our communities against the criminal element. Wealth is a component of free will, people are not truly free to make their own choices unless they have the ability to live with the consequences of those choices. If a choice takes away food, shelter, or security (or opens us up to the government's monopoly on the use of force), then is it really a free choice.[601] Wealth is

---

[598] 1 Tim 6:10.

[599] Kiernan, John (2017). "Is money the root of all evil? Experts pick sides." Wallet Hub at https://wallethub.com/blog/money-is-the-root-of-all-evil/31418.

[600] 1 Tim 6:10.

[601] See Contra, Letzing, John (2021). "Are Covid-19 Mandates Human Rights Violations?" World Economic Forum at https://www.weforum.org/agenda/2021/08/are-covid-19-vaccine-mandates-a-human-rights-violation/. In this article, the experts are the people choosing to

simply the ability to do what we choose, so those who are attacking wealth are simply saying that they are the only ones who deserve the right to choose.

Many of these people are people who are pushing the socialist/democratic socialist/communist systems. The idea that people are not smart enough to control their own wealth has been around for centuries. Marx and Engels merely weaponized it with groups who have classically been opposed to self-determination, unions, and universities. Unions like the control of telling people what to do, universities think that they are smarter than everyone else in the system. It was a match made in heaven. The reason that the system does not work; however, is that these groups preaching it do not want to do the work to maintain the system. They want to be the ones in the leadership roles that do nothing and still live a good lifestyle.[602]

On the other side of the spectrum, you have the despots preaching how pure capitalism is needed to make the world a better place. While the free exchange of goods is something that should be striving for, the idea of pure capitalism is scary for people who understand the system. Pure capitalism leads to plutocracy, where the richest person controls everything (similar to socialism in all honesty). In this system, the most powerful person can crush competitors using anti-capitalist measures, because they have the ability to afford it. This quickly degrades to a kleptocracy or corporate fascism, moving either towards anarchy or communism on the Quadralectic system.[603]

The need for a structure of the wealth in the metaverse system is

---

enforce the mandates. This is like asking the president of a country whether his country is abusing the human rights of a group that he or she is abusing- while that person is hitting these people with a whip. They are going to say no. This article is just proof that the system is very broken.

[602] Please note that this refers to the union leadership, not the union workers who make the world go round in cooperation with non-union workers.

[603] Smithmyer, Christopher (2014). Quadralectics. Dobbs & Brodeur: Miami. (Available at Nova Southeastern Library.)

imperative. However, the question of how that system should look is still up in the air. We can rule out socialism (which has been tried and failed many times, regardless of what your Liberal Arts 101 professor has told you), pure capitalism, fascism, communism, and about a dozen other "isms" that have failed throughout history. New space needs new management styles, and we should not force ourselves to work with a system that was made for the real world, when we are dealing the with the digital world.

Another concept that does not really have any place other than here is looking at the DGP. The digital gross production is the amount of wealth generated by the metaverse system. This calculation should stand apart from the gross national product because it comes from a different source. By knowing the digital gross product, the value of the metaverse can be established separately from the countries in which the metaverse operates.

Business, Service, and Entertainment in the New Space.

The metaverse is not that useful if no one is hanging out there. There have been several experiments in augmented reality, virtual reality, and digital socialization, but they all seemed to have failed early on. The metaverse seems to be taking hold for a simple reason, the utility of the system is being augmented by the number of people using the system. People are joining the system and finding use value there. For the system to continue to improve, the utility and opportunity in the system need to keep growing.

Digital entertainment is one of the key areas that draw people into the metaverse. In old iterations of VR and AR, there was not a lot of entertainment that helped people interact. You would awkwardly walk around with robotic motions, hoping to run into someone else to talk to. Since most were in a gaming environment, you also hoped that the person did not rob you or kill your avatar. It would be like wandering through a medieval forest, high risk, not that much reward. So, people stayed where they knew, in the dark ages they stayed at home and in towns, in the information age, they stayed in the real world. Now with the metaverse and the digital age, people have low risk, high utility options- now the metaverse can really shine. Entertainment is the thing that draws people in.

One people are there, watching movies and chatting is great but what does that really do for them personally. People need to be able to make money on the metaverse to keep up with what they are spending their money on. This means that they have to be able to offer services. The NFT market is the opening of this system, but other services being offered digitally can be a major boon for the metaverse. Once people can offer services on the metaverse platform (which people are starting to), businesses can start to take hold.

Once a digital business enters into the market, the market will stabilize. This will give the metaverse a permanent foothold in cyberspace. What type of businesses will do best in the area are unknown. Some promising areas we have already seen are education (charter), education (university), retail (its everywhere), and shared research and development. These will open doors to other areas, but it will be the entrepreneurs who define what businesses will be successful in cyberspace.

Giving value to the new Space.

Humanity has this bad habit of trying to give its own system of valuation to locations where there are already other people. North America, South America, Australia, Asia, the Middle East, Africa all have been "discovered" and conquered so many times that history does not even keep track of it. No race, ethnicity, or people is completely innocent when it comes to conquest. Now, as we move into the metaverse, we need to learn to respect the indigenous traditions of shared governance and leisure time that have made it so successful.

One of the first elements that we need to look at when evaluating space in the metaverse is the use-value. This is the big item that distinguishes the metaverse from its predecessors. The more that people can actually use the space that they are working in, the better. Each time a new and novel use develops on the metaverse, a new series of customers can be entered into the system. This grows the system and increases the value of the digital universe.

Expansion value is a hybrid type of valuation. How big can the metaverse get? This all depends on the size of the internet of things. Items that are generally not thought of as "connected" can be a powerful tool in giving more space for the metaverse to operate. Rather than using massive server farms that are destructive to the environment, an implanted chip that runs of the residual energy of a refrigerator, stove, or tv can process data in small amounts. Using this "waste" energy that vampire appliances exude, we can diminish waste and increase the expansion of the system. Regardless, the larger the space in the new frontier, the more value can be added as people populate that space.

The meeting place value rounds out the present value of the system. The ability to meet others online is important. As cartoon avatars give way to real people avatars, we have the ability to engage in real-time activities in the virtual space. The added benefit that people will be on a more level playing field also adds to the fun. Think of a football league where everyone is physically matched evenly, where the game comes down to the abilities of the mind and planning. An area where people who have a disability can compete on the same level as those who are normally able. This is a world where equality can suppose equity as the measure of how functional society is.

Just like other areas of the metaverse, we need to ensure that we look at history to see what has worked. New valuation methods should be based on systems that we have seen work. True, some elements that may have failed in the past may be functional in the new metaverse, but any system which has failed in the past should be vetted and have a theoretical reason why it should work. Building a better system means looking at the past and how it should work.

Building Off of Traditional Value Models but not Being Limited By them.

Underlying the entirety of human interaction is the social contract. Starting with, "I will not kill you if you do not kill me" and moving to "If you follow the terms of our legal contract, I too will do likewise." the system has grown since humankind first developed civilization. Basic rules such as "you shall not steal" underpin our entire civilization, but where should they be found in the metaverse. While we can agree that the last 8 of the 10 commandments are generally good advice, where do we see ourselves as a society?

One of the big elements that seem to work in society is that everyone is equal as the effort they put into life. We cannot say everyone is equal, because there are lazy people out there that do not put their effort in, but everyone that tries should be given a fair shake in the world. Most people can agree on that. Elements such as free speech, the right to associate, the right to bear arms, the right to free press, the right to religion that is not set up to attack people, and the right to make fun of elected leaders are sacrosanct to modern society. The right to have due process and the right to have a voice in your governance is important too. Basic rules like these should be maintained in the new social contract.

On the other hand, there are some things in human history that we are not proud of. First and foremost, of these should be discrimination based on a factor that a person cannot change. Racism, sexism, and ethnocentrism have no place in the social contract. Another element that needs to be eliminated is the elitism that we saw during the pandemic, where the wealthy had access to services (Newstrom, the Mayor of Chicago, Pelosi) that other people did not have access to. Having your hair styled is not necessary to run a government, look at Johnson. Discrimination based on choices people do make should be limited to discrimination on only things that affect other people (there will be arguments). Additionally, we might all agree that fascism does not really work.

As a crypto community, we need to make the world a better place. If we work together, we have the ability to do this. Crypto users run the gambit from despots to teachers, from doctors to murderers, from politicians to people who are actually honest. The voice of the best in the groups should be the voices that guide our progress. If we take the time to make the world a better place, it will be a better place.

Whether we can do better is not really a question, however, whether we will do better is always a challenge. As a crypto community, this is a choice that each of us needs to make. Are we going to be with the despots or the teachers? Will we support the doctors or the killers? Will we let politicians run roughshod over us, or will we stand up and fight for what is right? This choice comes down to each of us, and each of us must make this choice.

Conclusion to Part III

"What am I?" This is a question that is going to haunt the metaverse and cryptocurrencies for years. As the digital nomads that are moving through the metaverse discover new and exciting elements of the system, we must take a moment each time to see whether we are making the system better or worse. The crypto community is being dropped into a new world to make it what we believe is best. Will it be like the world we live in today, with crime and corruption? Will it be a digital utopia where children can learn, people can have 20-hour work weeks, and the Terran people can evolve to a new level of being? Or will we fail in this mission and have the world decay into a dystopia of people arguing over "what fan theory is best" and the sciences and arts will continue to degrade till hacks like the NIH rewrite the scientific journals and the only thing for entertainment would make the movie "Ideocracy" blush.

Stabilization of the system is the first element. Both cryptocurrency and the metaverse rely on having a stable system to ensure that the blockchain continues to function. We need to know that the valuation of the system is based on science, not on what people want it to be. The transitional value will continue to grow over time. The transactional value will grow as more businesses and governments enter into the system. Market value will show what people believe the system is worth; the more that the system grows, the more faith we will see. For those coins in the Stablecoin 2.0 system, the value will grow as the coin is used more. This creates an actual value in the system that will, one day, suppose the legacy of the fiat system that created it.

As the system grows, so too will the complexity of the system. Different types of derivatives will develop and be traded on the market. While options, warrants, futures, forwards, and swaps will undoubtedly lead the way, now and innovative metaverse derivatives will join the market for better security and stability. As more traders put more money into the system, it has the ability to become the system we all hoped that it will be.

Finally, we need to welcome the utility of the metaverse into the cryptoverse. It is coming whether we like it or not. The only say that we will have in the development of the system is how it comes to be. If we reject the metaverse, then it will become what others want it to become. If the crypto community accepts and welcomes the metaverse, then it has the potential to be the world that we hope it can be. As with everything, each of us has a choice to make. We hope you make the right choice on this issue.

Conclusion: Slaying the Dragons of the Digital Age

Dragons are one of the most interesting elements of human literary history. They, more than any other literary device (save humans), can take on any persona that we need them to take on. Dragons can be benevolent. Dragons can be evil. Dragons can be tricky. Dragons can be sage. These are the parts of the human mind that we want to make into something which we do not want to face, but do not want to admit is within our control. Beyond all else, the dragons we create are our creations. Slaying the troubles that they bring will help us realize that we are in control of our lives.

Benevolent dragons are often the most dangerous dragons that we see in literature. The gift of a dragon, in any culture, always comes with a cost. In the case of the digital age, the benevolent dragon looking to beguile us with gifts are governments seeking to control the digital age. They welcome people into the discussion, but then when talk turns serious, those who are not in power are regulated to the children's table, like at a family dinner. Here we watch as others make decisions for us, while we are powerless to respond. If we speak up, we are chastised for complaining and noted about how we are impertinent since we were given the privilege to be in the room, just not at the adult's table. The benevolent dragons of government give us the "right" to be present at the discussion, but not the full right to participate. The insidious nature of this form of governance is that they know we already have the right, that without the support of the people, these benevolent governments are nothing more than the benevolent dragons of old, figments of someone's imagination, given form, but a form that the people can remove at any time.

Evil dragons are another masterful set of imagery in ancient lore. These dragons strike fear into the people, destroying what they have created and carrying away what they need. In the digital age, these are the governments that tell people that they cannot be part of the digital world. "It is our world," they say, "that you must live in." Like any other dragons, it is our fear that gives them power. As the digital world evolves, if enough people rise against these evil governments, by using VPNs and participating anyway, their system will break and yours will replace it. It is true that evil only reigns when good people do nothing. To dispel this dragon, people need to work together- both nationally and internationally to make the world a better place.

Some dragons in history were tricksters. Dragons who gave the protagonist just enough information to get himself (or herself) into trouble. When the hero fails at what they were doing, because of the lack of information, the dragon chides the hero because the hero is a fool. Then the hero needs to live with the circumstance of their actions, even though it was the dragon's fault. In the digital age, these are the regulators who give us just enough information to get ourselves into trouble. By not following the current tax code, the governments allow traders, users, and businesses to accumulate wealth, then change the tone of the information and yank the rug out from under them. The courts are the system that should be used to fight these dragons, forcing governments to delineate the rules so that all are playing by an equal rulebook. The way to beat any trickster is to force them to play by their own rules.

The final dragon of lore is the dragon who is the great sage. Like the trickster, the dragon sages give the protagonist (us if you are following) information. Rather than reserve some information for the game, the sage gives all the information that the hero wants. This almost always turns out to be too much information (think Adam and Eve).[604] Knowledge without wisdom can be a curse, some governments are giving crypto users free reign without allowing the laws to support them. This grey area between law and reality allows for criminals to function. Free information is never free, when it is given by an unjust actor the cost is usually your soul. To slay this dragon, the community must work together to help people find wisdom in how to use the knowledge.

The spiderweb bridge is part of what helps us move past the traps of the ancient dragons. It allows members of the crypto community to work together, across all blockchains and beyond all borders to empower the

[604] Genesis.

people. When we realize that the dragons are problems of our own creation, our imaginations get out of control; we can shine the light on them and dismiss the mystique. Once we are dealing with governments without their scary appearance, we can ensure that the legal code is in the favor of freedom. The spiderweb bridges help bring all members of the crypto community together, the Stablecoin 2.0 gives the community the wherewithal to make positive change.

When the industry works together, they need to have forums where people can meet to discuss what needs to be done. Whether we follow an old leadership structure or create a new structure is up to the community, but we know that the regulators have their own structure. We need to organize to prevent the regulators from destroying the market, but we also must ensure that in organizing we do not give the representatives that we choose too much power over us. The strength of the crypto market and the metaverse is the decentralized nature of the system. While some dragons have multiple heads, they cannot be looking at all of us at once.

Fear of change is one of the ways that benevolent masters, evildoers, tricksters, and sages keep people in check. They act like they have control of the system. Benevolent masters threaten that they will take their gifts ways (they are already ours, so we can just take them). Evildoers threaten action if we change things (there are more of us than there are of them). Tricksters hope that we do not see that change may help us. Sages are the most afraid, because the change that we bring to the system can make their knowledge useless. We slay these dragons by allowing the system to move forward. Regulators only regulate based on the fear of the people who are oppressed; if the people show no fear, then it is the regulators who are afraid.

The more that people work together in any community, but especially the crypto community, the less the world around them seems scary. The only reason that we created government is that we wanted someone to keep others from abusing us. The system has come full circle and now it is the government that is locking people in their homes, telling them if and when they are sick, and telling them whether they can go to get food or work to support their family. The unrestrained monopoly on the use of force is a failed experiment in the digital age. Individuals, corporations, and associations should be given equal voice with governments in matters of world economic development.

It has taken an unnumbered thousands of years for humanity to get to the point where we do not have to appoint government toughs to defend us in our own space. When we empower the people and enforce the common-sense laws that are already on the books, both the real world and the metaverse can be a better place. Everything comes down to choice: are you going to let the dragons of the world control you- or will you dispel them as the children's fairytale they are and forge the world in the image of equality, progress, and the success of all humankind?

The Choice is Yours:

Tyranny of the Regulators Freedom of the People in Cyberspace

?

Glossary

Accessibility (Ability) - The ability of a document of presentation to be accessed by persons who are differently abled.

Accessibility (Crypto) - The ability of a member of the crypto community to access their assets at their discretion.

Active Reserve - The holdings of a company in a traded portfolio, bringing more value to the currency ecosystem.

Aggregate Market Value- The valuation taken from a weighted average of all trade on all markets within a system.

Air-gapped computer - A computer that is physically disconnected from the internet so that they data on the computer cannot be accessed remotely. In an air-gapped computer, there is no wife, Bluetooth, or direct internet connection. All interfaces are directly connected and also non-connected to the internet in any way.

Air-Gapped Storage - Storage of information on an air-gapped computer to ensure that the data on the system cannot be accessed except select connected terminals.

Alt-Coin - Generally any digital currency that is not bitcoin. In this text, the term is used concurrently with 2nd Wave cryptos. The technical difference between 2nd Wave cryptos and altcoin is that Ethereum is defined as a 1st Wave crypto, though in common parlance it is considered an altcoin.

American Option - A put or call option allowing the investor to enforce the option at any time up until the final execution date.

Anti-Trust - Anti-monopoly laws that were created to prevent one person or corporation from becoming too powerful and forcing others out of commercial space. (Clayton and Sherman Acts).

Anti-Whale Technology - Technology developed to prevent large holders within the system from manipulating the currency through large trades.

Ashe School of Thought - During a tiered ICO, when a tier sells out quickly, the following tier should be for a smaller amount of coin/token. The thought behind this is that the smaller tier levels will allow the coin/token to find its market value more quickly and the larger (later) launches can be set at the true market value. This mode is used to prevent day trading a speculation during the early release.

Arbitrage - The process of triangulating currency. When the currency is exchanged on multiple exchanges, the value on each exchange may be fractionally different. As such, there may be opportunities to buy on one exchange, convert to another currency, then sell the currency to convert back to the original currency at a favorable rate to increase the value of the holding. This was popular in the 1990s and is making a comeback in crypto trading.

Bargained For Exchange - One of the basic principles of contract law. If a person does not have the ability to bargain for their position, then it is not a contract which the parties freely entered into.

Batches - Groups of coins or tokens released together during an ICO.

Bear - A person who believes that the market or a specific asset will be in the decline and plays the market to make money off of that belief.

Bear Market - A market where the majority of the stocks are in a sell-off.

"Bilateral Contract - A contract in which both parties exchange a promise to preform."

Blacklist - The process of declaring a person or company should not be worked with by members of the community.

Borg Coins - Coins with the expressed purpose of assimilating all other coins on the market.

BPSAA - Blockchain Privacy, Security & Adoption Alliance, an association of cryptocurrencies working to improve the market through better practice in the field.

Bull - A person who believes that the market or a specific asset will rise and is buying to take advantage of that movement.

Bull Market - A market where a majority of the assets are rallying.

Burn - removing a set number of coins from the system in order to increase the value of the remaining coins.

Burning Coins - The process of removing coins from the system in order to increase the value of the remaining coins in the system. Burns can be conducted either in a simple or complex fashion.

Buying the Dip - When stock or crypto is in a downward trend and the holder believes that the decline will continue then rebound, the holder sells the coins on the way down then buys at a lower rate to increase their holdings in the stock or crypto.

Call Option - A type of option where the holder of the option has the opportunity on or before a specific date to buy up to a specific amount of asset or security for a set price.

Charity Shuffle - The process of giving out amounts of an initial currency offering to increase the use of the crypto in a given market. This works by benefiting the crypto (for having more users) and the charities (as a donation).

Choice of Law Clause - The portion of a contract that dictates what type of law will be used to resolve disputes. Choice of law clauses should have the area that the court is in and the jurisdiction of the law to be used. (ex. The court would be in the United States but the parties agree to be judged under U.K. law).

Click-Through Agreement - A Semi contract where a person can read the agreement or just click “ok” to accept the agreement. They are tenuous as a contract at best.

Coin - A type of cryptocurrency that has its own blockchain.

Cold Storage - The term for maintaining crypto in a wallet that cannot be accessed for normal trade or usage. Generally used in the staking process.

Conditional Burns - Burns that are set up by a series of cognitions, whether acute or chronic to reduce the number of coins. These burns are not static and are at the behest of the person who controls the crypto, or the community.

Conditional Staking - A system based on burns, where coins taken out of the system are placed in an active wallet to increase the value of the entire ecosystem. The coins are used to purchase stocks, bonds, property, other crypto, currencies, or other assets to act as a holding to increase the inherent value of the system.

Controller of a Crypto - The person or company who is responsible for the system management of a cryptocurrency.

Creator of a Coin - The person or persons who created the concept behind a given cryptocurrency.

Critical Mass - The point at which a standing burn system empties the *Black Wallet* into active wallets to increase the value of the system. This is done so that the *Black Wallet* is not a target for hacks.

Crypto - A short-hander term for cryptocurrencies including, but not limited to, coins, tokens, and NFTs.

Crypto Bill of Rights - A list of the rights that the crypto community agrees are needed for a fair global economy.

Cryptocurrency - Digital currencies, based off on or existing on a blockchain, used for transactions in the digital and real-world space.

Crypto diversity - The concept that the more cryptos that get created, the faster the system will be able to find the problems within specific models and create solutions to those problems.

Cryptonomics - The economics of the cryptos space, taking the best aspects of the field of economics, IT, and business finance and combining them into a functional system.

Cryptoverse - All digital space dealing with blockchain and crypto technology (including metaverse).

Dead Wallet - A 2nd Wave crypto concept where coins were burned to a wallet that the owner "lost" the key. This was used to reduce the number of coins or tokens without deleting coins. This system was effective till dead wallets started to activate again, which caused a market loss in late 2021.

Decentralized Finance - The concept that the economic system is more efficient when it is run by the market, rather than the Keynesian system where the market is manipulated by central banks or governments.

DeFi - See decentralized finance.

Derivative - A security that is based on the underlying value of another asset.

Derivative Variable - A variable that is used in the determination of the valuation of a system.

Determinative Variable - A valuation of a system based on another variable.

DGP - See digital gross product.

Diamond Hands - Traders who stick with a currency for the long term, ignoring the short-term rises and falls.

Digital Gross Product - The amount of commerce that a given digital system generates each year.

Dumps - The process of getting rid of all crypto that one person holds.

Economics - A liberal art that looks for patterns in the economic system and asserts grounded theory based on those observations.

Equal Distribution - In a re-release, a process where coins are returned to the holders and are distributed equally to everyone holding the coins, regardless of how many coins they are holding.

Equal Release (ICO) - An ICO where all batches are the same size.

Equitable Distribution - In a re-release, a process where coins are returned to the holders and are distributed based on the amount of coin that they are holding on a given partner platform.

Equitable Release (ICO) - An ICO where the batch size is dictated by the speed at which the previous level sold out (generally based on either the Ashe or Smithmyer school of thought).

European Option - An option that can only be executed at the end of the time period.

Exchanges - Platforms that allow the trade and exchange of currencies, stocks, cryptos, commodities, and other assets.

Family of Coins - A group of coins (regardless of platform) that work together to increase the value of an ecosystem.

Fear of Missing Out - See FOMO.

Fiat Currency - Central bank-issued currency which is only backed on the faith and credit of the government for which it is minted.

Five-Tiered ICO - A ICO where the crypto is released in five "batches"

First Wave Crypto - Bitcoin or Ethereum.

FOMO - Fear of Missing Out, something that drives people to get in on fads.

Forward - An agreement where a person has the right to purchase stock at the end of a period of time for a set amount of money. Forwards cannot be traded on the market and are settled at once.

Fungible Tokens - Tokens where each token is not different from any other token in the system.

Future - A derivative where a person has the obligation to purchase or sell a given amount of coin on a specific date for a specific amount. These are more restrictive than options and can also be traded on the open market.

Gas Fees- The amount that a user pays for a transaction for using the chain to confirm the transaction (these can get very steep on Ethereum).

General ICO - When a coin is introduced onto the market in one "batch" allowing the market to dictate the price at a later time.

GETs - See Global Exchange Tokens

General Burns - When a controller of a coin announces that a portion of the reserve will be removed from the market to increase the value of each individual coin/token. In most general burns the controller asks that the holders burn a like percentage.

Global Exchange Tokens - Tokens that are designed to allow traders and users to bridge different blockchains via the existence of partnerships within the system.

Hard Fork - A change in a blockchain system that all coins moving forward must use to maintain their status on the system.

Holder (Stock) - A person who possesses a stock. The holder has all the legal rights to the stock.

Holder (Derivative) - A person who has control over the execution of a derivative before the time on the derivative expires.

Hot Wallet - A wallet in a cryptosystem that is active (alternate meaning- A wallet in a system where the key has been stolen.

ICO - See Initial Coin offering.

Insider Trading - The process of a person acting on information, not generally available to the public, to make trades leveraging the special access to information to make a profit.

Into the Wild - When crypto is released from the compete for control of its creator/controller to the marketplace.

IPO - See Initial Public Offering.

Inherent Value - The value of a crypto within an ecosystem that has a holdings system. The holding system can either have percentile holdings (where the amount of the system is derivative of the market cap of each crypto in the system) or joint holdings, where the cryptos in the ecosystem have joint membership in the ecosystem (better for system management).

Initial Coin Offering - When a crypto (both coins and tokens) is offered to the public through an exchange or a brokerage.

Initial Public Offering - When a stock is first offered to the public through an exchange or a brokerage.

Japanese Candle - A way of following the market where the stock is shown by the high bid, the low bid, the high average, the low average, and the average in one infographic for some time. So named because it looks like a candle. On most platforms, ascending candles are green and descending candles are red.

Joint Holding Value - A system where a Stablecoin 2.0 ecosystem is valued based on the number of coins in the system and the value of the holdings shared by the family of coins.

KIROS Development Plan - The portion of the KIROS white pages looks at how the token will be distributed and developed.

KIROS White Paper - The operating plan for the KIROS Global Exchange Token Program.

Lemmings - People in the market that follow personalities on the market and do what they tell them (if you are invested in a system where a guru tells you what to do, you are a lemming). Lemmings can cause runs and rallies on the market.

Lipstick Politician - A politician that will say anything about a subject that they do not know, then do exactly what their donors tell them to do.

Longs - People who buy a stock for the long term, these people tend to hold stocks for weeks, months, or years, and in crypto people who hold cryptos for days, weeks, months, or years.

Margins - the amount of money that a person has in their brokerage account, basically a trader borrows from the brokerage the amount of money their account has as a net value and uses the borrowed amount to make trades that they do not have enough liquid value to trade.

Market Value - The valuation of what people are playing for crypto on a market. This can be a single market value or an aggregate market value.

Market Volume - The amount of trade that is being done in a specific coin on a given exchange or across multiple exchanges.

Mickey Bucks - A currency offered by Disney in its parks that was pegged to the dollar. Rubes could buy the currency for use in the park. As time went on, fewer and less stores in the park would accept the Mikey bucks turning the holders into bag holders for a novelty currency.

Monocurrency Reserves - Holdings where only one coin is maintaining its reserves (common in Stablecoin 1.0).

Monopoly - The process of a company having control over the means of production for all of one type of product. This can be illegal or legal in specific jurisdictions.

Multicurrency Reserves - When multiple cryptocurrencies work together to build holding which functions as a value base for all the coins in that group.

Multilateral Contract - A contract where multiple parties have interests, duties, and expectations.

Multilevel Portfolio - A portfolio with more than one type of asset in the portfolio (precious metals AND stocks, Commodities AND bonds, etc.)

National Favoritism - The process of a country giving preferential treatment to crypto or company that is founded or operates within its national borders.

NFT - See Non-Fungible Token

Non-Fungible Token - A token that is unique in its existence and the chain verifies that the holder has exclusive rights to that token.

Oligopoly - The process of a person or company obtaining the purchase rights for all of one type of good.

Option - A type of derivative where a person buys the “option” to sell (put) or buy (call) at a certain price on or before a named time. This option can then be traded on the open market with the option being executed when the holder calls in the option, or the option can expire rendering it worthless.

Optional Staking - The concept that a group of people, by action or by consent, can put away a portion of their holdings to increase the reserve of crypto.

OTC Trades - See over-the-counter trades.

Over the Counter Trades - Trades that are done person to person and not handled by any exchange.

Paper Hands - A person who sells at the first sign of a decline in the coin value.

Patterns (Stock) - movements in the market that traders look for when they want to know if there will be a market reversal.

Percentile Holding Value - The value of the holding reserve assigned to specific crypto in a family of coins related to the percentile value of the holdings of the ecosystem in relation to the market cap of the specific crypto.

Pre-Planned Release - This is a cycle in a tiered release where the number of coins in each "batch" is released at a specific price in a specific volume. This is generally the easiest system to use for a tiered ICO, but usually has the most difficulty finding the real market rate.

Proof of Stake - The ability of crypto or an ecosystem to prove that their holdings of the system (Stablecoin 1.0 or Stablecoin 2.0) have a value that can be measured or verified. This is needed to give an actual value calculation for a coin.

Proof of Utility - The ability to prove that a coin has a use for a process. Example: when a GET is used to trade coins across blockchains without paying gas fees on both chains.

Protected Information - Information that should not be released to the public, includes names and addresses of traders.

Pump and Dump - The process of running the value of crypto or stock up, only to sell the crypto or stock quickly causing the rate to fall. Organized schemes to do this are illegal in most markets.

Purchase Futures - Futures that create the obligation for a party to purchase a set amount of assets at a given time.

Put Option - In an option system, a put option allows you to "put" the goods on the market, selling them at a predetermined amount, which may be above or below the market rate (usually you do not execute a call option below the market rate). New investors must realize that they are only buying the option to do this action, not the actual stock spoke about in the option.

Rental Society - A society where more people rent and least goods than own them. This system is highly conditional on government support.

Reserves - The amount of coin or token that a system keeps out of play (or in controlled play) to maintain the stability of the system. This reserve can be active or passive and generally is directly related to the holdings.

Resistance - An indicator where many people have offered to sell stock at a given price that can cause problems during a rally as the resistance line tends to eat up all purchases, not letting the stock or crypto move past that point.

Reversal (Stock) - When a stock is moving one way, then following a pattern begins to move the other direction. A declining stock would reverse to an ascending stock.

Reversal (Wrestling) - When one wrestler is in a hold and moves out of the hold to take control of the match by putting the other wrestler in a hold.

Rug Pulls - The process of pumping up a coin and then devaluing the coin quickly either by the creators cashing out or some other means. Should be illegal in all asset markets.

Schrodinger's Box - A box with a cat in it where the cat could be alive and dead at the same time. If the cat was dead, we could not know it is dead because, in the process of opening the box, the cat would be killed. It represents a theoretical concept with only one outcome, where the people are afraid of the outcome (which is predestined) and thus are unwilling to take the steps that are needed to fix it. Fiat currency is dead, but we are unwilling to make changes to the system to improve the lives of people around the world because we may kill the fiat currency, which is dead.

Schrodinger's Wallet Fallacy - The idea that the coin in the wallet can be active and inactive at the same time. The use of a dead wallet implies that the coin is not destroyed but is inactive. As a coin that can be accessed may be accessed, then the coin cannot be active and inactive at the same time.

Second Wave Crypto - Any crypto built upon the principles of smart contract technology after Ethereum.

Sell Futures - Futures where a person has an obligation to sell a given number of assets at a given price at a given time.

Short Trade - The process of borrowing an asset from a holder, then selling the asset hoping that the price of the asset goes down so that the seller is then able to buy back the asset before the end of the term, at a lower rate, and pocket the difference.

Single Market Value - The value of crypto on a single exchange or market.

Smithmyer School of Thought - The school of thought that during a tiered ICO, when a tier sells out quickly, the next tier should be larger. The philosophy behind this is that more people will be able to get involved with the coin at a lower rate to increase the dynamic holdings in the Stablecoin 2.0 system.

Spiderweb Bridge - A concept that coins can be interconnected by the system, rather than code, and the interconnectivity of the system allows for crypto ecosystems to develop that are not based on one specific blockchain.

Social Contract - The agreement between people in a society to give a government a specific list of privileges and duties in exchange for specific restrictions being placed on individual rights. The idea behind a social contract is that the government may only function in the matter prescribed and can never increase its own power or gain rights of its own.

Soft Fork - An increase in efficiency for a specific blockchain that each coin or token on the chain has the option of participating in.

Spot Rate - The value that a stock or crypto is trading at any given moment.

Stablecoin 1.0 - A system where the value of crypto is based on its relationship to a fiat currency

Stablecoin 1.1 - A system where the value of crypto is based on its relationship to a single asset or family of assets.

Stablecoin 2.0 - A system where the value of the crypto is based on the combined/communal holdings of a crypto ecosystem. This system can include stocks, bonds, property, and other real-world or digital assets withstanding value.

Staking - The process of a member of the community (including the creator) holding a portion of their coins/tokens in cold storage to decrease the number of coins/tokens in play and increase the value of the system.

Standing Burn - A burn that is on every transaction. An idea replacing "gas fees" as a taxation system for the crypto ecosystem. It should never be more than 2% on any given trade.

Standing Burn System - A system defining the standing burn for crypto. Examples are "The standing burn will be between 0.5% and 1.5%" or "The burn rate will be set on a five-minute basis by [X] controlling company."

Starter Burn - A period of higher-than-normal crypto burning to ensure that people are no "pump and dumping" during the initial ICO.

Static Reserve - A reserve of coins or tokens that are kept in a separate account for the purpose of managing the liquidity of the cryptosystem.

Stock Swap - The process of exchanging one stock for another, usually used in mergers and/or acquisitions.

Support Line - The area where many buyers have placed an order setting a lower limit for a stock value. A support line tends to "eat up" all the sales which allow the price to maintain at that level.

Swaps (Derivatives) - The process of exchanging future value for present value in the derivative market. This can fall under other types of equity, but crypto only really looks at present value v. future value currently.

Swaps (Stocks) - The process of swapping one stock for another (usually in amounts along with the same value) during a stock transaction. This method is usually used in mergers.

Tag - A person's online name.

Ten-Tiered-ICO - An initial coin offering system where the coins are broken up into ten "batches" for release, looking for the market value of a specific coin or token.

Terran - A non-political term for a human being born on earth (so all of us).

Third Wave Crypto - Any coin or token based on the Stablecoin 2.0 platform, with a standing burn, willing to participate in the spiderweb bridge.

Tiered ICO - An initial coin offering where the coin is offered in "batches" allowing the coin to find market equilibrium for price. The two most common forms are five and ten tiered ICOs.

Token - A form of cryptocurrency that exists on a blockchain that is not its own. Unlike a coin, a token is an overlay that increases the functionality within a set of defined parameters and bases its value on that procedural increase.

Tokenomics - The practice of assessing the value of a cryptocurrency based on the valuation, the distribution, the application, the reserves, and the community of the coin.

Trade Confirmation - A digital document that confirms that a trade has been completed.

Transactional Value - The value of a currency is determined by the amount of "real world" or digital world goods that the token or coin can purchase.

Transitional Value - The value of a currency is determined by the amount of value-added to a process by the information passing through the block operating on the coin/tokens chain.

Trust (monopoly) - A group of companies working together to maintain a monopoly on a system.

Trust (Systems) - The amount of faith the users have in a system.

Uni-asset System - A system that maintains the inherent value in a portfolio by using a single asset such as gold.

Unilateral Contract - A contract where one party's completion can only be done by an action.

Uni-level Portfolio - A Portfolio that only has one family of assets to manage the inherent value of the system (precious metals, stocks, bonds, etc.).

Variable Burn Rate - A burn rate that is set between two points (usually percentage points), which can be changed by the controller of the coin to increase or decrease the burn rate to help with coin growth. In a Stablecoin 2.0 system, this process should be managed by an AI.

Virtual Private Network - A screening system used to help protect the identity of a person using a digital system.

The volume of Trade - The number of coins or tokens that are being traded in a given segment.

VPN - See virtual private network.

Utility of Trade - The relationship between the volume of trade and the price point for crypto. Crypto with a low volume and a high rate of movement are less reliable than crypto with a high volume of trade and a low movement level when looking for indicators and patterns.

Warrants - A type of crypto derivative (based on a stock derivative) where coins are released from a named reserve via a per sale of the coin, where the buyer buys the right to the crypto at the present price for a later date. These coins are coins released from the reserve.

Whale - A trader who purchases or sells large volumes and large values of coins.

White List - A group of companies or people with whom a system is willing to work.

White Paper - A document showing the creation, development, and distribution plan of a cryptocurrency.

Index

Appendix 1: Crypto Bill of Rights

The crypto community is one of the most egalitarian communities in the world. As such, we have found that the governments of the world misunderstand that certain self-evident truths are difficult to understand. Because of that error of the centuries, it falls upon generations, from time to time, to remind the governments of the world that certain rights are inalienable, endowed by God, to the people of the world. The purpose of the governments is to preserve these rights, as such, we support that all governments of the world remember each person has these rights.

Part I: Human Rights

As we are all human, governments of the world need to protect the people in their humanity. This includes the protection of all human life until death by natural causes or termination after due process. The rights of humanity are sacrosanct, the following are among the most important rights- though this list is not exhaustive.

§ 1: The Right to Life- All human beings have the right to live their lives within the bounds of the law. To pursue their goals and ambitions through whatever legal means that their skills allow. This life shall be protected from the time of life (heartbeat or first cell division) through their natural death. Governments shall protect their people from violent death, except those who are convicted of homicide, treason, pedophilia, or the trafficking of human beings.

§ 2: Right to Self Determination- Each person has an inherent right to self-determination, no person shall be forced to work for another person, except on punishment for a crime for which they have duly convicted. Persons also have the right to have elected leadership, in which all persons have an equal say in who advocates on our behalves through representatives.

§ 3: Right to Religion- No government shall restrict the rights of people to practice their recognized religion or to choose not to participate in a religion. Groups that have created a "religion" to attack another religion shall not be included in this, though they do have the right not to participate. Free exercise shall be unrestricted, but for actions that harm other people or attack another religion.

§ 4: Right to Free Speech- Governments are obliged to protect the free political speech of any person within their borders. While the free speech of non-citizens may be restricted, it may not be fully prohibited.

§ 5: Right to a Free Press- No government shall have a monopoly on news media, a free press is vital to ensure that human rights are protected. No person who has worked in government may work for or be married to, a member of the press.

§ 6: People have an inherent right to associate, no government may, by action or inaction, prevent the gathering of people for the purpose of presenting a political opinion.

§ 7: The Right to Petition- All people have the right to petition the government for justice from grievances. All governments must have a recall mechanism to remove corrupt representatives from office, originating with the people- not from the government itself (though the latter can be in addition to the prior).

§ 8: Access to the Internet- The internet has become a human right. All people should have access to news and information on the internet. Governments can, if need be, restrict access to certain types of information (Example:. pornography, hate speech) to meet with cultural norms, but all information about politicians, business, and international news may not be restricted, including information that may be embarrassing.

§ 9: Right to Valuation of Jobs- Every person has the right to know the value of their job, which includes being given a salary based on the number of hours they have labored.

§ 10: The Right to Travel- Every person, unless this right has been removed by due process, has the right to travel internationally. The restriction of non-criminals to travel from one country to another should not be restricted. During times of crisis, travel may be restricted, but for no longer than 30 calendar days from the declaration of the crisis. Persons traveling in any country shall be returned to their country to stand trial for any accusations in a foreign country (though the home country must agree to have a trial under the laws of the accusing country).

§ 11: The Right to Education (Not Indoctrination)- Every person has the right to an education. Any tax monies collected for education should follow the child to their parent's choice of schools. Choices shall include public school, private school, parochial school, or charter schools. All teachers must have requisite education: primary school- bachelor's degree, secondary school-master's degree, Undergraduate college, Ph. D (or terminal masters only), graduate degree (terminal degree and five years working in the field).

Part II: Due Process Rights

§ 1: Right to know what crime is- When accused, within 12 hours of arrest, every person has the right to know what the charges are against them and have the opportunity to meet with an attorney within the first 24 hours of arrest, for any crime, including crimes against the state.

§ 2: Right to appear in court (before seizure)- If a warrant is issued, the premises can be secured and the accused has a right to confront the cause for the warrant, in open court, prior to a search or seizure being conducted. This right must be asked for when the seizure is attempted, and the appearance before the court must take place within 12 hours of the request or the warrant is invalid.

§ 3: Right to a Lawyer- Every person has the right to be represented by the council. In a criminal case, the indigent will be represented by public lawyers. In civil cases, the council is at the party's own expense.

§ 4: Right to See a Warrant before the Information is Turned Over- Any person may request the right to see a warrant during a search and may stop the search to challenge the warrant. In the interim between the challenge and the ruling, the state may secure the premises and the accused may not enter unsupervised.

§ 5: Right to a Public Trial- All persons in society have the right that all cases involving no minors must be public. If the minor in question has reached the age of adulthood, all cases must be public.

§ 6: Right to a Speedy Trial- All trials must take place within 6 months (if a person is out on bail) or 3 weeks (if a person is still in custody) of the initial arrest. Failure to do this by the government will result in the case being dropped.

§ 7: Right to an Appeal- Every person has a right to appeal the facts or the law of a case. Appeals can be in writing or oral, in the choice of the appealing party. All appeals must be heard within 6 months of the initial court decision. The court does not have a right to turn down an appeal; however, if an appeal is deemed frivolous by the court, then the appellant will be responsible for the court costs. If the appellant is not able to pay the court costs, then they will have three years added to their term for non-violent offenses, and 10 years added to their term for violent offenses. In the case of life terms, if an appeal is frivolous, then the sentence is the death penalty.

§ 8: Right to Confront Accuser- All people have the right to face their accuser, in the cases where the accuser is a child, the questions will be taken by a third party to the witness in another room to be asked.

§ 9: No Double Jeopardy- A person cannot be tried multiple times for the same crime unless it is shown that they tampered with a witness (which results in a life term in all cases).

§ 10: Right to Access to All Court Cases- All court cases will be publicly accessible with the following redactions: account numbers, names of victims, names of witnesses, names of jurors, weapons designs, and names of agents of the government in other countries or undercover in the country of the trial. All other information is public.

Part III: Transactional Rights

§ 1: Right to Trade- all people in this world have the right to trade their skills, their property, and their wealth for currency, goods, services, and/or property. Individuals can work within a specific currency system, uncontrolled by the government, to aid in the flow of commerce.

§ 2: The Right to Contract- All people have the right to enter into free contracts for legal services, legal goods, and/or currencies.

§ 2: Right to Know How Platforms Work- Each person has a right to know how a trading platform works in which they trade goods, currencies, services, securities, or other assets.

§ 3: Right to Know how Currencies are Managed- Each person has the right to know how their wealth is being managed in a managed account.

§ 4: Right-to-Know Burn Procedures- When dealing with crypto, each person has the right to know what the burn procedures are, how they will be managed, and what will be done with the "burned" currency.

§ 5: Right to Know Storage Procedures- All people have the right to know and choose how their wealth will be stored and have a right to access those funds upon confirmation of identity.

Appendix 2: Crypto News Resources

21 Cryptos, https://21cryptos.com/

99 Bitcoin News, www.99bitcoins.com

Airdrop Alert Blog, https://blogs.airdropalert.com/

Altcoin buzz, www.Altcoinbuzz.io

AIthority, https://aithority.com/

AMB Crypto, www.AMBcrypto.com

BCG Blockchain, https://www.bcg.com/capabilities/digital-technology-data/blockchain

Be in Crypto, www.beincrypto.com

Better Traders, https://www.thebettertraders.com

Bitcoin, www.bitcoin.org

Bitcoin Exchange Guide, www.bitcoinexchangeguide.com

Bitcoin Magazine, https://bitcoinmagazine.com/

Bitcoin.com News, https://news.bitcoin.com/

Bitcoinik, www.bitcoinIK.com

Bitcoinist, https://bitcoinist.com

Bitdegree Tutorials, https://www.bitdegree.org/tutorials/

Bitfinex Blog, www.blog.bitfinex.com

Bitinfo Charts, www.bitinfocharts.com

Bitpanda, https://www.bitpanda.com.

Blockchain Blog, www.medium.com/blockchain

Blockchain Magazine, https://blockchainmagazine.net/

Blockchain.news, www.blockchain.news

Blockium, https://www.blockium.io/Home/Welcome

Blockonomi, www.blockonomi.com

BPSAA (Association), https://bpsaa.vision/.

Brave New coin, www.bravenewcoin.com/insights/latest

Brookings (Boomers). https://www.brookings.edu.

BTC Manager, www.btcmanager.com

Business Insider (MSM). https://www.businessinsider.com

BuyUCoin Blog, https://blog.buyucoin.com/

BuyUcoin Talks https://medium.com/buyucoin-talks

CCN, https://www.ccn.com/crypto/

Chainalysis, https://blog.chainalysis.com/.

Changelly, https://changelly.com/

Changenow Blog, https://changenow.io/blog

CMC, https://www.cmcmarkets.com.

CNN Business, (MSM) https://www.cnn.com.

Coinbase Blog, https://blog.coinbase.com.

Coin Bureau, www.coinbureau.com/blog

Coin Central, www.coincentral.com

Coin Checkup Blog, https://coincheckup.com/blog/

Coin Funda, www.coinfunda.com

Coin Gape, https://coingape.com/

Coin Idol, www.coinidol.com

Coin Market Cap, https://coinmarketcap.com/

Coin Market, www.coin.market

Coin monks, www.medium.com/coinmonks

Coin News, https://www.coinnews.net/

Coin Rivet, www.coinrivet.com

Cointelegence, www.cointelegence.com/content

Coin Speaker, https://www.coinspeaker.com/

Coin Telegraph, https://subscriptions.cointelegraph.com

Coinbase, http://www.coinbase.com

CoinChapter, www.coinChapter.com

Coindesk, https://www.coindesk.com/.

Coindoo, www.coindoo.com

Coinpedia, www.coinpedia.org.

Coinquora, www.coinquora.com

Coinspeaker, www.coinspeaker.com

Coinstats Blog, https://coinstats.app/blog/

Coinsutra Blog, https://coinsutra.com/blog/

Cryptoadventure, www.cryptoadventure.com/guides

Crypto briefing, https://cryptobriefing.com/

Cryptocompare, www.cryptocompare.com

Crypto News Australia, www.cryptonews.com/au

Crypto News Flash, www.crypto-news-flash.com

Crypto News Z, www.cryptonewsz.com

Crypto Ninja, https://www.cryptoninjas.net/

Crypto Potato, https://cryptopotato.com/

Cryptogon, www.cryptogon.com

CryptosRus, www.cryptosrus.com

Cryptoslate, https://cryptoslate.com/

Daily Coin, www.dailycoin.com

Econlib, https://www.econlib.org.

Economic Times, (India) https://economictimes.indiatimes.com.

Emirex, https://blog.emirex.com.

Ethereum, www.ethereum.org.

Ethereum World News, www.etheriumworldnews.com

EuroMoney, https://www.euromoney.com/cryptocurrencies

EuroNews, https://www.euronews.com.

Finance Magnates, https://www.financemagnates.com/

Heritage Foundation, https://www.heritage.org

HITC, https://www.hitc.com.

Investopedia, https://www.investopedia.com/

Kraken Blog, www.blog.kraken.com

Ledger, https://www.ledger.com/decentralized-finance- DeFi

Liquid Blog, https://blog.liquid.com/

Market Compass Technical View, https://themarketscompass.substack.com/

Marketplace, http://www.marketplace.org.

The Merkle, www.themerkle.com

Mintme.com, www.mintme.com

Motley Fool, https://www.fool.com.

NewsBTC, https://www.newsbtc.com.

Next Advisor (MSM), https://time.com/nextadvisor/.

Now Payments, https://nowpayments.io/

Paxful Blog, https://paxful.com/blog

Prices.org, www.prices.org

Quartz, https://qz.com/re/cryptocurrency/

Raconteur, https://www.raconteur.net.

Today on Chain, https://www.todayonchain.com/

Tezro, https://blog.tezro.com

Tron Weekly, www.tronweekly.com

U.Today, https://u.today/

Use the Bitcoin, www.usethebitcoin.com

WazirX Blog, https://wazirx.com/blog/

Zebpay Blog, https://zebpay.com/blog/

Zycrypto, https://zycrypto.com/

All website links worked at the time of the writing.

Made in United States
North Haven, CT
06 November 2026

21875929R00314